QUALITATIVE INQUIRY

The Path of Sciencing

Rosemarie Rizzo Parse, RN; PhD; FAAN

Loyola University Chicago

QUALITATIVE INQUIRY

The Path of Sciencing

Rosemarie Rizzo Parse, RN; PhD; FAAN
Loyola University Chicago

JONES AND BARTLETT PUBLISHERS

Sudbury, Massachusetts

BOSTON   TORONTO   LONDON   SINGAPORE

National League *for* Nursing

World Headquarters
Jones and Bartlett Publishers
40 Tall Pine Drive
Sudbury, MA 01776
978-443-5000
www.jbpub.com
info@jbpub.com

Jones and Bartlett Publishers Canada
2406 Nikanna Road
Mississauga, ON L5C 2W6
CANADA

Jones and Bartlett Publishers International
Barb House, Barb Mews
London W6 7PA
UK

Library of Congress Cataloging-in-Publication Data

Parse, Rosemarie Rizzo.
    Qualitative inquiry : the path of sciencing / Rosemarie Rizzo Parse.
        p. cm.
    "National League for Nursing."
    Includes bibliographical references and index.
    ISBN 0-7637-1565-4 (alk. paper)
    1. Qualitative research. 2. Nursing—Research—Methodology. I. National League for Nursing. II. Title.
    RT81.5 .P363 2001
    610.73'076—dc21

                                                                                    00-065652

Production Credits
Acquisitions Editor: Penny Glynn
Associate Editor: Christine Tridente
Production Editor: AnnMarie Lemoine
Editorial Assistant: Thomas Prindle
Manufacturing Buyer: Amy Duddridge
Cover Design: Alj Mary
Design and Composition: Carlisle Communications, Ltd.
Printing and Binding: Malloy Lithographing

ISBN 0-7637-1565-4 (soft cover)
ISBN 0-7637-1842-4 (hard cover)

Printed in the United States of America
04 03 02 01   10 9 8 7 6 5 4 3 2 1

CONTENTS

ORIGINAL CONTRIBUTORS   xv

TABLES   xvii

FIGURES   xx

PREFACE   xxiii

1

SCIENCING: A PROCESS OF INQUIRY   1

Assumptions About Sciencing   2

    To Question Is to Reach Beyond What Is With What Is Possible   2

    A Question in Itself Incarnates the Questioner's Attitudes, Beliefs, and Style and Points to Personal Projects   2

    Both Questions and Answers Are Set With the Boundaries of the Questioner's Understanding of the Phenomenon   3

    The Questioning Process and the Answers Are Intersubjective   4

Building Knowledge With Qualitative Research   4

References   12

2

DIMENSIONS OF THE RESEARCH PROCESS   15

Conceptual Dimension   18

    Frame of Reference   18

    The Phenomenon and the Research Question   19

Ethical Dimension   19

    Scientific Merit   19

    Protection of Participants   19

    Integrity   20

Methodological Dimension   22

Interpretive Dimension   22

References   30

3 GROUNDED THEORY   35
Ontology   35
Epistemology   36
Methodology   37
   Processes of the Method   37
References   40

4 NARRATIVE RESEARCH   43
Ontology   43
Epistemology   44
Methodology   44
   Processes of the Method   44
References   45

5 HEURISTIC RESEARCH METHOD   47
Ontology   47
Epistemology   47
Methodology   48
   Processes of the Method   49
References   49

6 THE HERMENEUTIC METHOD   51
Ontology   51
Epistemology   53
Methodology   53
   Processes of the Method   53
References   54

7 THE QUALITATIVE DESCRIPTIVE METHOD   57
Ontology   57
Epistemology   58
Methodologies   58
   Processes of the Methods   58
References   60

8 QUALITY OF LIFE FOR PERSONS LIVING WITH ALZHEIMER'S DISEASE:
THE HUMAN BECOMING PERSPECTIVE [REPRINTED]   61
Nursing Perspective   63

Research Question and Objectives 64

Participants and Setting 64

Data Gathering 65

Data Analysis-Synthesis 65

Findings 65

    Objective 1: Meaning 65

      Theme 1 65

    Objective 1: Meaning 66

      Theme 2 66

    Objective 2: Rhythmicity 68

      Theme 3 68

    Objective 3: Cotranscendence 69

      Theme 4 69

Discussion 70

Connection With Human Becoming Literature 73

Conclusion 74

References 75

9

THE PHENOMENOLOGICAL METHOD 77

Ontology 77

Epistemology 78

The Phenomenological Method and Its Modifications 79

    Processes of the Phenomenological Method 79

      Investigating Particular Phenomena 79

      Investigating General Essences 79

      Apprehending Essential Relationships 80

      Watching Modes of Appearing 80

      Watching the Constitution of Phenomena in Consciousness 80

      Suspending Belief in the Existence of the Phenomenon 80

      Interpreting Concealed Meanings of Phenomena 81

    van Kaam's Procedural Modification 81

    Giorgi's Procedural Modification 82

    Colaizzi's Procedural Modification 82

References 83

10

THE EXPERIENCE OF LAUGHTER: A PHENOMENOLOGICAL STUDY
[REPRINTED] 87

Researcher's Perspective 89

Participants   89
Data Gathering and Analysis   89
Findings   90
Discussion   91
Findings and Related Literature   93
Recommendations   94
References   94

11 THE RELENTLESS DRIVE TO BE EVER THINNER: A STUDY USING THE
PHENOMENOLOGICAL METHOD [REPRINTED]   97

Marc D. A. *Santopinto*, MScN

The Research Question   97
Researcher's Perspective   99
Methodology   100
Presentation of Data and Findings   101
Meaning Unit: Subject 1   101
Meaning Unit: Subject 2   101
Theme: Subject 1   102
Theme: Subject 2   102
Focal Meaning: Subject 1   102
Focal Meaning: Subject 2   102
Focal Meanings: Subject 1   102
Focal Meanings: Subject 2   103
Situated Structural Description: Subject 1   103
Situated Structural Description: Subject 2   104
General Structural Description   104
Discussion   105
Conclusions   106
Implications and Recommendations   107
References   108

12 THE LIVED EXPERIENCE OF SELF-TRANSCENDENCE IN WOMEN WITH
ADVANCED BREAST CANCER [REPRINTED]   111

Doris D. *Coward*, RN; PhD

Purpose and Research Design   113
Examining Researcher Presuppositions   113
Formulating the Question for Subjects   113

Phenomenological Analysis of the Data   114

Discussion of the Findings of the Study   122

Conclusions   123

Implications of the Study   123

Issues Related to the Study Findings   124

References   125

13 ETHNOGRAPHY AND ETHNONURSING   127

Ontology   127

Epistemology   128

Methodologies   128

Processes of the Methods   128

References   131

14 USE OF CULTURE CARE THEORY WITH ANGLO- AND AFRICAN AMERICAN
ELDERS IN A LONG-TERM TERM CARE SETTING [REPRINTED]   133

Marilyn R. McFarland, RN; PhD

Purpose, Goal, and Domain of Inquiry   134

Assumptive Premises of the Research   134

Theoretical Framework   135

Ethnonursing Research Method   135

Major Research Findings   137

Modes of Decision-Making and Anglo- and African American
Culture Care   141

Culture Care Preservation or Maintenance   141

Culture Care Accommodation or Negotiation   142

Cultural Care Repatterning or Restructuring   143

Discussion   143

Conclusion   144

References   144

15 RESEARCH AS PRAXIS METHOD   147

Ontology   147

Epistemology   148

Methodology   148

Processes of the Method   148

References   149

16 Life Patterns of Persons with Coronary Heart Disease
[Reprinted]   151

    Margaret A. Newman RN; PhD, and Susan Diemert Moch, RN; PhD

Procedures   152

Findings   153

   Similarities of Patterns   153

      The Need to Excel   153

      The Need to Please Others   154

      The Feeling of Being Alone   154

   Differences Among Individual Patterns   156

      Binding Stage   158

      Centering Stage   158

      Choice Stage   159

      Transcendent Stage   160

      Disorganization and Death   160

Pattern Conclusions   161

Implications for Practice   161

References   162

17 The Human Becoming Modes of Inquiry   165

Ontology   165

Epistemology   165

Methodologies   167

   The Parse Method   167

      Processes of the Method   170

   The Human Becoming Hermeneutic Method   172

      Processes of the Method   172

   The Qualitative Descriptive Preproject-Process-Postproject Method   174

      Processes of the Method   174

References   179

18 The Lived Experience of Contentment: A Study Using the
Parse Research Method   183

Nursing Perspective   188

Participant Selection and Protection of Participants' Rights   188

Methodology   189

   Myra's Story   190

Joan's Story 191

Judith's Story 191

Angela's Story 192

Marianne's Story 193

Janet's Story 194

Jeanine's Story 194

Elizabeth's Story 195

Anna's Story 195

Julie's Story 196

Propositions 197

Discussion of Findings 197

Satisfying Calmness Amid the Arduous 198

Resolute Liberty 199

Benevolent Engagements 199

Findings and Related Literature 200

New Knowledge 200

Recommendations 201

Summary 201

References 201

19 "Mendacity" as the Refusal to Bear Witness: A Human Becoming Hermeneutic Study of a Theme from Tennessee Williams' "Cat on a Hot Tin Roof" 205

William K. Cody, RN; PhD

The Hermeneutic Situation for the Study 206

Nursing Perspective: The Human Becoming School of Thought as the Horizon of Inquiry 208

Significance for Nursing Science 209

Methodology 209

Findings 210

Discussion 216

Emergent Meanings 218

References 219

20 Evaluation of the Human Becoming Theory in Practice in an Acute Care Psychiatric Setting [reprinted] 221

Deborah Thoun Northrup, RN; PhD
William K. Cody, RN; PhD

Selecting Parse's Theory of Human Becoming   222

Purposes of the Study   222

Method and Procedures   223

   Setting and Sample Selection   223

   Protection of Participants' Rights   224

   Data Collection   224

Introducing Parse's Theory-Based Practice   224

Presentation of Findings   225

   Nurse Descriptions   225

      Pre-Implementation: All Units   225

      Themes in the Change Process: Mid- and Post-Implementation   226

   Changes Described by Patients   229

      Unit One   229

      Unit Two   230

      Unit Three   230

   Manager and Supervisor Perceptions   231

      Unit One   231

      Unit Two   231

      Unit Three   231

   Changes in Documentation   233

Conclusions   234

      Unit One   234

      Unit Two   234

      Unit Three   234

Discussion   234

Recommendations   235

References   236

21 EMERGING QUALITATIVE METHODS OF THE SCIENCE OF UNITARY
HUMAN BEINGS   237

Ontology   237

Epistemology   238

Emerging Qualitative Methodologies   239

   Rogerian Process of Inquiry Method   239

      Processes of the Method 239

   Unitary Field Pattern Portrait Method   240

      Processes of the Method 240

Unitary Pattern Appreciation Case Method   241
  Processes of the Method   241
Contributions of the Methods   241
References   242

22 CRITERIA FOR CRITICAL APPRAISAL OF QUALITATIVE RESEARCH   243
Conceptual   244
Ethical   244
Methodological   246
Interpretive   246
References   247

23 CONSIDERING TOMORROW: PARSE'S THEORY-GUIDED RESEARCH
[REPRINTED]   249
  Sandra Schmidt Bunkers, RN; PhD
Significance and Research Question   250
Nursing Perspective   250
Research Method and Findings   251
  Participants and Setting   252
  Processes of the Method and Findings   252
Discussion of Findings   256
Considering Tomorrow, Health, and Quality of Life   260
Core Concepts and Related Literature   260
Implications for Research   262
Reflections   262
References   262

24 CRITICAL APPRAISAL OF "CONSIDERING TOMORROW: PARSE'S
THEORY-GUIDED RESEARCH"   265
Conceptual   265
Ethical   266
Methodological   267
Interpretive   269
Conclusion   270
References   270

25 EXAMPLE OF A QUALITATIVE RESEARCH GRANT PROPOSAL 271

Abstract 271

Background 271

Nursing Perspective 272

Related Research: Previous Work of Principal Investigator 273

Other Related Literature 273

Participant Selection and Protection of Participants' Rights 275

Methodology 275

Significance to Nursing and Other Health Disciplines 277

Evaluation 278

References 279

26 QUALITATIVE RESEARCH AND THE USE OF COMPUTERS 283

Debra A. Bournes, RN; PhD

The Possibilities 284

Storing, Handling, and Finding Multiple Documents Simultaneously 284

Searching Text 285

Coding and Retrieving Data 286

Links Between Objects [Hyperlinks] 288

Indexing, Graphing, or Modeling Information 289

Handling External Data 289

Annotating Data 290

Displaying and Developing Data in Rich Text Format 290

Facilitating Use of Data in Multiple Programs Using XML 290

Supporting Teamwork 291

Using Computers in Qualitative Research: Areas of Concern 291

Choosing the Right Tool(s): Ontological-Epistemological-
    Methodological Congruence 292

REFERENCES 298

CODA 301

SELECTED REFERENCES 303

Books 303

Articles and Book Chapters 312

Theses and Dissertations 329

AUTHOR INDEX 331

SUBJECT INDEX 335

ORIGINAL CONTRIBUTORS

Debra A. Bournes, RN; PhD
Assistant Professor
School of Nursing
York University
Toronto, Ontario, Canada

William K. Cody, RN; PhD
Associate Professor and Chairperson
Family and Community Nursing
University of North Carolina at Charlotte
Charlotte, North Carolina

TABLES

1–1   QUALITATIVE RESEARCH METHODS: ONTOLOGICAL-
       METHODOLOGICAL CONGRUENCE WITH DISCIPLINE-SPECIFIC
       FRAME OF REFERENCE   6

1–2   CONGRUENCE AMONG PHENOMENON, RESEARCH QUESTION,
       AND METHOD   8

1–3   ONTOLOGY, EPISTEMOLOGY, AND METHODOLOGY WITH
       DISCIPLINARY ORIGIN OF RESEARCH METHOD   10

2–1   DESCRIPTIONS OF QUALITATIVE RESEARCH PROCEDURES AND
       METHODS FOR THE HUMAN SCIENCES   16

2–2   SPECTRUM OF QUALITATIVE RESEARCH METHODS   24

8–1   PARADOXICAL RHYTHMS EMERGING FROM THE THEMES   72

9–1   DIFFERENCES IN PHENOMENOLOGICAL PHILOSOPHIES:
       HUSSERL AND HEIDEGGER   78

10–1   ELEMENTS COMMON TO THE EXPERIENCE OF LAUGHING WITH
       SOME DESCRIPTIVE EXPRESSIONS   91

12–1   REPRESENTATIVE ORIGINAL PROTOCOL   115

12–2   SIGNIFICANT STATEMENTS   116

12–3   THEME CLUSTERS AGGREGATED FROM THE FORMULATED
       MEANINGS   119

12–4   THE EXHAUSTIVE DESCRIPTION OF SELF-TRANSCENDENCE   121

12–5   THE FUNDAMENTAL STRUCTURE OF SELF-TRANSCENDENCE   122

16–1   PARTICIPANTS' DESCRIPTIONS OF ALONENESS, LACK OF
          CONNECTEDNESS   155

17–1   THE HUMAN BECOMING SCHOOL OF THOUGHT   166

17–2   HUMAN BECOMING MODES OF INQUIRY   168

17–3   DIFFERENCES BETWEEN THE PARSE RESEARCH METHOD AND
          SIMILAR QUALITATIVE RESEARCH METHODS   169

17–4   ASSUMPTIONS UNDERPINNING HERMENEUTICS AND THE
          HUMAN BECOMING HERMENEUTIC METHOD   173

17–5   THE HUMAN BECOMING THEORY IN PRACTICE   176

17–6   HUMAN BECOMING IN PRACTICE: SAMPLE DOCUMENTATION
          FORMAT   178

18–1   PROGRESSIVE ABSTRACTION OF THE CORE CONCEPTS
          OF THE LIVED EXPERIENCE OF CONTENTMENT   198

22–1   CRITERIA FOR APPRAISAL OF QUALITATIVE RESEARCH:
          CONCEPTUAL, ETHICAL, METHODOLOGICAL, AND
          INTERPRETIVE DIMENSIONS   245

23–1   EXTRACTION-SYNTHESIS PROCESS WITH RELATED
          PROPOSITIONS   253

23–2   PROPOSITIONAL STATEMENTS OF PARTICIPANTS   255

23–3   THE LIVED EXPERIENCE OF CONSIDERING TOMORROW   257

23–4   HEURISTIC INTERPRETATION: PROGRESSIVE ABSTRACTION OF
          CORE CONCEPTS OF CONSIDERING TOMORROW   257

26–1   USING A COMPUTER TO ASSIST WITH ORGANIZING A PARSE METHOD STUDY   294

26–2   GENERAL CAPABILITIES OF WELL-KNOWN QUALITATIVE SOFTWARE PACKAGES   296

26–3   ONLINE RESOURCES WITH UP-TO-DATE INFORMATION ABOUT QUALITATIVE RESEARCH SOFTWARE   298

FIGURES

2–1   SAMPLE CONSENT FORM   21

14–1   LEININGER'S SUNRISE MODEL TO DEPICT THE THEORY
OF CULTURE CARE DIVERSITY AND UNIVERSALITY   136

16–1   YOUNG'S SEQUENCING OF HUMAN EVOLUTION   157

On the brink of illumination,
the old ways are very seductive and liable to pull you back.

~ *Sri Ramakrishna*

As you go the way of life, you will see a great chasm.
Jump.
It is not as wide as you think.

~ *Joseph Campbell*

Novus ordo seclorum:
A new order of the ages is born.

~ *Virgil*

PREFACE

There is a notable shift in inquiry on health and quality of life in the discipline of nursing and in other human sciences. The shift is toward a desire for understanding humanly lived experiences. Finding answers to research questions about lived experiences requires the use of rigorous qualitative methods, since human experience cannot be quantified or held captive in reports with digital measures.

It is important to distinguish just what is meant by research and qualitative research as presented in this book. Research here refers to formal research conducted in a rigorous fashion following a well-defined method. It is differentiated from systematic inquiry and problem solving. Although both systematic inquiry and problem solving are essential in conducting formal research, neither is research in itself. Systematic inquiry is a library database search for information about a phenomenon. Problem solving, inherent in human living, is a trial-and-error process to resolve dilemmas and is often called research in instances where technical problems in nursing practice require solutions. Neither of these processes are considered research in this book.

It is necessary also to clarify the meaning of qualitative research as used in this book. Qualitative research is referred to by some researchers as the open-ended questions that may appear in a survey or at the end of a quantitative study. For purposes of this book, however, qualitative research is defined as *the systematic study of phenomena with rigorous adherence to a design, the data of which comprises oral, written, or artistic descriptions of human experiences, and for which there are no digital findings.*

The purpose of this work is sixfold: (1) to specify the assumptions of sciencing with qualitative research; (2) to describe the conceptual, ethical, methodological, and interpretive dimensions of qualitative research; (3) to present the ontology, epistemology, and methodology for selected qualitative approaches to research; (4) to present examples of some of the most frequently used qualitative research methods; (5) to set forth criteria for critical appraisal of qualitative research with demonstration of a critique; and (6) to present a well-developed qualitative grant proposal—including a budget and timetable.

Qualitative methods from the human science disciplines and qualitative methods unique to the discipline of nursing are presented. Established nursing methods (Leininger, 1985, 1988, 1995; Newman, 1994/2000; Parse, 1987, 1995, 1998) and emerging nursing methods (Butcher, 1996, 1998; Carboni, 1995; Cowling, 1998) from the science of unitary human beings (Rogers, 1970, 1994) are presented in their original form.

Faculty, graduate students, researchers, and practitioners of nursing, as well as other human science and health professionals, will find this book informative. This is especially true if they are interested in gaining an understanding of the elements of qualitative research methods, critiquing qualitative research, and writing grant proposals for the funding of qualitative research.

This work is offered in the spirit of scholarly dialogue and in an effort to foster rigor in qualitative inquiry.

REFERENCES

Butcher, H. K. (1996). A unitary field pattern portrait of dispiritedness in later life. *Visions: The Journal of Rogerian Nursing Science*, 4(1), 41–58.

Butcher, H. K. (1998). Crystallizing the processes of the unitary field pattern portrait research method. *Visions: The Journal of Rogerian Nursing Science*, 6(1), 13–26.

Carboni, J. T. (1995). The Rogerian process of inquiry. *Nursing Science Quarterly*, 8, 22–37.

Cowling, W. R. (1998). Unitary case inquiry. *Nursing Science Quarterly*, 11, 139–141.

Leininger, M. M. (Ed.). (1985). *Qualitative research methods in nursing*. Orlando, FL: Grune and Stratton.

Leininger, M. (1988). Leininger's theory of nursing: Cultural care diversity and universality. *Nursing Science Quarterly*, 1, 152–160.

Leininger, M. (Ed.). (1995). *Transcultural nursing: Concepts, theories, research, and practices* (2nd ed.). New York: McGraw-Hill.

Newman, M. A. (2000). *Health as expanding consciousness* (2nd ed.). Sudbury, MA: Jones and Bartlett/National League for Nursing Press. (Original work published 1994)

Parse, R. R. (1987). Nursing science: *Major paradigms, theories, and critiques*. Philadelphia: Saunders.

Parse, R. R. (Ed.). (1995). *Illuminations: The human becoming theory in practice and research*. New York: National League for Nursing Press.

Parse, R. R. (1998). *The human becoming school of thought: A perspective for nurses and other health professionals*. Thousand Oaks, CA: Sage.

Rogers, M. E. (1970). *An introduction to the theoretical basis of nursing*. Philadelphia: Davis.

Rogers, M. E. (1994). The science of unitary human beings: Current perspectives. *Nursing Science Quarterly*, 7, 33–35.

CHAPTER 1

SCIENCING

A PROCESS OF INQUIRY

Sciencing (White, 1938) is coming to know and understand the meaning of phenomena of concern to a discipline. It is the ongoing process of inquiry that specifies knowing as the continuous incarnating of the unfamiliar with the familiar. The term *sciencing* implies that knowing is ever-changing with new experiences. Sciencing is in stark contrast to science, which specifies inquiry as pursuing and achieving the absolute truth, as if there are undisputable, unchanging truths. The word *science* comes from the old French term *science*, which means knowledge, and from the Latin word *scientia*, a noun formed from the present participle of the verb *scire*, meaning "to know." It implies knowledge gained through study (Barnhart, 1995; Klein, 1967; Onions, Friedrichsen, & Burchfield, 1966).

All inquiry (science or sciencing) into human phenomena is conducted to gain an understanding of something in a systematic way, but the goals of various approaches and methodologies are different. For example, the notion of inquiry as *sciencing* is particularly useful in describing the approach to research that purports to study human experiences. This approach to inquiry is grounded in an ontology that focuses on human experiences as unitary and ever-changing, thus absolute truths are not sought. The congruent methodologies are used to discover the meaning of experiences as lived and described by the people living the experiences. This focus on human experiences arises from the human sciences (see, for example, Dilthey, 1961, 1894/1977a, 1927/1977b; Fahlberg & Fahlberg, 1994; Foucault, 1994; Gadamer, 1976, 1960/1998; Giorgi, 1968, 1970, 1986, 1992; Guba & Lincoln, 1990; Mitchell & Cody, 1992; Parse, 1981, 1998; Polkinghorne, 1983, 1986a, 1986b, 1988; Ricoeur, 1981; Secord, 1990; Taylor, 1985; van Kaam, 1993; Van Manen, 1997a, 1997b; Watson, 1988, 1999), which are different from the natural sciences (see,

1

for example, Bacon, 1561–1626/1996; Descartes, 1596–1650/1965; Hume, 1711–1776/1977; Kant, 1724–1804/1998; Laudan, 1996; Popper, 1959) in that the natural science methodologies have a causal ontology and elicit quantitative data from observable phenomena to confirm or reject causal relationships. "The working model of the natural sciences is constituted by the concepts of a causal order in a physical world and their particular methodology consists of procedures for discovering it" (Dilthey, 1961, p. 109).

Dilthey (1894/1977a, 1927/1977b; Ermarth, 1978) points to a concern that the natural science methodologies do not capture the meaning of life. He says that to understand meaning and pattern in life, study should be made of unitary human's participative experience with situations. The human sciences, according to Dilthey (1894/1977a, 1927/1977b), illuminate meanings, values, and relationships to gain understanding of human experiences. The ontological base of a research tradition that focuses on discovering the meaning of humanly lived phenomena is acausal, reflecting the idea that humans cocreate experiences in mutual process with the universe. The term *sciencing*, then, best describes the approach to inquiry with the qualitative research presented in this book.

ASSUMPTIONS ABOUT SCIENCING

There are four assumptions underpinning sciencing.

1. To question is to reach beyond what is with what is possible.
2. A question in itself incarnates the questioner's attitudes, beliefs, and style and points to personal projects.
3. Both questions and answers are set with the boundaries of the questioner's understanding of the phenomenon.
4. The questioning process and the answers are intersubjective.

To Question Is to Reach Beyond What Is With What Is Possible

Questions reflect what is and what might be. Humans are questioning beings who seek to comprehend or further understand what is given, while considering what is possible. Questioning is a way of rejecting what appears fixed; it is a way of contextualizing the moment in light of what might be possible.

A Question in Itself Incarnates the Questioner's Attitudes, Beliefs, and Style and Points to Personal Projects

A question presupposes a grasp of what is and what might be, that is, the individual's perspectival experience of the *what is* and *what is possible* all-at-once. All knowledge is personal knowledge, so one's understanding of a phenomenon is always perspectival; it is always from the individual's own frame of reference—which is imbued with personal meaning arising from the human-universe mutual process. Questions about a phenomenon can arise only from a knowing of that phenomenon. Questions both disclose and hide the questioner's personal projects and knowledge of phenomena. Questions thematize entities of significance and arise from the individual's life experience. For example, three people enter the forest and raise questions disclosing their projects:

The businessperson asks: "How can we move this lumber to the yard for sale?"

The environmentalist asks: "How can we preserve the trees?"

The hunter asks: "Where are the most frequent hiding places for deer?"

Which is the correct way of viewing the forest? Clearly, it depends on the questioner's knowledge and personal projects, since all are appropriate questions.

Both Questions and Answers Are Set With the Boundaries of the Questioner's Understanding of the Phenomenon

What and how questions are asked already prefigures and delineates the answers. A horizon expands and all-at-once confines personal visioning, since knowing is always perspectival. Human beings, as meaning givers, take a stance through questioning, which both opens and closes possibilities. For example, in a Catholic family there are four sons whose questions about the sacrament of reconciliation reveal the boundaries of potential answers:

The first son asks: "How can I better understand the meaning of and participate in the sacrament of reconciliation?" This son recognizes that this sacrament is integral to his history and he wants to know more.

The second son asks: "What does all this have to do with me?" This son acknowledges the sacrament of reconciliation as something significant, but not as an actuality related to his projects.

The third son asks: "What is all this?" This son sees the reconciliation ritual simply as what is, but does not grasp it as an entity of concern to him.

The fourth son does not ask any questions relevant to the sacrament of reconciliation. For this son it is not a phenomenon of significance, or an actuality of his knowing.

An individual's understanding is imbued with the presuppositions, preconceptions, and biases of his or her own belief system. The nature of the question foreshadows the possibilities of the answers.

The Questioning Process and the Answers Are Intersubjective

Questions lead to certain answers and answers reflect the questions. The researcher-researched dialectic gives rise to a cocreated horizon of meaning. The researcher (questioner) is part of the research in an explicit way, since he or she asks the question, plans the design, conducts the research, and interprets the findings.

The qualitative researcher is simultaneously an explorer, a cartographer, a synthesizer, and an interpreter, investigating a phenomenon to enhance understanding. The researcher as explorer combs the literature and dwells with the phenomenon to ascertain what research question to ask in a formal research project. The researcher as cartographer maps the plan, following a rigorous extant method specifying each phase of the design. The researcher as synthesizer dwells with the data, organizing and discovering essences, patterns, and themes. The researcher as interpreter creatively weaves the patterns and themes into a coherent description or explanation of the phenomenon under study. The researcher is inextricably connected with the researched and the project is marked with the researcher's uniqueness.

BUILDING KNOWLEDGE WITH QUALITATIVE RESEARCH

Knowledge is built in a discipline through discipline-specific research. Concepts in the knowledge world of any discipline emerge from a universe of discourse that can be divided into levels of abstraction and selected to create, explain, or describe a situation. Discourse has two elements: context (or situatedness) and novelty, which is what is being said about the uniqueness of the situation. The language of science is embedded in the disciplinary frameworks and theories, which are written at an abstract level explicating both the situatedness of concepts and their unique meanings. In order to build knowledge, research findings are interpreted in the language of science.

With qualitative research, the knowledge about human experiences arises from descriptions given by humans. The descriptions are in concrete language, and through the research process that language is gradually transposed over levels of discourse to the abstract language of science. For instance, in describing the lived experience of hope, a research participant might speak about *picturing accomplishments*. The researcher could then transpose *picturing accomplishments* to a higher level of abstraction as *envisioning triumphs*. Another participant might describe *persisting amid the ups and downs of life*. At a higher level of abstraction, the researcher could capture the ideas expressed by the participant as *pushing-resisting with the arduous*. A simpler example of transposing levels of discourse is Mary–person–individual–human. In moving up levels of abstraction, ideas become gradually more abstract and simultaneously less specific. Sound sciencing is conducted and reported respecting the levels of discourse. It begins with the choice of a phenomenon of interest.

The research question arises from the phenomenon of interest. It is what the researcher wants to know about the phenomenon. What the researcher wants to know about a phenomenon reveals the ontological grounding of that researcher. The research question leads to a method. Table 1–1 on page 6 shows qualitative research methods, the ontological origins of each method, and whether or not a discipline-specific theory may be used as a theoretical perspective with each particular method (Parse, 1996). Table 1–2 on page 8 shows examples of phenomena for study, research questions emanating from each phenomenon, and the qualitative method of choice to answer the question. Table 1–3 on page 10 illustrates the various qualitative research methodologies and specifies their disciplinary origin, ontology, and epistemology.

TABLE 1–1   QUALITATIVE RESEARCH METHODS: ONTOLOGICAL-
METHODOLOGICAL CONGRUENCE WITH DISCIPLINE-
SPECIFIC FRAME OF REFERENCE

METHOD	ORIGINAL ONTOLOGICAL BASE	DISCIPLINE-SPECIFIC FRAME OF REFERENCE
Grounded theory	Symbolic interactionism and pragmatism	Symbolic interactionism and pragmatism are the perspectives that guide grounded theory studies.
Narrative research	Human science	Discipline-specific theoretical perspective can be explicated as a guide to study.
Heuristic research	Humanistic psychology	Discipline-specific theoretical perspective can be explicated as a guide to study.
Hermeneutics	Literary science	Discipline-specific theoretical perspective can be explicated as a guide to study.
Qualitative descriptive	Social science	(Researcher specifies frame of reference with which s/he approaches the text.)
Phenomeno-logical	Method can follow one of two ontological paths as originated by	Discipline-specific theoretical perspective can be explicated as a guide to study.
	Husserl	Researcher holds in abeyance all beliefs about phenomenon.
	Heidegger	Researcher makes preconceptions about phenomenon explicit.
Ethnography	Anthropology	Discipline-specific theoretical perspective can be explicated as a guide to study.

TABLE 1–1   Qualitative Research Methods: Ontological-Methodological Congruence With Discipline-Specific Frame of Reference (Continued)

Method	Original Ontological Base	Discipline-Specific Frame of Reference
Established Nursing Methods: Basic Research		
Ethnonursing method	Nursing	Culture care theory
Research as praxis method	Nursing	Health as expanding consciousness
Parse research method	Nursing	Human becoming school of thought
Human becoming hermeneutic method	Nursing	Human becoming school of thought
Established Nursing Methods: Applied Research		
Qualitative descriptive preproject-process-postproject method	Nursing	Human becoming school of thought
Emerging Nursing Methods: Basic Research		
Rogerian process of inquiry	Nursing	Science of unitary human beings
Unitary field pattern portrait method	Nursing	Science of unitary human beings
Unitary pattern appreciation case method	Nursing	Science of unitary human beings

TABLE 1–2 CONGRUENCE AMONG PHENOMENON, RESEARCH QUESTION, AND METHOD

PHENOMENA FOR STUDY	EXAMPLE	RESEARCH QUESTION	METHOD
Changing patterns of social systems and processes	Nurse-person relationship	What are the social dynamics of nurse-person relationships?	Grounded theory
Human experience	Life process		Narrative research Descriptive Explanatory
		What truths arose from Ghandi's life story? Why did Ghandi's life unfold as it did?	
Human experience	Joy	What is joyful experience like?	Heuristic research
Human experience	Suffering	What is it like to be suffering as expressed in the Holocaust records?	Hermeneutics
Human experience	Feeling lonely	What is the meaning of feeling lonely?	Qualitative descriptive
Human experience	Loneliness		Phenomenological van Kaam Giorgi Colaizzi
		What is the structural definition of loneliness? What is the structural description of loneliness? What are the essential features of loneliness?	
Cultural patterns	Courage	What is courage like for Latino Americans with chronic health concerns?	Enthnography
		Established Nursing Methods: Basic Research	
Cultural care patterns	Cultural care patterns of Chinese Americans in Chicago	What are the cultural care patterns of Chinese people who live in Chicago?	Ethnonursing method

Life patterns	Life patterns after heart surgery	What are the life patterns of persons who have had heart surgery?	Research as praxis method
Universal lived experiences	Contentment	What is the structure of the lived experience of contentment?	Parse research method
Universal lived experiences	Being human	What does it mean to be human?	Human becoming hermeneutic method
		Established Nursing Methods: Applied Research	
Changing patterns	Changing patterns when the human becoming theory guides practice	What happens to nurses' beliefs and practices, persons' and families' experiences of nursing care, and multidisciplinary healthcare providers' opinions of nursing care when the human becoming theory is the basis for practice? Or What happens when the human becoming practice methodology is lived with individuals or groups?	Qualitative descriptive preproject-process-postproject method
		Emerging Nursing Methods: Basic Research	
Human-environment pattern manifestations	Nurse-client relationship	What is the pandimensional unitary field process in a nurse-client relationship?	Science of unitary human beings methods Rogerian process of inquiry method
	Dispiritedness	What is the unitary field pattern portrait of dispiritedness?	Unitary field pattern portrait method
	Despair	What is the pattern of a person experiencing despair as the dominant sensation of his/her experience?	Unitary pattern appreciation method

TABLE 1–3 ONTOLOGY, EPISTEMOLOGY, AND METHODOLOGY WITH DISCIPLINARY ORIGIN OF RESEARCH METHOD

DISCIPLINARY ORIGIN	ONTOLOGY	EPISTEMOLOGY	METHODOLOGY
Social sciences/social psychology	Symbolic interactionism and pragmatism	Changing patterns of social systems and processes	Grounded theory method
Human sciences	Discipline-specific ontology may be used	Human expressions, events, objects, ideas, or lived experiences	Narrative research method
Humanistic psychology	Discipline-specific ontology may be used	Meaning of human experiences surfacing from the personal questions, problems, or challenges of the researcher	Heuristic method
Literary science	Discipline-specific ontology may be used	Meaning of human projects and experiences as expressed in texts	Hermeneutic method
Social sciences	Discipline-specific ontology may be used	Patterns and themes of human experiences	Qualitative descriptive method
Philosophy and psychology	Husserlian-transcendental phenomenology Heideggerian-existential phenomenology	Essences of lived experience	Phenomenological method
Anthropology	Discipline-specific ontology may be used	Meanings of symbolic patterns arising in the language and activities of a cultural group	Ethnographic method

		Established Nursing Methods: Basic Research	
Nursing	Culture care theory	Cultural care patterns and values	Ethnonursing method
Nursing	Theory of health as expanding consciousness	Life patterns of the person-environment interaction	Research as praxis method
Nursing	Human becoming school of thought	Universal lived experiences of health from persons' descriptions	Parse research method
Nursing	Human becoming school of thought	Universal lived experiences of health from texts and artforms	Human becoming hermeneutic method
		Established Nursing Methods: Applied Research	
Nursing	Human becoming school of thought	Changing patterns	Qualitative descriptive preproject-process-postproject method
		Emerging Nursing Methods: Basic Research	
Nursing	Science of unitary human beings	Human-environment pattern manifestations	Science of unitary human beings methods
			Rogerian process of inquiry method
			Unitary field pattern portrait method
			Unitary pattern appreciation case method

REFERENCES

Bacon, F. (1996). *Collected works of Francis Bacon*. London: Routledge. (Original work written 1561–1626)

Barnhart, R. K. (Ed.). (1995). *The Barnhart concise dictionary of etymology* (p. 692). New York: HarperCollins.

Descartes, R. (1965). *A discourse on method and other works*. New York: Washington Square Press. (Original work written 1596–1650)

Dilthey, W. (1961). *Pattern and meaning in history*. New York: Harper & Row.

Dilthey, W. (1977a). Ideas concerning a descriptive and analytic psychology. In *Understanding* (pp. 23–120). The Hague: Martinus Nijhoff. (Original work published 1894)

Dilthey, W. (1977b). The understanding of other persons and their expressions of life. In R. M. Zaner & K. L. Heiges (Trans.), *Descriptive psychology and historical understanding* (pp. 123–144). The Hague: Martinus Nijhoff. (Original work published 1927)

Ermarth, M. (1978). *Wilhelm Dilthey: The critique of historical reason*. Chicago: University of Chicago Press.

Fahlberg, L. L., & Fahlberg, L. A. (1994). A human science for health: An overview. *Health Values, 18*(5), 3–12.

Foucault, M. (1994). *The order of things: An archeology of the human sciences*. New York: Vintage Books.

Gadamer, H.-G. (1976). *Philosophical hermeneutics* (D. E. Linge, Ed. & Trans.). Berkeley: University of California Press.

Gadamer, H.-G. (1998). *Truth and method* (2nd rev. ed.) (J. Weinsheimer & D. G. Marshall, Trans.). New York: Continuum. (Original work published 1960)

Giorgi, A. (1968). Existential phenomenology and the psychology of the human person. *Review of Existential Psychology & Psychiatry, 8*(2), 102–116.

Giorgi, A. (1970). *Psychology as a human science: A phenomenologically based approach*. New York: Harper & Row.

Giorgi, A. (1986). The "context of discovery/context of verification" distinction and descriptive human science. *Journal of Phenomenological Psychology, 17*(2), 151–166.

Giorgi, A. (1992). The idea of human science. *Humanistic Psychologist, 20*(2–3), 202–217.

Guba, E. G., & Lincoln, Y. S. (1990). Can there be a human science: Constructivism as an alternative. *Person Centered Review, 5*(2), 130–154.

Hume, D. (1977). *Philosophical essays concerning human understanding*. Indianapolis: Hackett. (Original work written 1711–1776)

Kant, I. (1998). *Critique of pure reason*. Cambridge, UK: Cambridge University Press. (Original work written 1724–1804)

Klein, E. (1967). *A comprehensive etymological dictionary of the English language* (Vol. II, L-Z, p. 1397). New York: Elsevier.

Laudan, L. (1996). *Beyond positivism and relativism: Theory, method, and evidence*. Boulder, CO: Westview Press.

Mitchell, G. J., & Cody, W. K. (1992). Nursing knowledge and human science: Ontological and epistemological considerations. *Nursing Science Quarterly, 5*, 54–61.

Onions, C. T., Friedrichsen, G. W. S., & Burchfield, R. W. (Eds.). (1966). *Oxford English dictionary of English etymology* (p. 797). Oxford: Clarendon Press.

Parse, R. R. (1981). *Man-living-health: A theory of nursing.* New York: Wiley.

Parse, R. R. (1996). Building knowledge through qualitative research: The road less traveled. *Nursing Science Quarterly, 9,* 10–16.

Parse, R. R. (1998). *The human becoming school of thought: A perspective for nurses and other health professionals.* Thousand Oaks, CA: Sage.

Polkinghorne, D. (1983). *Methodology for the human sciences: Systems of inquiry.* Albany: State University of New York Press.

Polkinghorne, D. E. (1986a). Changing conversations about human science. *Saybrook Review,* 6(1), 1–32.

Polkinghorne, D. E. (1986b). Conceptual validity in nontheoretical human science. *Journal of Phenomenological Psychology,* 17(2), 129–149.

Polkinghorne, D. E. (1988). *Narrative knowing and the human sciences.* Albany: State University of New York Press.

Popper, K. R. (1959). *The logic of scientific discovery.* London: Hutchinson.

Ricoeur, P. (1981). *Hermeneutics and the human sciences.* New York: Cambridge University Press.

Secord, P. (1990). The need for a radically new human science. In D. N. Robinson & P. L. Mos (Eds.), *Annals of theoretical psychology volume* 6 (pp. 75–87). New York: Plenum Press.

Taylor, C. (1985). Interpretation and the sciences of man: Philosophy and the human sciences. *Philosophical Papers,* 2, 15–57, New York: Cambridge University Press.

van Kaam, A. (1993). Psychology as a human science and the human science of transcendent formation. *Studies in Formative Spirituality,* 14(2), 247–270.

Van Manen, M. (1997a). From meaning to method. *Qualitative Health Research,* 7(3), 345–369.

Van Manen, M. (1997b). *Researching lived experience: Human science for an action sensitive pedagogy* (2nd ed.). London, Ontario: Althouse Press.

Watson, J. (1988). *Nursing: Human science and human care. A theory of nursing.* New York: National League for Nursing.

Watson, J. (1999). *Postmodern nursing and beyond.* New York: Churchill Livingstone.

White, L. (1938). Science is sciencing. *Philosophy of Science,* 5(4), 369–389.

CHAPTER 2

DIMENSIONS OF THE RESEARCH PROCESS

The qualitative research process has four major dimensions: conceptual, ethical, methodological, and interpretive. The logical flow of a research study depends on coherence among these dimensions. There is much debate over the way ontology, epistemology, and methodology are connected. One view perpetuates the idea that the ontology specifies the theoretical, the epistemology guides the focus, and the methodology is merely the procedure that best analyzes the data. From this view, even if the research question focuses on a unitary human pattern manifestation, the methodology may be quasi-experimental—which is grounded in a causal, nonunitary ontology (Barrett, 1996; Goodwin & Goodwin, 1984). The other view is that in order for inquiry to be logically coherent, the ontology dictates the epistemology and the methodology, and, thus, the links are internally consistent (Denzin & Lincoln, 1994, 2000; Guba & Lincoln, 1994; Mitchell & Cody, 1992; Parse, 1996a; Powers, 1987). For example, if the phenomenon of interest and the research question of a study are concerned with understanding a unitary humanly lived experience, then it follows that the methodology of choice is qualitative. The choice of a particular qualitative method depends on how the question is asked (see Tables 1–2 and 1–3 in Chapter 1) (Parse, 1996a).

In all qualitative research there is a phenomenon to be studied that is distinct and separate from the participant group. The choice of phenomenon reflects the ontological frame of reference of the researcher, and the research question arises from this frame of reference. The research question announces what the researcher is seeking to discover and which design is to be used in conducting the research study. Selection of and number of participants are decided by the researcher in conjunction with the specifications of the method. Ethical standards are honored throughout the research project.

Data-gathering and analysis processes are governed by the chosen method and are adhered to strictly. Interpretation of findings reflects the conceptualization of the study and specifies new discipline-specific knowledge. It is important to note that qualitative research methods are different from research procedures (see Table 2–1 for differentiation details).

TABLE 2–1   DESCRIPTIONS OF QUALITATIVE RESEARCH PROCEDURES AND
METHODS FOR THE HUMAN SCIENCES

GENERAL HUMAN SCIENCE PROCEDURES AND METHODS

Procedures

Content analysis is a procedure to determine numerical frequencies of words and phrases describing phenomena. This is primarily a quantitative process, though qualitative thematic induction in coding has resulted in it being classified with qualitative methods (see Denzin & Lincoln, 1994, 2000).

Conversational analysis is a procedure that uses casual conversations as the data, and the analysis leads to an understanding of social relationships. When the conversations are discourses from institutions, sociocultural organizations, films, art, CD ROMs, or texts, it may be called *discourse analysis* (see Denzin & Lincoln, 2000; Gubrium & Holstein, 2000; Silverman, 2000).

Feminist qualitative procedure focuses on women's concerns related to power, gender, economics, and other key issues (see Denzin & Lincoln, 2000; Olesen, 2000).

Interpretive phenomenology is a procedure used to analyze experiences in their social contexts (see Benner, 1994).

Methods

Grounded theory is a social science method used to study changing patterns of social systems and processes from the ontological base of symbolic interactionism and pragmatism (see Artinian, 1998; Charmaz, 2000; Corbin & Strauss, 1990; Glaser, 1978, 1995; Glaser & Strauss, 1967; Parse, 1996a; Strauss, 1987; Strauss & Corbin, 1994).

Narrative research is a linguistic production method providing insights into the whole structure of an event, idea, object, or lived experience (see Denzin & Lincoln, 2000; Parse, 1996a; Ricoeur, 1984, 1985, 1988).

Heuristic research is a formal method used to discover the meaning of human experiences surfacing from the personal questions, problems, or challenges of the researcher (see Moustakas, 1961, 1967, 1990; Parse, 1996a).

Hermeneutics is a method used to interpret text (see Cody, 1995; Dilthey, 1961, 1976, 1883/1988; Gadamer, 1976, 1960/1998; Heidegger, 1962; Parse, 1996a, 1998; Schleiermacher, 1805/1977).

Qualitative descriptive is a formal method used to intensively investigate a phenomenon to discover patterns and themes that can be interpreted in light of a nursing, or other human science, frame of reference. It may be called exploratory or case depending on the details of the procedures (see Parse, 1996a, 1996c).

TABLE 2–1   DESCRIPTIONS OF QUALITATIVE RESEARCH PROCEDURES AND
METHODS FOR THE HUMAN SCIENCES (CONTINUED)

GENERAL HUMAN SCIENCE PROCEDURES AND METHODS

Methods (continued)

Phenomenology is a formal method to uncover the meaning of lived
experiences (see Colaizzi, 1973, 1978; Giorgi, 1985, 1986a, 1986b, 1989,
1992a, 1997; Parse, 1996a; Spiegelberg, 1975, 1976, 1981, 1960/1982; van
Kaam, 1959, 1966; Van Manen, 1990).

Ethnography is a formal method whose origin is anthropology. It is the study
of cultural values of groups. It is sometimes called field research because
the milieu is a natural setting for participant observation (see Parse, 1996a;
P. J. Pelto, 1970; Pelto & Pelto, 1973, 1976, 1981, 1996, 1997; Spradley, 1979,
1980; Tedlock, 2000).

ESTABLISHED NURSING METHODS: BASIC RESEARCH

Ethnonursing is a method used to describe, explain, and predict cultural care
patterns (see Leininger, 1985, 1995, 1996; Parse, 1996a).

Research as praxis is a method used to describe the nature of the life patterns
of person-environment interactions (see Newman, 1997, 1999, 1994/2000;
Parse, 1996a).

Parse research method is a phenomenological-hermeneutic method used to
discover structures of universal lived experiences (see Parse, 1987, 1992,
1995, 1996a, 1996b, 1997a, 1997b, 1998, 1999a).

Human becoming hermeneutic method is a method of inquiry that focuses on
interpretation and understanding of texts and artforms from a human
becoming perspective (see Cody, 1995; Parse, 1998).

ESTABLISHED NURSING METHODS: APPLIED RESEARCH

Qualitative descriptive preproject-process-postproject method is a method to ascertain
what happens when human becoming is the guide to practice (see Parse,
1995, 1998).

EMERGING NURSING METHODS: BASIC RESEARCH

Rogerian process of inquiry is a method used "to investigate the dynamic
enfolding-unfolding of human field–environmental field energy field
patterns and the evolutionary change of configurations of field patterning by
the nurse and client" (Carboni, 1995, p. 28).

Unitary field pattern portrait method is a method used to "create a unitary
understanding of the dynamic kaleidoscope and symphonic pattern
manifestations emerging from the pandimensional human/environmental
mutual process" (Butcher, 1998, p. 14).

Unitary pattern appreciation case method is a method used to "comprehend the
essence or pattern of the case" and "focuses on knowing and appreciating
the unitary pattern of another through the creation of a mutually
participative exploration of pattern manifestations" (Cowling, 1998, p. 141).

There is another significant debate related specifically to qualitative research. There are those authors (Field & Morse, 1985; Glaser, 1978; Glaser & Strauss, 1967; Knaack, 1984; Morse, 1992; Strauss, 1987; Strauss & Corbin, 1990, 1997, 1998) who purport that qualitative research is purely inductive and that the theoretical perspective of the researcher must be absent in the conduction of the study. Yet there are other seasoned qualitative researchers (Giorgi, 1968, 1970, 1971, 1985, 1986a, 1986b, 1989, 1992a, 1992b, 1997, 2000; Guba, 1990; Guba & Lincoln, 1989, 1990; Leininger, 1985; Mitchell, 1994, 1996; Mitchell & Cody, 1993; Newman, 1997, 1994/2000; Parse, 1987, 1992, 1995, 1996a, 1997a, 1997b, 1998, 1999a) who believe that qualitative research expands disciplinary knowledge. Knowledge and understanding of phenomena are perspectival and theory laden (Butler, 1992; Cody, 1995; Gadamer, 1976, 1960/1998; Giorgi, 1968, 1970, 1971, 1985, 1986a, 1986b, 1989, 1992a, 1992b, 1997, 2000; Guba, 1990; Guba & Lincoln, 1989, 1990; Heidegger, 1962, 1975; Kockelmans, 1967, 1985; Mitchell, 1994; Parse, 1981, 1996a, 1998; Reeder, 1988; Ricoeur, 1976, 1981). There is no atheoretical approach to inquiry. Mitchell and Cody (1993) elaborate on this notion. They contend that with grounded theory, for example, "the actual role of *theory* is veiled in obscurity" (p. 171). Although Glaser and Strauss (1967) say that grounded theory studies must not begin with presuppositions about the phenomenon, they acknowledge that symbolic interactionism and pragmatism are the origins of their work and that the findings, that is, the theories generated from the studies, are social science. Mitchell and Cody (1993) further specify that ethnography and phenomenology—including both Husserl's (1913/1962, 1965, 1931/1991) and Heidegger's (1962) phenomenology and the methods of their followers (see for example, Colaizzi, 1973, 1978; Giorgi, 1989, 1997; van Kaam, 1959, 1966)—are theory laden. Mitchell and Cody also offer examples of research studies that implicitly illuminate the theoretical perspectives of the researcher in studies purported by the authors to be without presuppositions about the phenomena under study.

CONCEPTUAL DIMENSION

The conceptual dimension refers to three major areas related to the ontological and epistemological aspects of inquiry: the frame of reference, the phenomenon, and the research question. The frame of reference is the belief system from which the phenomenon and research question arise; it is the paradigmatic perspective of the researcher. The belief system, that is, the ontology, encompasses the basic assumptions about the phenomenon, and the question reflects the researcher's knowledge and particular interest in the phenomenon.

Frame of Reference

For researchers in the human sciences, the paradigmatic perspective encompasses a belief that human beings participate in creating the phenomenon of interest. "The human sciences are possible only because we directly participate in their subject matter" (Macquarrie, 1968, p. 36). The researcher's frame of reference shapes the study. It is the conceptualization that prefigures the pattern of the research. It is stated in the specific language of the discipline and makes explicit the researcher's theoretical view of the phenomenon under study.

The Phenomenon and the Research Question

The phenomenon of the research is the concept under study stated at an abstract level. For example, the phenomenon may be the experience of courage, hope, caring for someone, privacy, presence, joy, happiness, love, or loneliness, among others. The research question is the interrogatory statement specifying what the researcher wants to know about the phenomenon. For instance, *What is the experience of happiness?* or *What is the meaning of being loved?* Refer to Table 1–2 for examples of qualitative research methods appropriate for studying specific types of phenomena and for answering particular research questions.

ETHICAL DIMENSION

The ethical dimension includes three areas: scientific merit, protection of participants, and integrity.

Scientific Merit

Scientific merit is the correspondence, coherence, and pragmatics of the research process. A research study with scientific merit enhances the knowledge base of the discipline by focusing on a phenomenon from a frame of reference relevant to the discipline, using the language of the discipline throughout the research process, and preserving semantic consistency. Scientific merit is reflected in the logical coherence of the entire research process. This is evident when there is careful articulation of a focus on discipline-specific knowledge acquisition—from discussion of the frame of reference through discussion of the findings. The scientific merit of a study also is reflected in the pragmatics of exploring, mapping, and conducting the study and synthesizing the findings.

Protection of Participants

The protection of participants is ensured through careful measures to preserve confidentiality, anonymity, safety, and the right to withdraw from the research at any time. Studies should be reviewed and approved by an institutional review board set up specifically for the protection of human subjects. Persons interested in participating in a study should be given a detailed verbal and written description of the study and be informed of what participation in the study will entail. Whether persons choose to participate should have no effect on any future services they receive.

Consent should be obtained from all participants and a copy of the signed consent form should be given to each participant. To ensure that participants' welfare and rights are protected, full disclosure of the study's purposes, procedures, and intent should be given. Participants' rights of privacy, confidentiality, and anonymity must be honored. For instance, to ensure privacy, participants can be given the opportunity to choose where they feel comfortable speaking. To ensure confidentiality, audiotapes and/or videotapes and transcriptions can be kept in a locked cabinet and erased or shredded after completion of the study. To protect anonymity of participants, only code numbers, or code names, should be used to identify participants during the research process and in publications. A consent form must include details about these protections and the risks and benefits of participating. A sample consent form is shown in Figure 2–1.

Integrity

Integrity is the consistent adherence to a set of ethical principles. With the advancement of knowledge, integrity is concerned with at least three major areas: false reporting of research findings, duplicate publication, and plagiarism. The ethical standards that govern reporting of qualitative and quantitative research findings include clarity, accuracy, and truthfulness. *Clarity* in reporting—meaning without obfuscation of the research question, the design, or the methodological nuances of the data-gathering and analysis-synthesis processes—is essential to integrity in reporting. *Accuracy* in reporting refers to scrupulous exactness in adhering to facts in presentation. It is the meticulous laying bare of the research process. Deviation from the facts violates standards and places the integrity of a report in question. *Truthfulness* refers to unreserved veracity in reporting. It is the forthright presentation of unaltered details. Integrity in reporting research findings is a heavy responsibility for both budding and seasoned scholars (adapted from Parse, 1999b).

Duplicate publication is another concern in preserving the integrity in the advancement of knowledge. It occurs when the same material is published in two different refereed journals as a way of inflating the publication record of the author(s). The ethical standards that govern duplicate publication are related to appropriate use of disciplinary resources and trustworthiness of the author. When sending a similar but well-disguised manuscript to more than one journal, there is an inappropriate use of disciplinary resources, that is, compromising the coveted space in refereed journals and using the time of seasoned scholars, editors, and publishers who critically appraise the work and prepare it for publication. Use of resources in this way truncates the acquisition of knowledge and reflects directly on the trustworthiness of the author. The trustworthiness of the author is the creditability with which he or she will become known. Preserving integrity in the advancement of knowledge requires authors to consider carefully the appropriate use of disciplinary resources when examining their manuscripts for publication (adapted from Parse, 1999b).

Figure 2–1   Sample consent form

CONSENT

I am willing to participate in this study on having courage being conducted by _____ . The purpose and procedure of the study have been fully explained to me, and I realize that I can end my participation at any time without penalty.

I understand that I will be asked to bring a personal symbol, picture, piece of music, poem, or metaphor of my experience of having courage and that I will be asked to describe it as part of my description of my experience of having courage. If possible, a photograph will be taken of the symbol, picture, piece of music, poem, or metaphor of having courage that I bring to share. I understand that the discussion will last from 20 to 60 minutes depending on how long I want to participate. The discussion will be audio and video tape recorded, and these tapes will be erased once the study is complete. I also understand that a transcript of the discussion will be made and that the transcript will be shredded when the study is complete. I have been told that my name will not appear on the written transcripts, reports, or any published papers. However, quotations and symbols, pictures, pieces of music, poems, or metaphors of having courage from our discussion may be used anonymously in reports of the study.

I understand that there are no known risks or benefits to such a discussion. However, my descriptions may contribute to the enhancement of nursing knowledge.

I understand that I am free to not answer any question. If during the discussion I become uncomfortable, I have the option to stop and withdraw from the study, or stop and reschedule.

I understand that I may call _____ at any time to talk about any concerns or questions I may have about my participation in the study.

I also have been informed that whether or not I participate will have no effect on services that I or any member of my family may receive.

I freely and voluntarily consent to participate in this study, and will be given a copy of this consent form.

_____   _____
Participant's Signature   Date

_____
Researcher's Signature

Plagiarism is another concern when considering integrity in the advancement of knowledge. Plagiarism is the act of presenting the work of another person as one's own. It is appropriating ideas, either written or spoken, without giving credit to the original author. Plagiarism may occur when lifting the title, a passage, a paragraph, a sentence, or a phrase from a work without acknowledging the source appropriately. Knowledge development progresses by building on what is known in a discipline; thus, quoting the work of others is essential to the enhancement of ideas. The crucial point is giving credit to the author of these ideas. When in doubt, consider presenting the source to preserve integrity in the advancement of knowledge (adapted from Parse, 1999b).

Preserving integrity is a growing concern as the information superhighway becomes the major mode of transporting ideas. The monitoring of adherence to ethical standards on this highway is yet to be formalized. Thus, it is the profound responsibility of each scholar to be vigilant when making contributions to the advancement of knowledge (adapted from Parse, 1999b).

METHODOLOGICAL DIMENSION

The methodological dimension encompasses the data-gathering and data analysis-synthesis phases of the research process. These phases are determined by the research question that drives the design of the study. Data-gathering choices for qualitative research are governed by the particular details of the research method being used. These choices include structured and nonstructured interviews, observation, participant observation, dialogical engagement, storytelling, written prose or poetic descriptions, hand or computer drawings, and rhythmical expressions such as music or dance. The data analysis-synthesis phase flows from the data gathering and also is governed by the details of the particular method being used. Data analysis-synthesis procedures are unique for each method and may include processes for writing summative narratives; identifying and synthesizing themes and patterns; creating propositions; developing pattern profiles; identifying common elements; extracting-synthesizing essences; and describing domains, taxonomies, and components, among others.

INTERPRETIVE DIMENSION

The interpretive dimension encompasses the description of findings in light of disciplinary knowledge and demonstrates the value of the findings for the advancement of science through theory development, research, and, where pertinent, practice. Interpretation and dissemination of findings with regard to the discipline is a responsibility of the researcher, since it is important that the new knowledge derived from the research be available to scholars in the discipline.

Table 2–2 is an overview of the conceptual, ethical, methodological, and interpretive dimensions of the spectrum of qualitative research methods presented in this book. These dimensions of the research process are an important consideration for good sciencing and they are essential as a guide to sound critique. See Chapter 22 for critique criteria related to these dimensions.

TABLE 2–2   SPECTRUM OF QUALITATIVE RESEARCH METHODS

METHOD	CONCEPTUAL	
	Ontology (*Frame of Reference and Purpose*)	*Epistemology* (*Phenomena/Example of Research Question*)
Grounded theory method	Symbolic interactionism and pragmatism	Patterns and processes of social units
	To discover social theory and to interpret, predict, and explain the perspectives and actions of multiple participants.	What are the social dynamics of kinship relations?
Narrative research method*	Human science	Life process experiences and recorded events
	To discover, in linguistic form, the details of a life event and why an event occurred as it did.	Why did Ghandi's life unfold as it did?
Heuristic research method*	Humanistic psychology	Human experiences
	To discover the meaning of human experiences surfacing from the personal concerns of the researcher.	What is the experience of feeling joyful?
Hermeneutic method*	Literary science	Experiences expressed in texts
	To expand understanding of human experiences.	What is suffering like as recorded in the Holocaust records?
Qualitative descriptive method*	Social science	Social connections, interrelationships, life events
	To intensively study a phenomenon to discover patterns and themes about life events.	What is the meaning of feeling lonely?
Phenomenological method*	Philosophy and psychology	Lived experiences
	To discover patterns or structures of phenomena.	What is the structural description of loneliness?
Ethnographic method*	Anthropology	Symbols, rituals, customs
	To gain an understanding of the meanings a culture group attaches to symbols in organizing and interpreting their life experiences.	What is a birthday celebration like in Korean culture?

* Nursing perspective can be explicated as a guide to study.

ETHICAL	METHODOLOGICAL		INTERPRETIVE
	Data Gathering	*Data Analysis*	
	Interviewing, observing, questioning, theoretical sampling, coding, developing hypotheses	Coding, theoretical sampling, and developing hypotheses (proceeds simultaneously with data gathering)	
	Interviewing and dialoguing	Detecting patterns, identifying themes/core plots, and interpreting	
	Initial engaging, immersion, incubation, illumination	Explication and creative synthesis	
	Reading and re-reading text	Dwelling, interpreting, and synthesizing emergent themes	
	Interviewing, observing, questionnaires	Identifying themes and constructing a description of the phenomenon	
	Interviewing, written descriptions	Intuiting, analyzing, and describing	
	Participant observation and enthnographic inquiry (informal conversations and deliberate questioning)	Domain, taxonomic, componential, and theme analysis proceeds simultaneously with data gathering	

Scientific Merit; Integrity; and Protection of Human Subjects

Heuristic Relevance; Connecting with Nursing Theory and Research

TABLE 2–2 SPECTRUM OF QUALITATIVE RESEARCH METHODS (CONTINUED)

METHOD	CONCEPTUAL	
	Ontology *(Frame of Reference* *and Purpose)*	*Epistemology* *(Phenomena/Example* *of Research Question)*
ESTABLISHED NURSING METHODS: BASIC RESEARCH		
Ethnonursing method	Nursing—Culture care theory To gain an understanding of the meanings a culture group attaches to symbols in organizing and interpreting their care experiences.	Cultural care patterns What are the cultural care patterns of Russians who live in New York City?
Research as praxis method	Nursing—Theory of health as expanding consciousness To reveal participants' life patterns and participants' recognition and insight into their patterns for the purpose of expanding consciousness.	Life patterns What are the life patterns of persons who have had heart surgery?
Parse research method	Nursing—The human becoming school of thought To discover the meaning of lived experiences.	Universal lived experiences What is the structure of the lived experience of feeling confident?
Human becoming hermeneutic method	Nursing—The human becoming school of thought To discover emergent meanings of human experiences through a study of texts and artforms.	Universal lived experiences What does it mean to be human?
ESTABLISHED NURSING METHODS: APPLIED RESEARCH		
Qualitative descriptive preproject-process-postproject method	Nursing—The human becoming school of thought To evaluate what happens when human becoming is a guide to practice.	Patterns of practice What happens when the human becoming practice methodology is lived with individuals or groups?

ETHICAL	METHODOLOGICAL		INTERPRETIVE
	Data Gathering	*Data Analysis*	
	Observing, participating, interviewing, validating	Identifying and categorizing themes	
Scientific Merit; Integrity; and Protection of Human Subjects	Non-directive interviewing, diagramming sequential patterns, revising with participant feedback	Analyze in light of health as expanding consciousness, interpret using Young's spectrum, designate pattern similarities among participants as themes, and state in propositional form	*Heuristic Relevance; Connecting with Nursing Theory and Research*
	Dialogical engagement	Extractopm-synthesis of stories, essences, core concepts, propositions, and a synthesized structure of the lived experience	
	Dwelling with texts and/or artforms	Discoursing with penetrating engaging, interpreting with quiescent beholding, and understanding with inspiring envisaging	
	Pre-, mid-, and post-project information gathering— interviewing, observing documenting	Thematic conceptualizations of patterns of practice	

TABLE 2–2 SPECTRUM OF QUALITATIVE RESEARCH METHODS (CONTINUED)

METHOD	CONCEPTUAL	
	Ontology *(Frame of Reference and Purpose)*	*Epistemology* *(Phenomena/Example of Research Question)*
EMERGING NURSING METHODS: BASIC RESEARCH		
Rogerian process of inquiry method	Nursing—Science of unitary human beings	Human-environment pattern manifestations
	To discover pandimensional unitary field process patterns.	What is the pandimensional unitary field process in a nurse-client relationship?
Unitary field pattern portrait method	Nursing—Science of unitary human beings	Human-environment pattern manifestations
	To create a unitary understanding of the dynamic kaleidoscopic and symphonic pattern manifestations emerging from the pandimensional human/environment mutual process to enhance understanding of significant phenomena related to human well-being	What is the unitary field pattern portrait of dispiritedness?
Unitary pattern appreciation case method	Nursing—Science of unitary human beings	Human-environment pattern manifestations
	To gain an understanding of the human-environment mutual process.	What is the pattern of a person experiencing despair as the dominant sensation of his/her experience?

ETHICAL	METHODOLOGICAL		INTERPRETIVE
	Data Gathering	*Data Analysis*	
	Field notes, unitary instrumentation, interviewing	Synthesizing shared mutual understandings, developing a pandimensional unitary process report, developing theory	
	Interviewing, field notes, reflective journals	Unitary field pattern portrait construction through mutual processing, immersion/ crystallization, and evolutionary interpretation	
	Pattern appreciation— interviewing, observing, creative expression	Comprehending the pattern of the whole, recognizing features, developing a pattern profile, and verifying it with the participant	

Scientific Merit; Integrity; and Protection of Human Subjects

Heuristic Relevance; Connecting with Nursing Theory and Research

REFERENCES

Artinian, B. M. (1998). Grounded theory research: Its value for nursing. *Nursing Science Quarterly*, 11, 5–6.

Barrett, E. A. M. (1996). Canonical correlation analysis and its use in Rogerian research. *Nursing Science Quarterly*, 9, 50–52.

Benner, P. (Ed.). (1994). *Interpretive phenomenology: Embodiment, caring, and ethics in health and illness*. Thousand Oaks, CA: Sage.

Butcher, H. K. (1998). Crystallizing the processes of the unitary field pattern portrait research method. *Visions: The Journal of Rogerian Nursing Science*, 6(1), 13–26.

Butler, R. N. (1992). Quality of life: Can it be an endpoint? How can it be measured? *American Journal of Clinical Nutrition*, 55, 1267S–1270S.

Carboni, J. T. (1995). The Rogerian process of inquiry. *Nursing Science Quarterly*, 8, 22–37.

Charmaz, K. (2000). Grounded theory: Objectivist and constructivist methods. In N. K. Denzin & Y. S. Lincoln (Eds.), *Handbook of qualitative research* (2nd ed., pp. 509–535). Thousand Oaks, CA: Sage.

Cody, W. K. (1995). Of life immense in passion, pulse, and power: Dialoguing with Whitman and Parse—A hermeneutic study. In R. R. Parse (Ed.), *Illuminations: The human becoming theory in practice and research* (pp. 269–308). New York: National League for Nursing Press.

Colaizzi, P. F. (1973). *Reflection and research in psychology: A phenomenological study of learning*. Dubuque, IA: Kendall/Hunt.

Colaizzi, P. F. (1978). Psychological research as the phenomenologist views it. In R. S. Valle & M. King (Eds.), *Existential-phenomenological alternatives for psychology* (pp. 48–71). New York: Oxford University Press.

Corbin, J., & Strauss, A. (1990). Grounded theory research: Procedures, canons, and evaluative criteria. *Qualitative Sociology*, 13(1), 3–21.

Cowling, W. R. (1998). Unitary case inquiry. *Nursing Science Quarterly*, 11, 139–141.

Denzin, N. K., & Lincoln, Y. S. (1994). Introduction: Entering the field of qualitative research. In N. K. Denzin & Y. S. Lincoln (Eds.), *Handbook of qualitative research* (pp. 1–17). Thousand Oaks, CA: Sage.

Denzin, N. K., & Lincoln, Y. S. (Eds.). (2000). *Handbook of qualitative research* (2nd ed.). Thousand Oaks, CA: Sage.

Dilthey, W. (1961). *Pattern and meaning in history*. New York: Harper & Row.

Dilthey, W. (1976). *Selected writings* (H. P. Rickman, Trans.). Cambridge, UK: Cambridge University Press.

Dilthey, W. (1988). *Introduction to the human sciences* (R. J. Betanzos, Trans.). Detroit: Wayne State University Press. (Original work published 1883)

Field, P. A., & Morse, J. M. (1985). *Nursing research: The application of qualitative approaches*. Rockville, MD: Aspen Systems.

Gadamer, H.-G. (1976). *Philosophical hermeneutics* (D. E. Linge, Ed. & Trans.). Berkeley: University of California Press.

Gadamer, H.-G. (1998). *Truth and method* (2nd rev. ed.) (J. Weinsheimer & D. G. Marshall, Trans.). New York: Continuum. (Original work published 1960)

Giorgi, A. (1968). Existential phenomenology and the psychology of the human person. *Review of Existential Psychology & Psychiatry, 8*(2), 102–116.

Giorgi, A. (1970). *Psychology as a human science: A Phenomenologically based approach.* New York: Harper & Row.

Giorgi, A. (1971). Phenomenology and experimental psychology: II. In A. Giorgi, W. Fischer, & R. von Eckartsberg (Eds.), *Duquesne studies in phenomenological psychology* (Vol. 1, pp. 3–29). Pittsburgh, PA: Duquesne University Press.

Giorgi, A. (1985). Sketch of a psychological phenomenological method. In A. Giorgi (Ed.), *Phenomenology and psychological research* (pp. 8–22). Pittsburgh, PA: Duquesne University Press.

Giorgi, A. (1986a). The "context of discovery/context of verification" distinction and descriptive human science. *Journal of Phenomenological Psychology, 17*(2), 151–166.

Giorgi, A. (1986b). Theoretical justification for the use of descriptions in psychological research. In P. D. Ashworth, A. Giorgi, & A. J. J. deKoning (Eds.), *Qualitative research in psychology: Proceedings of the International Association for Qualitative Research in Social Science* (pp. 3–22). Pittsburgh, PA: Duquesne University Press.

Giorgi, A. (1989). One type of analysis of descriptive data: Procedures involved in following a systematic phenomenological method. *Annual Edition of Methods: A Journal for Human Science,* 39–61.

Giorgi, A. (1992a). Description versus interpretation: Competing alternative strategies for qualitative research. *Journal of Phenomenological Psychology, 23*(2), 119–135.

Giorgi, A. (1992b). The idea of human science. *Humanistic Psychologist, 20*(2–3), 202–217.

Giorgi, A. (1997). The theory, practice, and evaluation of the phenomenological method as a qualitative research procedure. *Journal of Phenomenological Psychology, 28*(2), 235–260.

Giorgi, A. (2000). Psychology as a human science revisited. *Journal of Humanistic Psychology, 40*(3), 56–73.

Glaser, B. (1995). A look at grounded theory: 1984 to 1994. In B. Glaser (Ed.), *Grounded theory: 1984–1994. Volume one* (pp. 3–17). Mill Valley, CA: Sociology Press.

Glaser, B. G. (1978). *Theoretical sensitivity: Advances in methodology or grounded theory.* Mill Valley, CA: Sociology Press.

Glaser, B. G., & Strauss, A. L. (1967). *The discovery of grounded theory: Strategies for qualitative research.* New York: Aldine.

Goodwin, L. D., & Goodwin, W. L. (1984). Qualitative vs. quantitative research or qualitative and quantitative research? *Nursing Research, 33,* 378–380.

Guba, E. G. (Ed.). (1990). *The paradigm dialogue.* Newbury Park, CA: Sage.

Guba, E. G., & Lincoln, Y. S. (1989). *Fourth generation evaluation.* Newbury Park, CA: Sage.

Guba, E. G., & Lincoln, Y. S. (1990). Can there be a human science? Constructivism as an alternative. *Person Centered Review, 5*(2), 130–154.

Guba, E. G., & Lincoln, Y. S. (1994). Competing paradigms in qualitative research. In N. K. Denzin & Y. S. Lincoln (Eds.), *Handbook of qualitative research* (pp. 105–117). Thousand Oaks, CA: Sage.

Gubrium, J. F., & Holstein, J. A. (2000). Analyzing interpretive practice. In N. K. Denzin & Y. S. Lincoln (Eds.), *Handbook of qualitative research* (2nd ed., pp. 487–508). Thousand Oaks, CA: Sage.

Heidegger, M. (1962). *Being and time* (J. Macquarrie & E. Robinson, Trans.). New York: Harper & Row.

Heidegger, M. (1975). *Poetry, language, and thought* (A. Hofstadter, Trans.). New York: Harper & Row.

Husserl, E. (1962). *Ideas: General introduction to pure phenomenology* (W. R. Boyce Gibson, Trans.). New York: Collier Books. (Original work published 1913)

Husserl, E. (1965). *Phenomenology and the crisis of philosophy.* New York: Harper & Row.

Husserl. E. (1991). *Cartesian meditations: An introduction to phenomenology* (D. Cairns, Trans.). Dordrecht: Kluwer Academic Publishers. (Original work published 1931)

Knaack, P. (1984). Phenomenological research. *Western Journal of Nursing Research,* 6(1), 107–114.

Kockelmans, J. J. (Ed.). (1967). *Phenomenology.* New York: Doubleday.

Kockelmans, J. J. (1985). *Heidegger and science.* Washington: Center for Advanced Research in Phenomenology and University Press of America.

Leininger, M. (Ed.). (1995). *Transcultural nursing: Concepts, theories, research, and practices* (2nd ed.). New York: McGraw-Hill.

Leininger, M. (1996). Culture care theory, research, and practice. *Nursing Science Quarterly,* 9, 71–78.

Leininger, M. M. (Ed.). (1985). *Qualitative research methods in nursing.* Orlando, FL: Grune & Stratton.

Macquarrie, J. (1968). *Martin Heidegger.* Richmond, VA: John Knox.

Mitchell, G. J. (1994). Discipline-specific inquiry: The hermeneutics of theory-guided nursing research. *Nursing Outlook,* 42 (5), 224–228.

Mitchell, G. J. (1996). Clarifying contributions of qualitative research findings. *Nursing Science Quarterly,* 10, 143–144.

Mitchell, G. J., & Cody, W. K. (1992). Nursing knowledge and human science: Ontological and epistemological considerations. *Nursing Science Quarterly,* 5, 54–61.

Mitchell, G. J., & Cody, W. K. (1993). The role of theory in qualitative research. *Nursing Science Quarterly,* 6, 170–178.

Morse, J. M. (1992). If you believe in theories. *Qualitative Health Research,* 2, 259–261.

Moustakas, C. E. (1961). *Loneliness.* Englewood Cliffs, NJ: Prentice-Hall.

Moustakas, C. E. (1967). Heuristic research. In J. F. T. Bugental (Ed.), *Challenges of humanistic psychology.* New York: McGraw-Hill.

Moustakas, C. E. (1990). *Heuristic research: Design, methodology, and application.* Newbury Park, CA: Sage.

Newman, M. A. (1997). Experiencing the whole. *Advances in Nursing Science,* 20(1), 34–39.

Newman, M. A. (1999). The rhythm of relating in a paradigm of wholeness. *Image: Journal of Nursing Scholarship,* 31(3), 227–230.

Newman, M. A. (2000). *Health as expanding consciousness* (2nd ed.). Sudbury, MA: Jones and Bartlett/National League for Nursing Press. (Original work published 1994)

Olesen, V. L. (2000). Feminisms and qualitative research at and into the millennium. In N. K. Denzin & Y. S. Lincoln (Eds.), *Handbook of qualitative research* (2nd ed., pp. 215–255). Thousand Oaks, CA: Sage.

Parse, R. R. (1981). *Man-living-health: A theory of nursing.* New York: Wiley.

Parse, R. R. (1987). *Nursing science: Major paradigms, theories, and critiques.* Philadelphia: Saunders.

Parse, R. R. (1992). Human becoming: Parse's theory of nursing. *Nursing Science Quarterly, 5,* 35–42.

Parse, R. R. (Ed.) (1995). *Illuminations: The human becoming theory in practice and research.* New York: National League for Nursing Press.

Parse, R. R. (1996a). Building knowledge through qualitative research: The road less traveled. *Nursing Science Quarterly, 9,* 10–16.

Parse, R. R. (1996b). The human becoming theory: Challenges in practice and research. *Nursing Science Quarterly, 9,* 55–60.

Parse, R. R. (1996c). Quality of life for persons living with Alzheimer's disease: The human becoming perspective. *Nursing Science Quarterly, 9,* 126–133.

Parse, R. R. (1997a). The human becoming theory: The was, is, and will be. *Nursing Science Quarterly, 10,* 32–38.

Parse, R. R. (1997b). Transforming research and practice with the human becoming theory. *Nursing Science Quarterly, 10,* 171–174.

Parse, R. R. (1998). *The human becoming school of thought: A perspective for nurses and other health professionals.* Thousand Oaks, CA: Sage.

Parse, R. R. (1999a). *Hope: An international human becoming perspective,* Sudbury, MA: Jones and Bartlett.

Parse, R. R. (1999b). Integrity and the advancement of nursing knowledge. *Nursing Science Quarterly, 12,* 187.

Pelto, G. H., & Pelto, P. J. (1976). *The human adventure: An introduction to anthropology.* New York: Macmillan.

Pelto, P. J. (1970). *Anthropological research: The structure of inquiry.* New York: Harper & Row.

Pelto, P. J., & Pelto, G. H. (1973). Ethnography: The fieldwork enterprise. In J. J. Honigmann (Ed.), *Handbook of social and cultural anthropology* (pp. 241–288). Chicago: Rand McNally.

Pelto, P. J., & Pelto, G. H. (1981). *Anthropological research: The structure of inquiry.* Cambridge, MA: Cambridge University Press.

Pelto, P. J., & Pelto, G. H. (1996). Research design in medical anthropology. In C. F. Sargent & T. M. Johnson (Eds.), *Medical anthropology: Contemporary theory and method* (pp. 293–324). Westport, CT: Praeger.

Pelto, P. J., & Pelto, G. H. (1997). Studying knowledge, culture, and behavior in applied medical anthropology. *Medical Anthropology Quarterly, 11*(2), 147–163.

Powers, B. A. (1987). Taking sides: A response to Goodwin and Goodwin. *Nursing Research, 36,* 122–126.

Reeder, F. (1988). Hermeneutics. In B. Sarter (Ed.), *Paths to knowledge: Innovative methods for nursing* (pp. 193–238). New York: National League for Nursing Press.

Ricoeur, P. (1976). *Interpretation theory: Discourse and the surplus of meaning.* Fort Worth: Texas Christian University Press.

Ricoeur, P. (1981). *Hermeneutics and the human sciences.* New York: Cambridge University Press.

Ricoeur, P. (1984). *Time and narrative, Vol. 1* (K. McLaughlin & D. Pellauer, Trans.). Chicago: University of Chicago Press.

Ricoeur, P. (1985). *Time and narrative, Vol. 2* (K. McLaughlin & D. Pellauer, Trans.). Chicago: University of Chicago Press.

Ricoeur, P. (1988). *Time and narrative, Vol. 3* (K. McLaughlin & D. Pellauer, Trans.). Chicago: University of Chicago Press.

Schleiermacher, F. (1977). *Hermeneutics: The handwritten manuscripts* (H. Kimmerle, Ed., & J. Duke & J. Forstman, Trans.). Atlanta, GA: Scholar Press. (Original work published 1805).

Silverman, D. (2000). Analyzing talk and text. In N. K. Denzin & Y. S. Lincoln (Eds.), *Handbook of qualitative research* (2nd ed., pp. 821–834). Thousand Oaks, CA: Sage.

Spiegelberg, H. (1975). *Doing phenomenology: Essays on and in phenomenology.* The Hague: Martinus Nijhoff.

Spiegelberg, H. (1976). *The phenomenological movement. Vols. I and II.* The Hague: Martinus Nijhoff.

Spiegelberg, H. (1981). *The context of the phenomenological movement.* Boston: Martinus Nijhoff.

Spiegelberg, H. (1982). *The phenomenological movement: A historical introduction* (3rd rev. and enlarged ed.). The Hague: Martinus Nijhoff. (Original work published 1960)

Spradley, J. P. (1979). *The ethnographic interview.* New York: Holt, Rinehart & Winston.

Spradley, J. P. (1980). *Participant observation.* New York: Holt, Rinehart & Winston.

Strauss, A. L. (1987). *Qualitative analysis for social scientists.* Cambridge: Cambridge University Press.

Strauss, A., & Corbin, J. (1990). *Basics of qualitative research: Grounded theory procedures and techniques.* Newbury Park, CA: Sage.

Strauss, A., & Corbin, J. (1994). Grounded theory methodology: An overview. In N. K. Denzin & Y. S. Lincoln (Eds.), *Handbook of qualitative research* (pp. 273–285). Thousand Oaks, CA: Sage.

Strauss, A., & Corbin, J. (1997). *Grounded theory in practice.* Thousand Oaks, CA: Sage.

Strauss, A., & Corbin, J. (1998). *Basics of qualitative research: Techniques and procedures for developing grounded theory* (2nd ed.). Thousand Oaks, CA: Sage.

Tedlock, T. (2000). Ethnography and ethnographic representation. In N. K. Denzin & Y. S. Lincoln (Eds.), *Handbook of qualitative research* (2nd ed., pp. 455–486). Thousand Oaks, CA: Sage.

van Kaam, A. L. (1959). Phenomenal analysis: Exemplified by a study of the experience of "feeling really understood." *Journal of Individual Psychology, 15,* 66–72.

van Kaam, A. L. (1966). Application of the phenomenological method. In *Existential foundations of psychology* (pp. 294–329). Pittsburgh, PA: Duquesne University Press.

Van Manen, M. (1990). *Researching lived experience: Human science for an action sensitive pedagogy.* Albany: State University of New York Press.

CHAPTER 3

GROUNDED THEORY

ONTOLOGY

Grounded theory was developed in the early 1960s (Strauss, 1987) and initially published by Glaser and Strauss in 1967. In creating the methodology, Glaser and Strauss (1967) were influenced by the works of scholars from two schools of thought—pragmatism and symbolic interactionism (Charmaz, 2000; Corbin & Strauss, 1990; Glaser & Strauss, 1967; Strauss, 1987; Strauss & Corbin, 1994). From pragmatism, Glaser and Strauss primarily drew from the works of Dewey (1916, 1937) and Mead (1917, 1934). Blumer (1931), Hughes (1971), Park and Burgess (1921), and Thomas and Znaniecki (1918) are cited as the major influences from the symbolic interactionism perspective (Corbin & Strauss, 1990; Glaser & Strauss, 1967). Pragmatism and symbolic interactionism, then, are the ontological bases of grounded theory, and the phenomena of concern are patterns and processes of social units.

Strauss and Corbin (1994) note that since the grounded theory methodology was first published "a number of guidelines and procedures have evolved" (p. 273). They believe that the central elements (for instance the use of constant comparisons) of grounded theory have not changed but that "additional ideas and concepts suggested by contemporary social and intellectual movements are entering analytically as *conditions* into the studies of grounded theory researchers" (Strauss & Corbin, 1994, p. 276). They also contend that multiple disciplines may use grounded theory as a theoretical perspective to guide research. Artinian (1998) and Glaser (1995) argue that a new form of grounded theory has emerged and that this "new form," suggested by

Strauss and Corbin (1994), is not consistent with the original grounded theory because it does not emphasize the production of theories. Others, such as Chenitz and Swanson (1986), believe that the only frame of reference for grounded theory is symbolic interactionism.

The grounded theory methodology is designed to expand understanding of symbolic interactionism, pragmatism, and social psychology (Glaser & Strauss, 1967; Parse, 1996) by answering research questions such as, "*What are the social dynamics of nurse-person relationships?*" The purposes of the method follow:

1. To discover social theory by systematically gathering and analyzing data, and developing and verifying distinct hypotheses about relationships between concepts (Artinian, 1998; Corbin & Strauss, 1990; Glaser, 1978, 1995; Glaser & Strauss, 1967; Parse, 1996; Strauss, 1987; Strauss & Corbin, 1994).
2. To interpret, predict, and explain the perspectives and actions of multiple subjects (Corbin & Strauss, 1990; Glaser, 1995; Glaser & Strauss, 1967; Strauss & Corbin, 1994) by clarifying "patterns of action and interaction between and among various types of social units" (Strauss & Corbin, 1994, p. 278).

The basic assumptions that underpin grounded theory follow:

1. Social phenomena are complex and continually changing in response to evolving conditions (Corbin & Strauss, 1990; Strauss, 1987).
2. Human behavior is understandable, predictable, and controllable (Corbin & Strauss, 1990; Glaser & Strauss, 1967).
3. Researchers' perspectives influence the research process (Corbin & Strauss, 1990; Glaser, 1978, 1995; Strauss, 1987; Strauss & Corbin, 1994).
4. Social theory is generated through comparative analysis of field data (Glaser & Strauss, 1967).

Epistemology

The entities for study with the grounded theory methodology are changing patterns of social systems and processes (refer to Table 1–2). For example, professional socialization (Broadhead, 1983), status passages (Glaser & Strauss, 1970), interactions between builders and would-be house owners (Glaser, 1972), and ovarian egg donation between sisters (Lessor, 1993) are all entities that have been studied using this method. The entities chosen for study lead to one of two kinds of theory: substantive or formal substantive (Glaser & Strauss, 1967). Substantive theory arises from an area of social inquiry such as patient care, nurse-patient relationships, and professional organization. Formal theory arises from conceptual areas of sociological inquiry with phenomena such as authority, power, or road rage (Glaser & Strauss, 1967).

METHODOLOGY

The grounded theory method is tailored to study a diverse array of phenomena by systematically gathering and analyzing multiple kinds of data from the field of study (Glaser, 1995, p. 6; Glaser & Strauss, 1967, p. 18; Strauss, 1987; Strauss & Corbin, 1994). The method leads to predictions, explanations, interpretations, and applications relevant to sociological inquiry (Glaser & Strauss, 1967). Participants are protected by standard ethical procedures (see Chapter 2 for details of standard ethical procedures and a sample consent form). There is no limit to the number of participants.

Processes of the Method

Grounded theory is "a general method of comparative analysis" (Glaser & Strauss, 1967, p. 1). It is a "style of doing qualitative analysis that includes a number of distinct features, such as theoretical sampling, and certain methodological guidelines, such as the making of constant comparisons . . . the use of a coding paradigm" (Strauss, 1987, p. 5), and the simultaneous gathering and analysis-synthesis of data (Corbin & Strauss, 1990) to ensure conceptual development and density (Strauss, 1987).

Data gathering and analysis-synthesis are interrelated processes and must be carried out simultaneously to afford appropriate theory generation (Corbin & Strauss, 1990). Data gathering involves "interviews and observations as well as such other sources as government documents, video tapes, newspapers, letters, and books—anything that might shed light on questions under study" (Corbin & Strauss, 1990, p. 5). It is conducted in ways that systematically seek multiple perspectives (Strauss & Corbin, 1994). Data gathering leads to coding and memoing—which in turn lead to searches for new data, more coding, and additional memoing. Data analysis-synthesis begins almost immediately and subsequent data gathering is informed by the questions, observations, or hypotheses generated about emergent categories and their relationships (Strauss, 1987). Analysis-synthesis also includes factors "broader than those that bear immediately on the phenomenon of central interest . . . [possibly including] economic conditions, cultural values, political trends, social movements, and so on" (Corbin & Strauss, 1990, p. 11).

The procedures of the grounded theory method "constitute guidelines that should help most researchers in their enterprises" (Strauss, 1987, p. 7). The guidelines emphasize certain operations that must be carried out in *discovering, verifying,* and *formulating* grounded theories. The basic *work processes* (Strauss,

1987, pp. 17–22) that arise with discovering, verifying, and formulating a grounded theory follow:

1. Raising generative questions (about possible hypotheses, concepts, and their relationships) (Strauss, 1987, p. 17).
   a. Generative questions begin with an insight that sparks interest in some phenomenon.
   b. Generative questions "stimulate the line of investigation in profitable directions; they lead to hypotheses, useful comparisons, the collection of certain classes of data, even to general lines of attack on potentially important problems" (Strauss, 1987, p. 22).
   c. Insights occur throughout the study, open up further questions about the phenomenon or about other phenomena, and guide theoretical sampling.
   d. Theoretical sampling is a "means whereby the analyst decides *on analytic grounds* what data to collect next and where to find them. The basic question in theoretical sampling is: W*hat* groups or subgroups of populations, events, activities (to find varying dimensions, strategies, etc.) does one turn to *next* in data collection. And for *what* theoretical purpose" (Strauss, 1987, pp. 38–39)? It is essential to draw samples of concepts with their properties and variations, and to keep track of theoretical ideas using theoretical memoing and sorting (Strauss, 1987). Theoretical memoing and sorting are processes by which the researcher records theoretical questions, hypotheses, and codes. They provide a major means for integrating theory (Strauss, 1987).
2. Ensuring the relevance of the coding—it must be linked with the examination and collection of data (Strauss, 1987). Coding proceeds theoretically. The researcher conceptualizes "how the substantive codes may relate to each other as hypotheses to be integrated into a theory" (Glaser, 1978, p. 72). T*heoretical coding* is enhanced by *theoretical sensitivity*—the disciplinary or professional knowledge, as well as both research and personal experiences, that the researcher brings to the inquiry (Glaser, 1978; Strauss & Corbin, 1994, p. 280). According to Glaser (1995), theoretical sensitivity means that researchers "[suspend their] own interests and prior knowledge to a level of sensitivity which enables catching on to what will surely emerge. The [researchers do] not go blank or give up [their] knowledge. [They go] sensitive with all [their] learning, alert to any possibility and then to how to formulate it with concepts" (Glaser, 1995, p. 9). There are three types of coding:
   a. *Open coding* is "the unrestricted coding of the data" (Strauss, 1987, p. 28) in which "events/activities/interactions are compared with others for similarities and differences. They are also given conceptual labels. In this way, conceptually similar events/activities/interactions are grouped together to form categories and subcategories" (Corbin & Strauss, 1990, p. 12).

    b. *Axial coding* "consists of intense analysis done around one category at a time" (Strauss, 1987, p. 32). "Categories are related to their subcategories, and the relationships tested against data" (Corbin & Strauss, 1990, p. 13).

    c. *Selective coding* "pertains to coding *systematically* and concertedly for the core category" (Strauss, 1987, p. 33). It is "the process by which all categories are unified around a 'core' category, and categories that need further explication are filled in with descriptive detail" (Corbin & Strauss, 1990, p. 14).

3. Making provisional linkages among discovered concepts (Strauss, 1987). Concepts, the basic units of analysis, are the researcher's conceptualizations of the raw data. They become more abstract as analysis-synthesis proceeds (Corbin & Strauss, 1990) and are incorporated as part of the generated theory only after they are repeatedly found to be present in the data.

4. Verifying linkages among concepts through collecting new data, generating new codes, and making constant comparisons (Strauss, 1987).

    a. Making constant comparisons is a process of examining the "similarities, differences, and degrees of consistency" (Strauss, 1987, p. 25) among empirical indicators. Empirical indicators are the "actual data, such as behavioral actions and events, observed or described in documents and in the words of interviewees and informants" (Strauss, 1987, p. 25).

    b. Making constant comparisons generates "an underlying uniformity, which in turn results in a coded category" (Strauss, 1987, p. 25). Coded categories are compared to the emergent concept, additional indicators are compared to the conceptual codes, and the codes are "sharpened to achieve their best fit to data . . . and further properties of categories are generated, until the codes are verified and saturated yielding nothing much new" (Strauss, 1987, p. 25). Categories contain similar concepts and are stated at higher levels of abstraction than concepts.

5. Integrating the dimensions, distinctions, and linkages that are the most salient to the evolving theory (Strauss, 1987), taking care to account for patterns and variations in the data (Corbin & Strauss, 1990).

    a. Core categories evolve and develop. They are representative of the central phenomenon of the study (Corbin & Strauss, 1990; Strauss, 1987) and are "identified by asking questions such as: What is the main analytic idea presented in this research? If my findings are to be conceptualized in a few sentences what do I say? What does all the action/interaction seem to be about? How can I explain the variation that I see between and among the categories" (Corbin & Strauss, 1990, p. 14)? Core categories are related to many other categories (more so than other categories) (Strauss, 1987), and they are substantive with "clear implications for a more general theory" (Strauss, 1987, p. 36). It is important to write and integrate ideas, making use of visual diagrams and devices when necessary, to make explicit the theory that has evolved from the research (Glaser, 1995; Glaser & Strauss, 1967; Strauss, 1987).

b. Hypotheses about relationships among categories are developed and should be checked both in the field and with experienced colleagues and revised as necessary (Corbin & Strauss, 1990).

Interpretation of the findings is written in light of symbolic interactionism and pragmatism and recommendations for further research are specified. For further details about the grounded theory method, with its procedures for data analysis-synthesis, see Glaser and Strauss (1967), Strauss (1987), Corbin and Strauss (1990), and Strauss and Corbin (1994). For an example of a study that used the grounded theory method, see Finfgeld (1998).

REFERENCES

Artinian, B. M. (1998). Grounded theory research: Its value for nursing. *Nursing Science Quarterly*, 11, 5–6.

Blumer, H. (1931). Science without concepts. *American Journal of Sociology*, 36, 515–533.

Broadhead, R. (1983). *Private lives and professional identity of medical students*. New Brunswick, NJ: Transaction.

Charmaz, K. (2000). Grounded theory: Objectivist and constructivist methods. In N. K. Denzin & Y. S. Lincoln (Eds.), *Handbook of qualitative research* (2nd ed., pp. 509–535). Thousand Oaks, CA: Sage.

Chenitz, W. C., & Swanson, J. M. (1986). *From practice to grounded theory: Qualitative research in nursing*. Menlo Park, CA: Addison-Wesley.

Corbin, J., & Strauss, A. (1990). Grounded theory research: Procedures, canons, and evaluative criteria. *Qualitative Sociology*, 13(1), 3–21.

Dewey, J. (1916). *Essays in experimental logic*. Chicago: University of Chicago Press.

Dewey, J. (1937). *Logic: The theory of inquiry*. New York: Holt.

Finfgeld, D. L. (1998). Courage in middle-aged adults with long-term health concerns. *Canadian Journal of Nursing Research*, 30(1), 153–169.

Glaser, B. (1972). *Experts versus laymen: A study of the patsy and the subcontractor*. New Brunswick, NJ: Transaction.

Glaser, B. (1978). *Theoretical sensitivity*. Mill Valley, CA: Sociology Press.

Glaser, B. (1995). A look at grounded theory: 1984 to 1994. In B. Glaser (Ed.), *Grounded theory: 1984–1994. Vol. 1* (pp. 3–17). Mill Valley, CA: Sociology Press.

Glaser, B., & Strauss, A. (1970). *Status passages*. Chicago: Aldine.

Glaser, B. G., & Strauss, A. L. (1967). *The discovery of grounded theory: Strategies for qualitative research*. New York: Aldine.

Hughes, E. (1971). *The sociological eye*. Chicago: Aldine.

Lessor, R. (1993). All in the family: Social processes in ovarian egg donation between sisters. *Sociology of Health and Illness, 15,* 393–413.

Mead, G. (1917). Scientific method and the individual thinker. In J. Dewey (Ed.), *Creative intelligence* (pp. 167–227). New York: Holt.

Mead, G. H. (1934). *Mind, self, and society.* Chicago: University of Chicago Press.

Park, R., & Burgess, E. (1921). *An introduction to the science of sociology.* Chicago: University of Chicago Press.

Parse, R. R. (1996). Building knowledge through qualitative research: The road less traveled. *Nursing Science Quarterly, 9,* 10–16.

Strauss, A. (1987). *Qualitative analysis for social scientists.* New York: Cambridge University Press.

Strauss, A., & Corbin, J. (1994). Grounded theory methodology: An overview. In N. K. Denzin & Y. S. Lincoln (Eds.), *Handbook of qualitative research* (pp. 273–285). Thousand Oaks, CA: Sage.

Thomas, W. I., & Znaniecki, F. (1918). *The Polish peasant in Europe and America.* Chicago: University of Chicago Press.

CHAPTER 4

NARRATIVE RESEARCH

ONTOLOGY

Narrative research, born out of the human sciences as a way to understand human expression, is a linguistic product with emphasis on the whole of an event, object, idea, or lived experience (Erikson, 1975; Parse, 1996; Polkinghorne, 1983, 1988, 1989; Ricoeur, 1974, 1976, 1975/1977, 1984, 1985, 1988, 1991). Narrative meaning organizes human experiences into episodes (Polkinghorne, 1988). Words and sentences are the media of presentation, but narrative is "discourse which is a unit of utterance: it is something that is written or spoken that is larger than a sentence" (Polkinghorne, 1988, p. 31). Discourse is language integrated in a way to convey meaning. Narrative discourse conveys stories of everyday living and discloses meanings through the linguistic choices made by the narrator. In this sense, narrative is meaning-making, and it is pervasive in human living. The researcher may identify a discipline-specific frame of reference as a guide to the study, and in so doing discloses the ontological lens of the narrative.

The purpose of narrative research is to discover, in linguistic form, the details of a life event and why an event occurred as it did. The assumptions underpinning this method follow:

1. In human existence, matter, life, and meaning are fused.
2. "Human experience is enveloped in a personal and cultural realm of non-material meanings and thought" (Polkinghorne, 1988, p. 15).
3. Experience is constructed through interpretation of meaningful recollections, perceptions, and expectations.
4. Stories about life events shed light on the meanings of human experiences.

EPISTEMOLOGY

Life process experiences and recorded events are the entities for study with the narrative research method. Descriptive narrative research studies are designed to answer questions such as *"What truths arose from Gandhi's life story?"* and explanatory narrative studies are designed to answer questions such as *"Why did Gandhi's life unfold as it did?"* Examples of narratives are myths, fairy tales, personal histories, novels, and human stories.

METHODOLOGY

There are two types of narratives: descriptive and explanatory. A *descriptive* narrative is a story told by individuals or groups recounting meaningful life events. This type of narrative also may be used by members of families or organizations to gain understanding of the evolution and purpose of the family or organization. The *explanatory* narrative is a linguistic account of how and why an event occurred. Narrative explanations are retrospective, bringing together various episodes of a story with time sequencing related to specific decisions that led to the event (Erikson, 1975; Guba & Lincoln, 1989).

Processes of the Method

Although the direct aim of these two types of narratives is different, the data-gathering and analysis processes are similar (Agar & Hobbs, 1982; Brooks, 1984; Denzin & Lincoln, 1994, 2000; Giorgi, Fischer, & Murray, 1975; Labov, 1982; Mishler, 1986; Pelto & Pelto, 1981; Polkinghorne, 1988; Ricoeur, 1984, 1985, 1988, 1991). The processes follow:

1. Interviewing in which the participant orders and sequences moments into whole stories that are grounded in context and explicate meaning.
2. Dialoguing with documents in which discrete explanations are related to situations and events.
3. Detecting patterns across stories derived from participants' interviews and documents.
4. Identifying common themes and core plots in the stories.
5. Interpreting core plots to describe and explain life processes or events.

The researcher interviews participants and examines documents to arrive at a story about an event that reflects the whole of the event. The researcher searches for common themes in the data, arrives at core plots, and interprets the remembered event in light of the core plots (Polkinghorne, 1983, 1988, 1989; Ricoeur, 1974, 1976). There is no limit to the number of participants with narrative research, and standard ethical procedures are honored (refer to Chapter 2).

For further information about narrative research see Polkinghorne (1983, 1988, 1989) and Ricoeur (1974, 1975/1977, 1984, 1985, 1988, 1991). Examples of published narrative research are Erikson's *Young Man Luther* (1958) and *Gandhi's Truth* (1969).

REFERENCES

Agar, M., & Hobbs, J. R. (1982). Interpreting discourse: Coherence and the analysis of ethnographic interviews. *Discourse Processes, 5,* 1–32.

Brooks, P. (1984). *Reading for the plot: Design and intention in narrative.* New York: Knopf.

Denzin, N. K., & Lincoln, Y. S. (Eds.). (1994). *Handbook of qualitative research.* Thousand Oaks, CA: Sage.

Denzin, N. K., & Lincoln, Y. S. (Eds.). (2000). *Handbook of qualitative research* (2nd ed.). Thousand Oaks, CA: Sage.

Erikson, E. H. (1958). *Young man Luther: A study in psychoanalysis and history.* New York: Norton.

Erikson, E. H. (1969). *Gandhi's truth: On the origins of militant nonviolence.* New York: Norton.

Erikson, E. H. (1975). *Life history and the historical moment.* New York: Norton.

Giorgi, A., Fischer, C. T., & Murray, E. L. (Eds.). (1975). *An application of phenomenological psychology.* Pittsburgh, PA: Duquesne University Press.

Guba, E. G., & Lincoln, Y. S. (1989). *Fourth generation evaluation.* Newbury Park, CA: Sage.

Labov, W. (1982). Speech actions and reactions in personal narrative. In D. Tannen (Ed.), *Analyzing discourse: Text and talk.* Washington, DC: Georgetown University Press.

Mishler, E. G. (1986). *Research interviewing: Context and narrative.* Cambridge, MA: Harvard University Press.

Parse, R. R. (1996). Building knowledge through qualitative research: The road less traveled. *Nursing Science Quarterly, 9,* 10–16.

Pelto, P. J., & Pelto, G. H. (1981). *Anthropological research: The structure of inquiry.* Cambridge, MA: Cambridge University Press.

Polkinghorne, D. E. (1983). *Methodology for the human sciences.* Albany: State University of New York Press.

Polkinghorne, D. E. (1988). *Narrative knowing and the human sciences.* Albany: State University of New York Press.

Polkinghorne, D. E. (1989). Phenomenological research methods. In R. S. Valle & S. Halling (Eds.), *Existential-phenomenological perspectives in psychology: Exploring the breadth of human experience* (pp. 41–60). New York: Plenum Press.

Ricoeur, P. (1974). *The conflict of interpretations: Essays in hermeneutics* (D. Ihde, Ed.). Evanston, IL: Northwestern University Press.

Ricoeur, P. (1976). *Interpretive theory: Discourse and the surplus of meaning.* Fort Worth, TX: Texas Christian University Press.

Ricoeur, P. (1977). *The rule of metaphor: Multi-disciplinary studies of the creation of meaning in language* (R. Czerny, K. McLaughlin & J. Costell, Trans.). Toronto, Ontario: University of Toronto Press. (Original work published 1975)

Ricoeur, P. (1984). *Time and narrative*, Vol. 1 (K. McLaughlin & D. Pellauer, Trans.). Chicago: University of Chicago Press.

Ricoeur, P. (1985). *Time and narrative*, Vol. 2 (K. McLaughlin & D. Pellauer, Trans.). Chicago: University of Chicago Press.

Ricoeur, P. (1988). *Time and narrative*, Vol. 3 (K. McLaughlin & D. Pellauer, Trans.). Chicago: University of Chicago Press.

Ricoeur, P. (1991). Life in quest of narrative. In D. Wood (Ed.), *On Paul Ricoeur: Narrative and interpretation* (pp. 20–34). London: Rutledge.

CHAPTER 5

HEURISTIC RESEARCH METHOD

ONTOLOGY

The ontology of the heuristic research method developed by Clark E. Moustakas (1961, 1967, 1972, 1975, 1981, 1988, 1990) arises from humanistic psychology. Heuristic, from the Greek *heuristein*, means to discover. This research method requires that the researcher's perspective be an essential element of the study. Thus, a theoretical perspective from nursing or another human science may guide the study. The researcher arrives at a phenomenon of interest while examining personal experiences. The phenomenon flows from the researcher's own awareness of meanings regarding issues of great concern.

The purpose of the heuristic research method is to discover the meaning of human experiences surfacing from the personal concerns of the researcher. The researcher seeks to understand the wholeness and unique patterns of experiences in a scientific, organized, and disciplined way (Moustakas, 1990, p. 16). The assumptions of the method follow:

1. Understanding of phenomena is deepened with the persistent, disciplined devotion of intense study.
2. The researcher's frame of reference, self-discipline, intuition, and indwelling are reliable sources for discovering the meaning of human experiences.

EPISTEMOLOGY

The heuristic research method focuses on studying human experiences in a unique way. The entities for study arise from the personal questions, problems, or challenges of the researcher. They surface as awarenesses of something that is of great interest but essentially unknown to the researcher, yet the researcher must have had a direct encounter with the phenomenon under study (Moustakas, 1990). The research question grows out of "an intense interest in a particular problem or theme" (Moustakas, 1990, p. 41). The characteristics of the research question follow:

1. It seeks to reveal more fully the essence or meaning of a phenomenon of human experience.
2. It seeks to discover the qualitative aspects, rather than quantitative dimensions, of the phenomenon.
3. It engages one's total self and evokes a personal and passionate involvement and active participation in the process.
4. It does not seek to predict or to determine causal relationships.
5. It is illuminated through careful descriptions, illustrations, metaphors, poetry, dialogue, and other creative renderings, rather than by measurements, ratings, or scores. (Moustakas, 1990, p. 42)

The following steps delineate the research question:

1. List all aspects of particular interests or topics that represent curiosities or intrigues. Do this freely, jotting down questions and thoughts even if they are not complete.
2. Cluster the related interests or topics into subthemes.
3. Set aside any subthemes that imply causal relationships, and any that contain inherent assumptions.
4. Look at all the remaining subthemes and continue to consider them thoughtfully until one basic theme or question emerges as central, one that passionately awakens your interest, concern, and commitment.
5. Formulate it in a way that specifies clearly and precisely what it is that you want to know. (Moustakas, 1990, p. 42)

Examples of research questions that would call the researcher to use the heuristic method are *What is the experience of feeling joyful?* and *What is the experience of living on death row?*

METHODOLOGY

The heuristic method is a systematic search, through self-inquiry and dialogue with others, to discover the meanings of human experiences. Participants, called coresearchers, are protected by standard ethical procedures (see Chapter 2 for details of standard ethical procedures). There is no limit to the number of coresearchers.

Processes of the Method

The concepts and processes of the method (Moustakas, 1990, pp. 15–27) follow:

Identifying with the focus of inquiry:	The researcher becomes one with the question.
Self-dialogue:	The researcher is open, receptive, and attuned to the phenomenon inviting apprehension of the whole.
Tacit knowing:	The invisible is welcomed as the basis for all knowledge.
Intuition:	Perceptiveness is essential in knowledge seeking to form patterns and themes.
Indwelling:	An inner-turning is necessary to find meanings of human experiences.
Focusing:	A relaxed inner attention, when sustained, unfolds central meanings of an experience.
The internal frame of reference:	The person having the experience can give a valid account of the experience.

There are six phases of the heuristic method (Moustakas, 1990, pp. 27–34):

1. *Initial engaging*: discovering a passionate concern for a phenomenon.
2. *Immersion*: living with the phenomenon in all ways, times, and places.
3. *Incubation*: detaching from close involvement to allow the tacit to speak.
4. *Illumination*: breaking through the unknowns to new awarenesses.
5. *Explication*: concentrating on themes, qualities, and components.
6. *Creative synthesis*: narrating or drawing unique combinations of all data from all coresearchers.

The validation of heuristic research confirms the meanings with the data through checking and judging the significance of the narrative or art depicting the experience. Interpretation of findings, in this case the creative synthesis about the phenomenon under study, is to be in light of the frame of reference of the researcher and is discipline-specific to enhance knowledge. New knowledge gained from the study should be specified and recommendations for further studies made.

For further information, details about the method, and examples of research studies conducted using the method, see Moustakas (1961, 1967, 1990).

REFERENCES

Moustakas, C. E. (1961). *Loneliness*. Englewood Cliffs, NJ: Prentice-Hall.

Moustakas, C. E. (1967). Heuristic research. In J. F. T. Bugental (Ed.), *Challenges of humanistic psychology*. New York: McGraw-Hill.

Moustakas, C. E. (1972). *Loneliness and love*. Englewood Cliffs, NJ: Prentice-Hall.

Moustakas, C. E. (1975). *The touch of loneliness*. Englewood Cliffs, NJ: Prentice-Hall.

Moustakas, C. E. (1981). *Rhythms, rituals, and relationships*. Detroit: Center for Humanistic Studies.

Moustakas, C. E. (1988). *Phenomenology, science, and psychotherapy*. Sydney, Nova Scotia: Family Life Institute, University College of Cape Breton.

Moustakas, C. E. (1990). *Heuristic research: Design, methodology, and application*. Newbury Park, CA: Sage.

CHAPTER 6

THE HERMENEUTIC METHOD

ONTOLOGY

The *hermeneutic method* is interpretive. Hermeneutics is an ancient, yet post-modern mode of inquiry derived from the Greek *hermeneuin*—meaning to interpret. The Greek god Hermes interpreted messages from the gods to the people. Hermeneutics was used as an interpretative process to critique poetry and other literary works, and as a method in religion to interpret biblical texts (Bleicher, 1980). Schleiermacher (1805/1977), a 19th-century German philosopher, implicitly suggests hermeneutics as important for the human sciences. His student Wilhelm Dilthey (1961, 1976, 1883/1988) posits and elaborates on hermeneutics as the primary mode of inquiry for the human sciences. He believes it is not to be relegated simply to biblical and historical studies. Dilthey (1883/1988) says that hermeneutic studies of expressions of life are an appropriate means for gaining an understanding of human experiences. These expressions are artforms (Parse, 1981, 1992, 1998), literary works, organizations, culture, and others (Dilthey, 1961, 1976, 1883/1988; Ermarth, 1978; Parse, 1981, 1992, 1998; Polkinghorne, 1983, 1986a, 1986b, 1988). Dilthey (1961, 1976, 1883/1988) writes of the importance of the hermeneutic circle in examining and interpreting words and sentences, the whole of an expression. Schleiermacher (1805/1977) and Dilthey (1961, 1976, 1883/1988) lay the foundation for Heidegger (1962), who moved their view of hermeneutics as epistemology and methodology to ontology. Heidegger (1962), then, is credited with the shift of hermeneutics from epistemology and methodology to ontology. Understanding, he says, is a fundamental form of human existence.

Gadamer (1976, 1960/1998), like Heidegger (1962), believes that hermeneutics extends understanding about human existence, and he brings this notion to a new level by positing that understanding is a primordial mode of being human. He introduces the notion of a fusion of horizons, which is the coming together of the vision arising from the interpreter's unique perspective with the description of the experience by the author of the work being interpreted, to shed light on the meaning of being human.

Gadamer (1976, 1960/1998) says that language is the medium of understanding and interpreting. Texts and artforms are created in language symbols, words, and sentences, and in drawings, movement, and other media (Parse, 1981, 1998). The hermeneutic mode is dialogical, and understanding emerges with the beckoning dialogue of researcher with artform, or researcher with text, as horizons of meaning continually change with insightful ponderings (Parse, 1981, 1998). Although Ricoeur's (1974, 1976, 1981, 1984, 1985, 1987, 1988, 1992) view of hermeneutics is somewhat different, he contends, along with Gadamer (1976, 1960/1998) and Parse (1981, 1998), that there is a surplus of meanings that overflow the moment and there is always more to understand. Ricoeur (1976, 1981) believes that written and oral narratives disclose meanings and contain the remembered, fixed with the imaginary to fill in the spaces of the now not observable (Ricoeur, 1984, 1985, 1988). He says that original patterns of language encode meaning, but there is always the possibility of new meaning in the dynamic interaction between the language system (langue) and the speech event (parole). According to Ricoeur (1976, 1981), the readers of text must take these ideas into account as well as considering their own intentions and prejudices.

Schleiermacher (1805/1977), Dilthey (1961, 1976, 1883/1988), Heidegger (1962), Gadamer (1976, 1960/1998), and Ricoeur (1974, 1976, 1981, 1984, 1985, 1987, 1988, 1992) are the shapers of hermeneutics as a method of interpretation for the human sciences. They do not, however, advocate using literary hermeneutics with interview data, but, rather, they generate their own texts through guided questions of their own creation.

The assumptions of hermeneutics, synthesized from the works of Heidegger (1962), Gadamer (1976, 1960/1998), and Ricoeur (1974, 1976, 1981, 1984, 1985, 1992) follow:

1. Language is the horizon of hermeneutic ontology.
2. Fore-knowing and prejudices are constituents of meaning.
3. There is a dynamic interaction between language style (langue) and speech event (parole).
4. The researcher-text dialectic arises with a fusion of horizons.
5. Situatedness is the context undergirding emergent understandings.

The researcher explicitly and implicitly shows a perspective as the interpretation of the text unfolds. Discipline-specific ontology is disclosed in the choice of language used in the study.

Epistemology

The entities for study with the hermeneutic method are experiences that are expressed in texts. Permission to use the texts may be required. The interpretation of the text is from the researcher's perspective and may answer questions such as, "*What is suffering like as recorded in the Holocaust records?*"

Methodology

Several hermeneutic approaches have been developed (Benner, 1985/1999; Cody, 1995; Diekelmann, Allen, & Tanner, 1989; Gadamer, 1976; Heidegger, 1962; Parse, 1998; Ricoeur, 1974, 1976, 1981, 1984, 1985, 1992), but the general processes are the same.

Processes of the Method

The general processes of the hermeneutic method include the following:

1. Dwelling with the text in search of the meaning of the phenomenon under study.
2. Interpreting the words, phrases, and sentences in light of the frame of reference of the researcher.
3. Synthesizing the ideas into a formal presentation of research findings.

Heidegger (1962), Gadamer (1976, 1960/1998), and Ricoeur (1974, 1976, 1981, 1984, 1985, 1992) present slightly different conceptualizations of the hermeneutic method. Heideggerian hermeneutics follows a three-strategy pattern: *searching* for the overall meaning; *interpreting* parts to the whole and whole to the parts; and *sharing* what is new (Heidegger, 1962). Gadamer (1976, 1960/1998) explicates the notion of *fusion of horizons*, which specifies that interpretation surfaces in the reader-text dialogue and is reflective of the reader's and author's prejudices.

Gadamer (1976, 1960/1998) believes that understanding emerges from the researcher's *fore-knowing* and it continually changes with the *dialogue* with the text. *Situatedness* is the context undergirding all understanding, but understanding is an emerging process. Whereas one's historicity embeds the context, there are infinite possibilities in the fusion of horizons of meanings as the researcher engages the unfamiliar and emerges with new meanings and yet a new situatedness. This is different from Ricoeur (1974, 1976, 1981, 1984, 1985, 1987, 1988, 1992), who suggests that the more distant the reader is from the text, the more true the interpretation.

Ricoeur's (1974, 1976, 1981, 1984, 1985, 1987, 1988, 1992) hermeneutics happens through the processes of *interpretation*, *distanciation*, and *appropriation*. Interpretation surfaces in reading and rereading in search of depth of meaning.

Distanciation is holding judgment in abeyance in order to separate what is said from what is actually being written about. This happens in the dialogue between "the world of the text and the world of the reader" (Ricoeur, 1988, p. 179). Ricoeur (1988) writes, "The more readers become unreal in their reading, the more profound and far-reaching will be the work's influence on social reality" (p. 179). After distanciation comes Ricoeur's (1988) appropriation, that is, the assimilation of the unfamiliar with the familiar for the purpose of expanding the understanding of the meaning of the text.

Nurse authors Benner (1985/1999) and Diekelmann, Allen, and Tanner (1989) purport to have Heideggerian hermeneutic methods. Benner uses a three-step strategy—paradigm cases, exemplar, and thematic analyses—in seeking to find meaning and understanding of practices and experiences. Diekelmann, Allen, and Tanner developed a seven-stage hermeneutic method to identify categories, relational themes, and constitutive patterns arising in texts. Neither of these methods is ontologic in form. Cody (1995) and Parse (1995, 1998) created the human becoming hermeneutic method in the Heideggerian-Gadamerian style. It is discussed in detail in Chapter 17.

For further information regarding the hermeneutic method, see Heidegger (1962), Gadamer (1976, 1960/1998), and Ricoeur (1974, 1976, 1981, 1984, 1985, 1992). For an example of a hermeneutic study see Gadamer (1980).

REFERENCES

Benner, P. (1999). Quality of life: A phenomenological perspective on explanation, predication, and understanding in nursing science. In E. C. Polifroni & M. Welch (Eds.), *Perspectives on philosophy of science in nursing* (pp. 303–314). New York: Lippincott. (Reprinted from *Advances in Nursing Science*, 8(1), 1985, 1–14)

Bleicher, J. (1980). *Contemporary hermeneutics: Hermeneutics as method, philosophy, and critique*. London: Routledge & Kegan Paul.

Cody, W. K. (1995). Of life immense in passion, pulse, and power: Dialoguing with Whitman and Parse, A hermeneutic study. In R. R. Parse (Ed.), *Illuminations: The human becoming theory in practice and research*. New York: National League for Nursing Press.

Diekelmann, N., Allen, D., & Tanner, C. (1989). *The NLN criteria for appraisal of baccalaureate programs: A critical hermeneutic analysis*. New York: National League for Nursing Press.

Dilthey, W. (1961). *Pattern and meaning in history*. New York: Harper & Row.

Dilthey, W. (1976). *Selected writings* (H. P. Rickman, Trans.). Cambridge, UK: Cambridge University Press.

Dilthey, W. (1988). *Introduction to the human sciences* (R. J. Betanzos, Trans.). Detroit: Wayne State University Press. (Original work published 1883)

Ermarth, M. (1978). *Wilhelm Dilthey: The critique of historical reason*. Chicago: University of Chicago Press.

Gadamer, H.-G. (1976). *Philosophical hermeneutics* (D. E. Linge, Ed. & Trans.). Berkeley: University of California Press.

Gadamer, H.-G. (1980). *Dialogue and dialectic: Eight hermeneutical studies on Plato* (P. C. Smith, Trans.). New Haven: Yale University Press.

Gadamer, H.-G. (1998). *Truth and method* (2nd rev. ed.) (J. Weinsheimer & D. G. Marshall, Trans.). New York: Continuum. (Original work published 1960)

Heidegger, M. (1962). *Being and time* (J. Macquarrie & E. Robinson, Trans.). New York: Harper & Row.

Parse, R. R. (1981). *Man-living-health: A theory of nursing.* New York: Wiley.

Parse, R. R. (1992). Human becoming: Parse's theory of nursing. *Nursing Science Quarterly, 5,* 35–42.

Parse, R. R. (Ed.). (1995). *Illuminations: The human becoming theory in practice and research.* New York: National League for Nursing Press.

Parse, R. R. (1998). *The human becoming school of thought: A perspective for nurses and other health professionals.* Thousand Oaks, CA: Sage.

Polkinghorne, D. E. (1983). *Methodology for the human sciences: Systems of inquiry.* Albany: State University of New York Press.

Polkinghorne, D. E. (1986a). Changing conversations about human science. *Saybrook Review, 6*(1), 1–32.

Polkinghorne, D. E. (1986b). Conceptual validity in nontheoretical human science. *Journal of Phenomenological Psychology, 17*(2), 129–149.

Polkinghorne, D. E. (1988). *Narrative knowing and the human sciences.* Albany: State University of New York Press.

Ricoeur, P. (1974). *The conflict of interpretations: Essays in hermeneutics* (W. Domingo et al., Trans.). Evanston, IL: Northwestern University Press.

Ricoeur, P. (1976). *Interpretation theory: Discourse and the surplus of meaning.* Fort Worth: Texas Christian University Press.

Ricoeur, P. (1981). *Hermeneutics and the human sciences.* New York: Cambridge University Press.

Ricoeur, P. (1984). *Time and narrative,* Vol. 1 (K. McLaughlin & D. Pellauer, Trans.). Chicago: University of Chicago Press.

Ricoeur, P. (1985). *Time and narrative,* Vol. 2 (K. McLaughlin & D. Pellauer, Trans.). Chicago: University of Chicago Press.

Ricoeur, P. (1987). *The rule of metaphor: Multidisciplinary studies of the creation of meaning in language* (R. Czerny et al., Trans.). Toronto: University of Toronto Press.

Ricoeur, P. (1988). *Time and narrative,* Vol. 3 (K. McLaughlin & D. Pellauer, Trans.). Chicago: University of Chicago Press.

Ricoeur, P. (1992). *History and truth* (C. A. Kelbley, Trans.). Evanston, IL: Northwestern University Press.

Schleiermacher, F. (1977). *Hermeneutics: The handwritten manuscripts* (H. Kimmerle, Ed., & J. Duke & J. Forstman, Trans.). Atlanta, GA: Scholar Press. (Original work published 1805)

CHAPTER 7

THE QUALITATIVE DESCRIPTIVE METHOD

ONTOLOGY

The qualitative descriptive research method is explained in a variety of general qualitative research resources (see, for example, Denzin & Lincoln, 1994, 2000; Gubrium & Sankar, 1994; Marshall & Rossman, 1998; Mason, 1996; Maxwell, 1996; Morse & Field, 1995; Munhall & Boyd, 1993) but in less detail than is presented here. Although this method has its origin in the social sciences, a discipline-specific theoretical perspective, such as a theory of nursing, can be used as a conceptual framework to guide the research study (refer to Table 1–3). Appropriate conceptualization of the research project is crucial, since it frames the entire study and lays the foundation for sound sciencing. The researcher determines the phenomenon of interest. The researcher's perspective is the view of the chosen phenomenon of interest synthesized with an extant discipline-specific theory. The objectives for qualitative descriptive studies arise directly from the perspective.

The purpose of the qualitative descriptive method is to study intensely a phenomenon to discover patterns and themes about life events when the researcher has specific questions about the phenomenon. The research question drives the study plan. It is an interrogatory statement that includes only the phenomenon of interest, not the participant group. For example, *What is the meaning of feeling lonely*? (see also Table 1–2). Assumptions underlying the qualitative descriptive method follow:

1. Humans create social networks.
2. Humans can describe retrospective and prospective life events.
3. Patterns and themes surface through intense study of phenomena.

EPISTEMOLOGY

The nature of the research for the qualitative descriptive method focuses on social connections, interrelationships, life events, and other matters concerned with the social sciences. The entities for discipline-specific study in nursing, consistent with the ontologies of theoretical frames of reference of the simultaneity paradigm, for example, are quality of life (Bournes, 1997; Fisher & Mitchell,1998; Mitchell, 1998; Parse, 1996; Pilkington, 1999); laughing at oneself (Malinski, 1991); the meaning of retirement (Davis & Cannava, 1995); living with persistent pain (Carson & Mitchell, 1998); having no place of your own (Baumann, 1994); the meaning of being an elder (Jonas, 1992); the meaning of living with AIDS (Nokes & Carver, 1991); and deliberative, mutual patterning (Nellett, 1998).

METHODOLOGIES

There are two qualitative descriptive approaches, the *exploratory* study and the *case* study. An exploratory study is an investigation of the meaning of a life event for a group of people. The case study is an investigation of one social unit, for example, a person or a family.

Processes of the Methods

Processes for the exploratory study and the case study follow:

1. Planning a coherent design to ensure scientific merit.
2. Specifying the participant group.
3. Planning for the protection of participants' rights.
4. Gathering data by
   a. Using open-ended questions derived from the objectives.
   b. Using only questions pertinent to the research question.
   c. Eliciting information through:
      (1) Interview,
      (2) Observation, and/or
      (3) Questionnaire.
5. Analyzing-synthesizing data by
   a. Identifying major themes according to the objectives in the language of the participant(s).
   b. Reading the transcribed text of the interview while listening to the audiotape and viewing the videotape.
   c. Identifying and separating major ideas contained in the data about the phenomenon of concern.
   d. Identifying and separating major ideas common to all participants.

  e. Naming representative themes of the major ideas common to all participants.

  f. Stating major themes according to the objectives in the language of the researcher.

  g. Constructing a description of the phenomenon from a synthesis of the themes in the language of the researcher.

  h. Moving the description to the level of science in the discipline—for example, nursing.

6. Discussing findings in light of the disciplinary perspective guiding the study.

7. Recommending further research.

The researcher plans a coherent scientifically sound design to investigate the phenomenon. A scientifically sound design means that the ontology, epistemology, and methodology are congruent. The participant group is selected from the population that the researcher wishes to engage in the study. There is no set number of participants required by this method. Standard procedures for protection of participants are followed (see Chapter 2). A consent form including the purpose of the study, the time and nature of the questions involved, the risks and benefits, the assurance of confidentiality and anonymity, and the right to withdraw at any time without repercussions is signed by all participants. If participants are unable to sign the consent, verbal consent is obtained and documented. For a sample consent form refer to Chapter 2.

Data may be gathered through interview, observation, or questionnaire. The interview is a face-to-face discussion between the researcher and participant during which the researcher asks the open-ended questions that were derived from the objectives of the study. Interviews are audiotaped and videotaped. Observation, which may be audio and video recorded, is the direct witnessing of an event related to the objectives of the study. The questionnaire is a formal structure containing succinctly stated, open-ended questions related to the objectives of the study. It is completed in written form. Audiotapes and videotapes are transcribed verbatim. Data are analyzed and synthesized by contemplating the transcripts, audio and video recordings, or records of the observations, which contain answers to the data-gathering questions, and by identifying major themes according to the study objectives— in the language of the participants and in the language of the researcher. The themes are synthesized to construct a descriptive statement in the language of the researcher. The researcher moves this descriptive statement up levels of abstraction to the level of science in the discipline.

Interpretation of the findings is to be done in light of the original conceptualization and requires connecting the identified themes to the discipline-specific frame of reference and elaborating on the new knowledge gained from the study. Recommendations are made for further research to continue the line of inquiry. An example of a qualitative descriptive study using a nursing frame of reference is in Chapter 8.

REFERENCES

Baumann, S. L. (1994). No place of their own: An exploratory study. *Nursing Science Quarterly, 7,* 162–169.

Bournes, D. A. (1997). Quality of life: Exploring the perspective of patients with congestive heart failure (Master's thesis, University of Toronto, 1997). *Masters Abstracts International, 36*(06), 1583.

Carson, M. G., & Mitchell, G. J. (1998). The experience of living with persistent pain. *Journal of Advanced Nursing, 28*(6), 1242–1248.

Davis, D. K., & Cannava, E. (1995). The meaning of retirement for communally-living retired performing artists. *Nursing Science Quarterly, 8,* 8–16.

Denzin, N. K., & Lincoln, Y. S. (Eds.). (1994). *Handbook of qualitative research.* Thousand Oaks, CA: Sage.

Denzin, N. K., & Lincoln, Y. S. (Eds.). (2000). *Handbook of qualitative research* (2nd ed.). Thousand Oaks, CA: Sage.

Fisher, M. A., & Mitchell, G. J. (1998). Patients' views of quality of life: Transforming the knowledge base of nursing. *Clinical Nurse Specialist, 12*(3), 99–105.

Gubrium, J. F., & Sankar, A. (Eds.). (1994). *Qualitative methods in aging research.* Thousand Oaks, CA: Sage.

Jonas, C. M. (1992). The meaning of being an elder in Nepal. *Nursing Science Quarterly, 5,* 171–175.

Malinski, V. M. (1991). The experience of laughing at oneself in older couples. *Nursing Science Quarterly, 4,* 69–75.

Marshall, C., & Rossman, G. B. (1998). *Designing qualitative research* (3rd ed.). Thousand Oaks, CA: Sage.

Mason, J. (1996). *Qualitative researching.* Thousand Oaks, CA: Sage.

Maxwell, J. A. (1996). *Qualitative research design: An interactive approach.* Thousand Oaks, CA: Sage.

Mitchell, G. J. (1998). Living with diabetes: How understanding expands theory for professional practice. *Canadian Journal of Diabetes Care, 22*(1), 30–37.

Morse, J. M., & Field, P. A. (1995). *Qualitative research methods for health professionals* (2nd ed.). Thousand Oaks, CA: Sage.

Munhall, P., & Boyd, C. O. (Eds.). (1993). *Nursing research: A qualitative perspective* (2nd ed.). New York: National League for Nursing Press.

Nellett, G. H. (1998). The caregiver's experience of deliberative mutual patterning with pain-ridden substance users (Doctoral dissertation, Loyola University Chicago, 1998). *Dissertation Abstracts International, 59*(06B), 2685.

Nokes, K. M., & Carver, K. (1991). The meaning of living with AIDS: A study using Parse's theory of man-living-health. *Nursing Science Quarterly, 4,* 175–179.

Parse, R. R. (1996). Quality of life for persons living with Alzheimer's disease: The human becoming perspective. *Nursing Science Quarterly, 9,* 126–133.

Pilkington, F. B. (1999). A qualitative study of life after stroke. *Journal of Neuroscience Nursing, 31*(6), 336–347.

CHAPTER 8

QUALITY OF LIFE FOR PERSONS LIVING WITH ALZHEIMER'S DISEASE: THE HUMAN BECOMING PERSPECTIVE[1]

The purpose of this research was to ascertain the meaning of quality of life for persons living with Alzheimer's disease. The human becoming theory was the nursing perspective for this descriptive-exploratory study in which 25 people, designated as having mild to moderate Alzheimer's disease, were asked to describe their quality of life. Findings showed that quality for these participants is *a contentment with the remembered and now affiliations that arises amidst the tedium of the commonplace, as an easy-uneasy flow of transfiguring surfaces with liberating possibilities and confining constraints, while desiring cherished intimacies yields with inevitable distancing in the vicissitudes of life, as contemplating the ambiguity of the possibles emerges with yearning for successes in the moment.* Implications for further research and practice are also discussed.

Who can determine the quality of a person's life? Baltimore Orioles' shortstop Cal Ripkin Jr. created a new record on September 6, 1995, for the number of consecutive games played. The man whose record he broke was Lou Gehrig, first baseman of the New York Yankees, who was in the prime of his career when he was diagnosed with the debilitating neuromuscular disease that now bears his name. In a speech in Yankee Stadium in 1939, Gehrig said, "Fans, for the past two weeks you have been reading about a bad break I got. Yet today I consider myself the luckiest man on the face of the earth. . . . I might have had a bad break, but I have an awful lot to live for" (Robinson, 1990, pp. 263, 264). Who can determine the quality of a person's life? From the perspective of the

[1]Rosemarie Rizzo Parse, Quality of life for persons living with Alzheimer's disease: The human becoming perspective, *Nursing Science Quarterly*, 9, 126–133, copyright © 1996 by Chestnut House Publications. Reprinted by permission of Sage Publications, Inc.

human becoming theory, only the person's own description discloses his or her quality of life. Only the person—*there*—living the life can describe its quality (Parse, 1994b). This is true of all persons—even those who have been designated by medical diagnoses as having some "cognitive impairment."

While little attention has been given to quality of life for special groups such as the elderly and disabled (Clark, 1988; Cohen, 1991; Dossa, 1989; Nickel et al., 1996), some research studies have been conducted in settings where the majority of clients have been considered to have some cognitive impairment (Aller & Coeling, 1993; Clark & Bowling, 1990; Cox, Kaeser, Montgomery, & Marion, 1991; Grant & Reimer, 1991; Kayser-Jones, 1990; Malott & McAiney, 1995; Minkler, 1984; Oleson, Heading, Shadick, & Bistodeau, 1994; Turner, 1993). For example, in one study in Ontario, Canada, experts including nurses, family caregivers, family physicians, psychiatrists, psychologists, and social workers were asked to identify factors that they believed contributed to the quality of life of residents medically diagnosed with dementia (Malott & McAiney, 1995). The preliminary findings identified important factors related to quality of life for the resident, family, staff, and facility. The factors pertaining to residents were freedom from pain, low level of agitation, and ability to communicate needs in some manner. Family factors were quality of visits, healthy family functioning, and knowledge about dementia; staff factors were desire to work with residents with dementia, knowledge about dementia, and specific skills training; and facility factors were commitment to quality, adequate number of staff, and special programs (Malott & McAiney, 1995, p. 12).

Another study by Oleson and colleagues (1994) compared perceptions of quality of life for ten residents and nine nursing staff of a long-stay institution in England, using a semi-structured interview approach. They found similar themes for both residents and nurses. According to these researchers, however, residents' perceptions tended to be more personal and were sometimes negative, whereas those of nurses tended to be more positive and were more reflective of professional duties. Aller and Coeling (1993) interviewed eight residents of a long-term care facility in Ohio, using a semi-structured format. They identified the following as areas influencing the residents' quality of life: (a) ability to communicate with other residents and staff within the facility, (b) ability to care for self, and (c) ability to help others.

Kitwood and Bredin (1992), social psychology researchers with the Bradford Dementia Research Group in England, have described indicators of wellbeing which they conceptualize as quality of life in persons medically diagnosed with dementia, based on extensive observations. The 12 indicators of well-being were not written at the same level of discourse, making the findings difficult to interpret, but the significance of the findings is that they are based on the human actions and values as expressed by those observing the situation closely. Kitwood and Bredin also identified four global sentient states which these indicators express: (a) sense of personal worth, (b) sense of agency, (c) social confidence, and (d) hope.

While these studies focused on quality of life with cognitively impaired persons, very little research has been done on the quality of life phenomenon from the perspective of persons designated as having Alzheimer's disease. And there have been only a few brief descriptive and personal accounts of this experience in the literature (Danforth, 1984; Winters-Miner, 1989). There are, however, a number of books written by experts for caregivers of persons with Alzheimer's. While these books illuminate the meanings and complexities of life for caregivers, they do not explore meanings and complexities for persons living with Alzheimer's disease.

Two yet unpublished qualitative descriptive exploratory studies on quality of life for persons living with Alzheimer's disease or related disorders were completed using the human becoming theory (Parse, 1981, 1987, 1992, 1995) as a guide. Mitchell (1993) conducted a pilot study in a chronic care setting in which approximately half of the 22 participants were medically diagnosed with Alzheimer's disease or a related disorder. She identified three themes in the transcripts of all the participants. The themes are complex and reflect the depth of descriptions offered by participants. The first theme was *uplifting involvements amidst oppressive restrictions and loss illuminates priorities as changing situations surface comfort-discomfort.* The second theme was *the turbulent-calm of intimate engaging surfaces harmony-discord amidst shifting views of communion-aloneness.* The third theme was *uncertain anticipation and confident knowing converge in understandings that fortify resolve for moving beyond.*

Mitchell and Jonas-Simpson (1995) conducted a study on quality of life framed by the human becoming theory (Parse, 1981, 1987, 1992, 1995) with 80 participants from the same chronic care facility as Mitchell's (1993) pilot study. The majority of the participants were over the age of 65, and some of them were medically diagnosed as having Alzheimer's disease or a related disorder. The first theme that emerged from the data was "treasured involvements with family and friends confirm a connectedness with the world" (Mitchell & Jonas-Simpson, 1995, p. 12). The second theme was "uplifting times of humor and genuine concern emerge with the suffering of disregard" (p. 25). The third theme was "shifting patterns of restriction-freedom reflect the struggle between wanting to care for self while having to rely on others" (p. 49). Findings from these two studies shed light on the meaning of quality of life as human becoming.

NURSING PERSPECTIVE

The nursing perspective from which this study emerged and through which the findings are interpreted is the human becoming theory (Parse, 1981, 1987, 1992, 1995), the principles of which are:

1. *Structuring meaning multidimensionally* is cocreating reality through the languaging of valuing and imaging.

2. *Cocreating rhythmical patterns of relating* is living the paradoxical unity of revealing-concealing and enabling-limiting while connecting-separating.
3. *Cotranscending with the possibles* is powering unique ways of originating in the process of transforming.

This theory specifies that "one's lived experiences incarnate quality of life; thus, only the person living the life can describe it" (Parse, 1994b, p. 17). "Quality of life is the meaning one gives to one's life at the moment in cocreation with the universe" (p. 18). The meaning is what one chooses to attend to in the process of cocreating a personal reality. A description of quality of life as a personal reality discloses and hides all-at-once the connecting and separating with the universe of people, ideas, objects, and situations, which simultaneously enables and limits movement. In living quality of life, humans forge ahead and hold back in cocreating new ways of being like others yet unique, with the certainty and uncertainty inherent in choosing the changing of patterns of health.

RESEARCH QUESTION AND OBJECTIVES

The research question of this descriptive-exploratory study was: What is the meaning of the experience of quality of life? The three objectives of the study with related interview questions were:

1. To describe the significance of quality of life.
    a. What is life like for you?
    b. What contributes to your quality of life?
    c. What may diminish your quality of life?
    d. What are your priorities right now?
2. To describe patterns of relating connected to quality of life.
    a. Who is most important to you?
    b. What changes in your routine or relationships might change your quality of life?
3. To describe concerns, plans, hopes, and dreams related to quality of life.
    a. How would you like to change your quality of life?
    b. What can you do to make this happen?
    c. What are your concerns?
    d. What are your hopes and dreams?

PARTICIPANTS AND SETTING

The participants of the study were 5 men and 20 women who were identified as persons who had been medically diagnosed with beginning or moderate

Alzheimer's disease. This population is traditionally considered incompetent to give accurate information. From the human becoming perspective, however, all persons are considered able to share the meanings of their situations in some way. It was found that the participants in this study could talk about their quality of life. Sometimes their sentence structure was not clear and at times they did not complete a sentence, but the messages of their stories were clear as the interviewer spent time talking with them. Standard measures to protect the rights of participants, approved by a human subjects' review board, were implemented. Most interviews took place in the private rooms of the participants at a multilevel care facility located in the midwest. Two interviews took place in the private homes of the participants.

DATA GATHERING

Open-ended questions in relation to the objectives were used to begin discussions with participants. The interviewer sought depth and clarity through being sensitive to the flow of the conversation as guided by the descriptions given by the participants. Most interviews lasted 15–30 minutes. Discussions were tape recorded and transcribed.

DATA ANALYSIS-SYNTHESIS

Data analysis-synthesis was conducted according to the scientific process of the descriptive exploratory method (Parse, Coyne, & Smith, 1985). Transcripts were read and reread and major themes by objective were identified in the language of the participants. These themes were synthesized in the language of the researcher and the findings, the answer to the research question, were interpreted in light of the human becoming theory.

FINDINGS

The findings of this study are presented showing the themes in the language of the participants and the themes in the language of the researcher by objective with examples from the participants' descriptions that led to the cocreation of the themes.

Objective 1: Meaning

Theme 1

Language of Participants: An appreciation of family and old and new friends resides along with living the humdrum routine day-to-day.

Language of Researcher: Contentment with the remembered and now affiliations arises amid the tedium of the commonplace.

Participant Statement

Day to day, life is average, nothing special, not as good as it used to be with family and friends. Friends of mine have all gone here, there, and everywhere. Well, I have a family yet. I have three, four [children]—I don't know anymore. . . . [I care] when it's something with my family. [One friend] calls me, then I do her, but she's that kind of person, kind of loyal. We've known one another since [I got married]. She lets me know she has been on a trip . . . and she will always send a card. And she is very good . . . and sometimes when I can't quite get the words out to her . . . she knows that I have this . . . but I don't care.

Participant Statement

Life is fine. It's nothing very exciting, just ordinary goings-on. Just to get along from day to day. I like to read, and go out and shop, and to go to the movies and theater. I don't go out too much, I'll be honest with you, but I do once in a while. It all sounds kind of dull, but it really isn't. And friends and relatives are still important, though I haven't too many relatives around anymore. [They contribute to my quality of life] just being there by me, I guess, somebody to talk with when you want to talk. Going to the theater used to mean going to the city, but there isn't much theater anymore.

Participant Statement

Life is pretty dull now. I listen to the radio. I'm not with people very much. I still have a wonderful family, but they're all busy. . . . Anything that I want to do is up to me to do it. I don't enjoy much, to be very truthful. Just being with my children.

Participant Statement

Life is humdrum, and exciting. It is quite different here—different from home. We have a group of four or five young women, and they're called the Activities Committee. They plan all these things that they have an idea that we can do. It's the silliest thing you ever saw. It's a bunch of old ladies sitting in a circle on chairs, and we hardly ever get out of the chair. But . . . it's quite a workout, and [we] enjoy it. . . . This is a great place. There's a lot of happy people here, and . . . some develop friendships. You just talk with people, and you get so you laugh at the same things, and maybe discuss certain topics that you're both interested in. You just feel your way. Some develop friendships very quickly, and others are slower, and some people you rather dislike and avoid. It's just like it is anywhere.

Objective 1: Meaning

Theme 2

Language of Participants: The smooth and troublesome struggles of change arise with opportunities and limitations.

Language of Researcher: The easy-uneasy flow of transfiguring surfaces with liberating possibilities and confining constraints.

Participant Statement

[Life] is not as good as it used to be. I have this illness now, and of course, I'm older, and that also doesn't help. The disease . . . what I have that hasn't done much for me . . . because I can't do these things anymore . . . . I don't have [old] friends anymore . . . and that makes a difference. Things have changed a lot . . . but I do have family . . . they're the only ones I have to go to, and yet, they get me mad at times. Oh, I just get kind of crabby, probably, and there are times I just get sick of it all. I hate to be this way with my family—they can't do anything. (*Crying*). I don't earn my keep because I can't do that much anymore. I used to wash and iron, and everything, and now I don't really do that, and that makes a difference. . . . I used to do things around the house; I always liked to keep things in place, and now, I don't do much of that anymore. I used to like to talk, and these things have changed. When you talk to people some-times . . . then . . . you just can't . . . and then you feel embarrassed . . . people will watch you . . . so enjoy life while you can. Yes, yes, enjoy! You don't know what's going to be knocking at your door, eventually. I never thought this would have [happened]. Naturally, when you get old, you get various prob-lems, and things like that. But you never expect them to happen [to you]. If it's going to happen, it's going to happen to somebody else, not you. . . . I guess you think yours is the worst . . . but I realize that there are a lot of people that have plenty [not just me].

Participant Statement

The worst part is the eyesight. I don't know how I can improve my eyesight. It's gone. It's just old age, but that's my problem. Oh yes, I can hear; my hearing is going too, but I can still hear music. I enjoy music; otherwise there is nothing else to do. Of course, it's no good complaining, because there's nothing that nobody can do about it. I can't read the newspapers and see what's going on. So basically, I'm in lousy, rotten shape. Because I used to enjoy reading the newspaper, and finding out the news. I can't do that; I can't see this damn TV. . . . But oh, in the summer, I wait for the summertime, out in the rose gar-den there. I always enjoy that, to go and sit out there when the sun is out, and it's beautiful. Oh yes, I can't wait to go outside.

Participant Statement

So, my life has changed quite a bit now, because I'm here. This is one week only, and I'm finding out a lot of things. At first, it was a little hectic, and I didn't know what to do, but I got used to it, and I like it now. And the people here are nice to you, and you don't have to worry about if something goes wrong, or you get sick. They take care of you here, and that I like. . . . And I like it here. I was wondering if I would, but I'm satisfied. . . . It's better than being alone, like I was at home, in my own house. I was alone, and it wasn't good. I couldn't drive anymore, and I'd have to ask my neighbors all the time.

Objective 2: Rhythmicity

Theme 3

Language of Participants: Wishing for family closeness mingles with a gentle acceptance of being apart.

Language of Researcher: Desiring cherished intimacies yields with inevitable distancing in the vicissitudes of life.

Participant Statement

So my family has to do all this stuff. Maybe to an extent, I wish I could do it again, and yes, I know, there's some things I could do better around the house, but I don't like it anymore. Who needs housework? That doesn't do anything [for me]; I've had a lifetime of that. Oh, maybe it was different because then many things were yours and many things were new. When I was a child, we had aunts, and uncles, and cousins, and things happened. It used to be fun, and now they're all gone. I don't have any family, except [our immediate family] here. Probably if I didn't have my family, I would be in a real problem. Sometimes I wonder maybe it is easier going into a nursing home. Well, what happens happens!

Participant Statement

I worship that son of mine. He's a bright boy, and he has gotten honors. He graduated from the military school, and he was very fortunate to have that. He's always been a joy to us. He is older now, that we can talk very frankly about things. He is living near—that's why I am here; he found this place. And now my son and his wife are going down to Florida. Well, I've had my time down in Florida; I've been down there a number of times, but they're not asking me to go, and I can understand why, because I'm an old person, and I wouldn't be doing all those things the youngsters do, you know; they're in swimming, and they're doing all those things that I would be, so I am happy about that.

Participant Statement

I have twin daughters that live in California, and then I have two sons that live here. And they come to see me. Of course, the girls, I don't get to see very often, maybe once every two years or so. Their children all live in California, too, so I don't get to see them very often. . . . Of course, you know, with the boys, they don't have time. My oldest son took over our business after my husband retired. And then, my youngest son travels; he's not home very much. So I don't get to see them as often as I'd like, but then, after all, they have families too. . . . I'd leave the children, because they have their families and their children, and it isn't up to me to tell them what to do, so I just . . . they live their lives and I live mine.

Objective 3: Cotranscendence

Theme 4

Language of Participants: Considering the sureness-unsureness of what's next arises with wishes for simple immediate accomplishments.

Language of Researcher: Contemplating the ambiguity of the possibles emerges with yearning for successes in the moment.

Participant Statement

I wish this would all change, but it's not going to. Things have changed a lot, and I wish they would find something, a miracle thing, but that doesn't seem too likely. Oh, I'm sure some day they'll find out what to do. But after all, who am I when President Reagan, even if somebody such as he—so there's nothing much you can do. . . . Well, naturally, it would be better probably; I wish I could be out more . . . just be outside.

Participant Statement

I really love life, but I accept whatever is, for all of us. Right now, well, I'm in my 90s, and I expect that I'm not going to live a long time, but I'm not dwelling on it . . . and I will be—whatever.

Participant Statement

[What would change my quality of life is] just that I enjoy myself a little more. Get better acquainted here, and see my family more frequently. Just meeting people, I suppose. When you are new, it's difficult to meet up with different people, so that takes a little time. So far, [it's going] very nicely. For my future, I hope that everything goes well. Let's hope that I continue to function properly. And my dreams are of another world, I guess, when I'm long gone. When you pass away—whatever is ahead of you.

The findings of this study, then, are the themes arising from the descriptions of participants:

1. Contentment with the remembered and now affiliations arises amid the tedium of the commonplace.
2. The easy-uneasy flow of transfiguring surfaces with liberating possibilities and confining constraints.
3. Desiring cherished intimacies yields with inevitable distancing in the vicissitudes of life.
4. Contemplating the ambiguity of the possibles emerges with yearning for successes in the moment.

The answer to the research question is: quality of life is *a contentment with the remembered and now affiliations that arises amidst the tedium of the commonplace, as an easy-uneasy flow of transfiguring surfaces with liberating possibilities and confining constraints, while desiring cherished intimacies yields with inevitable distancing in the vicissitudes of life, as contemplating the ambiguity of the possibles emerges with yearning for successes in the moment.*

DISCUSSION

Theme 1, *contentment with the remembered and now affiliations arises amid the tedium of the commonplace*, surfaced in discussions with all participants as they talked about how their lives now compared to how they used to be. Their conversations reflected an appreciation for family and old and new friends as they described the humdrum of everyday by sharing the details about the unchanging routines. This theme was not apparent in the extant literature on quality of life in general nor in the research literature on quality of life for persons with cognitive impairment (Aller & Coeling, 1993; Clark & Bowling, 1990; Cox, Kaeser, Montgomery, & Marion, 1991; Grant & Reimer, 1991; Kayser-Jones, 1990; Malott & McAiney, 1995; Minkler, 1984; Oleson, Heading, Shadick, & Bistodeau, 1994; Turner, 1993).

Theme 2, *the easy-uneasy flow of transfiguring surfaces with liberating possibilities and confining constraints*, arose as participants spoke of the smooth and troublesome struggles in their changing patterns of living. They noted that there were many limitations in the now, but they hastened to add that opportunities were also present. Most participants could foresee gradual changes on the horizon, and, while most did not want to become dependent on others, they believed they would be safe. This theme indirectly reflected two global states (sense of personal worth and hope) of the four identified from the 12 indicators of well-being specified by Kitwood and Bredin (1992) as quality of life for persons medically diagnosed with dementia. The participants in this study believed in themselves and, even with the troublesome struggles, could envision hope for the not-yet as they repeatedly pointed to other possibilities.

Theme 3, *desiring cherished intimacies yields with inevitable distancing in the vicissitudes of life*, emerged as participants spoke of wishing for family closeness yet gently accepting being apart. All participants spoke fondly of family relationships. Most wanted to see their relatives more often but recognized that their children, nieces, and nephews had lives of their own. This theme did not surface in the general literature on quality of life or in the literature on quality of life for persons medically diagnosed with dementia.

Theme 4, *contemplating the ambiguity of the possibles emerges with yearning for successes in the moment*, surfaced in participants' discussions when they thought about and considered what would be next in their lives. All participants said they knew they would change, yet were unsure of what would happen as they got older and wished for simple accomplishments in the immediate. This theme was not apparent in the general literature on quality of life but was alluded to in personal accounts of living with Alzheimer's disease (Danforth, 1984; Winters-Miner, 1989).

All four themes shed light on the meaning of quality of life in general and in particular for persons living with Alzheimer's disease.

The synthesized definition of quality of life arising from the descriptions of participants has four major paradoxical rhythms lived all-at-once as the was and will-be appear in the now. These rhythms are expressed at a higher level of abstraction and flow directly from the themes (see Table 8–1), surfacing in the context of contentment with the remembered and the now amidst the tedium of the commonplace. They are (a) calm-turbulence, (b) freedom-restriction, (c) certainty-uncertainty, and (d) togetherness-aloneness. These paradoxical rhythms of quality of life can be connected to the human becoming theory. The calm-turbulence rhythm of transfiguring arises with the shifting patterns of freedom-restriction amidst the certainty-uncertainty of togetherness-aloneness.

These paradoxical rhythms are ways the human structures meaning, cocreates rhythmical patterns, and cotranscends with the possibles at many realms of the universe. The meaning of quality of life for the participants, who were designated as having beginning to moderate Alzheimer's disease, in this study was articulated in their stories of the ease and unease of change as new priorities were forged with deep appreciation for family closeness and friendships, even though the humdrum of the routine was ever-present with the lulls and agitations of ongoing change. The explicit knowings of their evolving situations were made clear in their descriptions of constraints in the now and the about-to-be. The constraints were discussed in light of new opportunities envisioned as participants were enabled and limited all-at-once. Some participants told of the remembered in stories of working, driving their cars, taking care of their homes, and helping others as they reflected on the changes in the now that restricted their movement.

The participants confirmed and did not confirm certain options as ways of changing. They spoke and were often silent in languaging their thoughts about the quality of their lives as they expressed concern about moving—being-still and about their patterns of relating with family and friends—telling some things and not others. Their attention to surroundings and activities is the way they connected and separated with their worlds, through the remembered, the anticipated, and the now all-at-once. They spoke about connecting and separating with events (exercise and shopping), ideas (reading books, watching TV), people (family and friends), and objects. The participants propelled their way through situations by pushing-resisting while creating new ways of becoming as they tried to conform yet not conform to what others desired. They wondered what was next as they contemplated what might happen to them, yet simultaneously they focused on cherished immediate successes and said they were ready for what might happen as the unfamiliar gradually changed to the familiar.

TABLE 8–1 PARADOXICAL RHYTHMS EMERGING FROM THE THEMES

Themes (participants' language)	Smooth-troublesome	Opportunities-limitations	Sureness-unsureness	Close to–apart from
	↓	↓	↓	↓
Themes (researcher's language)	Easy-uneasy	Liberating possibilities–confining constraints	Ambiguity	Intimacy-distancing
	↓	↓	↓	↓
Paradoxical rhythms at the theoretical level	Calm-turbulence	Freedom-restriction	Certainty-uncertainty	Togetherness-aloneness

Quality of life for the participants in this study is incarnated in the calm-turbulent flow of the day-to-day as changing priorities cocreate different ultimate meanings in life while anticipated freedoms and restrictions arise in the moments of being together with and apart from others. Quality of life is inextricably woven with the certain and uncertain possibles that lie ahead—the not knowings of what is really next lingers with the knowings embedded in plans for the next day, the next meeting with family, or the next call from a friend.

CONNECTION WITH HUMAN BECOMING LITERATURE

Three of the four rhythms arising from the themes in the descriptions of participants in this study are consistent with findings in the two other descriptive exploratory studies on quality of life guided by the human becoming theory with persons designated as living with Alzheimer's disease and related disorders (Mitchell, 1993; Mitchell & Jonas-Simpson, 1995). These are togetherness-aloneness, freedom-restriction, and calm-turbulence. Participants in all three studies in some way made explicit the closeness and distance with family and friends, the opportunities and constraints in transfiguring, and the ups and downs in the humdrum of the commonplace. The one rhythm, certainty-uncertainty, found in the present study is also explicit in the Mitchell (1993) study; participants in these two studies spoke of anticipated uncertainties simultaneously with confident knowings. All four paradoxical rhythms were also somewhat consistent implicitly with some of the non–research-based personal accounts of persons living with Alzheimer's disease reported in the extant literature (Danforth, 1984; Winters-Miner, 1989).

The paradoxical rhythm of restriction-freedom was the phenomenon of interest in a Parse research method study with 12 persons between 75 and 92 years of age conducted by Mitchell (1995). The structure of the lived experience of restriction-freedom was found to be "anticipating limitations with unencumbered self-direction while yielding to change fortifies resolve for moving beyond" (p. 175). The descriptions by participants from Mitchell's (1995) study are consistent with those descriptions that led to the identification of freedom-restriction in the present study. The participants, who were generally in the same age range in both studies, recognized their constraints yet envisioned other possibles. Participants in both studies offered descriptions that reflected yielding to change yet moving beyond with the small successes in the now. The ideas of freedom-restriction and calm-turbulence were also found in the structure of the lived experience of struggling through a difficult time, a study conducted by Smith (1990) with unemployed persons. The structure stated that "struggling through a difficult time was sculpting new lifeways in turbulent change through affirming self while feeling expanded by assets and restricted by obstacles in the midst of grieving the loss of what was cherished" (pp. 22–23). The paradoxical rhythm of togetherness-aloneness is one that has surfaced in several studies guided by the human becoming theory. The phenomena of concern in these studies were grieving (Cody, 1991, 1995; Pilkington, 1993), suffering (Daly, 1995), retirement (Davis & Cannava, 1995), and laughing and health (Parse, 1994a). In all of these studies participants in some way made explicit the importance of being with and apart from others.

Clearly, the paradoxical rhythms found in the present study on quality of life are present in other lived experiences as evidenced in these research findings. As more research is conducted on various lived experiences and on quality of life, some synthesis of findings will be necessary to shed light on quality of life as the human's lived experiences of health at the moment (Parse 1994b).

CONCLUSION

Persons designated as having beginning to moderate levels of Alzheimer's disease described the quality of their lives with much detail, and, while at times they had difficulty getting words together in a sentence, they did tell their stories. The themes and four emergent paradoxical rhythms from this study provide the world of science with new knowledge about quality of life for persons living with Alzheimer's disease and about quality of life in general.

The new knowledge enhances the human becoming nursing theory by enriching understanding of human experiences and it adds substantial information to the extant general literature on quality of life which to date does not reflect these ideas. The findings from this study along with those from the Mitchell (1993) and the Mitchell and Jonas-Simpson (1995) studies begin to build a substantive human science knowledge base about quality of life which sheds light on unitary human becoming different from the particulate perspective that now dominates the literature on this phenomenon. The new knowledge connected to the human becoming theory offers nurses a broader base from which to guide their practice. Knowing about the themes and paradoxical rhythms will guide the nurse as s/he moves with the rhythms of persons and families as they tell of their experiences, hopes, and dreams. Further research on quality of life from the human becoming perspective is necessary since the goal of nursing from this view is quality of life. Each one of the paradoxical rhythms uncovered in this study could be investigated further and then examined in light of the findings from other studies guided by the human becoming theory.

Dimsdale and Baum (1995) in their work "Quality of Life in Behavioral Medicine Research" ask, "Is there a way of quantifying quality of life?" and "Is consensus possible about how to define quality of life?" (p. xi). And, this author asks, Who can describe the quality of a person's life? Who? The answer is— only the person living the life.

REFERENCES

Aller, L. J., & Coeling, H. (1993). Quality of life: Its meaning to the long-term care resident. *Journal of Gerontological Nursing, 19,* 20–25.

Clark, P. G. (1988). Autonomy, personal empowerment, and quality of life in long-term care. *The Journal of Applied Gerontology, 7*(3), 279–297.

Clark, P. G., & Bowling, A. (1990). Quality of everyday life in long stay institutions for the elderly: An observational study of long stay hospital and nursing home care. *Social Science and Medicine, 30,* 1201–1210.

Cody, W. K. (1991). Grieving a personal loss. *Nursing Science Quarterly, 4,* 61–68.

Cody, W. K. (1995). The lived experience of grieving for families living with AIDS. In R. R. Parse (Ed.), *Illuminations: The human becoming theory in practice and research* (pp. 197–242). New York: National League of Nursing.

Cohen, D. (1991). The subjective experience of Alzheimer's disease: The anatomy of an illness as perceived by patients and families. *The American Journal of Alzheimer's Care and Disorders and Research, 6*(3), 6–11.

Cox, C., Kaeser, L., Montgomery, A., & Marion, L. (1991). Quality of life nursing care: An experimental trial in long-term care. *Journal of Gerontological Nursing, 17,* 6–11.

Daly, J. (1995). The lived experience of suffering. In R. R. Parse (Ed.), *Illuminations: The human becoming theory in practice and research* (pp. 243–268). New York: National League of Nursing.

Danforth, A. (1984). *Living with Alzheimer's—Ruth's story.* Falls Church, VA: The Prestige Press.

Davis, D. K., & Cannava, E. (1995). The meaning of retirement for communally-living retired performing artists. *Nursing Science Quarterly 8,* 8–17.

Dimsdale, J. E., & Baum A. (Eds.). (1995). *Quality of life in behavioral medicine research.* Hillsdale, NJ: Lawrence Earlbaum Associates.

Dossa, P. A. (1989). Quality of life: Individualism or holism? A critical review of the literature. *International Journal of Rehabilitation Research, 12*(2), 121–136.

Grant, N. K., & Reimer, M. (1991). *Indicators of quality of care as perceived by residents, significant others, and nursing staff in long term care agencies.* Calgary, Alberta: The University of Calgary.

Kayser-Jones, J. (1990). The environment and quality of life in long-term care institutions. *Nursing and Health Care, 10,* 121–130.

Kitwood, T., & Bredin, K. (1992). Towards a theory of dementia care: Personhood and well-being. *Ageing and Society, 12*(3), 269–287.

Malott, O. W., & McAiney, C. (1995). Improving quality of life for residents with dementia. *Long Term Care, 4*(3), 10–12.

Minkler, M. (1984). Health promotion in long-term care: A contradiction in terms? *Health Education Quarterly, 11*(1), 77–89.

Mitchell, G. J. (1993). *Quality of life: Exploring the client's perspective.* Paper presented at The First International Colloquium on Qualitative Research, Sponsored by Loyola University Chicago, Chicago, IL, October 28–29, 1993.

Mitchell, G. J. (1995). The lived experience of restriction-freedom in later life. In R. R. Parse (Ed.), *Illuminations: The human becoming theory in practice and research* (pp. 159–195). New York: National League for Nursing.

Mitchell, G. J., & Jonas-Simpson, C. (1995). Quality of life: Exploring the client's perspective. Unpublished manuscript, The Queen Elizabeth Hospital, Ontario, Canada.

Nickel, J. T., Salsberry, P. J., Caswell, R. J., Keller, M. D., Long, T., & O'Connell, M. (1996). Quality of life in nurse case management of persons with AIDS receiving home care. Research in Nursing & Health, 19, 91–99.

Oleson, M., Heading, C., Shadick, K. M., & Bistodeau, J. A. (1994). Quality of life in long-stay institutions in England: Nurse and resident perceptions. Journal of Advanced Nursing, 20(1), 23–32.

Parse, R. R. (1981). Man-living-health: A theory of nursing. New York: Wiley.

Parse, R. R. (1987). Nursing science: Major paradigms, theories, and critiques. Philadelphia: Saunders.

Parse, R. R. (1992). Human becoming:Parse's theory of nursing. Nursing Science Quarterly, 5, 35–42.

Parse, R. R. (1994a). Laughing and health: A study using Parse's research method. Nursing Science Quarterly 7, 55–65.

Parse, R. R. (1994b). Quality of life: Sciencing and living the art of human becoming. Nursing Science Quarterly, 7, 16–21.

Parse, R. R. (1995). Illuminations: The human becoming theory in practice and research. New York: National League for Nursing.

Parse, R. R., Coyne, A. B., & Smith, M. J. (1985). Nursing research: Qualitative methods. Bowie, MD: Brady.

Pilkington, F. B. (1993). The lived experience of grieving the loss of an important other. Nursing Science Quarterly 6,130–140.

Robinson, R. (1990). Iron Horse: Lou Gehrig in his time. New York: Norton.

Smith, M. C. (1990). Struggling through a difficult time for unemployed persons. Nursing Science Quarterly 3, 18–28.

Turner, P. (1993). Activity nursing and the changes in the quality of life of elderly patients: A semi-quantitative study. Journal of Advanced Nursing, 18(11), 1727–1733.

Winters-Miner, L. A. (1989). Family reactions: Plight of Alzheimer's victims and caregivers. In G. D. Miner, L. A. Winters-Miner, J. P. Blass, R. W. Richter, & J. L. Valentine (Eds.), Caring for Alzheimer's patients: A guide for family and healthcare providers (pp. 217–225). New York: Plenum.

CHAPTER 9

THE PHENOMENOLOGICAL METHOD

ONTOLOGY

Phenomenology as a philosophical method of inquiry was first described by Franz Brentano in the late 19th century (Spiegelberg, 1960/1965, 1975, 1976, 1981, 1960/1982). It is a noncausal method that relies on description to enhance understanding of human experiences. It is a method of discovery, not verification. Brentano's student, Edmund Husserl, refined the method (Husserl, 1931/1962, 1965, 1990). Husserl's (1931/1962, 1965, 1990) philosophical method leads to uncovering the true essence of phenomena. It happens through bracketing personal biases and dwelling with descriptions of the phenomenon until pure meaning surfaces. Martin Heidegger (1962), a colleague of Husserl's, further specified the phenomenological method. He departed from Husserl's notion of bracketing, because he believes that humans cannot bracket personal biases, but in fact it is these biases that create the lens through which the researcher views the phenomenon (see Table 9–1). Heidegger's 20th-century works brought together Husserl's ideas on phenomenology, with modifications, and the ideas of 19th-century existential philosopher Sören Kierkegaard (1960, 1987), thus birthing the philosophical science of existential phenomenology. Many German and French philosophers expanded the phenomenological movement. Jean-Paul Sartre (1963, 1966), Maurice Merleau-Ponty (1963, 1973, 1974), and Gabriel Marcel (1956, 1978) are preeminent French philosophers whose works moved forward the phenomenological method. These authors, along with literary artists Franz Kafka (1949, 1952, 2000), Albert Camus (1946, 1995), and others shaped and fostered the phenomenological movement, enhancing specificity and diversity of thought. Other preeminent scholars fostering the movement are Binswanger (1963),

TABLE 9–1   DIFFERENCES IN PHENOMENOLOGICAL PHILOSOPHIES:
HUSSERL AND HEIDEGGER

HUSSERL	HEIDEGGER
Transcendental phenomenology	Existential phenomenology
Epistemological	Ontological
Meaning is pure.	Meaning is coconstituted.
Bracketing avoids bias.	Prejudicial understandings are biases that cannot be avoided.
Trustworthiness is preserved with bracketing to achieve objectivity.	Trustworthiness arises in laying a clear path of inquiry.
The finding is the meaning of the phenomenon, "the thing itself."	The finding is the meaning of the phenomenon arrived at through the researcher-phenomenon dialectic.

Kockelmans (1967), Colaizzi (1973, 1978), Giorgi (1971, 1985, 1986, 1989, 1992, 1997), Schutz (1975), and van Kaam (1959, 1966).

Phenomenology, as a scientific method, grew as an alternative to the traditional natural science methods of inquiry, which do not take into account personal descriptions of lived experiences. The purpose of the phenomenological method is to discover structures of lived experiences to shed light on their meaning. The goal is to arrive at a comprehensive description of the phenomenon under study. The assumptions underpinning phenomenology as a scientific method (Spiegelberg, 1960/1965, 1975, 1976, 1981, 1960/1982) and its modifications (Colaizzi, 1973, 1978; Giorgi, 1971, 1985, 1986, 1989, 1992, 1997, 2000); van Kaam, 1959, 1966) follow:

1. Humans coconstitute situations.
2. Knowledge about human experience is expanded by allowing essences of phenomena to appear through descriptions without predictable prescriptions.
3. Knowledge about human experience is gained from retrospective descriptions of lived experiences.

EPISTEMOLOGY

The entities for study with the phenomenological method are lived experiences. Phenomenologists seek to discover the patterns or structures of phenomena, which are the experiences as lived. For example, phenomena for study with the phenomenological method include waiting for a heart transplant, being attentively present to a loved one, or grieving the loss of someone close, among others.

THE PHENOMENOLOGICAL METHOD AND ITS MODIFICATIONS

Spiegelberg (1960/1965, 1975, 1976, 1981, 1960/1982) set forth the essential processes of phenomenology, which are adhered to generally in all of the scientific procedural modifications that have emerged. The most common modifications are those by van Kaam (1959, 1966), Giorgi (1971, 1985, 1986, 1989, 1992, 1997, 2000), and Colaizzi (1973, 1978).

Processes of the Phenomenological Method

The essential processes of phenomenology set forth by Spiegelberg (1976) follow:

1. Investigating the particular phenomenon.
2. Investigating general essences.
3. Apprehending the essential relationships among essences.
4. Watching modes of appearing.
5. Watching the constitution of a phenomenon in consciousness.
6. Suspending belief in the existence of the phenomenon.
7. Interpreting the meaning of the phenomenon. (p. 659)

Investigating Particular Phenomena.   Three major processes—*intuiting, analyzing,* and *describing* (Spiegelberg, 1976)—are involved in investigating particular phenomena. These processes are closely related and, though discrete in operation, occur all-at-once. *Intuiting* is the process of coming to know the phenomenon as described by the participants. It happens through deep contemplation and strict adherence to the surfacing meaning of the phenomenon as it shows itself in the participants' descriptions. Each description is read and reread to grasp the uniqueness of the phenomenon. *Analyzing* is the intentional examining of elements of the phenomenon, distinguishing characteristics, and unraveling the connections to other phenomena. Analyzing is "the general examination of the structure of the phenomenon according to its ingredients and configuration" (Spiegelberg, 1976, p. 671) to understand the whole of the lived experience. *Describing* is integral to intuiting and analyzing. It is the process of affirming a connection between the phenomenon and everything that is denoted or connoted by way of the terms used in reference to it (Spiegelberg, 1976, p. 673). Describing involves attending to major manifestations of the phenomenon and setting forth the essences and beyond, specifying the meaning of a lived experience in a structure. The processes of intuiting, analyzing, and describing are fundamental to the phenomenological method and permeate the other six activities of the method.

Investigating General Essences.   Through examining the particulars, general essences are investigated. Interrogation of the particulars involves contemplating the experience as written and seeking the details through probing what the phenomenon really is showing as its essence. For example, "Using the particular red of an individual rose as a point of departure we can see it as an instance of a certain shade of red in general. But we can also see it as exemplifying redness and finally color as such" (Spiegelberg, 1976, p. 677). Thus, examining particulars leads to the apprehension of general essences.

Apprehending Essential Relationships.   Apprehending essential relationships occurs through examining relations among the particulars within a single general essence, and among several general essences. The purpose for apprehending essential relationships is to discover the nature of the general essences. The process, called *imaginative variation*, is achieved by studying both the internal connections and external connections of the essences (Spiegelberg, 1976, p. 680). It answers the question, "*What is the nature of the essences, general and particular, of the phenomenon?*" Entities compatible with the essences of a phenomenon should be specified in the description; those not essential to the nature of the phenomenon should be omitted. Thus, a deep understanding of the phenomenon can be achieved.

Watching Modes of Appearing.   The way in which a thing appears is significant to the understanding of the phenomenon as a whole (Spiegelberg, 1976, p. 685). Watching modes of appearing focuses on the way a phenomenon presents itself to participants, as shown in the descriptions, and to the researcher through *dwelling* with the descriptions. The descriptions of all participants reveal a profile of the phenomenon.

Watching the Constitution of Phenomena in Consciousness.   The way a phenomenon constitutes itself in consciousness can be explored through a process of integrating the unfamiliar with the familiar. "Constitutional exploration consists of determining the way in which a phenomenon establishes itself and takes shape in our consciousness" (Spiegelberg, 1976, p. 688). The constitution of a phenomenon is significant to its meaning, and knowledge of it expands understanding. For example, the knowledge of a stranger's personality grows from the links one makes, beginning with the first impression and continuing with subsequent meetings. The connectedness among the links constitutes the pattern, which is the stranger's personality (Spiegelberg, 1976, p. 689).

Suspending Belief in the Existence of the Phenomenon.   Suspending belief in the existence of a phenomenon is called *bracketing*. Bracketing is the process of holding in abeyance the meaning of the phenomenon for the researcher as different from the phenomenon as it appears. The researcher makes explicit his or her beliefs about the phenomenon and sets these aside when approaching participants' descriptions. It is important in "phenomenology that we consider all of the data, real or unreal or doubtful, as having equal rights, and investigate them without fear or favor" (Spiegelberg, 1976, p. 672). Bracketing, then, is an attempt to ensure that the various perspectives of the participants are considered in uncovering the essences of the phenomenon under study. Whereas Husserl (1931/1962, 1965, 1990) believes bracketing must be complete to achieve the true meaning of the phenomenon, Heidegger (1962) believes that bracketing is never achieved fully, because humans are bound to see phenomena from their perspectival view.

Interpreting Concealed Meanings of Phenomena.   Hermeneutic interpretation arises in dwelling with descriptions and going beyond by shifting the level of discourse from the concrete to the abstract. Inferences are made joining the hidden and disclosed meanings. "Hermeneutics is an attempt to interpret the 'sense' of certain phenomena" (Spiegelberg, 1976, p. 695). This activity requires the researcher "to dwell with the subjects' descriptions and to go beyond what is directly given" (Spiegelberg, 1976, p. 695). This leads to the construction of a structure of the lived experience that captures the meaning that participants give to the phenomenon, but it is stated in disciplinary language (Giorgi, 1985).

As noted previously, several modifications of the phenomenological method, as described by Spiegelberg (1976), have emerged. There is no required number of participants for phenomenological research, but all participants are to be protected by the ethical standards specified in Chapter 2 of this book. The most commonly used procedural modifications—those developed by van Kaam (1959, 1966), Giorgi (1971, 1985, 1986, 1989, 1992, 1997), and Colaizzi (1973, 1978)—are presented in the following sections.

van Kaam's Procedural Modification

van Kaam (1959, 1966) sets forth six scientific operations of phenomenological analysis to be used to gain an understanding of lived experiences by answering research questions such as *"What is the structural definition of loneliness?"* These operations follow:

1. Eliciting descriptive expressions.
2. Identifying common elements.
3. Eliminating expressions not related to the phenomenon.
4. Formulating a hypothetical definition of the phenomenon.
5. Checking the hypothetical definition with the original descriptions.
6. Specifying the structural definition.

The researcher invites participants to "describe a situation in which you experienced loneliness. Share all the thoughts and perceptions you can recall until you have no more to say about the phenomenon." The descriptions are written. Through *intuiting, analyzing,* and *describing,* the researcher identifies *descriptive expressions,* which are statements about the lived experience under study. *Common elements* are identified as the researcher dwells with the descriptive expressions, synthesizing clusters of congruent ideas. These are stated in abstract language and are the major themes arising from dwelling with the descriptive expressions. The common elements are synthesized into a *hypothetical definition* that is compared to each description to ascertain whether the common elements appear explicitly or implicitly in each description. The definition is then modified if necessary to reflect all common elements arising from the descriptive expressions. This becomes the *structural definition*, which is the major finding of the study. Seasoned researchers with experience in the phenomenological method and a congruent frame of reference to that underpinning the study are asked to judge the accuracy of the path of inquiry.

Giorgi's Procedural Modification

Giorgi (1971, 1985, 1986, 1989, 1992, 1997, 2000) sets forth a procedural modification of phenomenology as a scientific method to uncover the meaning of a lived experience by answering research questions such as *"What is the structural description of loneliness?"* The procedural modification includes:

1. Dwelling with the description to get a sense of the whole.
2. Returning to the participant for elaboration on ambiguous areas of the description.
3. Identifying natural meaning units.
4. Identifying themes.
5. Identifying focal meanings.
6. Synthesizing a situated structural description.
7. Synthesizing a general description.

Like van Kaam's (1959, 1966) procedure, the researcher using Giorgi's (1971, 1985, 1986, 1989, 1992, 1997, 2000) modification of the phenomenological method invites participants to describe a situation in which they experienced the phenomenon. The descriptions are written or audiotaped. The researcher dwells with written descriptions, or the transcripts, and returns to the participant to elaborate on any part of the description that the researcher finds unclear. The completed description is then called the elaborated description. Through *intuiting, analyzing,* and *describing,* the researcher identifies natural meaning units (context-laden constituents of the phenomenon under study) from which themes are identified in the language of the participant. Focal meanings move the theme to the language of the researcher, and a situated structural description is synthesized for each participant. The situated structural descriptions of all participants are synthesized to form the general structural description—which answers the research question and is the meaning of the lived experience.

Colaizzi's Procedural Modification

Colaizzi (1973, 1978) sets forth a procedural modification of the scientific phenomenological method to uncover the meaning of lived experience through answering research questions such as *What are the essential features of loneliness?* The procedural modification includes the following:

1. Reading all participants' descriptions.
2. Extracting significant statements.
3. Formulating meanings (hidden and disclosed).
4. Clustering themes for each description through
   a. Validating the themes with the original descriptions; and
   b. Relying on a tolerance for ambiguity.
5. Developing an exhaustive description.
6. Formulating the exhaustive description into an unequivocal statement of identification of the structure.
7. Validating the findings (the structure) with the participants.
8. Integrating information from the validating interview into the final description.

Like van Kaam (1959, 1966) and Giorgi (1971, 1985, 1986, 1989, 1992, 1997, 2000), Colaizzi (1973, 1978) seeks descriptions of the phenomenon under study, but his modification requires asking the participants, in an interview, detailed questions about the experience as lived. The questions are constructed by the researcher while the researcher dwells with and listens to his or her own presuppositions about the phenomenon. These questions then are asked to the participants and the answers are audiotaped. The transcribed descriptions are read and through *intuiting, analyzing,* and *describing,* the researcher identifies the significant statements, formulates meanings into themes, and clusters the themes—validating them with the original description of the participant. An exhaustive description is developed from a synthesis of themes from all participants, and the findings are validated by asking the participants whether the description fits their experience (Colaizzi, 1978, p. 62). Any new information from participants in the validation interview must be integrated into the final description, which answers the research question.

These three modifications of the phenomenological method are used the most frequently. For further details about the phenomenological method and these three modifications see Spiegelberg (1960/1965, 1975, 1976, 1981, 1982), van Kaam (1959, 1966), Giorgi (1971, 1985, 1986, 1989, 1992, 1997, 2000), and Colaizzi (1973, 1978). An example of each modification follows in Chapters 10 (van Kaam), 11 (Giorgi), and 12 (Colaizzi).

REFERENCES

Binswanger, L. (1963). *Being-in-the-world: Selected papers of Ludwig Binswanger* (J. Needleman, Trans.). New York: Basic Books.

Camus, A. (1946). *The stranger.* New York: Random House.

Camus, A. (1995). *The first man* (D. Hapgood, Trans.). New York: Knopf.

Colaizzi, P. F. (1973). *Reflection and research in psychology*: A *phenomenological study of learning*. Dubuque, IA: Kendall/Hunt.

Colaizzi, P. F. (1978). Psychological research as the phenomenologist views it. In R. S. Valle & M. King (Eds.), *Existential phenomenological alternatives for psychology* (pp. 48–71). New York: Oxford University Press.

Giorgi, A. (1971). Phenomenology and experimental psychology: II. In A. Giorgi, W. Fischer, & R. von Eckartsberg (Eds.), *Duquesne studies in phenomenological psychology* (Vol. I, pp. 3–29). Pittsburgh, PA: Duquesne University Press.

Giorgi, A. (1985). Sketch of a psychological phenomenological method. In A. Giorgi (Ed.), *Phenomenology and psychological research* (pp. 8–22). Pittsburgh, PA: Duquesne University Press.

Giorgi, A. (1986). Theoretical justification for the use of descriptions in psychological research. In P. D. Ashworth, A. Giorgi, & A. J. J. deKoning (Eds.), *Qualitative research in psychology: Proceedings of the International Association for Qualitative Research in Social Science* (pp. 3–22). Pittsburgh, PA: Duquesne University Press.

Giorgi, A. (1989). One type of analysis of descriptive data: Procedures involved in following a systematic phenomenological method. *Annual Edition of Methods: A Journal for Human Science*, 39–61.

Giorgi, A. (1992). Description versus interpretation: Competing alternative strategies for qualitative research. *Journal of Phenomenological Psychology*, 23(2), 119–135.

Giorgi, A. (1997). The theory, practice, and evaluation of the phenomenological method as a qualitative research procedure. *Journal of Phenomenological Psychology*, 28(2), 235–260.

Giorgi, A. (2000). Concerning the application of phenomenology to caring research. *Scandinavian Journal of Caring Science*, 14, 11–15.

Heidegger, M. (1962). *Being and time* (J. Macquarrie & E. Robinson, Trans.). New York: Harper & Row.

Husserl, E. (1962). *Ideas: General introduction to pure phenomenology* (W. R. B. Gibson, Trans.). New York: Collier Macmillan. (Original work published 1931)

Husserl, E. (1965). *Phenomenology and the crisis of philosophy*. Philadelphia: Harper & Row.

Husserl, E. (1990). *The idea of phenomenology* (W. Alston & G. Nakhnikian, Trans.). Boston: Kluwer Academic Press.

Kafka, F. (1949). *The castle*. New York: Knopf.

Kafka, F. (1952). *Selected short stories* (W. Muir & E. Muir, Trans.). New York: Modern Library.

Kafka, F. (2000). *The metamorphosis, In the penal colony, and other stories: With two new stories*. New York: Scribner.

Kierkegaard, S. (1960). *The diary of Sören Kierkegaard* (P. Rohde, Ed.). New York: The Wisdom Library.

Kierkegaard, S. (1987). *Either/or* (S. L. Ross, Ed., & G. L. Stengren, Trans.). New York: Harper & Row.

Kockelmans, J. J. (Ed.). (1967). *Phenomenology*. New York: Doubleday.

Marcel, G. (1956). *The philosophy of existentialism*. Secaucas, NJ: Citadel.

Marcel, G. (1978). *Mystery of being: Reflection and mystery* (Vol. 1). South Bend, IN: Gateway Editions.

Merleau-Ponty, M. (1963). *The structure of behavior.* Boston: Beacon.

Merleau-Ponty, M. (1973). *The prose of the world.* Evanston, IL: Northwestern University Press.

Merleau-Ponty, M. (1974). *The phenomenology of perception* (C. Smith, Trans.). New York: Humanities Press.

Sartre, J.-P. (1963). *Search for a method.* New York: Knopf.

Sartre, J.-P. (1966). *Being and nothingness.* New York: Washington Square Press.

Schutz, A. (1975). *On phenomenology and social relations.* Chicago: University of Chicago Press.

Spiegelberg, H. (1965). The essentials of the phenomenological method. In H. Spiegelberg, *The phenomenological movement: A historical introduction*: Vol. 1 (2nd ed., pp. 653–701). The Hague: Martinus Nijhoff. (Original work published 1960)

Spiegelberg, H. (1975). *Doing phenomenology: Essays on and in phenomenology.* The Hague: Martinus Nijhoff.

Spiegelberg, H. (1976). *The phenomenological movement* (Vols. I and II). The Hague: Martinus Nijhoff.

Spiegelberg, H. (1981). *The context of the phenomenological movement.* Boston: Martinus Nijhoff.

Spiegelberg, H. (1982). *The phenomenological movement: A historical introduction* (3rd rev. and enlarged ed.). The Hague: Martinus Nijhoff. (Original work published 1960)

van Kaam, A. L. (1959). Phenomenal analysis: Exemplified by a study of the experience of "feeling really understood." *Journal of Individual Psychology, 15,* 66–72.

van Kaam, A. L. (1966). Application of the phenomenological method. In A. L. van Kaam, *Existential foundations of psychology* (pp. 294–329). Pittsburgh, PA: Duquesne University Press.

CHAPTER 10

THE EXPERIENCE OF LAUGHTER: A PHENOMENOLOGICAL STUDY[1]

The purpose of this research was to uncover a structural definition of laughing in persons over 65. The structural definition that arises from this study is: laughing is a *buoyant immersion in the presence of unanticipated glimpsings prompting harmonious integrity which surfaces anew through contemplative visioning*. This definition is congruent with some of the current literature and practices related to laughter and health. It corresponds to the principles of Parse's human becoming theory and thus expands understanding of human experiences related to structuring meaning, living in relation to others, and viewing the familiar in a new light.

Laughter has historically been considered regenerative, degenerative, and derisive (Holland, 1982), as well as a social corrective. Shakespeare often included a court jester, who acted as the chorus or commentary, lightening the heaviness of a tragedy like *King Lear* and confirming the comedy in *As You Like It* (Rowse, 1978). Jonathan Swift used humor as satire (Rosenheim, 1959). In more recent times, comedians have been an important part of entertainment in Western society. Charlie Chaplin memorialized satire in a number of silent movies. Jay Leno and his compatriot late-night hosts make their living by the use of humor.

Laughter is a uniquely human experience; persons of all ages smile and laugh. People say they "feel good" when they laugh, yet laughter as a phenomenon has not been examined extensively in either qualitative or

[1]Rosemarie Rizzo Parse, The experience of laughter: A phenomenological study. *Nursing Science Quarterly*, 6, 39–43, copyright © 1993 by Chestnut House Publications. Reprinted by permission of Sage Publications, Inc.

quantitative research studies. Nevertheless, there do exist some quantitative research reports on humor as well as a common store of anecdotal information that indicates the value and use of laughter. There have been numerous attempts to define humor (Mindess, 1987; Berlyne, 1972) and to relate it to other characteristics such as creativity (Wicker, 1985). Freud (1905/1960) specifically examined humor in relation to the unconscious. According to the literature, the benefits of humor range from tension release by allowing persons to express themselves (Young & Frye, 1966) to broadening thoughts and facilitating insights (Heuscher, 1980) to putting pain in perspective (Tooper, 1984). Shared laughter, it has been noted (Block, Browning, & McGrath, 1983), can promote intimacy, belongingness, warmth, and friendliness.

A body of opinion has accumulated about laughter, written for the most part by psychologists, sociologists, anthropologists and philosophers. It is thought by psychologists and anthropologists to have evolved as a device that may have served to thwart aggression, spread information, and preserve social unity (Black, 1984; Gordon, 1969). It is considered to be culturally universal (Eibl-Eibesfeldt, 1972) and is thought to be innate: studies of blind and deaf children have demonstrated that even without visual or auditory stimulation from the social environment, children laugh (Goodenough, 1931).

It is known that laughter can arise from tickling (Stearns, 1972), or from comical thoughts (Shultz & Horibe, 1974), and that gender, age, education, language, and culture are factors related to whether or not a person will laugh in a given situation (Omwake, 1937). It is known that laughter can relieve tension (Goodenough, 1931) and that it increases as social density increases (Freedman & Perlick, 1979) but that it can occur in solitary situations (Berlyne, 1972), indicating that it is not strictly a social phenomenon. Laughter has been seen as a safety valve for surplus energy (Spencer, 1860) or psychic energy (Freud, 1905/1960), as aggressive in nature (Avner, 1984), as a signal of well-being (Darwin, 1890), as reflective of anger and hostility (Fry & Salameh, 1987), as a mediator of the stress response for people who are depressed (Nezu, Nezu, & Blissett, 1988), as stemming from a sense of superiority (Morreall, 1987), as a response to incongruity (Morreall, 1987), and as "therapeutic" (Cousins, 1976). Laughter can occur in so many different situations that it is difficult to determine one definition that can fit all cases (Black, 1984). Further difficulty stems from the uses, values, and origins of laughter, which have been for centuries a matter of debate and disagreement.

Norman Cousins (1979) popularized the notion of laughing to improve health, as he participated in his own healing through planned periods of laughter. Consistent with Cousins (1979), Malinski (1991) noted in a report of her qualitative study of laughing in older couples that "observations of people who laugh at themselves indicated they seemed happier, more self-assured, and more at ease with themselves than those who were not able to do so. Laughing at oneself seemed to serve as a key to 'unbox' the person, disclosing possibilities for transforming situations, especially those with potentially adverse effects on confidence, self-esteem, and well-being" (p. 69). Both

Cousins (1979) and Malinski (1991) link laughing and health or well-being. This statement reflects the general opinion about laughing as it is viewed in the '90s, with negative views of this phenomenon currently relegated to historical reference. The researcher agrees with Malinski (1991) and Cousins (1979, 1989) that laughter and health are intertwined and that laughing is in fact connected to one's experience of health. This contention has been reinforced by anecdotal accounts of people who say such things as "laughing made me feel better" or "a good laugh leaves you happy."

This study was implemented to uncover a structural definition of laughter as it is experienced in everyday life for persons over 65. van Kaam's (1969) modification of the phenomenological method was used since it is congruent with both the intent of the inquiry (to uncover the meaning of a lived experience) and the phenomenon being studied. The research question in this study was: What is the structural definition of the experience of laughing?

RESEARCHER'S PERSPECTIVE

The researcher views laughing as a lived experience characterized by an uplifting self-immersion sparked by the recognition of some incongruence, prompting a happy feeling. Laughter erupts when the person experiences an amusing event or when something calls up in the person humorous images of a remembered connectedness which reflects lived values. The connecting-separating with the images incarnates the *was*, the *is*, and the *will be* all-at-once, which propels one beyond the now to the not-yet. The laughing experience transforms the moment and lingers, creating a happy feeling and prompting a sense of oneness and contentment often reflected in personal descriptions of health.

PARTICIPANTS

The participants of this study were men and women (N = 30) over 65 years of age who could write and understand English. They were informed of the nature of the study, the time commitment required, and the manner in which they would be involved. The only demographic data requested were age and gender. Anonymity was guaranteed. No names were attached to the descriptions. Writing the description requested was considered consent to participate; no written consent form was utilized. The procedure for informed consent was approved by a university review board for the protection of human subjects.

DATA GATHERING AND ANALYSIS

An invitation to participate in the study was distributed to approximately 50 people via the researcher and her colleagues. Specifically, participants were asked: "Describe a situation in which you experienced 'laughing your heart out.' Share all your thoughts and feelings about the situation." Descriptions were mailed or personally returned to the researcher.

Thirty participants' descriptions were analyzed through the processes of intuiting, analyzing, and describing using the six operations of scientific explication of phenomenological analysis detailed by van Kaam (1969), as follows:

1. *Quantitative and qualitative listing of descriptions.* The researcher read and dwelled with each participant's description and, through the processes noted above, identified the descriptive expressions. She then listed the expressions from each participant's description in the individual's own language. (A descriptive expression is a statement that completes an idea about the lived experience being described.)

2. *Identification of common elements of experience.* The researcher then determined the elements common to all participants' descriptions. A common element is an abstract statement describing a major theme which appears explicitly or implicitly in most descriptions and is compatible with all. Common elements were then stated in the language of the researcher, representing a move up the ladder of abstraction.

3. *Elimination of expressions not related to the phenomenon being examined.* In this study, all descriptive expressions by the 30 participants were included.

4. *Hypothetical definition of the phenomenon.* A hypothetical definition was then derived from the specific common elements. This definition was conceptualized by the researcher and written in the language of science.

5. *Application of the hypothetical definition to the original descriptions.* Subsequently, each description was studied in relation to the hypothetical definition, to be certain it was explicitly or implicitly compatible.

6. *Final identification of the structural definition.* A structural definition of laughing was identified.

FINDINGS

Four elements common to the experience of laughing, as determined by the analysis of the statements of the 30 participants, were identified: *buoyant immersion, harmonious integrity, contemplative visioning,* and *unanticipated glimpsings.* Some descriptive expressions leading to these common elements, as voiced by the participants are included in Table 10–1. When these common elements were synthesized, the structural definition of laughing was: *Laughing is a buoyant immersion in the presence of unanticipated glimpsings, prompting harmonious integrity which surfaces anew in contemplative visioning.*

TABLE 10–1	ELEMENTS COMMON TO THE EXPERIENCE OF LAUGHING WITH SOME DESCRIPTIVE EXPRESSIONS
ELEMENT	**DESCRIPTIVE EXPRESSIONS**
Buoyant immersion	"Laughed hard till it hurt."
	"Made me feel high."
	"When I laughed real hard, tears flowed."
	"Brought tears to my eyes that blinded my vision."
	"Like swimming—you move every muscle of your body."
Harmonious integrity	"A sense of oneness."
	"Sense of calm."
	"Feels good to laugh."
	"Become relaxed afterwards."
	"Makes me feel good."
Contemplative visioning	"Still laugh at the event now."
	"Just thinking about the event, I get a happy feeling."
	"Happy memories when thinking of my kids."
	"Remembering creates the laughter all over again."
	"Laughing my heart out when reliving the event."
Unanticipated glimpsings	"Occurred when reminiscing about the unexpected happenings."
	"Occurred when many were required to share personal privacies unexpectedly."
	"Laughter arose with another in an unusual unexpected happening."
	"Occurred in anticipation of a comedic ending."
	"Occurred while watching another in an unusual unexpected situation."

DISCUSSION

The four elements emerging in this study correspond to the principles of the human becoming theory (Parse, 1981, 1992). Themes of meaning, rhythmicity, and cotranscendence are reflected in the definition.

In the current study, the principle "Cotranscending with the possibles is powering unique ways of originating in the process of transforming" (Parse, 1981, p. 69) is connected with the experience of laughing as a *buoyant immersion*. Buoyant immersion is paradoxical in that it refers to plunging-down-rising-up all-at-once. The plunging-down-rising-up is deeply sinking into the experience while simultaneously being uplifted. Buoyant refers to a light floating, and immersion refers to a sinking into deeply. This simultaneous occurance prompts a change in perspective. The participants' descriptive expressions showed a propelling beyond the moment while deeply embedded in the now of the laughter. The participants noted an uplifting movement reflected in the hilarity, hysteria, and giggling during the remembered event. The upsurging high feeling implies movement to different heights. This is related to powering the possibilities, an aspect of cotranscendence. The idea of being "immersed" surfaced in descriptions of the self moving with the rhythms of the laughter, a feeling of being breathless and a sense of swimming in the mirth. Buoyant immersion reflects powering through originating a transforming and is thus linked to this principle of the human becoming theory.

Unanticipated glimpsings (also linked to the cotranscendence principle, particularly to the concept of transforming) refers to seeing things from a different perspective. Unanticipated glimpsings are the split-second insights that confirm the unusual as real, as one yields to a buoyant immersion. These unanticipated glimpsings can arise where there is a juxtaposition of two unusual happenings or ideas shedding a new light on a situation. The descriptive expressions reported by participants show that laughing occurs in the presence of an incongruous happening, something unanticipated, like a comedic ending to a serious story or unexpectedly having to share privacies with others. The unanticipated glimpsings transform the now through the laughter and shift the perspective, prompting consideration of new possibilities. The transforming arises from powering originating in cotranscending with the possibles.

Harmonious integrity is linked to another principle of the human becoming theory (Parse 1981, 1992), "Cocreating rhythmical patterns of relating is living the paradoxical unity of revealing-concealing and enabling-limiting while connecting-separating" (Parse, 1981, p. 69). Harmonious integrity is the sense of being in tune with others and the universe. It is the feeling of calm that arises through a satisfying experience. Laughing cocreates such an experience. The descriptive expressions demonstrate these experiences of the rhythmical human-universe process in ideas expressed by participants related to calmness, openness, and feeling more relaxed. There surfaced a sense of unity in connecting-separating with the amusing phenomenon as participants were enabled-limited in revealing-concealing their ways of being with laughing. Thus it appears from the descriptions in this study that laughing fosters harmonious integrity as humorous rhythmical patterns of relating are cocreated.

Contemplative visioning is linked to the principle "Structuring meaning multidimensionally is cocreating reality through the languaging of valuing and imaging" (Parse, 1981, p. 69). It is the reflection on images that were once lived and are now lived in memory. These images kindle anew the meaning of the situation. The descriptive expressions in this study reflected a picturing of the *was* in the remembrances, the laughing about it again, and the happy feeling experienced when thinking about a humorous event. Picturing an event in which incongruities arose creates laughter bringing new meaning to a situation. The laughing surfaces through the remembered moment; thus, laughing is lived multidimensionally as the languaging of valuing and imaging structure meaning.

FINDINGS AND RELATED LITERATURE

The structural definition of the lived experience of laughing, *a buoyant immersion in the presence of unanticipated glimpsings prompting harmonious integrity which surfaces anew in contemplative visioning*, is consistent with the researcher's own view of laughing. The common elements which emerged directly from the participants' descriptions are evidenced in the self-immersion, the sense of intuneness, and glimpsing images of other times that the researcher articulated in the researcher's perspective. The definition is also consistent with views about laughing espoused by May (1975), who said that humor was connected to one's own selfhood, an expression of the core of the person. The definition from this study also reflects Frankl's (1969) belief that laughing is a way of putting distance between self and world and that humor helps one rise above or transcend the moment toward a new view.

The structural definition of laughing arising in this study is closely connected with the structural definition of health uncovered in a phenomenological study of health of 400 subjects between the ages of 7 and 93 (Parse, Coyne, & Smith, 1985). The three elements in the structural definition of health are *harmony, plenitude* and *energy*. In the 100 participants over age 66 in the study, these elements were specified as *transcendent vitality, generating completeness,* and *synchronous contemplation. Transcendent vitality* can be linked to *buoyant immersion* and *unanticipated glimpsings,* all of which are connected to the principle "Cotranscending with the possibles." Feeling uplifted, the surge of energy, and an expression of ah! ah! are related to transcending with a new view. These ideas are related to powering and transforming. *Synchronous contemplation* and *generating completeness* from the health study can be linked with *harmonious integrity* and *contemplative visioning* from the laughter study. These connect with the other two principles of the human becoming theory since the sense of oneness, the remembered images, and the feeling of being satisfied are clearly related to cocreating rhythmical patterns and structuring meaning multidimensionally.

The findings of this study are complementary to Malinski's (1991) finding that for twenty elderly couples, "the experience of laughing at oneself was a natural spontaneous form of expression that came with maturity, brought couples closer together, helped them to maintain a positive attitude, and promoted feelings of youthfulness, health, and well-being" (p. 72). These participants made a connection between laughing and health. Information gathered from the current study suggests that laughing creates an uplifting feeling of oneness and that there is a connection between laughter and health.

RECOMMENDATIONS

The experiences of laughing and health, as described by the people living them, are closely related. There is an uplifting burst in each, a sense of intuneness and a satisfying picturing. The structural definition of laughing as it is connected to the structural definition of health relates closely to the meaning of health set forth in the human becoming theory, that health is a process of becoming, a set of value priorities emerging and changing. It is *not* the absence of disease *nor* its opposite (Parse, 1981). There are shared common elements in both the experience of laughter and the experience of health, and further research is required to enhance understanding of the link. A research study on laughing and health is being implemented using Parse's (1987; 1990; 1992) research methodology. Common elements of laughing such as contemplative visioning might also be studied to enhance understanding of its meaning.

The knowledge about laughter as connected to the human becoming theory expands the knowledge base for nursing practice, where the nurse might foster contemplative visioning of a humorous event with persons who raise this as a possibility. The contemplative visioning may lead to harmonious integrity and a sense of "feeling good" with self. Knowing the connection between laughing and health, the nurse would be alert for opportunities to move with a person in a buoyant immersion related to unanticipated glimpsings which surface as a sense of oneness with the universe.

Qualitative research studies such as this one on laughing are essential for enhancing nursing's knowledge base on lived experiences of health. Expanding understanding of human living is a worthy aim of nursing research when the primary goal of nursing is quality of life.

REFERENCES

Avner, Z. (1984). *Personality and sense of humor.* New York: Springer-Verlag.

Berlyne, D. E. (1972). Humor and its kin. In Goldstein, J. H., & McGhee, P. E. (Eds.), *The psychology of humor.* New York: Academic Press.

Black, D. W. (1984). Laughter. *The Journal of the American Medical Association, 252,* 2995–2998.

Block, S., Browning, S., & McGrath, G. (1983). Humor in group psychology. *British Journal of Medical Psychology, 56,* 89–97.

Cousins, N. (1976). Anatomy of an illness (as perceived by the patient). *New England Journal of Medicine, 295,* 1459–1463.

Cousins, N. (1979). *Anatomy of an illness as perceived by the patient: Reflections on healing and regeneration.* New York: Norton.

Cousins, N. (1989). *Head first: The biology of hope.* New York: Dutton.

Darwin, C. (1890). *Expression of the emotions in man and animal* (2nd ed.). New York: Appleton.

Eibl-Eibesfeldt, I. (1972). Expressive movements. In R. A. Hind (Ed.), *Non-verbal communication* (pp. 297–324). Cambridge, MA: Cambridge University Press.

Frankl, V. E. (1969). *The will to meaning.* New York: New American Library.

Freedman, J. L., & Perlick, D. (1979). Crowding, contagion, and laughter. *Journal of Experimental Social Psychology, 15,* 295–303.

Freud, S. (1960). *Jokes and their relation to the unconscious.* New York: Norton. (Original work published 1905)

Fry, W. F., Jr., & Salameh, W. A. (Eds.). (1987). *Handbook of humor and psychotherapy: Advances in the clinical use of humor.* Sarasota, FL: Professional Resource Exchange.

Goodenough, F. L. (1931). Expressions of emotion in a deaf-blind child. *Journal of Abnormal Social Psychology, 27,* 328–333.

Gordon, G. (1969). *The language of communication.* New York: Hastings House.

Heuscher, J. E. (1980). The role of humor and folklore themes in psychotherapy. *American Journal of Psychiatry, 137,* 1546–1549.

Holland, N. N. (1982). *Laughing: A psychology of humor.* Ithaca, NY: Cornell University Press.

Malinski, V. M. (1991). The experience of laughing at oneself in older couples. *Nursing Science Quarterly, 4,* 69–75.

May, R. (1975). *The courage to create.* Toronto, Ontario, Canada: McLeod.

Mindess, H. (1987). The panorama of humor and the meaning of life. *American Behavioral Scientist, 30,* 82–95.

Morreall, J. (1987). *The philosophy of laughter and humor.* Albany, NY: University of New York Press.

Nezu, A. M., Nezu, C. M., & Blissett, S. E. (1988). Sense of humor as a moderator of the relation between stressful events and psychological distress: A prospective analysis. *Journal of Personality and Social Psychology, 54,* 520–525.

Omwake, L. (1937). A study of sense of humor: Its relationship to sex, age, and personal characteristics. *Journal of Applied Psychology, 21,* 688–704.

Parse, R. R. (1981). *Man-living-health: A theory of nursing.* New York: Wiley.

Parse, R. R. (1987). *Nursing science: Major paradigms, theories, and critiques.* Philadelphia: Saunders.

Parse, R. R. (1990). Parse's research methodology with an illustration of the lived experience of hope. *Nursing Science Quarterly, 3,* 9–17.

Parse, R. R. (1992). Human becoming: Parse's theory of nursing. *Nursing Science Quarterly, 5,* 35–42.

Parse, R. R., Coyne, A. B., & Smith, M. J. (1985). *Nursing research: Qualitative methods.* Bowie, MD: Brady.

Rosenheim, E., Jr. (Ed.). (1959). *Jonathan Swift: Selected prose and poetry.* New York: Rinehart.

Rowse, A. L. (Ed.). (1978). *The annotated Shakespeare*. New York: Potter.

Shultz, T. R., & Horibe, F. (1974). Development of the appreciation of verbal jokes. *Developmental Psychology, 10*, 13–20.

Spencer, H. (1860). The physiology of laughter. *MacMillan's Magazine, 1*, 395–402.

Stearns, F. (1972). *Laughing*. Springfield, IL: Charles C. Thomas.

Tooper, V. O. (1984). Humor as an adjunct to occupational therapy interactions. *Occupational Therapy in Health Care, 1*(1), 49–57.

van Kaam, A. (1969). *Existential foundations of psychology*. New York: Doubleday.

Wicker, F. W. (1985). A rhetorical look at humor as creativity. *The Journal of Creative Behavior, 19* (3), 175–184.

Young, R. D., & Frye, M. (1966). Some are laughing; some are not—why? *Psychological Reports, 18*, 747–754.

CHAPTER 11

THE RELENTLESS DRIVE TO BE EVER THINNER: A STUDY USING THE PHENOMENOLOGICAL METHOD[1]

Marc D. A. Santopinto, MScN

The relentless drive to be thinner is an experience lived by many individuals in the present sociohistorical context. Since fundamental questions concerning the structure of this lived experience remain unanswered in the literature, theory-based approaches to nursing practice have yet to be conceptualized for these individuals. The investigator was unable to find even a single nursing study related to the target phenomenon. The present study addresses the foundational question: What is it like to live the experience of the relentless drive to be ever thinner? Retrospective written and verbal accounts from two women who had lived this experience were analyzed using the Giorgi modification of the phenomenological method. The central finding of this study was: The relentless drive to be ever thinner is a persistent struggle toward an imaged self lived through withdrawing-engaging. This theoretical proposition was found to be congruent with Parse's theory of nursing. The study findings suggest directions for innovative nursing research and support Parse's theory as a useful perspective for the investigation of health experiences.

The relentless drive to be ever thinner is an experience lived by many individuals in the present sociohistorical context (Szekely, 1987). Women, in particular, may view themselves as failures if they are not ultrathin or at least

[1]Marc D. A. Santopinto, The relentless drive to be ever thinner: A study using the phenomenological method. *Nursing Science Quarterly*, 2, 29–36, copyright © 1989 by Williams & Wilkins. Adapted and reprinted by permission of Sage Publications, Inc.

losing weight (Szekely, 1987). Indeed, the personal focus upon becoming thin has become commonplace in the western world (Lucas, 1982). This phenomenon is increasingly reflected by the print and electronic media, which portray ultrathinness as a valued ways of being (Garner, Garfinkel, & Olmstead, 1983).

Foundational questions concerning the structure of this lived experience remain unanswered in the literature, and practice approaches grounded in nursing science have yet to be conceptualized. If innovative theory-based approaches to nursing practice with these individuals are to be found, it is important that nurses understand what it is like to live the relentless drive to be ever thinner.

How can an investigator attend with fidelity to the description of an experience-as-lived, without reducing it to experience-as-observed? This is possible only if (a) the subjects' descriptions are allowed to emerge in a natural setting with a minimum of external interference, (b) the subjects' descriptions are interpreted in a manner which accounts for the investigator's theoretical presuppositions, and (c) study subjects are encountered within a framework of engagement rather than detachment (Sandelowski, 1986). The present study used a rigorous methodology fulfilling these criteria. Use of the phenomenological method enabled the investigator to collect and interpret narrative data describing what it is like to actually live the relentless drive to be ever thinner. Phenomenological investigators seek the essence of lived experiences (Parse, Coyne, & Smith, 1985). This method of inquiry is implemented within a context of discovery rather than within the quantitative context of verification (Giorgi, 1985).

There is a paucity of literature related to the lived experience of the relentless drive to be ever thinner. Boss (1963) and Binswanger (1958) provided independent phenomenological studies of the experiences of two subjects. Boss (1963) viewed the experience as grounded in being-with-others, while Binswanger (1958) viewed the self as cut off from a social world. Binswanger viewed the relentless drive as a unique way of being-in-the-world, while Boss (1963) viewed the self as ontologically indistinguishable from other individuals. Both investigators situated the experience within the person's shrinking universe of meaning. Thus, Binswanger (1958) described the individual as narrowed down to a shrinking number of possibles, and Boss (1963) described the self as reduced to a single aspect of being-with-world and unable to unfold.

Both investigators described the relentless drive as an incomplete way of being-with-world. Boss (1963) described a loss of freedom to choose, and Binswanger (1958) posited a basal inauthenticity of the individual. Both investigators described the self as living in the past, and cut off from a sense of future. Binswanger (1958) and Boss (1963) described living the relentless drive to be ever thinner as a descent into the tomb-world of self-as-fat.

The Research Question

The present study addressed the foundational question: What is it like to live the relentless drive to be ever thinner? The purpose of the study was to uncover the meaning of the experience as it was lived by two women. The knowledge generated from this study may expand nurses' understanding of this phenomenon and enhance nursing's knowledge of how people live the value priorities of personal health (Parse, 1987). Nursing research serves to expand the knowledge base of the discipline. This study, evolving from Parse's human science nursing perspective, may strengthen nursing science in an area of human experience which remains unexplicated by nurse researchers.

RESEARCHER'S PERSPECTIVE

By rendering all personal beliefs and assumptions explicit, the investigator helps the reader to follow the decision trail of data interpretation (Guba & Lincoln, 1981; Spiegelberg, 1971). The investigator's prestudy beliefs about the relentless drive to be ever thinner were found to be congruent with Parse's (1981) theory of nursing. As the investigator has not personally lived the relentless drive to be ever thinner, experiential beliefs were not described in this study.

From the investigator's perspective, the relentless drive to be ever thinner is a unique way of choosing to be with one's world. As such, the study phenomenon is an experience of lived health, a coconstituted and nonlinear process of becoming (Parse, 1981). Viewed from this perspective, the relentless drive is neither a disease nor an adaptation to stressors, but rather a nexus of unfolding personal choices situated within one's world.

Living the relentless drive to be ever thinner is coexisting with one's personal world in a process of simultaneous and constant interchange. Together with important others, one creates a unique personal reality while imaging many different possibles. Through one's unique way of speaking and moving, one images self, giving meaning to all interrelationships (Parse, 1981). Thrown into situations (Heidegger, 1962), yet freely choosing, one cocreates a fluid meaning-matrix of opportunities and limitations (Binswanger, 1958). This takes place explicitly and tacitly all-at-once as one becomes aware of hidden aspects of self (Parse, 1981). One's images of self emerge through interrelationships with other people.

Powering is the pushing-resisting of human encounter in the face of imaged nonbeing (Parse, 1981). Living the relentless drive to be ever thinner, one struggles to assert self as one encounters the possibility of loss of self (Heidegger, 1962). The constant struggle evolves in complexity as one attempts to integrate images of the unfamiliar with the familiar. For the person living the relentless drive to be ever thinner, nonbeing may be imaged as fatness. Rejecting this image in the struggle toward imaged thinness, one interacts with important others in a pattern of pushing-resisting. Conflict ebbs and flows as one moves toward a personal dream which may not be shared or even understood by one's family and friends.

Cocreating rhythmical patterns of relating surface in the paradoxical unity of enabling-limiting (Parse, 1981). The person living the relentless drive to be ever thinner makes choices within a shifting matrix of possibles. The ebb and flow of feeling enabled and limited in situations defines all-at-once the ambiguity and clarity of the relentless drive to be ever thinner.

Having explicated all personal presuppositions concerning the phenomenon, the investigator synthesized these into the following statement: Living the relentless drive to be ever thinner is *powering the imaging of enabling-limiting*. This means that the person struggles to assert self against images of nonbeing, freely choosing opportunities and limitations which confirm the meaning of the now. These assumptions were methodologically held in abeyance by the investigator as the data collection process began.

METHODOLOGY

The study method selected was the Giorgi (1985) modification of phenomenological inquiry. The investigator elicited written and verbal retrospective descriptions of the study phenomenon from persons who had lived the experience. The subjects' descriptions were then rigorously analyzed and interpreted to uncover the meaning of the lived experience.

Phenomenological researchers study very small samples (Bogdan & Taylor, 1975; Parse et al., 1985). Parse et al. (1985) state that samples of two to five subjects have been found to yield data redundancy or saturation, an accepted indicator of sample size sufficiency. The sample for this study consisted of two women between the ages of 18 and 35. Both subjects were English speaking, and both stated that they had lived the experience of the relentless drive to be ever thinner. The purpose of the study was explained to each subject by the investigator. After all questions about the study were answered by the investigator, each subject signed a declaration of informed consent. Subjects' rights to anonymity, confidentiality, and the right to withdraw at any time were explained by the investigator. Each subject was given the following written statement: "Please describe your experience of the relentless drive to be ever thinner." The investigator refrained from elaborating upon the meaning of the question, inviting the subjects to simply respond as they saw fit. No guidelines were given concerning the length of the descriptions or length of time to be taken for writing.

The subjects were informed that they would later be asked questions about areas of the written description needing further clarification. They were further informed that their answers would be tape recorded and that the recordings would be electromagnetically erased after final transcription by the investigator. Subjects were invited to contact the investigator should discomfort arise from recollecting the experience.

After the original descriptions were carefully read and studied by the investigator and areas of ambiguity were identified in each text, the investigator returned to the subjects and obtained further narrative data. Both stages of data collection were combined as an elaborated written description for each subject. Each step of the data analysis-synthesis process is described for the reader within the following section.

PRESENTATION OF DATA AND FINDINGS

The raw data of the study are the elaborated descriptions of the relentless drive to be ever thinner. The study findings emerged from a rigorous process of intuiting, analyzing, and describing in which the raw data were raised to increasingly higher levels of discourse in the language of science.

The raw data were first examined for spontaneously occurring shifts in meaning. Discrete passages of text, called meaning units, were thus identified. Meaning units are context-laden constituents, rather like words in a paragraph (Giorgi, 1975). Meaning units do not actually exist in the raw text; they are constituted perceptually by the researcher who actively searches for emerging meaning (Giorgi, 1985). Two meaning units from this study are:

Meaning Unit: Subject 1

I was just existing. I wasn't a normal human being, someone who lived and laughed, experienced things and had emotions and feelings. I denied myself any kind of pleasure and alienated myself from anyone who used to mean something to me (family and friends). My motto was: "If you don't let anyone close to you, they can't hurt you."

Meaning Unit: Subject 2

I could not believe what terrible physical condition I was in—I was ashamed. I vowed I'd never stop exercising and allow myself to deteriorate to that extent ever again. As I began exercising regularly I began to feel a lot better. As my weight dropped, my spirits rose. I would worry if I missed a single day of exercise for fear I would become fat again. I also worried that I wasn't doing enough, and began to increase my exercise and swimming program. When I hit a plateau with my weight, I dropped my caloric intake even further. Friends and family began complimenting me on my will power and told me I was looking great.

Meaning units were read repeatedly in a spirit of contemplative dwelling (Parse et al., 1985) and then reformulated by the investigator in the language of the subject. This reformulation, called a theme, encapsulates the essence of the meaning unit. The themes corresponding to each of the foregoing meaning units follow.

Theme: Subject 1

Afraid of being hurt by others, the subject denied herself pleasure and removed herself from family and friends.

Theme: Subject 2

The subject felt pleased as others began to compliment her on her will power and appearance, and she increased attention to her regimen lest she again become fat.

The themes were then raised to a higher level of discourse and were reformulated by the investigator as focal meanings. An intuitive leap takes place at this level of analysis, as the investigator uncovers meaning that may have been tacit in the raw data (Spiegelberg, 1971). The focal meanings which emerged from the foregoing two themes are explained in the following sections.

Focal Meaning: Subject 1

The subject took flight inward, living withdrawing-engaging all-at-once.

Focal Meaning: Subject 2

Buoyant with the reaffirmation of others concerning her new self, the subject intensified the struggle in a leap beyond past images of who she was.

In this manner, eight focal meanings were identified in the themes which emerged from the elaborated description provided by Subject 1. Eleven focal meanings were identified in the data of Subject 2. All focal meanings are presented:

Focal Meanings: Subject 1

1. The subject lived the relentless drive to be ever thinner as an agony understood only superficially by others.
2. The subject recalls existing at a distance from her world.
3. The subject experienced time speeding as she imagined profiles of her cherished ways of being with the world, dwelling constantly with the not-yet.
4. The subject took flight inward, living withdrawing-engaging all-at-once.
5. Unfocused and despondent, the subject struggled to defend the integrity of her private world while glimpsing the possibles.
6. Awareness of self as existing in a private world surfaced through relating with others in a pattern of confrontation-rejection.
7. Living the unacceptable costs of her narrowing universe, the subject struggled to hide and disclose all-at-once her driven way of being-with-world.
8. Driving self relentlessly in an effort to incarnate intentions, the subject bitterly pursued the only images of self that she could cherish.

Focal Meanings: Subject 2

1. The subject lived the relentless drive to be ever thinner in mutual interrelationship with others as she became aware of how they saw her.
2. Buoyant with the reaffirmation of others concerning her new self, the subject intensified the struggle in a leap beyond past images of who she was.
3. The subject steadfastly confirmed her way of being with the world, living a pattern of skirmish and encounter with her important others.
4. Feeling increasingly distanced from others in an ever vanishing now, the subject sought shelter in veiling emerging aspects of self.
5. Bitter and resolute all-at-once, the subject lived her intentions veiled from others.
6. The subject struggled to protect the integrity of her way of being with world, hiding her own growing doubts.
7. The subject felt her move toward a cherished image of self was being blocked by others.
8. The subject found ways to dupe others regarding her inexorable struggle toward thinness, made ever more complex by those seeking to change who she was.
9. Never free of the struggle and ever uncertain of its meaning, the subject found solace in moving beyond the moment.
10. Feeling bound to a lingering predicament, the subject created a new reality by choosing to view the familiar differently.
11. Constantly aware of the was, the subject moved toward the will-be, choosing opportunities that expanded her horizons of meaning.

Each set of focal meanings was then synthesized as a situated structural description. The situated structural descriptions grasp the meaning of the relentless drive to be ever thinner as lived by each subject.

Situated Structural Description: Subject 1

The subject lived the relentless drive to be ever thinner as an agony understood only superficially by others. Existing at a distance from her world, the subject experienced time speeding. She cherished her ways of being with the world, dwelling constantly with the not-yet. She took flight inward by living withdrawing-engaging all-at-once. Unfocused and despondent, she struggled to defend the integrity of her private world while glimpsing the possibles. She became aware of existing in a private world as she related with others in a pattern of confrontation-rejection. Living the unacceptable costs of her narrowing universe, the subject struggled to hide and disclose all-at-once her driven way of being with the world. Driving self relentlessly in an effort to incarnate intentions, she bitterly pursued the only images of self that she could cherish.

Situated Structural Description: Subject 2

The subject lived the relentless drive to be ever thinner in mutual interrelationship with others as she became aware of how they saw her. Buoyant with the reaffirmation by others of her new self, she intensified the struggle in a leap beyond past images of who she was. Steadfastly confirming her way of being with the world, she lived a pattern of skirmish and encounter with close others. Feeling increasingly distanced from them in an ever vanishing now, she sought shelter by veiling emerging aspects of self. Bitter and resolute all-at-once, she lived her intentions hidden from others. She struggled to protect the integrity of her way of being-with-world, hiding her growing doubts. Feeling her move toward a cherished image of self blocked by others, she found ways to dupe them. Her inexorable struggle was made ever more complex by those seeking to change who she was. Never free of her struggle and ever uncertain of its meaning, she found solace in moving beyond the moment. Feeling bound to a lingering predicament, she created a new reality by choosing to view the familiar differently. Constantly aware of the was, she moved toward the will-be, choosing opportunities that expanded her horizons of meaning.

Both situated structural descriptions were then synthesized as one general structural description. The general structural description captures the most general meaning of the relentless drive to be ever thinner (Giorgi, 1985).

General Structural Description

The relentless drive to be ever thinner is a lived agony emerging in mutual interrelationship with others. One becomes aware of being seen in different ways by others who understand the experience only superficially. Buoyant with the reaffirmation of a new self, one intensifies the struggle to be ever thinner in a leap beyond one's images of the past. Steadfastly confirming this way of being-with-world, one lives a pattern of skirmish and encounter with close others. Living at a distance from the world in an ever-vanishing and speeding now, one dwells constantly with the not-yet, seeking shelter by veiling emerging intentions. Bitter and resolute all-at-once, one lives the unacceptable costs of a narrowing universe, concealing growing doubts from others. Driving self relentlessly in an effort to incarnate intentions, one bitterly pursues the only images of self that one cherishes. Unfocused and despondent, one is never free of the struggle to be thin and ever uncertain of its meaning. One struggles constantly to protect one's world from those seeking to change who one is, even as one glimpses other possibles. Finding ways to dupe other people, one encounters the world in a pattern of confrontation-rejection. Becoming aware of one's private world through relating with others, one takes flight inward, living withdrawing-engaging all-at-once. Struggling all-at-once to hide and disclose the drivenness of the struggle, one feels bound to a lingering predicament and seeks solace in moving beyond the moment. Ever aware of the was, one moves toward the will-be, choosing opportunities that expand horizons of meaning. The person living the relentless drive to be ever thinner creates a new reality by choosing to view the familiar differently.

DISCUSSION

Rigorous analysis of the general structural description yielded three central concepts: withdrawing-engaging, persistent struggle, and imaged self. Words and phrases such as seeking shelter, veiling doubts, protecting, and the many references to relating with others all disclose the central concept, withdrawing-engaging. The theme of persistent struggle surfaces repeatedly in phrases such as lived agony emerging through interrelationship, intensified struggle, skirmish and encounter, bitter yet resolute pursuit, relentless driving of self, constant struggle, and struggle-as-driven. Finally, the theme of imaged self emerges in language such as: being seen in different ways by others; new self; past images of self; way of being-with-world; dwelling with the not-yet; cherished images of self; awareness of self; and new reality. The three emergent concepts are disclosed in the very language of the general structural description. The concepts of persistent struggle, imaged self, and withdrawing-engaging are not homogeneous throughout the text but rather accrue new levels of meaning with each different expression.

The concept of persistent struggle, embodied in the general structural description, bears rich meaning transcending the limited insights of the investigator's theoretical presuppositions. For example, persistent struggle is lived in an ever vanishing, speeding now, as one dwells with the not-yet. This lived time perspective, not explicated with clarity in the researcher's perspective, is congruent with Parse's (1981) concept of powering. Powering, like the persistent struggle of the general structural description, is oriented toward the not-yet. Both concepts embody the critical attribute of conflictual interrelationship. In the concept of persistent struggle, conflict emerged as confrontation-rejection. In Parse's concept of powering, this attribute is called pushing-resisting. The paradox of powering is manifest in persistent struggle as the person, bitter and resolute all-at-once, chooses to live the unacceptable in struggle toward a cherished dream. Further paradox is manifest in the person's awareness of driving forward, yet being driven, all-at-once.

Imaged self emerges as a central concept from the text of the general structural description. It is conceptually congruent with Parse's (1981) concept of imaging. Both constructs show how individuals experience a shift in the way they see themselves while they interrelate with others. Both concepts reveal that individuals create images of self at both prearticulate and explicit levels of awareness. Imaged self emerges rich in meaning: the dream of self-as-thin is the cherished image that one chooses to live. In imaging self-as-thin, one concretizes the meaning of multidimensional experience in a simultaneous incarnation of explicit and tacit knowing (Parse, 1981).

The third central concept to emerge from the study findings is the paradoxical concept of withdrawing-engaging. The fabric of the general description shows how one lives with the world by choosing to create a new reality together with others. Living a pattern of skirmish and encounter, one distances from and engages with one's world, veiling intentions, and seeking shelter. Never apart from others, one takes flight inward through withdrawing-engaging. Withdrawing-engaging corresponds closely to Parse's (1981) concept connecting-separating. As togetherness with one's world evolves in ever greater diversity, one connects and separates with the other, all-at-once (Parse, 1981).

The propositional statement emerging from the general structural description was seen to be: The relentless drive to be ever thinner is a persistent struggle toward an imaged self lived through withdrawing-engaging. This propositional statement, grounded in the study data, was critically compared with Parse's (1981) theory of nursing. This analysis has disclosed conceptual congruence between the three central themes, on the one hand, and Parse's (1981) concepts of powering, connecting-separating, and imaging, on the other. Accordingly, at the highest level of abstraction, the data of this study support the following theoretical proposition: The relentless drive to be ever thinner is lived as powering the imaging of connecting-separating. The study findings are therefore supportive of Parse's (1981) theory of nursing.

CONCLUSIONS

Both Binswanger (1958) and Boss (1963) described the relentless drive to be ever thinner as a tomb-world of fatness and black despair. While profiles of pain, isolation and discomfort are present in the general structural description of the experience in this study, these phrases are consistently embodied in the textual context of social interconnectedness and choosing. The despair and helplessness of earlier phenomenological findings were not supported by the present study. Instead, a chosen and paradoxical unity of solitude and social interrelationship surface in the study findings. Despair is not revealed in the general structural description. There is, however, a nexus of cherished images pursued at any cost. The fear of fat surfaces only secondarily as the images of one's past. The primary existential focus of the experience is the imaged not-yet of self as ever thinner. The general stance of the person living this experience is accordingly not one of fear or dread, but one of longing. It may be useful to incorporate this focus in healing exploration with individuals living the relentless drive to be ever thinner.

Both Binswanger (1958) and Boss (1963) described the relentless drive to be ever thinner as lived primarily in the past, cut off from any personal sense of future. The findings of the present study support inner time awareness as a special way of being-with-world for the person living this experience. But the pattern of this lived time is different from that described by Binswanger (1958) and Boss (1963). One lives withdrawn from and engaged with the world in a vanishing, speeding now, while dwelling constantly with the not-yet. One's primary orientation toward the not-yet is a basal structure of powering (Parse, 1981). While Binswanger (1958) and Boss (1963) described the experience as separation from a personal future, the findings of the present study reveal a dwelling with possibles as seen from the shifting strata of the vanishing now, while ever aware of the imaged was. An awareness of how one experiences time may help nurses to understand the lived meaning of the relentless drive to be ever thinner.

Binswanger (1958) suggested that people living the relentless drive to be ever thinner are ontologically cut off from the world of others. The present study supports the richly paradoxical nature of this flight inward. One struggles within a private world sustained only through constant interrelationship with others. This study finding may have significant implications for bridge building with people living the relentless drive to be ever thinner. Explicitly, clients may choose to talk about the intense isolation they feel. At a more tacit level, they may be living a primordial and radical interconnectedness with others.

Binswanger (1958) described the relentless drive to be ever thinner as a unique way of being-in-the-world, while Boss (1963) emphatically affirmed the universal profiles of the experience. The findings of the present study suggest that the relentless drive to be ever thinner is lived as universal and particular all-at-once. While some phrases of the general structural description seem to apply only to people living the relentless drive to be ever thinner, other phrases of the scientific description seem to have indiscriminate application to the human condition in general. An important conclusion of this finding is that nurses may foster a sense of interconnectedness in their clients by being present to both particular and universal aspects of the relentless drive to be ever thinner.

The findings of this study are supportive of Parse's (1981) theory of nursing and corroborate its usefulness as a framework for the study of human experiences. The general structural description of the relentless drive to be ever thinner is congruent with Parse's theory, and new approaches for nursing research and practice with these individuals may now be derived from the theory itself.

IMPLICATIONS AND RECOMMENDATIONS

Research . . . implications are grounded in the congruence of the study findings with Parse's (1981) theory of nursing. . . .

Implications for research from this study include using a different population living the relentless drive to be ever thinner. Research is also needed concerning other lived experiences associated with eating and awareness of self. Future research may also focus upon sustained exercising as a way of caring about self.

The Giorgi modification of the phenomenological method used in this study was developed by the non-nursing human sciences. It is important that bridging methodologies link these research approaches to the special perspectives of nursing science. A new method of scientific inquiry developed within nursing is the man-living-health research methodology (Parse, 1987). New studies of health experiences such as the relentless drive to be ever thinner may be usefully conducted using this new method specific to nursing science.

Finally, qualitative investigation of other human experiences is needed to provide further empirical support for Parse's (1981) theory. As human experiences are explored for possible congruence with man-living-health, the theory will be tested and expanded, thus enhancing nursing knowledge. The growth of nursing theory is necessary if nurses are to be present to people choosing ways of being-with-world in the last decade of the twentieth century and beyond.

REFERENCES

Binswanger, L. (1958). The case of Ellen West: An anthropological-clinical study. In R. May, E. Angel, & H. Ellenberger (Eds.), *Existence: A new dimension in psychiatry and psychology*. New York: Basic Books.

Bogdan, R., & Taylor, S. (1975). *Introduction to qualitative research methods: A phenomenological approach to the social sciences*. New York: Wiley.

Boss, M. (1963). *Psychoanalysis and daseinsanalysis*. New York: Basic Books.

Garner, D., Garfinkel, P., & Olmstead, M. P. (1983). An overview of the sociocultural factors in the development of anorexia nervosa. In P. Darby, P. Garfinkel, D. Garner, & D. Coscina (Eds.), *Anorexia nervosa: Recent developments in research* (pp. 65–82). New York: Liss.

Giorgi, A. (1975). An application of phenomenological method in psychology. In A. Giorgi, C. Fischer, & E. Murray (Eds.), *Duquesne studies in phenomenological psychology* Vol. II. Pittsburgh: Duquesne University Press.

Giorgi, A. (1985). *Phenomenology and psychological research*, Pittsburgh: Duquesne University Press.

Guba, E. G., & Lincoln, Y. S. (1981). *Effective evaluation: Improving the usefulness of evaluation results through responsive and naturalistic approaches*. San Francisco: Jossey-Bass.

Heidegger, M. (1962). *Being and time*. New York: Harper & Row.

Lucas, A. (1982). Bulimia and vomiting syndrome. *New York State Journal of Medicine 6*, 398–399.

Parse, R. R. (1981). *Man-living-health: A theory of nursing*. New York: Wiley.

Parse, R. R. (1987). *Nursing science: Major paradigms, theories and critiques*. Philadelphia: Saunders.

Parse, R. R., Coyne, A. B., & Smith, M. (1985). *Nursing research: Qualitative methods*. Bowie, MD: Brady.

Sandelowski, M. (1986). The problem of rigor in qualitative research. *Advances in Nursing Science*, 8, 27–37.

Spiegelberg, H. (1971). *The phenomenological movement: A historical introduction* Vol. II (2nd ed.). The Hague: Martinus Nijhoff.

Szekely, E. (1987). Women's anxious pursuit of attractive appearance. *Phenomenology and Pedagogy* 5, 108–118.

CHAPTER 12

THE LIVED EXPERIENCE OF SELF-TRANSCENDENCE IN WOMEN WITH ADVANCED BREAST CANCER[1]

Doris D. Coward, RN; PhD

The purpose of this exploratory study was to describe the lived-experience of self-transcendence in women with Stage IV breast cancer. A phenomenological approach was chosen for the research design and analysis. Five women who had lived with metastatic disease from 2 to 7 years described experiences from which they derived an increased sense of self-worth, purpose in life, and interconnectedness with others. The self-transcendent experiences involved an effort on the part of the participants to reach out beyond themselves to help other women, to permit others to help them, or to "just accept" unchangeable situations. The results indicated that participants found meaning in their lives in the face of life-threatening illness. Although nurses can not be expected to create self-transcendent experiences for their patients, they may be able to establish and maintain conditions in which the phenomenon occurs.

Self-transcendence is the capacity to reach out beyond oneself, to extend oneself beyond personal concerns and to take on broader life perspectives, activities, and purposes. Reaching out beyond oneself, without devaluing the self, leads to finding meaning in life. Self-transcendence, as defined above, is discussed in the disciplines of humanistic and transpersonal psychology

---

(Frankl, 1963, 1966, 1969; Maslow, 1968, 1971; May, 1981; Yalom, 1982), theology (Buber, 1961; Tillich, 1952), and nursing (Parse, 1981; Reed, 1987, 1989a, 1989b).

Frankl's view of self-transcendence was based on his analyses of human experiences of meaning in life. His conclusions were that the capacity for self-transcendence was a basic characteristic of being human and that human existence was not meaningful unless lived in terms of self-transcendence (Frankl, 1966, 1969). His description of the life of prisoners in Nazi concentration camps (Frankl, 1963) was an example of how humans will find meaning and purpose even within the most inexplicable and degrading of circumstances.

Frankl (1969) believes that a person finds meaning in life through self-transcendence in three ways. The first is giving to the world through creativity, such as in family, occupation, and creative works. The second is taking from the world by being receptive to others and to one's environment. The third is finding meaning in the attitude one takes to one's predicament when faced with an unchangeable situation. Life can never cease to have meaning because, even when one is deprived of both the creative and experiential ways to find meaning, there remains the opportunity to determine the manner in which one faces adversity.

Reed has studied the relationship of self-transcendence to mental health in the elderly (Reed, 1986, 1989a, 1989b). Her view of self-transcendence comes from a dialectical life span developmental framework that proposes that adults, through their life experiences, have had opportunity to accrue insight and energy for furthering personal development (Hultsch & Deutsch, 1981; Riegel, 1976). Adults may bring together transcendent perspectives that they have developed throughout their life to help them to continue to find meaning and sense of well-being even in the face of adversity.

The presence of self-transcendent views and behaviors in the elderly were found to be associated with emotional well-being (Reed, 1986, 1989a, 1989b). Self-transcendence also may be associated with emotional well-being in persons with life-threatening diseases. Steeves and Kahn (1987) described transcendent experiences in hospice patients and their loved ones. The experiences were closely tied to suffering and were a source of comfort and meaning. Hospice nurses observed that persons who recounted these experiences appeared to manage their suffering better than persons who did not appear to have them.

Breast cancer in women is often a slowly evolving disease. Even after metastases occur, up to 30% survive for more than 2 years and an additional 5 to 10% live for 5 years or longer (Keys, Bakemeier, & Savlov, 1983; Stoll, 1982). Awareness of how women continue to find purpose, meaning, and a sense of well-being during this time is of interest to health care providers who work with this population. However, no one has studied self-transcendence in women with breast cancer.

PURPOSE AND RESEARCH DESIGN

The purpose of this study was to describe the essential features of the lived experience of self-transcendence in women with advanced breast cancer. A phenomenological approach was chosen for the research design and analysis. This approach was appropriate for the investigation because the researcher wished to explore self-transcendence as it was lived by the individuals experiencing it. The research question was: What are the essential features of self-transcendence in women with advanced breast cancer?

Examining Researcher Presuppositions

The research was planned and conducted using the phenomenological research method as described by Colaizzi (1978). The first step was for the researcher to examine her presuppositions about the topic to be investigated. In her experience with seriously ill patients, she had been puzzled by the considerable variation in the manner people faced illness. Why did some patients, although seriously ill, appear to perceive meaning in their lives, maintain control over certain aspects of their care, and continue to initiate efforts to enhance self-esteem, while other patients, also seriously ill, perceived their situations as devoid of personal meaning, believed they lacked control over any aspect of their lives, and compared themselves only with those more fortunate than themselves?

In recent observations as facilitator of a breast cancer support group, the researcher noticed that some group members appeared to have found meaning in their lives *because* of their illness experience. They had confronted their illness, and had moved beyond their own concerns to provide help to other women with breast cancer. This transcending of self seemed to have resulted from willingness and effort to manage both the physical and emotional effects of their disease.

Paterson and Zderad (1976) proposed in their humanistic nursing theory that the concern of nursing is not merely with a person's well-being, but also with more-being, with becoming as much as is possible within a particular life situation. The researcher wondered if self-transcendence might be an indicator of more-being in women in crisis situations such as life-threatening illness. Self-transcending views and behaviors would indicate that a woman was actualizing her potential for personal development. Knowledge of those views and behaviors might assist the researcher, and other nurses, to plan interventions to promote more-being in women with advanced breast cancer.

Formulating the Question for Subjects

The above explication of the researcher's perspective is the necessary first step in phenomenological research. The second step is to formulate the question for the subjects. The success of the question depends on the extent to which it taps the subjects' experiences of the phenomenon rather than their theoretical knowledge of it. The question posed to participants in this study was, "Describe a situation in which you experienced self-transcendence. Describe the situation as you remember it, including your thoughts, feelings, and perceptions at the time. Continue to describe the experience until you feel it is fully described." Self-transcendence was defined for potential participants as an experience of a sense of well-being, purpose in life, and interconnectedness with others.

Colaizzi (1978) states that, given a successful question, anyone who has experience with the concept of interest and who is articulate would qualify as a subject. For this study, subject criteria also included women with Stage IV (metastatic) breast cancer. It was important to gain knowledge of the features of the self-transcendence specific to these women in order to plan interventions specific to their needs.

Descriptions of self-transcending experiences were obtained from five women with Stage IV breast cancer. Four of the descriptions were written by the participants and one was obtained on an audiotape. Three of the participants were members of a breast cancer support group. The fourth participant was a terminally ill woman who was provided contact and support by a group member. (This description was audiotaped by the investigator.) The fifth participant was a health care professional. The ages of the women ranged from 48 to 72 years, with a mean age of 62.6 years. One woman was single and living alone, two were widowed and living alone, and two were married and living with spouses. The length of time since diagnosis of Stage IV disease was 2 years ($n = 2$), 3 years ($n = 2$), and 7 years. Two participants described their cancer prognosis as good, two as limited, and one as poor. One woman described herself functionally as fully active, three reported being active but restricted in physically strenuous activity, and one was capable of only limited self-care.

Phenomenological Analysis of the Data

There are several analysis techniques described in the phenomenological research literature (Colaizzi, 1978; Giorgi, 1975; van Kaam, 1969). The technique used in this study was the one described by Colaizzi. Colaizzi's technique was previously used by Haase (1987) to identify components of courage in chronically ill adolescents and Reimen (1986) to describe the essential structure of a caring situation. In Colaizzi's technique the analysis consists of seven steps.

1. *Reading of all of the subjects' descriptions.*

The transcription of the interview and the written descriptions (called protocols) were each read several times in order to get a sense of their total content. An example of one protocol is found in Table 12–1.

2. *Extracting significant statements.*

Phrases or sentences directly pertaining to self-transcendence were extracted from the protocols and written on separate index cards. Colaizzi ad-

TABLE 12–1 REPRESENTATIVE ORIGINAL PROTOCOL

Experiencing four major losses in 2 years, part of my body, my husband, finances, and my daughter moving to Arizona, I sought counseling. Through this, a fairly long process, I learned I had to "get out of myself." I took my classes and college courses and became very aware of new awakenings within myself. I truly learned that by helping others I helped myself.

One course was exceptional. I was trained to become a volunteer on a crisis line. I experienced self-transcendence by the knowledge I had helped someone in crisis. One experience I will relate is: After working with a caller for over one and one-half hours I felt such a sense of being needed again. It was a homosexual suicide call. I struggled with the caller through much grief-sorrow in losing his lover. He was calling from a phone booth and my main objective at first was to not have him hang up but to "hang on." I put my whole self into this call. All my energies, compassion, and understanding were at a very high level. When I finally got him to make a "contact" with me, to wait until the next day to make a decision, I was ecstatic. I felt such an accomplishment. I felt I was needed and my feeling of self-worth was at its highest pitch—the highest I could remember for a long time. My body felt light. My shoulders felt free of burden. I actually walked lighter and more easily—almost floating—but not really. I stepped out into the night, the sky was clear, stars bright and twinkling. To inhale felt good. To breathe felt like a heavenly experience. I felt no bodily hurt or ache. My whole being was in a glorious state. My self was in touch with my total feelings which was of such pleasure I didn't want it to end. In the 15-minute drive home, I slid back the roof on my car, turned on the heat, looked at the sky, stars in all their wonderment, and felt physically and mentally in touch with God, or a supreme being. This was a beautiful experience—one I shall never forget. A feeling of lightness and contentment, the first I had had since I had had my mastectomy and lost my husband.

I gave of my whole self to that unknown young man on the phone line that evening. However, I feel I received much more. A wonderful memory as I recall it now that still gives me some of those same feelings which I have described. I feel it was a totally out of my body experience which I now know to be very healing—over and over again.

vocates eliminating statements that are the same or similar across several protocols. Sixty-five statements from the five protocols were reduced to the 51 significant statements presented in Table 12–2. Colaizzi also suggests that statements need not be repeated verbatim, but may be put into a more general form. For example, the statement, "This thought—a memory of astonishing strength—the feeling of being uplifted and sustained has stayed with me" was rewritten as "Continues to remember the feeling of being uplifted and sustained that she had during the self-transcending experience."

TABLE 12–2   SIGNIFICANT STATEMENTS

1. Gave her a boost when she could help the kids who worked with her.
2. Experienced self-transcendence (ST) when told how much a phone call had meant to another woman who had just had a mastectomy.
3. Feels glad when able to answer questions, provide reassurance, and give helpful suggestions.
4. Believes she is guided by the Lord to serve him in a special way.
5. Is on her way toward accomplishing a new life long focus.
6. Now tries to live each day to its fullest.
7. Now is able to take comfort from little things.
8. Acceptance of dying gives each day of life a value to be savored and enjoyed.
9. No longer afraid of death. Death now viewed as "the reward, the rest, the peaceful sleep."
10. Death not a worry because she has enjoyed a good life.
11. Reaching out to help others gives a little more purpose to life.
12. Feeling of purpose is to do duties joyfully.
13. Has strong positive feelings of being healed.
14. Learned she needed to "get out of herself" during counseling after major personal losses.
15. Through coursework, became aware of new awakenings in herself.
16. Putting all of self into helping another.
17. Experienced ST through the knowledge she had helped someone in crisis.
18. Feeling in touch with her total feelings was so pleasurable that she did not wish it to end.
19. Physical experience of feeling light, free of burden, almost floating.
20. Felt physically and mentally in touch with God or a supreme being.
21. Experienced increased self-worth from being needed.
22. Successful experience in Reach-to-Recovery led to increased self-confidence.
23. Validation of self-worth when friend continues to seek assistance.
24. Touching is one of her ways of expressing love.
25. Gets outside of self by loving and being loved.
26. She needs help now and feels wonderful when someone helps her.
27. ST was experienced at several points in her life, and was triggered by different things.

TABLE 12–2   Significant Statements (Continued)

28. Felt physically lifted above her pain.
29. Acceptance that things do not always work out as expected.
30. Rather than dwelling in anger, she used negative experiences with health care providers in a positive way.
31. She kept asking, "Why me?"
32. Her own experiences with cancer have broadened her understanding.
33. ST followed periods of great pain.
34. Continues to remember the feeling of being uplifted and sustained she had during the ST experience.
35. Did not contact old friends because she "did not wish to worry them." Now realizes that was unfair because they want to help her.
36. Learned that by helping others she helped herself.
37. ST experience was healing.
38. Although she had given much of herself, she believed she got back much more than she gave.
39. Feels compassion for others who suffer and wants to share her insight with them.
40. Was afraid when she first reached out to help another.
41. Now assists other women with breast cancer to have more self-esteem and be more assertive with health care providers.
42. Lacks stamina for physical volunteer work, but has found a new purpose and sense of meaning in counseling others.
43. Was drowning in misery when she recalled a helpful line of poetry.
44. The ST experience continues to be remembered and reexperienced through its memory.
45. ST experiences, during moments of pain, reward her by a return to tranquility.
46. Gives others pleasure by telling funny stories.
47. Looking at the sky and stars was a beautiful experience.
48. Expectation that things will work out for the best leads to feeling good.
49. She doesn't ask why things happen to her and doesn't think there is a reason. She just accepts it.
50. Believes she had a good life. But life moves on and she has to move with it. She just accepts.
51. Has come to terms with a situation (death) which most people avoid even contemplating.

3. *Creating formulated meanings*.

The next step was to spell out the meaning of each significant statement. Here, the investigator determined the underlying meaning of each statement. Colaizzi cautions that this step is a "precarious leap" and requires "creative insight" (Colaizzi, 1978, p. 59). The formulated meanings were written on the back of each index card containing the significant statements. Both the significant statements and their formulated meanings were then validated with a colleague who had read the protocols and who was experienced in phenomenological analysis. The formulated meanings (followed by numerical references to the significant statements from which they originated) are listed with the themes in Table 12–3. This is a validation step suggested by Hycner (1985).

4. *Aggregating formulated meanings into clusters of themes*.

The next step in analysis was to form clusters of themes that were common to all the protocols. The formulated meanings were sorted into groups that represented specific themes (Table 12–3). For example, one theme cluster was identified as "Self-transcendence may be reexperienced through reminiscence." Formulated meanings sorted into that category referred to feeling good when reliving self-transcending experiences. The aggregated clusters of themes were validated with a colleague. The theme clusters then were referred back to the original protocols to validate them. Anything in an original protocol not accounted for in a theme was reexamined. Anything proposed in a theme, but not implied in a protocol was also reevaluated.

Colaizzi (1978) points out that discrepancies may be noted among the clusters and that the researcher may feel uncomfortable with such contradictions. However, the researcher should trust the data and refuse the temptation to ignore data or themes that seem not to fit. The researcher must have a tolerance for ambiguity and "proceed with the solid conviction that what is logically inexplicable may be existentially real and valid" (Colaizzi, 1978, p. 61). Contradictory themes emerging from the present data were: acceptance of one's situation leads to self-transcendence, and self-transcendence leads to acceptance. These themes seemed at first to be mutually exclusive, but were validated by referring back to the protocols.

5. *Writing an exhaustive description*.

The next step was to integrate the significant statements, the formulated meanings, and the clusters of themes into a narrative exhaustive description. The exhaustive description of self-transcendence is found in Table 12–4.

6. *Identifying the fundamental structure of the concept*.

The sixth step was to describe, from the exhaustive description of the phenomenon, as unequivocal a statement of its fundamental structure as possible. The fundamental structure of self-transcendence in Table 12–5 is an integration and synthesis of its components as identified in the exhaustive description. The exhaustive description and the fundamental structure were then validated with the expert in phenomenological analysis.

TABLE 12–3   THEME CLUSTERS AGGREGATED FROM THE FORMULATED MEANINGS

Self-transcendence (ST) is associated with a crisis such as great loss or physical or emotional pain.

1. Anger associated with breast cancer diagnosis. (30, 31)
2. Many personal losses in addition to breast cancer. (14)
3. Negative experiences with health care providers. (30)
4. Physical pain. (28, 33, 43, 45)
5. Threat of death. (8–10, 51)
6. A period of great depression. (14, 25)

ST is creating new means to find purpose and meaning in life when the old ways are no longer appropriate.

1. Attended classes to learn how to do crisis counseling. (15)
2. Focused on a new purpose. (5, 41, 42)
3. Reaching out to help others brought more purpose to life. (11, 39)
4. Purpose now is to do duties joyfully. (12)

ST is a result of much effort.

1. Risked failure when first reached out to help another. (40)
2. Put all of self into trying to help another. (16)
3. Came to terms with a situation that most people avoid even thinking about, death. (51)

ST is experienced through helping others.

1. Learned that by helping others she helped herself. (36)
2. Although she had given of her whole self, she felt that she received much more in return. (38)
3. Feels compassion for others with breast cancer and wants to share her insights with them. (32, 39)
4. Found a new part of self through learning how to counsel others in crisis. (14–17)
5. Found pleasure by giving others pleasure by telling them funny stories. (46)
6. Felt good when helping younger people at her work. (1)
7. Feeling pleased when learning how much she was appreciated when reaching out to assist a new mastectomy patient. (2, 3, 22)
8. Assists other women with breast cancer to have increased self-esteem and to be assertive. (41)

ST is experienced when being open to receiving help from others.

1. Accepting help from friends indicated a change in perspective and personal growth on the part of the subject. (35)
2. Appreciating assistance provided by church and visiting nurses when unable to meet own self-care needs. (26)

TABLE 12–3   THEME CLUSTERS AGGREGATED FROM THE FORMULATED
MEANINGS (CONTINUED)

ST *eases pain and fear related to the prospect of dying.*

1. No longer afraid of death. (9, 51)

2. Had a good life and has no regrets. (10, 50)

ST *includes an emotional awareness of a sense of well-being that includes a physical sense of lightness.*

1. Seemed physically lifted above pain. (28, 34)

2. Mental uplifting and physical feeling of lightness, freedom from burden and pain. (19)

3. So pleasurable that one doesn't want it to end. (18)

4. May be experienced more than once and in different ways. (27)

ST *is associated with an increased sense of self-worth.*

1. Being needed leads to increased sense of feeling valued. (21)

2. Previous success led to feeling confident in reaching out again to help another. (15, 22)

3. Effort is validated when friend continues to seek her out. (23)

ST *is associated with connectedness to others and God.*

1. Feeling mentally and physically in touch with God or a supreme being. (20)

2. Expressing love through touching another. (24)

3. Getting outside of self by loving and being loved. (25)

4. Feeling emotionally supported through long-term friendships. (35)

5. Feeling guided by God to serve him in a special manner. (4)

ST *is associated with increased appreciation of things dear and with the environment.*

1. Now tries to live each day to its fullest. (6)

2. Now is able to find comfort in little things. (7)

3. Looking out at the sky and stars was a beautiful experience. (47)

4. Each day is valued as something to be savored and enjoyed. (8)

ST *leads to acceptance of personal circumstances.*

1. Acceptance of dying. (8–10)

2. Acceptance that things are not always as expected, but that they will work out for the best. (29, 48)

3. Acceptance of circumstances (life-threatening illness) without seeking reasons. (49)

4. Coming to terms with the situation. (51)

TABLE 12–3 THEME CLUSTERS AGGREGATED FROM THE FORMULATED MEANINGS (CONTINUED)

ST *may be reexperienced through reminiscence.*

1. Continues to be remembered and reexperienced through its memory. (44)
2. Continues to remember the feeling of being uplifted and sustained. (34)
3. Feels good when remembering past happy times and occasions when she was able to help younger people. (1, 50)

ST *is a healing experience.*

1. ST experience was very healing—over and over again. (37)
2. Has strong positive feelings of being healed. (13)

TABLE 12–4 THE EXHAUSTIVE DESCRIPTION OF SELF-TRANSCENDENCE

1. Self-transcendence is associated with an incident that generates intense negative feelings and emotions. These are experiences of physical and emotional pain, fear of death, and anger. Despair over personal losses—independence, a body part, family and friends, and the closeness of death encourage one to look for ways to "get out of oneself" and find new meaning in and purpose for living.
2. Self-transcendence is associated with great effort on the part of the one who experiences it. There are new skills to be learned: the risks of failure in first using them, the need to put all of oneself into the task, and the need to confront one's fears.
3. The experiences of self-transcendence are healing. There is an emotional sense of well-being accompanied by a sense of physical lightness and relief of burden. The experience is pleasurable and serves to lessen pain, fear, and regrets associated with dying.
4. Self-transcendence is experienced both through helping another and in accepting help from others when unable to do for self. There is a sense of receiving in return more than is given to another, even when helping another has required much effort. Helping is directed toward other women who have breast cancer and consists of sharing of experiences, answering questions, and providing reassurance. Allowing another to help means acceptance of one's dependence and understanding that letting another help allows the other to experience the pleasure of giving.

TABLE 12–5   The Fundamental Structure of Self-Transcendence

Self-transcendence, in women with Stage IV breast cancer, is an increased understanding of self and a moving beyond self that is associated with rising above crisis situations such as physical and emotional pain due to ill health, loss, and the threat of loss. Self-transcendence is accompanied by a sense of feeling uplifted, a physical lightness and relief of burden, a closeness to others, environment, and to God, a commitment to a purpose, and acceptance of inescapable circumstances. It is obtained through acceptance of inescapable circumstances, as well as through helping others, by permitting others to help, and through reminiscence of past self-transcendent experiences. The experience of self-transcendence leads to a sense of being healed, to increased valuing of self, to easing the fear and pain of loss, and to savoring of the small moments in life.

---

7. *Returning to subjects for validation.*

A final validating step was to return to the participants with the results of the analysis. They were asked if the fundamental structure of the phenomenon contained the essence of their original experiences. The three women who responded agreed that the fundamental structure of self-transcendence included the aspects they themselves had experienced.

DISCUSSION OF THE FINDINGS OF THE STUDY

Self-transcendence is the capacity of a person to move beyond self concerns without devaluing the self. The capacity to better understand themselves as well as the acquiring of broader perspectives, activities, and purposes appeared to assist the women in this study to find meaning when faced with unchangeable adverse life circumstances.

The women identified several instances in which they had searched for new purposes in their lives after life events that caused them emotional and physical pain, loss, and the threat of loss. Self-transcendence occurred after much effort on the part of the women. The effort involved learning new ways to help others, helping others, learning to be receptive to help from others, and changing their attitudes toward their illness.

The greatest effort on the part of the women took place on the level of acceptance when adverse situations could not be changed. As one woman said during the validation step of the analysis, "The hardest thing to learn is that when you can't do, then just be."

Although willingness and personal effort was required, the reward was well worth the effort in terms of increased valuing of self and a sense of being healed. There were physical feelings which were pleasurable—lightness, almost floating, uplifted, freedom from burden, lifted above pain, and return to tranquility. There was a strong and pleasant sense of connectedness to other women who suffered, to old friends, to the beauty in nature, and to God. There was a new sense of purpose in doing duties joyfully and in providing assistance to other women with breast cancer.

The reminiscence of previous transcendent experience was pleasurable and assisted the women to accept their present circumstances. Remembering how good she felt in the past when she helped others gave one woman the insight she needed to gracefully allow others to help her now. For another, death no longer was viewed with fear, but as a reward for having lived a good life. Reliving previous experiences also renewed feelings of self-worth and the sense of being healed.

CONCLUSIONS

The women in this study experienced meaning through self-transcendence in each of the ways discussed by Frankl (1969). They found purpose in helping other women with breast cancer and were receptive to help from others and to experiencing pleasure from their environment. The two women who were the most ill had come to terms with the closeness of death and had accepted its inevitability. Acceptance of inescapable situations also had promoted self-transcendence by causing the participants to look for new ways to find meaning.

The dialectical life span developmental model appeared to explain the phenomenon in the study participants (Riegel, 1976). The participants used an adverse life situation as an opportunity for personal development. They used previous experience, as well as newly learned skills, to reach beyond themselves for new challenges that led to personal growth.

Self-transcendence also appeared to be an indicator of more-being as described by Paterson and Zderad (1976). More-being, the potential for becoming as much more as is humanly possible within a particular life situation, is fostered through relationships with others. Making choices to reach out beyond themselves and exercising effort to implement those choices led to increased personal growth, and a sense of self-worth, as well as a redefinition of purposes in the lives of the study participants.

IMPLICATIONS OF THE STUDY

If the capacity for self-transcendence is inherent in humans, and if self-transcendence is necessary for fulfillment of meaning in life, what are the implications of this concept for nurses? First, nurses, as humans themselves, need awareness of self-transcendence as means of fulfilling their own meaning in life. Nurses need to recognize the ways they personally find meaning and assess the appropriateness of those ways in specific situations. (Is it not difficult for nurses, when they "can't do, to just let be?")

Second, nurses may wish to assess patients for components of self-transcendence with the aim of planning appropriate interventions to increase patients' ability to make choices that may lead to an increased sense of self-worth and meaning in life. In so doing, nurses accept the challenge of Paterson and Zderad to concern themselves not just with their patients' physical well-being, but with their more-being. Paterson and Zderad propose that more-being may be promoted through authentic contact between nurses and their patients. Authentic contact provides the means for fostering the awareness that assists a nurse to enhance the potential of a patient to make choices within the limits of her individual situation.

ISSUES RELATED TO THE STUDY FINDINGS

As is common in phenomenological research, there were few participants in this study and their selection was not random. The results are not meant to be generalized; the intent is to illuminate the lived experience of self-transcendence in a specific group of women with Stage IV breast cancer. In investigating a phenomenon in even a few individuals, one may be able to understand the experience in human beings in general.

A second issue is the accuracy of the descriptions of the phenomenon and the validity of the researcher's interpretation. Hycner (1985) suggests that in phenomenological research what is wanted is the knowledge of how participants experience a situation. Unless there is reason to believe that a participant is defensive about an experience, the description provided the researcher should be considered reliable. There was no evidence that participants in this study were defensive or guarded in their descriptions of their experiences. However, it is possible that the experiences described were presented in a socially desirable manner to the researcher.

The question of validity of the findings ultimately will be decided by the amount of consensual validation obtained for the results. The primary validity check was with the participants themselves. They validated that the derived fundamental structure of self-transcendence did capture the essence of their descriptions. A second check was the sharing of the descriptions and the steps of the analysis with an experienced colleague. A third check was to compare the results with the literature on self-transcendence. The final validity check is to submit the results and as much of the data as is possible to the scientific and lay community.

The results of this study on self-transcendence in women with advanced breast cancer are presented so that the findings may be evaluated and discussed from a larger number of perspectives. Additional questions may be asked related to the concept of self-transcendence. Is self-transcendence a phenomenon nurses observe in other seriously ill patients? Can nurses plan interventions to facilitate the capacity for self-transcendence? If so, what are those interventions? Does the experience of self-transcendence lead to an increased sense of emotional well-being in all seriously ill patients?

REFERENCES

Buber, M. (1961). The way of man according to the teachings of Hasidism. In W. Kaufmann (Ed.), *Religion From Tolstoy to Camus* (pp. 425–441). New York: Harper Torchbooks.

Colaizzi, P. (1978). Psychological research as the phenomenologist views it. In R. Valle & M. King (Eds.), *Existential-phenomenological alternatives for psychology* (pp. 48–71). New York: Oxford University Press.

Frankl, V. (1963). *Man's search for meaning: An introduction to logotherapy*. New York: Pocket Books.

Frankl, V. (1966). Self-transcendence as a human phenomenon. *Journal of Humanistic Psychology, 6*, 97–106.

Frankl, V. (1969). *The will to meaning*. New York: New American Library.

Giorgi, A. (1975). An application of phenomenological method in psychology. In A. Giorgi, C. Fischer, & E. Murry (Eds.), *Duquesne studies in phenomenological psychology Vol. 2* (pp. 6–103). Pittsburgh: Duquesne University Press.

Haase, J. (1987). Components of courage in chronically ill adolescents: A phenomenological study. *Advances in Nursing Science, 9*, 64–80.

Hultsch, D., & Deutsch, F. (1981). *Adult development and aging: A lifespan perspective*. New York: McGraw Hill.

Hycner, R. (1985). Some guidelines for the phenomenological analysis of interview data. *Human Studies, 8*, 279–303.

Keys, H., Bakemeier, R., & Savlov, E. (1983). Breast cancer. In P. Rubin (Ed.), *Clinical oncology: A multidisciplinary approach* (6th ed.). American Cancer Society.

Maslow, A. (1968). *Toward a psychology of being*. New York: Van Nostrand Reinhold.

Maslow, A. (1971). *Farther reaches of human nature*. New York: Viking.

May, R. (1981). *Freedom and destiny*. New York: Dell.

Parse, R. (1981). *Man-living-health: A theory for nursing*. New York: Wiley.

Paterson, J., & Zderad, L. (1976). *Humanistic nursing*. New York: Wiley.

Reed, P. (1986). Developmental resources and depression in the elderly. *Nursing Research, 36*, 368–374.

Reed, P. (1987). Spirituality and well-being in terminally ill hospitalized adults. *Research in Nursing and Health, 10*, 335–344.

Reed, P. (1989a). Mental health of older adults. *Western Journal of Nursing Research, 11*, 143–163.

Reed, P. (1989b May). *Relationship of patterns of self-transcendence to depression in the oldest old.* Paper presented at the 22nd Communicating Nursing Research Conference, San Diego, CA.

Riegel, K. (1976). The dialectics of human development. *American Psychologist, 31,* 689–700.

Reimen, D. (1986). The essential structure of a caring interaction: Doing phenomenology. In P. Munhall & C. Oiler (Eds.), *Nursing research*: A *qualitative perspective* (pp. 85–108). Norwalk, CT: Appleton-Century-Crofts.

Steeves, R., & Kahn, D. (1987). Experience of meaning in suffering. *Image,* 19, 114–116.

Stoll, B. (1982). Management of disseminated breast cancer. In E. Wilkes (Ed.), *The dying patient.* Lancaster, UK: MT Press.

Tillich, P. (1952). *The courage to be.* New Haven, CT: Yale University Press.

van Kaam, A. (1969). *Existential foundations of psychology.* New York: Doubleday.

Yalom, I. (1982). The "terrestrial" meanings of life. *International Forum for Logotherapy,* 5, 92–102.

CHAPTER 13

ETHNOGRAPHY AND ETHNONURSING

ONTOLOGY

The ethnographic and ethnonursing research methods have their origins in the discipline of anthropology and are concerned with culture groups (Atkinson & Hammersley, 1994; Boyle, 1994; Leininger, 1970, 1985, 1988, 1991, 1995, 1996; P. J. Pelto, 1970, 1973; Pelto & Pelto, 1973, 1976, 1979, 1981, 1996, 1997; Ragucci, 1972; Spradley, 1970, 1979, 1980; Spradley & McCurdy, 1972; Sturtevant, 1968; Tedlock, 2000). Any group of people who share goals, customs, rituals, objects, or events is considered a culture (Spradley, 1979, 1980). Though the focus is on cultural patterns for ethnography, a theoretical perspective from nursing or another human science discipline may be used as a guide to the study. The researcher specifies a phenomenon of interest and synthesizes it with an extant discipline-specific theory to set forth the overall conceptualization of the study to preserve standards of sound sciencing (Parse, 1996). Similarly, ethnonursing is guided by the sunrise model (Leininger, 1991, 1996). Here, the researcher specifies a phenomenon of interest and explicates it in relation to the sunrise model. There are significant differences among scholars as to the role of theory in the ethnographic method (Mitchell & Cody, 1993). Some authors believe that no connection with theory is necessary (Cohen & Tripp-Reimer, 1988, 1989; Field & Morse, 1985; Morse, 1989/1991; Munhall & Oiler, 1986).

The general purpose of ethnography and ethnonursing is to gain an understanding of the meanings a culture group attaches to symbols in organizing and interpreting their life experiences (Hammersley, 1992; Leininger, 1985, 1988; Spradley, 1979, p. 93; Tedlock, 2000; Wing, Crow, & Thompson, 1995). The specific purpose of each study may change as the study progresses

127

depending on what surfaces in the field. For example, Becker (1961) conducted an investigation with the initial purpose of studying the organization of medical schools and ended up studying the "level and direction of academic effort" (pp. 419–423) because of the data arising during the research project. The assumptions underpinning these methods follow:

1. Humans disclose patterns of practice in rituals, symbols, and customs.
2. Humans are culture-bound and exhibit folkways representative of an original aculturization.

EPISTEMOLOGY

The nature of the ethnographic and ethnonursing methods focuses on the exploration of symbols, rituals, and customs of a culture group. The entities for study are varied, for example, celebration rituals among aboriginal Australians or culture care patterns among Japanese living in the United States. Researchers would choose ethnography if they were interested in studying group interrelationships. The ethnonursing method (Leininger, 1985, 1988) would be the method of choice if an understanding of cultural care patterns was sought. Examples of research questions that lead to use of these methods are *What is a birthday celebration like in the Korean culture?* and *What are the cultural care patterns of Russians who live in New York City?*

METHODOLOGIES

Ethnography and ethnonursing are very similar in all methodological procedures. The difference with the ethnonursing method is in the use of the sunrise model (Leininger, 1991, 1996). See Chapter 14 of this book for an example of a research study in which ethnonursing is used.

Processes of the Methods

Ethnography and ethnonursing have two major processes, which combine the data-gathering and data-analysis phases of the methods. These processes are participant observation and ethnographic inquiry. These are carried out to create an ethnographic record, which consists of materials such as field notes, tape recordings, pictures, and symbols that document the informants' experiences with the phenomenon under study. Participant observation and ethnographic inquiry involve both the *emic* and *etic* views. The emic view is the insider's view, meaning that interpretations come from the informant's descriptions of the phenomenon under study (Frake, 1964; Harris, 1968; P. J. Pelto, 1970; Pelto & Pelto, 1973, 1976, 1979, 1981, 1996, 1997). The etic view is the outsider's interpretation of the cultural behavior exhibited in relation to the phenomenon under study (Pelto & Pelto, 1976,

1979, 1981, 1997). Both views are integrated in the methods to gain an understanding of the meanings of symbolic patterns that arise in the language structure of a culture.

Participant observation and ethnographic inquiry occur through an involved watching, discussing, questioning, and validating. The involved watcher participates in the cultural phenomenon under study and records what is happening (Atkinson & Hammersley, 1994; Hammersley & Atkinson, 1983; Spradley, 1979, 1980; Tedlock, 2000). The participants are called informants, *general* and *key*. Key informants are the major participants and persons the researcher relies on for validation of data. General informants are those persons who contribute information, but whose participation is not as intense as the key informant's. There is no set number of informants required by this method. All informants are given the option to withdraw at any time and are protected by standard procedures for protection of human subjects (see Chapter 2). Informants share information about the phenomenon under study in one of three types of settings, *free entry*, *limited entry*, and *restricted entry* (Spradley, 1980). A free entry setting is a public place where permission to gather data is not necessary. A limited entry setting is a place such as a school, office, or health center where permission is required of some official person. A restricted entry setting is one that requires agreement to enter by those participating (for example, closed political meetings).

Ethnographic inquiry is conducted with informal conversations and deliberate focused questioning directed toward eliciting meanings related to the phenomenon under study. Three major types of questions are used for interviewing (Spradley, 1979):

1. Descriptive questions are general, open ended, and explore the participants' representations of the phenomenon.
2. Structural questions are designed to discover what participants know and how the participants organize what they know about the phenomenon.
3. Contrast questions are used to show differences and similarities. They are formulated when the researcher notices differences in the way informants describe the phenomenon under study.

Participant observation and ethnographic inquiry increase in complexity as data gathering continues simultaneously with the various levels of analysis-synthesis.

1. Domain analysis is designed to uncover semantic relationships among terms and phrases used to describe the phenomenon under study in order to determine patterns that can be categorized in the linguistic framework of universal semantic relationships. Some universal semantic relationships are spatial, strict inclusion, attribution, means-end, and rationale (Spradley, 1979). Descriptive questions are used to discover the domains.

2. Taxonomic analysis is designed to uncover a single semantic relationship within a domain. A taxonomy illuminates the internal organization of a domain. Analysis may be done with all domains identified from the original search or the researcher may select one or two domains to investigate in-depth. Taxonomies are developed for each domain, with levels of description becoming ever more specific. Descriptive and structural questions are used to expand the taxonomies with verification and validation from informants (Spradley, 1979).

3. Componential analysis is directed toward the examination of meaning components. Components are the attributes of the phenomenon under study that surface in relation to differences rather than similarities among the categories in each domain. Contrast questions are used to validate the researcher's findings, but descriptive and structural questions also are used to verify the ethnographic record (Spradley, 1979).

4. Theme analysis leads to uncovering cultural conceptualizations that connect domains describing the phenomenon under study in a unique way. The themes arise through careful concentration in an immersion with the data related to the phenomenon under study. The recurring themes are major ideas that arise with verification from the informants. The informants' views of the phenomenon under study are fused with the researcher's discipline-specific perspective as themes are synthesized into hypothetical propositions as they are moved to higher levels of abstraction to contribute to science (Spradley, 1979).

Although these processes are peculiar to ethnography and ethnonursing, six specific steps for ethnonursing are listed here to make more explicit the ethnonursing research method for studying caring patterns in various cultures (Leininger, 1985, pp. 33–73; Wing et al., 1995):

Step 1:   Identify a domain of inquiry (a phenomenon to be studied).

Step 2:   Explore the literature.

Step 3:   Prepare research plans and approach.

Step 4:   Identify the sample.

Step 5:   Undertake data gathering and documenting with observing, participating, interviewing, and validating.

Step 6:   Perform data analysis (emic and etic) including pattern, contextual, and thematic analyses by

    a. Documenting data (list cognitive and contextual patterns).

    b. Describing data in extended accounts (combining patterns).

    c. Identifying and categorizing themes.

    d. Synthesizing themes into higher order statements and models.

    e. Summarizing findings with theoretical formulations.

The data analysis-synthesis may be facilitated by use of computer programs (see Leininger, 1985, 1988). The use of computers for qualitative research is discussed in detail in Chapter 26. Interpretation of findings is to be discipline-specific in light of the frame of reference of the researcher. New knowledge gained from the study should be specified and recommendations should be made for further research to continue the line of inquiry.

For further information about the details of the ethnographic method see Spradley (1979, 1980), P. J. Pelto (1970), Pelto and Pelto (1973, 1976, 1979, 1981, 1996, 1997), and Tedlock (2000). For additional information about the ethnonursing method see Leininger (1985, 1988, 1991, 1995, 1996). An example of a study using the ethnonursing method appears in Chapter 14 of this book.

REFERENCES

Atkinson, P., & Hammersley, M. (1994). Ethnography and participant observation. In N. K. Denzin & Y. S. Lincoln (Eds.), *Handbook of qualitative research* (pp. 248–261). Thousand Oaks, CA: Sage.

Becker, H. S. (1961). *Boys in white: Student culture in medical school*. Chicago: University of Chicago Press.

Boyle, J. S. (1994). Styles of ethnography. In J. A. Morris (Ed.), *Critical issues in qualitative research methods* (pp. 158–185). Thousand Oaks, CA: Sage.

Cohen, M. Z., & Tripp-Reimer, T. (1988). Research in cultural diversity: Qualitative methods in cultural research. *Western Journal of Nursing Research, 10*(2), 226–228.

Cohen, M. Z., & Tripp-Reimer, T. (1989).Qualitative methods in cultural research II. *Western Journal of Nursing Research, 11*(4), 495–497.

Field, P. A., & Morse, J. M. (1985). *Nursing research: The application of qualitative approaches*. Rockville, MD: Aspen Systems.

Frake, C. O. (1964). A structural description of Subanun "religious behavior." *Bobbs-Merrill reprint series in social sciences* (pp. 111–129). Indianapolis: Bobbs-Merrill. [Reprinted from *Explorations in cultural anthropology*, by W. H. Goodenough (Ed.), 1964, New York: McGraw-Hill].

Hammersley, M. (1992). *What's wrong with ethnography? Methodological explorations*. London: Routledge.

Hammersley, M., & Atkinson, P. (1983). *Ethnography: Principles in practice*. London: Tavistock.

Harris, M. (1968). *The rise of anthropological theory*. New York: Thomas & Crowell.

Leininger, M. (1970). *Nursing and anthropology: Two worlds to blend*. New York: Wiley.

Leininger, M. (Ed.). (1985). *Qualitative research methods in nursing*. Orlando, FL: Grune & Stratton.

Leininger, M. (1988). Leininger's theory of nursing: Cultural care diversity and universality. *Nursing Science Quarterly, 1*, 152–160.

Leininger, M. (1991). *Culture care diversity and universality: A theory of nursing*. New York: National League for Nursing Press.

Leininger, M. (Ed.). (1995). Transcultural nursing: Concepts, theories, research, and practices (2nd ed.). New York: McGraw-Hill.

Leininger, M. (1996). Culture care theory, research, and practice. Nursing Science Quarterly, 9, 71–78.

Mitchell, G. J., & Cody, W. K. (1993). The role of theory in qualitative research. Nursing Science Quarterly, 6, 170–178.

Morse, J. M. (Ed.). (1991). Qualitative nursing research: A contemporary dialogue (rev. ed.). Newbury Park, CA: Sage. (Original work published 1989)

Munhall, P. L., & Oiler, C. J. (1986). Nursing research: A qualitative perspective. Norwalk, CT: Appleton-Century-Crofts.

Parse, R. R. (1996). Building knowledge through qualitative research: The road less traveled. Nursing Science Quarterly, 9, 10–16.

Pelto, G. H., & Pelto, P. J. (1976). The human adventure: An introduction to anthropology. New York: Macmillan.

Pelto, G. H., & Pelto, P. J. (1979). The cultural dimension of human adventure. New York: Macmillan.

Pelto, P. J. (1970). Anthropological research: The structure of inquiry. New York: Harper & Row.

Pelto, P. J. (1973). The snowmobile revolution: Technology and social change in the Arctic. Menlo Park, CA: Cummings.

Pelto, P. J., & Pelto, G. H. (1973). Ethnography: The fieldwork enterprise. In J. J. Honigmann (Ed.), Handbook of social and cultural anthropology (pp. 241–288). Chicago: Rand McNally.

Pelto, P. J., & Pelto, G. H. (1981). Anthropological research: The structure of inquiry. Cambridge, MA: Cambridge University Press.

Pelto, P. J., & Pelto, G. H. (1996). Research design in medical anthropology. In C. F. Sargent & T. M. Johnson (Eds.), Medical anthropology: Contemporary theory and method (pp. 293–324). Westport, CT: Praeger.

Pelto, P. J., & Pelto, G. H. (1997). Studying knowledge, culture, and behavior in applied medical anthropology. Medical Anthropology Quarterly, 11(2), 147–163.

Ragucci, A. T. (1972). The ethnographic approach and nursing research. Nursing Research, 21, 485–490.

Spradley, J. P. (1970). You owe yourself a drunk: An ethnography of urban nomads. Boston: Little Brown.

Spradley, J. P. (1979). The ethnographic interview. New York: Holt, Rinehart & Winston.

Spradley, J. P. (1980). Participant observation. New York: Holt, Rinehart & Winston.

Spradley, J. P., & McCurdy, D. W. (1972). The cultural experience: Ethnography in complex society. Chicago: Science Research Associates.

Sturtevant, W. C. (1968). Studies in ethnoscience. In R. A. Manners & D. Kaplan (Eds.), Theory in anthropology: A sourcebook (pp. 475–499). Chicago: Aldine.

Tedlock, T. (2000). Ethnography and ethnographic representation. In N. K. Denzin & Y. S. Lincoln (Eds.), Handbook of qualitative research (2nd ed., pp. 455–486). Thousand Oaks, CA: Sage.

Wing, D. M., Crow, S. S., & Thompson, T. (1995). An ethnonursing study of Muscogee (Creek) Indians and effective health care practices for treating alcohol abuse. Family & Community Health, 18(2), 52–64.

CHAPTER 14

USE OF CULTURE CARE THEORY WITH ANGLO- AND AFRICAN AMERICAN ELDERS IN A LONG-TERM CARE SETTING[1]

Marilyn R. McFarland, RN; PhD

The purpose of this study was to discover the care expressions, practices, and patterns of elderly Anglo- and African American elders. The domain of inquiry was the cultural care of elderly residents within the environmental context of a long-term care institution. The ethnonursing qualitative research method was used to conduct the study which was conceptualized within Leininger's theory of culture care diversity and universality. Four major themes were discovered: (a) Residents expressed and lived generic care to maintain their preadmission lifeways; (b) The nursing staff provided aspects of professional care to support satisfying lifeways for residents; (c) Institutional care patterns and expressions were viewed as a continuing life experience but with major differences between the apartment section and nursing home units; and (d) An institutional culture of the retirement home was discovered which reflected unique lifeways and shared care and health expressions and practices. These themes substantiated the culture care theory and revealed new modes of care for the elderly in an institutional setting.

In the United States, the number of elderly persons with care needs who live in nursing homes, retirement homes, apartment complexes for the aged, retirement communities, and special residential facilities is markedly

[1]Marilyn R. McFarland, Use of culture care theory with Anglo- and African American elders in a long-term care setting, *Nursing Science Quarterly*, 10, 186–192, copyright © 1997 by Chestnut House Publications. Adapted and reprinted by permission of Sage Publications, Inc.

increasing. Over one million elderly citizens live in some type of retirement community (Pastalan, 1985), and there are increasing numbers of older adults who choose to live in these communities (Nettig & Wilson, 1987). The national rate of nursing home use by the elderly (over 64) has almost doubled (from 2.5 to 5%) since the introduction of Medicare and Medicaid in 1966 (Kemper & Murtaugh, 1991). Historically fewer African Americans than Anglo-Americans have used nursing homes, but the proportion of elderly African Americans admitted to nursing homes is increasing and actually doubled from 2% to 4% from 1974 to 1985 (Burr, 1990). Researchers project that the number of elderly living in nursing homes in the United States will increase by 76% in the next 30 years (Sloan, Shayne, & Conover, 1995).

Many researchers, including nurses, have studied the care of the elderly in long-term care institutions in the United States. However, most of these studies have been conducted with homogenous populations where cultural factors were not considered. No transcultural nursing studies of elder care in institutional settings were discovered in an extensive review of the literature.

PURPOSE, GOAL, AND DOMAIN OF INQUIRY

The domain of inquiry for this transcultural nursing study was the cultural care of elderly Anglo- and African American residents within the environmental context of a long-term care institution. The purpose of this study was to discover, describe, and systematically analyze the care expressions, practices, and patterns of elderly Anglo-American and African American residents in two settings within one long-term care institution. The goal of this study was to identify traditional generic (folk) and professional care factors that promote health (well-being) and beneficial lifeways for elderly residents and to explore ways to use both types of care to plan and implement culturally congruent nursing care within a long-term care institution.

ASSUMPTIVE PREMISES OF THE RESEARCH

The following assumptions which guided the researcher in this investigation were derived from 4 of the 13 assumptive premises of the culture care theory (Leininger, 1991b).

1. Cultural care for elders in a long-term care institution is essential for health, well-being, growth, and survival, and to face handicaps or death (derived from Leininger, 1991b).
2. Cultural care constructs of elderly residents can be identified within the long-term care institution, revealing some similarities and differences between cultural groups (derived from Leininger, 1991b).

3. Nurses and other staff members can reveal generic (folk) and professional views of care that influence health (derived from Leininger, 1991b).
4. An institutional culture of a long-term care setting for elders with its own cultural care values, beliefs, and practices which are embedded in the institution's worldview, social structure, and environmental context exists but is largely undiscovered data (derived from Leininger, 1991b).

THEORETICAL FRAMEWORK

The theory of culture care diversity and universality was selected to guide this study because it provides one of the most comprehensive and holistic means to discover and understand multiple universal and diverse factors that can influence elder care in an institution. The theory directs nurses to study and identify important broad holistic dimensions of humanistic culture care which include ". . . worldview, ethnohistory, religious (or spiritual) orientation, kinship patterns, material (and non-material) cultural phenomena, the political, economic, legal, educational, technological, and physical environment, language, and folk and professional care practices" (Leininger, 1991b, p. 23). The Sunrise Model (Figure 14–1) was conceptualized and developed by Leininger to depict different dimensions of the theory that needed to be considered to explicate largely covert and embedded culture care influences on individuals, groups, families, or institutions as related to the major premises of the culture care theory (1991a).

ETHNONURSING RESEARCH METHOD

The ethnonursing method as defined by Leininger (1991a) is

> . . . a qualitative research method using naturalistic, open discovery, and largely inductively derived emic modes and processes with diverse strategies, techniques, and enabling tools to document, describe, understand, and interpret the people's meanings, experiences, symbols, and other related aspects bearing on actual or potential nursing phenomena. (p. 79)

The ethnonursing research method has philosophical and research features that fit well with the culture care theory and with the goal and purposes of this study. Leininger developed the ethnonursing method to systematically study the culture care theory; it is focused on the people's viewpoints (1991a) and has supported the discovery of people truths in human living contexts (1988). The prefix ethno means *the people* and the suffix nursing refers to *a discipline focused on human care* (1991a). Accordingly, data were gathered from an emic (people-centered or insiders' views from the residents) and etic (professional

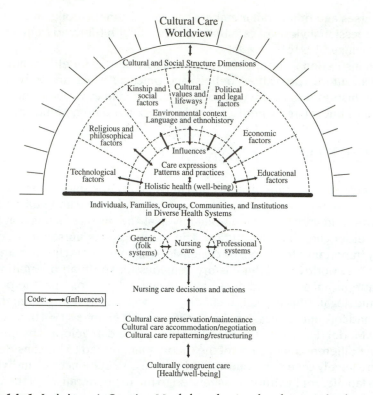

Figure 14–1 Leininger's Sunrise Model to depict the theory of culture care diversity and universality
Source: From Culture Care Diversity and Universality: A Theory of Nursing (p. 43, Fig. 1, Sunrise Model), by M. M. Leininger, 1991, New York. National League for Nursing Press. Copyright 1991 by National League for Nursing Press. Adapted with permission.

or outsiders' views from the staff) perspective over a 2-year period. The retirement home, which included a traditional nursing home as well as apartments for more independent living, was located in a large midwestern city in the United States.

Key and general informants have been a major source for nurse researchers to learn about people, their cultural care, health (well-being), and general lifeways (Leininger, 1991a). Informants were carefully and purposefully selected by the researcher based on who might be the most knowledgeable about the domain of inquiry. Key informants were generally more knowledgeable about the domain of inquiry, and general informants had general ideas about the domain and could offer data that was reflective on how similar and different their ideas were from key informants (Leininger, 1985, 1991a).

Fourteen key informants and twenty-six general informants (a total of forty informants) participated in this study. Fourteen Anglo-American (five key and nine general) and twelve African American (four key and eight general) resident informants were selected from the nursing home and apartment settings of the retirement home. Seventeen of the resident informants were women and nine were men. Five Anglo-American (two key and three general) and nine African American (three key and six general) nursing staff informants (nine registered nurses, three licensed practical nurses, and two nursing assistants) who were employed in the nursing home and/or in the apartment section of the retirement home were selected. Verbal consent was obtained from all resident informants, and written consent was obtained from all nursing staff informants.

Leininger's (1991a) Phases of Ethnonursing Analysis for Qualitative Data was used to rigorously analyze the data. The qualitative criteria of credibility, confirmability, meaning-in-context, recurrent patterning, saturation, and transferability (Leininger, 1991a) were consistently used in the analysis.

Major Research Findings

Four major themes were formulated by the researcher from the data analysis. The themes are presented with supportive examples of generic care patterns and descriptors.

The first theme formulated was *Anglo- and African American residents viewed, expressed, and lived generic care to maintain their preadmission generic lifeways and to maintain beneficial and healthy lifeways in the retirement home*. Although this institutional generic care theme tended toward universality, some diversities as well as commonalities were present in the culture care patterns of Anglo- and African American generic care that supported this theme.

The institutional generic care pattern of *doing for others* was obtained from repeated observations and descriptors of the residents from both cultural groups caring for other residents in many different ways. Elders focused inward on their own daily lifeways rather than toward a dangerous outside world, which influenced residents to provide collective care and individual care practices for other residents. The care pattern of doing for others was buttressed by the residents' kinship and religious values which had encouraged elders in the past to care for their families, their fellow church members, and others.

Many descriptors from Anglo- and African American residents confirmed the care pattern of doing for others, such as: "We get together every Tuesday all year and a group of us works on the crafts to sell at the bazaar . . . [and] She helps Mrs. K. to the dining room because Mrs. K. is not too alert." "I help her [referring to another resident] on and off the elevators. . . . You can't live here and just be concerned with individuality."

The generic care pattern of *families helping their elderly relatives* enhanced the health and lifeways of the residents and was reaffirmed in the preadmission lifeways of both the Anglo- and African American cultures. Anglo-American residents received help from their spouses or adult children. Descriptors from Anglo-Americans such as the following confirmed this care pattern: "I have my daughter, Mary, to bring things down to me. . . . My son calls me every week to check on me." In contrast with the Anglo-American findings, African American spouses and children, extended families, and nonkin who were considered family reflected the care pattern of families helping elderly residents. Grandchildren, great grandchildren, nieces, nephews, grandnieces, and grandnephews as well as church members or friends who were considered family and referred to as brothers, sisters, or daughters were involved in caring for African American elders. Verbatim descriptors supporting this finding were "I'm looking for my great granddaughter to visit this week" and "People at my church are like our brothers and sisters . . . a deacon comes from the church and brings me my mail every week."

The institutional generic care pattern of *spiritual or religious helping* was universal for both cultural groups but had some diverse aspects rooted in their respective cultures. Care as spiritual or religious help was received by African American residents from their church friends as direct personal help in a variety of ways. Church friends ran errands, did banking, paid bills, did laundry, brought communion to the residents, and visited with residents, which confirmed this care pattern. Anglo-American residents also received spiritual or religious help from their churches, but they were provided with less personal religious care than African Americans. Many Methodist churches in the area provided a more formal type of care by sending a minister to the institution to do a worship service, a choir to entertain the residents, or one of their women's groups to direct a craft activity.

A universal institutional generic care pattern shared by Anglo- and African American residents was *care as watchfulness or surveillance of others*. Descriptors from key and general informants from both cultural groups established the credibility of this care pattern. Descriptive statements related to care as surveillance were "There are three ladies on the fifth floor . . . they look after each other. They leave their doors unlocked so they can look in on each other" and "We all watch for absences in the dining room."

The second theme formulated was *Anglo- and African American professional nurses, licensed practical nurses, and nursing assistants provided aspects of professional care to support beneficial and satisfying lifeways to residents in the retirement home.* Although this professional care theme was common to many nursing staff members, there were some universal (common) and diverse aspects in the care patterns supporting this theme. Professional Anglo-American nursing staff learned some African American generic culture care practices from African American nursing staff and residents which reflected the care pattern of *linking professional care with generic care.* African American nursing staff tended to link selected professionally learned skills with their generic family-based care and lifeways, which reinforced the quality of elder care.

The professional care pattern of *presence or availability of care* was valued by Anglo-American and African American residents and staff and was a universal institutional finding. Several residents came to the institution before they required care just to have care available to them when they needed it. Descriptors, such as, "I know that nursing is here if I need it" and "Here in the apartments, you are on your own but if you need care, it is right here," supported the professional care pattern of presence.

The professional care pattern of *protection* was important to African American residents but not to Anglo-American residents. This diversity was related to the differences in the safety and security of the homes that the residents had left when they came to the retirement home. Although all residents felt safe and secure within the walls of the long-term care institution, most African American informants had left homes which were in unsafe neighborhoods and had in part moved for this reason. Statements by African Americans, such as, "My neighborhood really deteriorated and it was not safe to be by myself" and "It became dangerous around our house so we moved here," supported this care pattern for African American residents. African American staff recognized the importance of protective care and often accompanied African American residents when they wanted to go outside.

All residents and nursing staff valued the professional care pattern of *direct physical help* at the retirement home and believed it was essential to the residents' health and maintaining their beneficial lifeways. All the Anglo- and African American resident informants in the apartments and nursing home valued the tasks provided by the nursing staff such as dispensing medications, bed making, skin care, grooming, bathing, and dressing. However, African American nursing staff integrated the generic care pattern of *visiting* into their professional care practices. As the African American nursing staff gave direct physical help to the residents, they visited with them. Verbatim descriptors from African American residents, such as, "A caring nurse [nursing assistant] is kind, nice, and talks to me" and "I would like them to visit with him more [referring to the nursing assistants who care for her husband in the nursing home unit]," confirm visiting as a desired aspect of professional care. Descriptive statements from the African American nursing staff that confirmed their knowledge of this generic care practice were "I sometimes have tea with one of the residents in the afternoon when I take her medicine up to her and we visit" and "When I make a resident's bed, I like to talk to the resident . . . joking . . . visiting . . . that is something nurses should do." Anglo-American nursing staff were kind and friendly to residents from both cultural groups but seemed to be less knowledgeable than African American staff members about this culture-specific care practice.

The third theme discovered was *retirement home care patterns were expressed and viewed within the daily and nightly environmental context as a continuing life experience but with major differences between the apartment section and nursing home units*. All resident informants found life in the apartments more satisfactory and more congruent with their traditional and preadmission lifeways than life in the nursing home. In the nursing home residents shared a room with a roommate. There was little space for personal possessions, most personal possessions could not be secured, and there was little privacy. These and similar findings reflected the pattern of *the physical environment of the nursing home being less satisfying to both Anglo- and African American residents than the apartments.*

Another pattern discovered was that *social factors affected the residents' satisfaction with their lifeways in the nursing home.* Anglo- and African Americans were distressed by the number of confused and wandering residents in the nursing home. Descriptive statements, such as, "I found that confused lady in my bed one night" and "My room is open so anyone can go in," confirmed this pattern. Anglo-American residents even described life in the apartments as very much like their preadmission lifeways in their own homes.

Anglo- and African American residents of the nursing home setting found it difficult to eat with residents who were confused and had objectionable table manners, and residents were more satisfied with the food and the context in which meals were eaten in the apartments setting. Apartment residents who ate in the main dining room were offered choices of foods from a menu, whereas nursing home residents were served their meals on trays prepared by the dietary staff. African Americans in both settings missed their traditional cultural foods. African Americans were particularly dissatisfied with the formal dress code in the main dining room. It had always been the tradition to formally dress for meals in the main dining room, and Anglo-Americans who were long-term residents valued this practice. African Americans as newcomers to the home found this particularly incongruent with their previous lifeways.

The fourth theme formulated was *an institutional culture of the retirement home was discovered which reflected some unique lifeways and shared care and health expressions, patterns, and practices for elderly residents which were embedded in a worldview that focused inward on their daily lifeways.*

A pattern which supported this normative cultural and institutional theme was that *elderly residents spent more time with other residents and staff than their own families or other individuals.* Spending time together gave residents the opportunity to learn, share, and transmit institutional cultural values, beliefs, and lifeway practices related to care and health. Anglo-Americans were the first residents of the retirement home nearly 30 years ago. When African Americans began coming to the retirement home, the institutional cultural norms and values were in place. Anglo-American residents shared the care and lifeway practices of the institutional culture to a greater extent than African American residents, which was partially related to their relatively short length of time in the home. African Americans, as newcomers to the home, gradually brought their own cultural beliefs and values with them, which reflected some similarities and differences from those of Anglo-Americans. Culture is never completely static but is always dynamic, and the researcher observed some African American cultural beliefs, values, and practices such as serving African American foods and the relaxation of the formal institutional dress code gradually becoming an integral part of the institutional culture. Data from this study supported an institutional culture that was focused on care, health, and lifeway practices which were slowly changing.

MODES OF DECISION-MAKING AND ANGLO- AND AFRICAN AMERICAN CULTURE CARE

The culture care theory (Leininger, 1991b) predicts that care via the three modes of culture care preservation or maintenance, culture care accommodation or negotiation, and culture care repatterning or restructuring would guide nurses in providing culturally congruent care. These modes are discussed in relation to the findings and can serve as guidelines for nurses who give care to elders in long-term care settings.

Culture Care Preservation or Maintenance

Culture care preservation or maintenance refers to assistive, facilitative, and/or supportive actions and decisions that help elderly residents to retain their relevant care values so they can maintain their health (well-being) (derived from Leininger, 1991b). Anglo- and African American religious beliefs and practices were maintained as a source of strength and support to help residents face living in a retirement home with increasing disabilities related to aging and handicaps, and even the prospect of death. The nursing staff recognized the importance of family and maintained family involvement in the care of residents and attempted to preserve this cultural-specific care practice for residents of both cultural groups.

Nurses were considered by the elderly residents to be good nurses and to give good care if they visited and were friendly with the residents as they carried out the tasks of caregiving. Nursing staff should continue to preserve and link such generic care practices with professional care practices, since this pattern was supported by residents from both cultural groups. Residents valued the presence of nursing staff members who were readily available and willing to give care when it was needed, and this care practice should continue to be maintained.

The importance of giving care to others has been documented in previous transcultural nursing studies with dying clients (Gates, 1991), with Greek Canadian widows (Rosenbaum, 1990), and with HIV-positive African (Baganda) women (MacNeil, 1996). This care pattern was valued by both Anglo- and African American residents and maintained by the nursing staff. Anglo- and African American residents valued caring for others, and they often gave care to individual residents but also practiced collective care whereby residents gave care that benefited the entire retirement home. The focus on institutional collective care versus self-care is a form of cultural congruent care that residents desired in order to maintain healthy and beneficial lifeways in an institutional setting.

Culture Care Accommodation or Negotiation

In this study culture care accommodation refers to assistive, supportive, and/or facilitative actions and decisions that helped elderly residents adapt within the institutional context to maintain their health (well-being) (Leininger, 1991b). An important finding in this study was that the lifeways in the nursing home were much less satisfying than in the apartments, and the care patterns were less culturally congruent with the elders' preadmission lifeways. Nurses and residents had made numerous efforts to adapt or accommodate care patterns to work toward achieving care and an environmental context for care in the nursing home setting that was more like care in the apartments or even more like care in the residents' own homes. Residents in the nursing home were encouraged to bring in small personal items from their own homes. They brought in colorful afghans for their beds, small chests for storing belongings, and of course their own clothes. The nursing staff made great efforts to protect and secure these personal belongings, but efforts directed toward securing them were only partially successful. However, residents recognized that nursing staff members were continually attempting to accommodate their desire to keep and secure their personal belongings in the nursing home.

African American residents were less satisfied with the food than Anglo-Americans. Residents who ate in the day room on the nursing home units were less satisfied with the food than residents of the apartments, who ate in the main dining room. Residents of the nursing home complained about dining with other residents who would eat with their fingers or grab food off other residents' plates. Residents often complained about being awakened early in the morning to get ready for breakfast. Subsequently, the staff arranged for residents in the nursing home to be awakened at a later hour, and the nursing staff offered residents a breakfast of cold cereal and milk at any hour of the morning. Also, the nursing staff members made efforts to arrange for residents who were alert to eat together and placed residents who had objectionable table manners in a separate area.

Many African Americans missed foods that have traditionally been a part of their culture. They yearned for foods such as pork, greens, grits, and sweet potato pie and mentioned that foods were not salted and seasoned in the way they had prepared them in their own homes. The nursing home staff worked to include more traditional African American foods in the meals offered at the retirement home while still maintaining a healthy diet.

Since both Anglo- and African American residents viewed the neighborhood around the retirement home as hostile and unsafe, the nursing staff made efforts to take the residents outside the home to sit on the small grass strip around the perimeter of the parking lot. However, during the course of this study, the administrators of the home proposed a plan to convert a vacant lot next to the retirement home to an outdoor courtyard which would be accessible to those using wheelchairs and walkers and where residents could walk and sit. This would be a major cultural care accommodation in the residents' physical environment to benefit their health and lifeways.

Residents in this study talked about their health and satisfaction with their lifeways improving when they selectively embraced the professional supportive care expressions, patterns, and practices of the institutional culture and linked them with their own generic care and lifeways. Cultural care accommodation was evident when residents of both cultural groups supported linking generic and professional care practices. However, certain cultural conflicts became evident when African Americans attempted to negotiate to bring some of their cultural practices into the retirement home. Some of the long-term Anglo- American residents were particularly distressed about the relaxation of the dress code in the main dining room which was an accommodation to the African Americans who were relative newcomers to the home. The nursing staff attempted to accommodate both cultural groups to provide culturally congruent care while recognizing that cultural care accommodation which involved negotiation or compromise for both cultural groups was a valuable care practice that minimized cultural conflicts.

Cultural Care Repatterning or Restructuring

Culture care repatterning or restructuring refers to actions and decisions that helped elderly residents change or modify their lifeways for a new and different beneficial healthcare pattern (derived from Leininger, 1991b). Nurses need to be involved as co-participants in restructuring lifeway practices and the environmental context in which care is provided. Based on the finding that the care and the lifeways of residents in the nursing home were less satisfying than in the apartments, nurses must propose some major changes in the care practices and environmental context in which care is provided in nursing homes. Changes are needed in care routines, privacy considerations, room designs, and the way many services are scheduled for elderly residents of nursing homes. These changes can be accomplished only by nurses assuming an advocacy role for the residents and by working with other departments within the retirement home as well as with governmental and private agencies which provide the funding and make the rules and regulations that affect long-term care.

DISCUSSION

The culture care theory with the Sunrise Model as a conceptual and cognitive guide facilitated the researcher in discovering four common universal themes with diversities and commonalities within the patterns supporting the themes and was valuable in obtaining holistic, comprehensive, and yet specific findings related to culture care. The findings of both universality and diversity within the patterns related to the themes supported the assumptive premise of Leininger's (1991b) theory that "culture care concepts, meanings, expressions, patterns, processes, and structural forms of care are different (diversity) and similar (towards commonalities) among all cultures of the world" (p. 45).

The universal institutional theme of generic care being essential for the residents to maintain healthy and beneficial lifeways in an institution supported the assumptive premise of the culture care theory that states "care is essential for well-being, health, healing, growth, survival, and to face hardships or death" (Leininger, 1991b, p. 44). With the increase in the numbers of elderly from diverse cultures being admitted to nursing homes, the importance of generic elder care specific to each cultural group will be important to transcultural nurse gerontologists who practice in long-term care institutions. Generic elder care in a long-term care institution was found to be essential for the residents' health and beneficial lifeways, which meant that cultural care was grounded in the traditional culture of the residents and with the cultural norms of the institution. Cultural congruent care was contingent upon the nursing staff's being sensitive to elderly generic care and using this sensibility in professional care.

CONCLUSION

The research findings of this study offer direction as well as give insight as to the breadth and depth of the changes that are needed in long-term care in our society in caring for elders in long-term care settings. These findings substantiated the culture care theory and revealed new modes of care for the elderly in an institutional context. The findings revealed that some nurses are becoming aware of the diverse cultural values and beliefs of the elderly, but more research-based knowledge and education are imperative to make transcultural care values and beliefs a cognitive and integral part of elder care in an institutional setting.

REFERENCES

Burr, J. (1990). Race/sex comparisons of elderly living arrangements: Factors influencing the institutionalization of the unmarried. *Research on Aging*, 12(4), 507–530.

Gates, M. (1991). Transcultural comparison of hospital and hospice as caring environments for dying patients. *Journal of Transcultural Nursing*, 2(2), 3–15.

Kemper, P., & Murtaugh, C. (1991). Lifetime use of nursing home care. *The New England Journal of Medicine*, 324(9), 595–629.

Leininger, M. (1985). Ethnography and ethnonursing: Models and modes of qualitative data analysis. In M. Leininger (Ed.), *Qualitative research methods in nursing* (pp. 33–72). Orlando, FL: Grune & Stratton.

Leininger, M. (1988). Leininger's theory of nursing: Cultural care diversity and universality. *Nursing Science Quarterly*, 1, 152–160.

Leininger, M. (1991a). Ethnonursing: A research method with enablers to study the theory of culture care. In M. Leininger (Ed.), *Culture care diversity and universality: A theory of nursing* (pp. 73–118). New York: National League for Nursing Press.

Leininger, M. (1991b). The theory of culture care diversity and universality. In M. Leininger (Ed.), *Culture care diversity and universality: A theory of nursing* (pp. 5–68). New York: National League for Nursing Press.

MacNeil, J. M. (1996). Use of culture care theory with Baganda women as AIDS caregivers. *Journal of Transcultural Nursing*, 7(2), 14–20.

Nettig, F. E., & Wilson, C. C. (1987). When religion and health care meet: The church-related home. *Journal of Religion & Aging*, 3, 101–114.

Pastalan, L. A. (1985). Retirement communities. *Generations*, 9(2), 26–30.

Rosenbaum, J. N. (1990). Culture care of older Greek Canadian widows within Leininger's theory of culture care. *Journal of Transcultural Nursing*, 2(1), 37–48.

Sloan, F., Shayne, M., & Conover, C. (1995). Continuing care retirement communities: Prospects for reducing institutional long-term care. *Journal of Health Politics, Policy, and Law*, 20(1), 75–98.

CHAPTER 15

RESEARCH AS
PRAXIS METHOD

ONTOLOGY

The research as praxis method was derived from Newman's (1986, 1997a, 1997b, 1999, 1994/2000a) theory of health as expanding consciousness. In creating the theory of health as expanding consciousness, Newman (1986, 1994/2000a) was influenced by the works of several scholars—including Martha E. Rogers (1970), Bohm (1980), Prigogine (1976), and Young (1976a, 1976b). In the theory of health as expanding consciousness, humans are considered unitary and continuous with the undivided universe; meaning evolves and can be shown as sequential patterns over time; and health, the process of expanding consciousness, is the evolving pattern of the whole person-environment interaction (Newman, 1986, 1997a, 1997b, 1994/2000a). Health encompasses conditions known as disease, which are manifestations of the underlying pattern of the person-environment interaction (Newman, 1997a).

Researchers using the research as praxis method must know and understand Newman's theory, because the process requires that they embody it in their interactions with the participants (Newman, 1997a). Although the method evolved from and is consistent with Newman's theory of health as expanding consciousness, Newman (2000b) recently suggested that the researcher may approach the research process with a theoretical perspective other than the theory of health as expanding consciousness. As long as it is ontologically consistent with the research as praxis method, the researcher's theoretical perspective may be any theory from nursing or another human science. Researchers must specify their theoretical perspective and synthesize a view of the phenomenon of concern in light of that perspective.

The research as praxis method was designed to answer research questions such as *"What are the life patterns of persons who have had heart surgery?"* The purposes of the method are to reveal participants' life patterns, and to facilitate participants' recognition and insight into their patterns so that they may change them. Thus, researchers participate in the research to help the participants understand their situations with the potential for action (Newman, 1997a, 1994/2000a)—"they are seeking knowledge that illuminates transformation from one point to another" (Newman, 1997b, p. 38). The following tenets of health as expanding consciousness guide the research as praxis method:

1. There is mutuality of interaction between nurse and client.
2. Each client situation is characterized by uniqueness and wholeness of pattern.
3. The life process moves toward higher consciousness (Newman, 1997b, p. 35).

The assumptions underlying the method follow:

1. "The process of nursing practice is the content of nursing research" (Newman, 1994/2000a, p. 92).
2. Pattern recognition is emancipatory; it "accelerates the evolution of consciousness" (Newman, 1997a, p. 23).

EPISTEMOLOGY

The entities for study with the research as praxis method are life patterns (refer to Table 1–2). For example, life patterns of persons with coronary artery disease (Newman & Moch, 1991), the process of pattern recognition as a nursing intervention with persons with ovarian cancer (Endo, 1998), life patterns of people with chronic obstructive pulmonary disease (Jonsdottir, 1994), and life patterns of persons with cancer (Newman, 1995) are all entities that have been studied using this method.

METHODOLOGY

Research as praxis is a hermeneutic-dialectic method (Newman, 1994/2000a). The processes of the method are fluid and evolve uniquely with each researcher-participant relationship (Newman, 1997a). There is no limit to the number of participants in each study. All participants are protected by standard ethical procedures (refer to Chapter 2).

Processes of the Method

The processes of negotiation, reciprocity, and empowerment permeate the research as praxis method (Newman, 1994/2000a, pp. 147–149), which follows:

1. The interview.
   a. Begins with an open-ended statement, such as *"Tell me about the most meaningful experiences or persons in your life,"* to establish mutuality in the process of inquiry.
   b. Proceeds with no agenda in a nondirective manner.
2. Transcription.
3. Development of narrative.
   a. Select statements deemed most important to the participant.
   b. Arrange statements in chronological order to highlight the most significant events (written in the participant's language).
4. Draw a diagram that shows sequential events over time (no interpretation is made).
5. Follow-up.
   a. Share the diagram with the participant for clarification and/or revision.
   b. Note the participant's expressions and indications of pattern recognition and proceed with reflections and subsequent interviews until no further insights emerge (sometimes no signs of pattern recognition emerge and that is the pattern for that person—it should not be forced).
6. Application of the theory.
   a. Complete the interviews and then analyze the data in light of the theory of health as expanding consciousness (or another compatible theory explicated in the design phase as the guide for the study).
   b. Evaluate and interpret sequential patterns of interaction according to the participant's position on Young's (1976a, 1976b) spectrum of consciousness. Young's spectrum involves several stages—binding, centering, the choice point, decentering, and unbinding—through which humans move on to higher levels of consciousness.
   c. Designate pattern similarities among participants as themes and state them in propositional form.

For further information about Newman's theory of health as expanding consciousness and the research as praxis method, refer to Newman (1986, 1997a, 1997b, 1999, 1994/2000a). An example of a study using the research as praxis method can be found in Chapter 16 of this book.

REFERENCES

Bohm, D. (1980). *Wholeness and the implicate order.* London: Routledge & Kegan Paul.

Endo, E. (1998). Pattern recognition as a nursing intervention with Japanese women with ovarian cancer. *Advances in Nursing Science*, 20(4), 49–61.

Jonsdottir, H. (1994). Life patterns of people with chronic obstructive pulmonary disease: Isolation and being closed in (Doctoral dissertation, University of Minnesota, 1994). *Dissertation Abstracts International*, 56(03B), 1346.

Newman, M. A. (1986). *Health as expanding consciousness*. St. Louis: Mosby.

Newman, M. A. (1995). Recognizing a pattern of expanding consciousness in persons with cancer. In M. A. Newman, A *developing discipline: Selected works of Margaret A. Newman* (pp. 159–171). New York: National League for Nursing Press.

Newman, M. A. (1997a). Evolution of the theory of health as expanding consciousness. *Nursing Science Quarterly*, 10, 22–25.

Newman, M. A. (1997b). Experiencing the whole. *Advances in Nursing Science*, 20(1), 34–39.

Newman, M. A. (1999). The rhythm of relating in a paradigm of wholeness. *Image: Journal of Nursing Scholarship*, 31(3), 227–230.

Newman, M. A. (2000a). *Health as expanding consciousness* (2nd ed.). Sudbury, MA: Jones and Bartlett/National League for Nursing Press. (Original work published 1994)

Newman, M. A. (2000b, June). *The science of nursing practice*. Paper presented at the University of Minnesota Revealing Meaning for Nursing and Health II: A Conference on Phenomenology and Hermeneutics, Minneapolis, MN.

Newman, M. A., & Moch, S. D. (1991). Life patterns of persons with coronary heart disease. *Nursing Science Quarterly*, 4, 161–167.

Prigogine, I. (1976). Order through fluctuation: Self-organization and social system. In E. Jantsch & C. H. Waddington (Eds.), *Evolution and consciousness* (pp. 93–133). Reading, MA: Addison-Wesley.

Rogers, M. E. (1970). *An introduction to the theoretical basis of nursing*. Philadelphia: Davis.

Young, A. M. (1976a). *The geometry of meaning*. San Francisco: Robert Briggs.

Young, A. M. (1976b). *The reflexive universe*. San Francisco: Robert Briggs.

CHAPTER 16

LIFE PATTERNS OF PERSONS WITH CORONARY HEART DISEASE[1]

Margaret A. Newman, RN; PhD
Susan Diemert Moch, RN; PhD

This study of person-environment patterns of people with coronary heart disease was undertaken as an explication of Margaret Newman's theory of health as expanding consciousness. A method of cooperative inquiry was used involving eleven clients in a cardiac rehabilitation center, a cardiovascular nursing specialist, and the investigators. The clients were asked to describe the most meaningful times in their lives. Narratives of the evolving patterns based on the clients' descriptions were confirmed or revised by the clients. Similarities among patterns were supportive of some of the previously reported behaviors associated with coronary heart disease: the need to excel, a tendency to be repressed and externally controlled. Differences between individuals were explained by their position on Arthur Young's spectrum of human development. The mutual process of pattern recognition engaged in by nursing researchers and clients is seen as a model for practice.

A critical dimension of the theory of health as expanding consciousness is the assumption that disease, when present, is a manifestation of the evolving pattern of the whole (Newman, 1979, 1986, 1990). This assumption is supported by

---

Bohm's theory of wholeness and the implicate order (Bohm, 1980). Bohm contends that the pattern which is manifest (in this case, the disease pattern) is an explication of the underlying implicate pattern of the whole. Likewise, from another perspective, there is evidence from fractal theory that gross patterns repeat themselves in greater and greater detail of pattern at sub-microscopic levels (Briggs & Peat, 1989). The position taken in this study is that the pattern of disease is a gross manifestation of an underlying pattern that can be seen in behavioral patterns and in the pattern of inner experience of the person.

The pattern varies according to the unique configuration of each person-environment situation, however, the similarity of the disease pattern suggests that there will be similarity of patterns among persons with similar medical diagnoses. The objectives of this study were to describe the individual patterns of interaction of persons with coronary heart disease (CHD), to discern similarities and differences among the individual patterns, and to interpret these findings in terms of the conceptual congruence of the overall pattern with the theory of health as expanding consciousness.

Pattern identification is central to the theory and its application. Practicing nurses seek to recognize the individual, evolving pattern of the client in order to facilitate the client's insight and synchronization with the pattern. The significance of the study is twofold: (a) to illuminate the evolving patterns of this group of participants, and (b) to serve as a process guide for practicing nurses.

PROCEDURES

In selection of the sample, the medical diagnosis of CHD was chosen because of its prominence as a major health problem. A convenience sample of eleven persons (7 men and 4 women) who were clients in a cardiac rehabilitation program were interviewed while involved in the program. They were invited to participate in the study by a cardiovascular nursing specialist on the basis of her evaluation of their ability and readiness to be interviewed. Age and gender were not factors in the selection process; however, comparison of these factors indicated that the sample was reasonably representative of the clinic population. The mean age of the sample was 56 with women comprising 36% of the sample. The mean age of the women was 67, compared to 49 for the men. The mean age of the clinic population was 59 with women comprising 37% of the total; women's ages generally were approximately ten years older than the men.

Even though the investigators were aware, in general, of the literature regarding the personality types associated with heart disease, this study was undertaken in phenomenological fashion without specific attention to those types and with the intent of exploring in an open-ended way the participants' patterns of interaction over time. Interviews were conducted by the second author in offices at the center. As a step toward implementing an action research approach in which researcher and practitioner collaborate in carrying out the research, the cardiovascular nursing specialist in the rehabilitation center was considered a co-researcher and was co-interviewer as her schedule permitted. The nature and purpose of the interview as a collaboration between researchers and clients to understand the individual's overall life pattern was explained. Clients who were willing to participate signed a consent form in which the nature of the study and participants' rights to withdraw were described. All names used in this report are fictitious.

The interview began by asking the client to describe the most meaningful persons and events in her or his life. If prompting was needed, the participants were encouraged to think back over their lives and try to identify the persons or events that were most meaningful to them (Bramwell, 1984). The interviewers focused on what was meaningful to the client and followed the direction of the client in elaborating these experiences. The interviews were audiotaped, and after the initial interview, the tapes were reviewed and the data were organized into a chronological sequence of events and portrayed in a diagram of interpersonal relationships at critical points in their lives. (See Newman, 1987, for examples of this process.) The nature of the evolving pattern was contemplated and discussed by the authors prior to a second interview, during which the interviewer shared the joint perception of the pattern with the interviewee and solicited feedback regarding its accuracy and relevance. The recorded pattern was revised as indicated by the feedback from the participant.

A second, more intensive analysis of the transcripts of the interviews was conducted to articulate the pattern of the individual's relationships over time and to identify common themes in the evolving pattern of relationships. This analysis involved: (a) identifying the most important interactions and feelings described by the participant, (b) characterizing these highlights as themes of the individual pattern, (c) identifying themes common across several participants' patterns, and (d) identifying differences in the individual patterns. This process was repeated on a minimum of three occasions separated by one to two-month intervals.

FINDINGS

Similarities of Patterns

Three main themes surfaced as similar among the participants: (a) the need to excel, (b) the need to please others, and (c) the feeling of being alone.

The Need to Excel.   A predominant theme which emerged was the participants' need to excel: to be *"the best," "first," "No. 1."* The satisfaction of being better than others and of winning was important to their sense of well-being. The *drive for perfection* was accompanied by their pleasure in being recognized for their accomplishments and in being the center of activity and in control. Here are some of their comments:

". . . anything I do . . . I do it right. . . . I'm somewhat of a perfectionist . . . I never took a back seat to anybody."

"I always liked to win in sports . . . I didn't want to be just good, but better than whoever I competed with."

" . . . one of the biggest highlights in life was I was the No. 1 mechanic in the shop. . . . the highlight of my life was I made my goal. . . . I felt like I had really made a mark in life."

"I loved [playing hockey] . . . the contact, . . . and getting out there and accomplishing, showing them you could do it. Hearing the fans, you know, your friends, rooting them on. That was great. I loved that. It's good for the ego."

"If you want something done right, you've got to do it yourself."

The Need to Please Others.   There was a strong need to please others and difficulty in expressing one's own feelings, especially in situations of conflict:

"I like to have other people satisfied with me and who I am. I like to satisfy other people."

"I had already done things that I didn't want to do [to please his wife] . . . I had made a lot of compromises. . . . I get very uncomfortable when I am in the middle of an argument."

"I always feel kind of obligated to help wherever help is needed."

". . . I never really talked to my girlfriend about anything like this [fear of dying in surgery]. We never really discuss anything, anything real important . . . you know, like life and death sort of thing."

"I never followed through with [hockey]. I was asked to leave the team because I was smoking, got me mad, ego trip, and I never went back out again, to play hockey for a team, but I should have."

"I'm a peaceful person, basically . . . sensitive. It's just I don't show it a lot . . . I just don't want enemies or hurt feelings between me and other friends people. . . . I'm a people pleaser."

The Feeling of Being Alone.   An even more pervasive theme was the feeling of being alone and a lack of connectedness to others. Several participants specifically described themselves as "loners." They described remembrance of an isolated childhood often within a family characterized by conflict, deprivation, alcoholism, or verbal abusiveness. They often experienced painful, seemingly loveless childhoods and they described experiences of being isolated and disconnected from their parents, siblings, and schoolmates. As adults they had conflictive or merely instrumental relationships with their spouses and children. They were usually more connected to their work or other community activities than to their families. A pattern of repeated episodes of disconnectedness could be seen in both their personal and work relationships over time, with alcoholism a common accompaniment to their difficulties. (See Table 16–1).

Theoretically the similarities of pattern should reflect the pattern of the disease. Early research regarding behavioral patterns of persons with CHD portrayed them as being involved aggressively in "an incessant struggle to

TABLE 16–1 PARTICIPANTS' DESCRIPTIONS OF ALONENESS, LACK OF
CONNECTEDNESS

Allen*: Was the youngest in a large family and was designated the "last" to eat, so was afraid he would not get enough food. He described dissension with his siblings both as a child growing up and as an adult. His work was the most important thing in his life. His first wife left him because of the priority his work held in his life. He remarried. Began drinking heavily after first heart attack.

Bob: Said that he had no strong connections to anyone during childhood and adolescence. His parents fought frequently and divorced when he was age 13. He married at age 25 but always connected more to his work than to people. He drifted from his wife and began drinking heavily.

Carl: Referred to himself as always a loner, never interested in being with a gang: "I don't miss the crowd." He was one of nine children—a family in which it was emphasized that he was on his own.

Darlene: Her parents died when she was quite young, at which time she was separated from her siblings and sent to live with their aunt and uncle. She said that she had been lonely all her life.

David: Felt alone in performing chores around the house (sister and brother did not help). Said that he wished he could establish closeness in his own family (wife and two sons) but in talking about his wife's job, he expressed his wish not to participate in any way in her work. There was conflict with and distancing from his sons.

Ed: Said that his family was not close during childhood; he was scared of his abusive father and didn't have much respect for his mother. "The whole family was alcoholic." He has relied heavily on alcohol his entire life.

Frank: Talked about a painful, loveless childhood. Both parents were alcoholics. He said his father was a loner, "just like me." He felt pressured by his wife and had a tendency to "roam" to get away from the pressure and to seek solace in alcohol. He was separated from his wife and family for three years. His world was the bottle—he had no God, no relationship to anyone. But then he went back to his wife: "no place else to go."

Gary: Described himself as a loner. Felt disconnected from his family as a child and left home at age 15. After service in WWII he tried unsuccessfully to connect with father and siblings. He was married but saw it as a relationship of mutual exchange; he wanted meaningful connectedness with others but was unsure as to how to get it. He used alcohol to withdraw from others.

*All names are fictitious.

achieve more and more in less and less time," labeled as Type A (Friedman & Rosenman, 1974). They were thought to be motivated to assert and maintain control over their environment in order to avoid the fear of failure, and they were thought to have more stressful work experiences and marital relationships than their non-CHD counterparts. Further examination of the behavior of the coronary-prone person revealed the propensity to display hostility in explosive vocal mannerisms, and this characteristic was thought to be a discriminating factor (Dimsdale, 1988; Matthews, Glass, Rosenman, & Bortner, 1977). Dembroski and Costa (1988) delineated the type of hostility associated with CHD as antagonistic hostility, as seen in cynical, manipulative, and antagonistic attitudes and behavior.

Friedman and his associates, continuing to investigate the personality patterns associated with CHD, have indicated that it is not simply a matter of the characteristics of the Type A, hard-driving, fast-moving, job-involved persons, versus Type B (the opposite of Type A), but that persons with CHD in *both* categories were *more repressed, more tense, illness-prone, and externally controlled*. Within the Type B category, the individuals with CHD may be motivated to be the center of attention but not have the social skills to accomplish their goal. They are seen as having poor coping behaviors and other traits that lead to frustration. They are characterized by "thwarted motives and high emotionality, which do not achieve suitable expressions" (Friedman, Hall, & Harris, 1985, p. 1313).

These latter findings are particularly consistent with the data of this study. The participants were not easily dichotomized in a Type A or Type B classification. Nearly all of them were motivated to excel, to be the center of attention and in control of their situations, but some often were thwarted in their ability to achieve success by their inability to assert themselves, their desire to please others, and often their escape into alcoholism.

The physical form that coronary heart disease takes may be envisioned grossly as a narrowing of the lumen of the arteries resulting from a buildup of the wall of the vessels, a situation which gradually decreases the blood supply (energy) to the heart. The functioning of the system may deteriorate gradually and may be disrupted precipitously by occlusion of the vessel. An analogous closing in on the life flow and expression of self in interpersonal relationships was illustrated in the interview data. The potential for opening up in a more expressive way was considered desireable. The crisis brought about by heart disease was viewed in different ways. One explanation stems from the participants' locations on the developmental spectrum.

Differences Among Individual Patterns

Young's spectrum of human development is integral to the theory of health as expanding consciousness and provides an explanation for the differences observed in individual patterns (Newman, 1986; 1990; Young, 1978). Figure 16–1 depicts Young's (1978) sequencing of human evolution. The first stage of de-

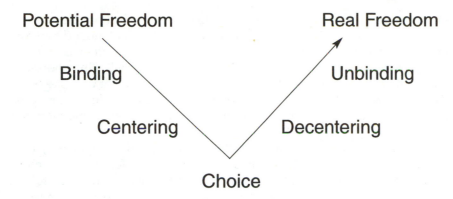

Figure 16–1 Young's sequencing of human evolution

velopment, according to Young, is characterized by *binding*, a phase in which everything is regulated for the individual who is sacrificed for the sake of the collective. There is very little individual identity or choice here.

The second stage, *centering*, is one in which the individual seeks to establish her or his identity by striving for success in the material and power sense. The stage is characterized by self-determination, competitiveness, and seeking control over others.

The next stage in Young's spectrum, *choice*, comes about when something happens that forces the individual to recognize that these self-determined strivings do not work anymore, that they are not really bringing about the "progress" they were seeking. It is a time of choice, a turning point at which the task of the individual is to discover how things work in this new reality and to move beyond the old ways to a reality not limited by the space-time dimensions of the physical world. The crisis of a heart attack or coronary surgery may represent such an event. This stage is central as an explanatory theory for practicing nurses as they encounter persons facing these choices. The transcendent phase of Young's spectrum begins when there is a shift from emphasis on self to concern with development beyond self.

The individual patterns seen in this study cluster around the binding, centering, and choice phases of Young's spectrum, differing by the extent to which participants were able to establish their identity. There were glimpses of a shift to the transcendent arm of the spectrum in the participants who experienced the coronary event as an opportunity to consider major life changes. Also, two older women whose individual patterns revealed well-integrated patterns seemed to have progressed beyond the self-centered characteristics of the binding and centering stages (Barbara and Darlene). Two other participants who died during the period of the study revealed the disorganization and turbulence that occurs in a system prior to transformation (see descriptions of Ann and Ed on page 160).

Binding Stage.   There were several examples of individual patterns depicting the binding stage. Carol, Frank, and David felt they had missed their opportunity to pursue a meaningful career and seemed to be still searching for who they were and how to relate to others. They felt controlled by others, and Carol particularly felt as though she had sacrificed her life for the sake of her family. They recognized their physical condition as a reminder of their mortality and limited life span, and they were unable to see beyond the bind they were in:

CAROL (age 59) saw herself as limited by her obligations to her family, both when she was a child and presently as a mother and wife. She felt she had "missed the boat" regarding the development of a career and never accomplished anything for herself. She felt she was expected to be available to her family. She regarded her capabilities as limited: that she was inadequate as wife and mother and a failure because two of her children had turned away from her teachings. She saw herself as going round in circles, like "a squirrel in a cage."

FRANK (age 41) referred to himself as a "people pleaser." When he "started moving along and getting involved" (in AA), he was sober and happy, but then his wife thought he was putting too much into it, and he started easing up, skipping meetings, and started drinking again: "I let her get to me."

For DAVID (age 44), his experience as a hockey player in high school was the highlight of his life. He revelled in his ability to win, to show what he could do. All of that came to a halt when he was kicked off the team for smoking. He got mad and sulked away without ever trying to get back on the team. In the interview David expressed regret that he "never followed through with [the hockey]" ". . . That's probably what I should have done right from the beginning . . . stay with it . . . and get on with what you want to do." David felt that his life pretty much stopped following coronary artery bypass surgery. His inactivity was depressing to him, made even more so by the realization that he may not have much time left.

Centering Stage.   The experiences of Allen and Carl represent examples of individual patterns depicting the centering stage. Allen and Carl were able to accomplish what they had set out to do in their careers, but then experienced the disruption and loss of this ability due to physical limitations related to heart disease.

The most important thing to ALLEN (age 57) was that he be intensely involved in things and get them done "right." He has worked hard all his life to satisfy other people and to be highly regarded in the community. He has worked his way up to being the head of the family business. He said he "didn't take a back seat to anybody." In addition, he became the administrator of the volunteer fire department. This work was the "biggest part" of his life. He prided himself in being the first person on the scene for twenty years.

He expressed pride and satisfaction in being in the center and at the helm of helping activities, and although he had to cut down on his work activities after his acute episode of coronary heart disease, he was still enjoying first place as a "supergrandpa" to his grandson.

CARL (age 46) did not know what to do next. His entire life had been devoted to following his mother's admonitions to find the "right" job and become the best at what he did. He went through a great many jobs before becoming an auto mechanic and working up to be the No. 1 mechanic. Carl also became very involved in lodge activities and became the "No. 1" man and was "known all over [the state]." He enjoyed the sense of being in charge and seeing the whole picture. He was pleased with his role in helping and advising others and found his relationship to his lodge brothers very meaningful.

Choice Stage.   Some participants were able to move beyond their current situation and view the heart attack or the bypass surgery as a critical time of re-evaluation of the meaning and direction of their lives. Bob, for example, epitomized someone who had experienced all of the same strivings for the top position and for perfection as did Allen and Carl. But, Bob was moving on and clearly experiencing the disruption in his life brought on by the heart attack as a *turning point*, a choice point, from which he could move beyond the space-time limitations of his past into a higher dimension of being.

As a boy BOB (age 38) developed skills in both music and sports and enjoyed excelling in what he did. He liked the competition and liked to win, to be better than everyone else. He said he was never closely connected to anyone but did marry at the age of 25. His love for and commitment to his music as a career took precedence over his marriage. For a while he had made decisions regarding his work to please his wife, but later was unwilling to compromise what he wanted to do, and they divorced. Bob played with a series of bands, going from one to the other, thinking he would find the perfect one but eventually they all ended up in bickering and would break up. He began drinking heavily, after his separation from his wife, as part of the lifestyle of his work.

Bob's heart attack was like a *"turning point"* for him. He had been questioning what the message was in this, what the reasons were for things happening. He felt like he was becoming more spiritual:

"I do believe that there is a higher power. I am open to all kinds of different concepts. Maybe it's time for a change . . . Maybe this is something I should take advantage of, maybe there is something I can contribute. I just don't know where to begin."

"I think of things because I have had a heart attack that . . . I would never be thinking . . . I'd be having the time of my life right now probably . . . I'm thinking of possibly doing something else than what I am doing up to this point, and you know, if I hadn't had the heart attack, I wouldn't be considering anything else. . . . This could be the best thing that ever happened to [me]."

GARY (age 60), too, had already been experiencing the need to "remodel" his life at the time of his heart attack and showed signs of transcending his previous limitations. He was in the process of remodeling his home when he had a heart attack. He had quit drinking and was getting ready to retire when it occurred. He expressed a sense of "wanting more" from his relationships with his family and the possibility that "maybe [he just hasn't] grown up yet." He was seeking a closer relationship with his family and related greater affectionate expressiveness.

Transcendent Stage.   BARBARA and DARLENE were both considerably older than the other participants (70s compared to primarily 40s and 50s). They expressed some of the characteristics already described, but were more connected with their families and community than the other participants and seemed to have less need for control. They presented a more fully integrated pattern that probably falls somewhere on the transcendent arm of Young's spectrum. Their heart attacks, viewed from the vantage point of long lives of complex relationships and events, did not seem to represent the same degree of disruption as it did for the others.

The greater integration of the patterns of these two women's lives may relate to their age and socialization as women. Bateson (1989) has described the ability of women, by virtue of their responsibilities to husband and children, to integrate interruptions in their personal and career development.

Disorganization and Death.   Two participants died during the conduct of the study. The first was a woman 56 years old. Prior to her heart attack the most important thing in ANN's life had been being able to take care of her own affairs, run her home, maintain order, and keep things running smoothly. But she was no longer able to do that. For the past six months she had been unable to run her home and deal with her affairs. She felt disconnected, disordered. She was afraid of everything, had lost her confidence in her ability to do anything. She felt as though her "world has collapsed right on top of [her]." The evening after Ann was interviewed, she collapsed and died at home.

ED, 59 years old, had been experiencing fatigue, depression, and no motivation to go on following his heart attack. In the days prior to his death, he had decided not to undergo further treatment but was unable to follow through with that decision. He reported several days of irritability and nights of insomnia, and expressed disgust at becoming a cardiac cripple. Ed's personal distress was intense; he wanted to go home or take a vacation. He didn't care about the consequences. With recurrent chest pain, however, he did not leave the hospital. Instead he underwent bypass surgery, during which he died.

The place of disorder in the self-organizing capacity of the living system is relevant (Prigogine, 1976). Turbulence, the point of shift from order to disorder, is a sign of the system's deep interconnectedness with the whole and is a critical point in a person's transformation (Briggs & Peat, 1989). Both of the above participants evidenced turbulence in their lives prior to their deaths.

Pattern Conclusions

The theory of health as expanding consciousness incorporates positions regarding pattern that appear paradoxical. The theory is based on the assumption of pattern as identifying the unique, evolving wholeness of the person. At the same time the theory embraces disease as a manifestation of the pattern of the person. These statements imply that each individual is characterized by a unique configuration of person-environment interaction over time, and that individuals who have the same disease manifest the same pattern. It is this paradox that this study intended to address. The findings support both sides of the paradox: The individual patterns were unique to each individual's situation, and there were patterns of interaction that were similar among the participants of the study. The similar patterns represent developmental tasks related to the first rung of Young's (1978) theory of human evolution. When those developmental needs were frustrated or when individuals were caught in a repetitive cycle of self-aggrandizement characteristic of the centering stage, the blocks to movement along the spectrum experienced by the participants were mirrored in the blocks in the disease process. The individual differences were apparent as some participants moved further along in the spectrum of development, and the differences were accentuated when participants faced the critical choice point that the manifestation of the disease represented. If they reached the choice point early enough and still had enough resources to confront their pattern and allow the meaning of their pattern to unfold, they had the potential of transcending the physical limitations and moving beyond themselves to a higher level of consciousness. If they had reached the limits of their resources, death was "the transformative door" (Moss, 1981, p. 101) to higher consciousness. One might speculate that if participants had experienced this process of pattern identification prior to the manifestation of the disease, they could have gotten in "sync" with their patterns before it became necessary for the pattern to emerge in the form of disease.

Implications for Practice

According to J. Huebsch, the cardiovascular nursing specialist involved in this study, this process of pattern identification can be easily incorporated into clinicians' daily activities with clients. Huebsch points out that the interviews "added enormously to the information base of each patient even when I thought I knew the patients." The process can be engaged in by the nurse to open up the experience of the clients and to connect authentically as person to person to the clients' situations. Huebsch emphasizes the importance of clinicians experiencing the process and recommends that for future research the schedule be set up to incorporate a staff member in each interview.

Huebsch examined the pattern conclusions of this study in light of her personal knowledge of the participants, and agreed that the patterns described fit the data but cannot be construed to fit all coronary heart disease patients. Most of the research on interpersonal patterns in relation to CHD does seek to generalize to the entire population and is aimed at detection of persons at risk for CHD for the purpose of preventing the disease. In addition, there are certain lifestyle changes related to diet, exercise, smoking, and stress management that are considered important in the prevention of, and rehabilitation from, the disease (Frenn, Borgeson, Lee, & Simandl, 1989).

This study offers a different perspective, one that emphasizes the meaning of the disruption that CHD represents for each person. The emphasis is on the unfolding pattern of the individual person's life and the importance of helping the individual get in touch with her or his pattern and express herself or himself more fully. The things that were most meaningful to the participants of this study were: (a) a sense of who they were, (b) a need to develop better relationships with members of their family, and (c) a desire to discover a new way of life. But often they did not know how to go about pursuing these objectives.

That's where nursing practice comes in. The presence of another person who is sensitive to self and to the environment can facilitate accomplishment of these objectives by mirroring the client's pattern. Participating in the client's pattern recognition, and what it represents in terms of the individual's stage of human development, opens the way to movement along the evolutionary spectrum.

The practice implications of this study relate more to the process than to the content. The process enacted through this research occurs as a nurse and client come together and form a shared consciousness (Newman, 1986, 1989). This rhythmic process of coming together and moving apart occurs until the client is able to see clearly and take action to express her or his "truth."

REFERENCES

Bateson, M. C. (1989). Composing a life. New York: Atlantic Monthly.

Bohm, D. (1980). Wholeness and the implicate order. London: Routledge & Kegan Paul.

Bramwell, L. (1984). Use of the life history in pattern identification and health promotion. Advances in Nursing Science, 7, 37–44.

Briggs, J., & Peat, F. D. (1989). Turbulent mirror. New York: Harper & Row.

Dembroski, T. M., & Costa, P. T. (1988). Assessment of coronary-prone behavior: A current overview. Annals of Behavioral Medicine, 10, 60–63.

Dimsdale, J. E. (1988). A perspective on type A behavior and coronary disease. The New England Journal of Medicine, 318, 110–112.

Frenn, M. D., Borgeson, D. S., Lee, H. A., & Simandl, G. (1989). Life-style changes in a cardiac rehabilitation program: The client perspective. Journal of Cardiovascular Nursing, 3, 43–55.

Friedman, H. S., Hall, J. A., & Harris, M. J. (1985). Type A behavior, nonverbal expressive style, and health. *Journal of Personality and Social Psychology, 48,* 1299–1315.

Friedman, M., & Rosenman, R. H. (1974). *Type A behavior and your heart.* New York: Knopf.

Matthews, K. A., Glass, D. C., Rosenman, R. H., & Bortner, R. W. (1977). Competitive drive, pattern A, and coronary heart disease: A further analysis of some data from the western collaborative group study. *Journal of Chronic Disease, 30,* 489–498.

Moss, R. (1981). *The I that is we.* Millbrae, CA: Celestial Arts.

Newman, M. A. (1979). *Theory development in nursing.* Philadelphia: Davis.

Newman, M. A. (1986). *Health as expanding consciousness.* St. Louis: Mosby.

Newman, M. A. (1987). Patterning. In M. Duffy & N. J. Pender (Eds.), *Conceptual issues in health promotion.* A report of proceedings of a Wingspread conference. Indianapolis: Sigma Theta Tau.

Newman, M. A. (1989). The spirit of nursing. *Holistic Nursing Practice, 3*(3), 1–6.

Newman, M. A. (1990). Newman's theory of health as praxis. *Nursing Science Quarterly, 3,* 37–41.

Prigogine, I. (1976). Order through fluctuation: Self-organization and social system. In E. Jantsch & C. H. Waddington (Eds.), *Evolution and consciousness* (pp. 93–133). Reading, MA: Addison-Wesley.

Young, A. M. (1978). *The reflexive universe: Evolution of consciousness.* San Francisco: Robert Briggs.

CHAPTER 17

THE HUMAN BECOMING
MODES OF INQUIRY

ONTOLOGY

The human becoming school of thought is a unique paradigm explicating the human-universe process (Parse, 1981, 1987, 1992, 1995, 1996b, 1997a, 1997c, 1998, 1999a, 1999b). The ontology of the human becoming school of thought is specified in its philosophical assumptions and principles (see Table 17–1). In this ontology, the human-universe process is mutual; the human structures personal meaning from multidimensional options; the human is free to choose in situation; the human lives paradoxical patterns of relating; and the human moves beyond with possibles. The epistemology and methodologies congruent with human becoming all evolve from the ontology.

EPISTEMOLOGY

Nursing inquiry for all of the basic research methods evolving from the human becoming ontology focuses on entities related to human lived experiences. These entities are universal lived experiences of health and quality of life, meaning that all persons experience the phenomenon (Parse, 1987, 1998). For example, appropriate for study with these methods are phenomena such as joy, sorrow, laughing, feeling peaceful, feeling confident, having courage, feeling understood, feeling alone, and feeling sad. Inquiry for the human becoming applied research method focuses on changing patterns when human becoming guides practice.

TABLE 17–1 The Human Becoming School of Thought

Assumptions About the Human and Becoming	Assumptions About Human Becoming	Principles of Human Becoming
The human is coexisting while coconstituting rhythmical patterns with the universe.	Human becoming is freely choosing personal meaning in situation in the intersubjective process of living value priorities.	*Structuring meaning multidimensionally* is cocreating reality through the languaging of valuing and imaging.
The human is open, freely choosing meaning in situation, bearing responsibility for decisions.	Human becoming is cocreating rhythmical patterns of relating in mutual process with the universe.	*Cocreating rhythmical patterns of relating* is living the paradoxical unity of revealing-concealing and enabling-limiting while connecting-separating.
The human is unitary, continuously coconstituting patterns of relating.	Human becoming is cotranscending multidimensionally with emerging possibles.	*Cotranscending with the possibles* is powering unique ways of originating in the process of transforming.
The human is transcending multidimensionally with the possibles.		
Becoming is unitary human-living-health.		
Becoming is a rhythmically coconstituting human-universe process.		
Becoming is the human's patterns of relating value priorities.		
Becoming is an intersubjective process of transcending with the possibles.		
Becoming is unitary human's emerging.		

Source: Parse, R. R. (1998). *The human becoming school of thought*. Thousands Oaks, CA: Sage.

166

METHODOLOGIES

With the human becoming school of thought, the basic research methods are the *Parse method* (Parse, 1987, 1992, 1995, 1996b, 1997a, 1997c, 1998, 1999a) and the *human becoming hermeneutic method* (Cody, 1995a, Parse, 1998). The applied research method is the *qualitative descriptive preproject-process-postproject method* (Parse, 1995, 1998) (see Table 17–2). These methods were developed using the following principles of methodology construction developed by Parse (1987, p. 173):

1. The methodology is constructed to be in harmony with and evolve from the ontological beliefs of the research tradition.
2. The methodology is an overall design of precise processes that adhere to scientific rigor.
3. The methodology specifies the order within the processes appropriate for inquiry within the research tradition.
4. The methodology is an aesthetic composition with balance in form.

The basic research methods, the *Parse method* and the *human becoming hermeneutic method*, enhance the substance of the school of thought by expanding understanding of human experiences. The applied research method, the *qualitative descriptive preproject-process-postproject method*, enhances knowledge about human becoming practice. Ethical standards for fostering the rights of participants are adhered to in all of the human becoming modes of inquiry.

The Parse Method

The *Parse research method* is a phenomenological-hermeneutic method used to discover the meaning of lived experiences through a study of persons' descriptions of experiences. The *Parse method* was first published in 1987 to answer research questions such as "*What is the structure of the lived experience of having courage?*" and is unique among phenomenological methods (see Table 17–3) in four ways:

1. The entities for study are universal lived experiences of health and quality of life. This means that all persons can, in some way, describe the experience. All persons have experiences such as joy, sorrow, suffering, laughing, waiting, and others. Participants are persons who can describe the meaning of the experience under study with words, symbols, metaphors, poetry, photography, drawings, music, or rhythmic movements.
2. The data-gathering process is a dialogical engagement, which arises as a true presence, researcher with participant. It is not an interview.
3. The analysis-synthesis is the extraction-synthesis, which moves the original dialogue gradually to higher levels of abstraction—from essences in the participants' language to essences in the researcher's language, to propositions for each participant, to core concepts, and to the structure of the lived experience.
4. The heuristic interpretation connects the findings to the principles of human becoming.

TABLE 17-2 Human Becoming Modes of Inquiry

	Basic Research		Applied Research
Purpose:	To advance the science of human becoming.		To evaluate what happens when human becoming guides practice.
Methods:	*Parse Method*	*Human Becoming Hermeneutic Method*	*Qualitative Descriptive Preproject-Process-Postproject Method*
Phenomena:	Lived experiences (descriptions from participants)	Lived experiences (descriptions from published texts and artforms)	Changing patterns (descriptions from participants and documents)
Processes:	Dialogical engagement Extraction-synthesis Heuristic interpretation	Discoursing with penetrating engaging Interpreting with quiescent beholding Understanding with inspiring envisaging	Preproject information gathering by evaluator. Teaching-learning on the human becoming practice methodology with health professionals, or living the human becoming practice methodology with individuals or groups. Midway information gathering by evaluator. Teaching-learning sessions and/or human becoming practice with individual or group participants (continued). Postproject information gathering by evaluator. Analysis-synthesis of themes from each information source. Synthesis of themes from all information sources.
Discover:	The structure of the experience (the paradoxical living of the remembered, the now moment, and the not-yet all-at-once)	Emergent meanings of human experiences	Thematic conceptualizations
Contributions:	New knowledge and understanding of humanly lived experiences to guide further research and practice.		Knowledge about what happens when human becoming guides practice in order to fortify this theory as a basis for practice in a variety of settings.

Source: Adapted from Parse, R. R. (1998). *The human becoming school of thought.* Thousand Oaks, CA: Sage.

TABLE 17–3   DIFFERENCES BETWEEN THE PARSE RESEARCH METHOD AND
SIMILAR QUALITATIVE RESEARCH METHODS

RESEARCH DIMENSIONS	PARSE METHOD	SIMILAR QUALITATIVE METHODS
Conceptual	Phenomena for study are universal human health experiences.	Phenomena may be lived experiences.
Ethical	Scientific integrity is preserved, and participants' rights are protected.	Scientific integrity is preserved and participants' rights are protected.
Methodological	Dialogical engagement is a researcher-participant dialogue that elicits descriptions. It is true presence, not an interview.	Retrospective descriptions, participant observation, and structured and unstructured interviews are used to elicit descriptions from participants.
	Extraction-synthesis is the process of moving participants' descriptions to synthesized structures of lived experiences.	Analysis-synthesis processes are used to move data from concrete descriptions to themes.
Interpretive	Heuristic interpretation is the process of weaving the structure with the human becoming theory and beyond, through structural transposition and conceptual integration, to enhance understanding of phenomena and expand knowledge of human experiences.	Conclusions are drawn and hypotheses are generated through logical abstraction, sometimes to provide a basis for quantitative research.

Source: Adapted from Parse, R. R. (1998). *The human becoming school of thought*. Thousand Oaks, CA: Sage.

The basic assumptions underlying the Parse method follow:

1. Humans are open beings in mutual process with the universe. The construct *human becoming* refers to the human-universe-health process.
2. Human becoming is uniquely lived by individuals and groups. People make reflective-prereflective choices in connection with others and the universe that incarnate their health.
3. Descriptions of lived experiences enhance knowledge of human becoming. Individuals and groups can describe their own experiences in ways that shed light on the meaning of health.
4. Researcher-participant dialogical engagement discovers the meaning of phenomena as humanly lived. The researcher, in true presence with the participant, can elicit authentic information about lived experiences.
5. The researcher, through inventing and abiding with logic while adhering to semantic consistency during the extraction-synthesis and heuristic interpretation processes, creates structures of lived experiences and weaves the structure with the theory in ways that enhance the knowledge base of nursing (Parse, 1992, p. 41).

Processes of the Method.   The processes of the Parse method are dialogical engagement, extraction-synthesis, and heuristic interpretation (Parse, 1987, 1992, 1995, 1996b, 1997a, 1997c, 1998, 1999a).

1. **Dialogical engagement** is a true presence of the researcher with the participant. It is not an interview. Dialogical engagement focuses on the phenomenon under study as it is described by the participant. Studies with four or more participants have discovered structures of lived experiences using the Parse method. The dialogues are audiotaped and, when possible, videotaped. The researcher centers prior to the engagement with each participant and, after the appropriate consent for protection of participants is signed, opens the dialogue with a comment such as "Please tell me about your experience of. . . ." The researcher enters the flow with each participant as the participant relates a description about the phenomenon under study. The researcher stays in true presence with the participant without interjecting questions but may move the discussion by saying something such as "Go on," or "Please say more about your experience of . . . ," or "Can you think of anything else that would help me understand your experience of . . . ," or "Please relate what you are saying with your experience of. . . ."

2. **Extraction-synthesis** involves constructing a story of essential ideas about the phenomenon from each participant's dialogue, culling the essences from the dialogue in the language of the participant, and conceptualizing these essences in the language of science to form a structure of the experience. The structure (the paradoxical living of the remembered, the now moment, and the not-yet all-at-once) is the answer to the research question. The remembered, the now moment, and the not-yet are incarnated all-at-once in

the participants' descriptions, since humans live and describe multidimensional realities. The extraction-synthesis happens through *dwelling with* the transcribed audiotaped and videotaped dialogues in deep concentration to elicit the meaning of the experience as described by participants and by *inventing* through abiding with logic, while adhering to semantic consistency. The extraction-synthesis process follows:

a. Constructing a story that captures the core ideas about the phenomenon of concern from each participant's dialogue.

b. Extracting-synthesizing essences in the participant's language from recorded and transcribed descriptions. The essences are succinct expressions of the core ideas about the phenomenon of concern as described by the participants.

c. Synthesizing-extracting essences in the researcher's language. These essences are expressions of the core ideas conceptualized by the researcher at a higher level of abstraction.

d. Formulating a proposition from each participant's essences. A proposition is a nondirectional statement conceptualized by the researcher joining the core ideas of the essences in the researcher's language. The essences arise directly from the participants' descriptions.

e. Extracting-synthesizing core concepts from the formulated propositions of all participants. Core concepts are ideas (written in phrases) that capture the central meaning of the propositions.

f. Synthesizing a structure of the lived experience from the core concepts. A structure is a statement conceptualized by the researcher joining the core concepts. The structure as evolved answers the research question.

3. **Heuristic interpretation** weaves the structure with the principles of human becoming and beyond to enhance the knowledge base and create ideas for further research (Parse, 1987, 1992, 1995, 1997a, 1997c, 1998, 1999a). *Structural transposition* and *conceptual integration* are the processes of heuristic interpretation that move the discourse of the structure to the discourse of the theory (for further details regarding the method, see Parse, 1987, 1992, 1995, 1996b, 1997a, 1997c, 1998, 1999a).

The findings from studies conducted using the Parse research methodology contribute new knowledge and understanding of human experiences, adding to the unique knowledge base of nursing. Researchers using the Parse research method have conducted numerous studies on universal lived experiences of health (see, for example, Allchin-Petardi, 1998; Baumann, 1996; Beauchamp, 1990; Blanchard, 1996; Bournes, in press; Bunkers, 1998; Cody, 1991, 1995b, 1995c; Daly, 1995; Gouty, 1996; Jonas-Simpson, 1998; Kelley, 1991; Kruse, 1999; Liu, 1994; Milton, 1998; Mitchell, 1990, 1995b; Mitchell & Heidt, 1994; Mitchell & Lawton, 2000; Northrup, 1995; Parse, 1990, 1994, 1997b, 1999a; Pilkington, 1993, 1997, 2000; Smith, 1990; Thornburg, 1993; Wang, 1997).

The Human Becoming Hermeneutic Method

The *human becoming hermeneutic method* (Cody 1995a, Parse 1998) was created in the Hedeggerian-Gadamerian tradition to answer research questions such as *What does it mean to be human?* The basic assumptions underlying this method further specify ideas from the assumptions underpinning hermeneutics (see Table 17–4). The basic assumptions follow:

1. Human perspective is personal meaning cocreated with the human-universe mutual process.
2. Human creations and interpretations of texts and artforms are perspectival.
3. The rhythmical process of researcher-text and researcher-artform dialogue coconstructs meaning moments.
4. New understandings of lived experience arise with interpretations of texts and artforms.
5. Understandings transfigure the researcher's life patterns.

Processes of the Method.   The *human becoming hermeneutic method* is a unique nursing method to discover emergent meanings of human experiences through a study of texts and artforms (Cody, 1995a; Parse 1998). It has unique processes that arise all-at-once. These are *discoursing with penetrating engaging, interpreting with quiescent beholding,* and *understanding with inspiring envisaging.*

Discoursing with penetrating engaging is piercing the hidden and disclosed all-at-once. It is conversing with the sharp glare of graceful attentiveness to untangle the knots of ambiguity in and among the lines, surfacing the cocreated meanings of researcher with text, or researcher with artform. The researcher is all-at-once in dialogue with the text or artform and also with the author of these media.

Interpreting with quiescent beholding is silent pondering, a dwelling close to the medium of the artform, or the words and sentences of the text, while explicitly-tacitly immersing in the appropriating-disappropriating of the surfacing meanings. It is a disciplined drifting with the rational-intuitive ebb and flow through the labyrinths of meanings in the researcher-text or researcher-artform dialogue. The researcher is expanding understanding while coconstructing meanings through moments with the text or artform in a rhythmical process.

Understanding with inspiring envisaging is springing forth with new visions—horizons fused with the warp and woof of the fabric unfolding in the researcher-text, or researcher-artform dialogue. It is climbing beyond with a deep apprehension of the surfacing meanings that are woven with and transfigure the researcher's explicit-tacit knowing of the phenomenon alive in the text or artform—yet there remains a knowing that the vessel of inquiry can never be filled. There is always the veil of mystery, the barely seen, as the researcher-text or researcher-artform dialogue moves beyond the moment of immediate contact. These processes are congruent with

TABLE 17–4   Assumptions Underpinning Hermeneutics and the Human Becoming Hermeneutic Method

Assumptions Underpinning Hermeneutics*	Assumptions Underpinning the Human Becoming Hermeneutic Method
Language is the horizon of hermeneutic ontology.	Human perspective is personal meaning cocreated with the human-universe mutual process.
Fore-knowing and prejudices are constituents of meaning.	Human creations and intepretations of texts and artforms are perspectival.
There is a dynamic interaction between language style (langue) and speech event (parole).	The rhythmical process of researcher-text and researcher-artform dialogue coconstructs meaning moments.
The researcher-text dialectic arises with a fusion of horizons.	New understandings of lived experience arise with interpretations of texts and artforms.
Situatedness is the context undergirding emergent understandings.	Understandings transfigure the researcher's life patterns.

*Synthesized from Heidegger (1962), Gadamer (1976, 1960/1998), and Ricoeur (1974, 1976, 1981, 1984, 1985, 1992)

Heidegger's (1962) idea of hermeneutics as having an ontological grounding and Gadamer's (1976, 1960/1998) notion of fusion of horizons, which Parse (1996a) says arises "when the text and interpreter meet in dialogue" (p. 12).

After necessary approval is granted, the researcher approaches the text or artform gently contemplating the phenomenon under study. In sinking deep into immersion with engaging and beholding over time, the researcher invites visions to surface of the connectedness of the phenomenon with human becoming. The researcher's ideas are recorded by marking passages of the text or areas of the artform with human becoming concepts for consideration in relation to the whole work. Meanings shift as each penetrating engaging and quiescent beholding with the phenomenon brings to the surface new inspiring visions that are the emergent meanings of the moment. These too are recorded in a journal, or marked in a copy of the text, or on the artform, for further contemplation along with the emergent meanings that arise at other times with the lingering presence of the intense engagements. The emergent meanings are synthesized and written in a creative narrative expressing the author's unique understanding as new visions are fused with the warp and woof of the fabric of understanding of the human experience under study.

The Qualitative Descriptive Preproject-Process-Postproject Method

The *qualitative descriptive preproject-process-postproject method* is an applied research method to evaluate what happens when human becoming is the guide to practice. It was created to answer research questions such as *What happens to nurses' beliefs and practices, persons' and families' experiences of nursing care, and multidisciplinary healthcare providers' opinions of nursing care when the human becoming theory is the basis for practice?* or *What happens when the human becoming practice methodology is lived with individuals or groups?* The basic assumptions underlying the method follow:

1. Value priorities are cherished beliefs that guide actions.
2. New experiences shed light on the familiar-unfamiliar.
3. New understandings are appropriated-disappropriated and woven with explicit-tacit knowings all-at-once.
4. Fulfilling satisfaction arises with recognition and living cherished beliefs.

Processes of the Method.   The processes of the method follow:

1. Preproject information gathering by the evaluator.
2. Teaching-learning sessions on the human becoming theory in practice for nurses and other healthcare providers; or living the human becoming practice methodology with individuals or groups (as appropriate to answer the research question guiding the study).
3. Midway information gathering by an evaluator.
4. Teaching-learning sessions and/or human becoming practice with individuals or groups (continued).
5. Postproject information gathering by an evaluator.
6. Analysis-synthesis of themes from each information source.
7. Synthesis of themes from all information sources.
8. Thematic conceptualizations.

Information is gathered before the initiation of the project, midway, and at the end of the project. Information sources, selected as appropriate to answer the research question guiding the study, include direct observation of nurses' documentation; written and tape-recorded interviews with nurses regarding their beliefs about humans, health, and nursing; tape-recorded interviews with persons and their families regarding their experiences with nursing care; and tape-recorded interviews with nurse managers, physicians, and other multidisciplinary healthcare providers. There is no limit to the number of participants in studies using this method. An evaluator who is not engaged in the day-to-day activity of the setting makes a record of the responses from the information sources before the regular teaching-learning process, or living the human becoming practice methodology begins, midway through the study, and at the end of the project. After preproject information gathering is completed a human becoming nurse (depending on the research question guiding the study) either teaches the theory to study participants, that is nurses and other healthcare providers, or lives the human becoming practice methodology with individual or group participants.

Practice consistent with the human becoming theory follows the practice methodology of illuminating meaning, synchronizing rhythms, and mobilizing transcendence (see Table 17–5) (Parse, 1987, 1992, 1995, 1997a, 1997c, 1998). When the study participants are healthcare professionals, they learn the methodology along with the basic beliefs set forth in the human becoming school of thought. When the participants are individual or group recipients of healthcare, they coparticipate in a nurse-person or nurse-group process with a human becoming nurse living the practice methodology.

Committing to practice from a human becoming perspective is a paradigm shift, takes concentrated study over time, and is reflected in the care with and documentation about those receiving service. In settings where formal documentation is required, a personal health description; patterns of becoming; nurse-person activities; and plans, goals, and priorities for change are included in an easy-to-access format that can be designed by nurses (see, for example, Table 17–6). *Personal health descriptions* include the meanings of the situation, the relationship with close others, and the hopes and wishes articulated by the recipient of care. *Patterns of becoming* are paradoxical themes surfacing in discussion over time. They guide nurse-person activities. *Activities* are those in which the nurse participates, as decided by the recipient of care. P*lans, goals, and priorities for change* in personal patterns of becoming are written from the perspective of the recipient of care. Changing patterns are described by the person and may be recorded by the nurse or the person (Parse, 1998).

After the end-of-project information gathering is completed, each set of descriptions is analyzed and synthesized to arrive at themes from each source. These themes are further synthesized to answer the research question. Thematic conceptualizations arise from this synthesis.

Findings from these applied research studies add knowledge and understanding about what happens when the human becoming theory guides practice. All the published studies have shown that the human becoming theory in practice created satisfaction and that there are major changes in nurses' beliefs about people and healthcare practices. Opinions about nursing from multidisciplinary healthcare providers also changed (see, for example, Jonas, 1995; Legault & Ferguson-Paré, 1999; Mitchell, 1995a; Northrup & Cody, 1998; Santopinto & Smith, 1995).

The three methods—the Parse method, the human becoming hermeneutic method, and the qualitative descriptive preproject-process-postproject method—are discipline-specific. In Chapter 18 there is an example of the Parse method with a study on contentment; Chapter 19 presents an example of the human becoming hermeneutic method with a study on mendacity and the refusal to bear witness in Tennessee Williams' *Cat on a Hot Tin Roof*; and Chapter 20 provides an example of the qualitative descriptive preproject-process-postproject method.

TABLE 17–5   THE HUMAN BECOMING THEORY IN PRACTICE

GOAL OF THE DISCIPLINE OF NURSING	CONTEXTUAL SITUATIONS	NURSE-PERSON PROCESS
Quality of life as described by the person, family, and community.	Nurse-person participation in person's home, heathcare centers, conference rooms, on walks, or on rides. Nurse-group participation in family homes, healthcare centers, recreation rooms, conference rooms, on walks, or on rides. All contexts in which structured and unstructured discussions arise in general or through storytelling, gardening, listening to poetry, listening to music, viewing films, patterned moving, and imagining.	True presence emerges in the nurse-person process as a special way of *being with* in which the nurse is attentive to moment-to-moment changes in meaning as s/he bears witness to the person's or group's own living of value priorities. Witnessing is beholding, an attending to with unconditional presence. It is a *dwelling with* incarnating availability. Witnessing is a non-intrusive gentle glimpsing in reaching beyond to honor the other as human dignity. The gentle glimpsing is a nonjudgmental gaze embracing the other as a unique cocreation. Embracing is an unadorned intending acknowledging the significance of the other's choices; it is a standing with during a journey. Witnessing is living true presence. Coming-to-be-present requires preparation and attention.

Source: Adapted from Parse, R. R. (1998). *The human becoming school of thought.* Thousand Oaks, CA: Sage.

PRACTICE METHODOLOGY	DOCUMENTATION

In true presence, the nurse lives the dimensions and processes of the practice methoodology:

Illuminating meaning is explicating what was, is, and will be. *Explicating is making clear what is appearing now through languaging.*

Synchronizing rhythms is dwelling with the pitch, yaw, and roll of the human-universe process. *Dwelling with is immersing with the flow of connecting-separating.*

Mobilizing transcendence is moving beyond the meaning moment with what is not-yet. *Moving beyond is propelling with envisioned possibles of transforming.*

Personal Health Description
The meaning of the situation, patterns of relating with close others, and the hopes and wishes are articulated by the person/family/community.

Patterns of Becoming
Themes surfacing in discussion are paradoxical and guide nurse-person/nurse-family/nurse-community activities.

Activities
Activities with nurse-person/nurse-family/nurse-community process are decided by the person/family/community.

Plans, Goals, Priorities, for Change
Plans for changing certain patterns of becoming are written specifically from the perspective of the person/family/community.

Description of Change
The person/family/ community's descriptions and evaluations are recorded. Recording may be done by the nurse or the person/family/community.

TABLE 17-6 HUMAN BECOMING IN PRACTICE: SAMPLE DOCUMENTATION FORMAT

PERSONAL HEALTH DESCRIPTION	PATTERNS OF BECOMING	ACTIVITIES
The meaning of the situation, patterns of relating with close others, and the hopes and wishes are articulated by the person/family/community.	Themes surfacing in discussion are paradoxical and guide nurse-person/ nurse-family/nurse-community activities.	Activities with nurse-person/nurse-family/nurse-community process are decided by the person/family/community.

PLANS, GOALS, PRIORITIES FOR CHANGE

Plans for changing certain patterns of becoming are written specifically from the perspective of the person/family/community.

DESCRIPTION OF CHANGE

The person/family/community's descriptions and evaluations are recorded. Recording may be done by the nurse or the person/family/community.

Source: Adapted from Parse, R. R. (1989). Parse's man-living-health model and administration of nursing service. In B. Henry, C. Arndt, M. DiVincenti, & A. Marriner-Tomey (Eds.), *Dimensions of nursing administration: Theory, research, education, practice* (pp. 69–74). Boston: Blackwell Scientific.

REFERENCES

Allchin-Petardi, L. (1998). Weathering the storm: Persevering through a difficult time. *Nursing Science Quarterly*, 11, 172–177.

Baumann, S. L. (1996). Feeling uncomfortable: Children in families with no place of their own. *Nursing Science Quarterly*, 9, 152–159.

Beauchamp, C. (1990).The lived experience of struggling with making a decision in a critical life situation (Doctoral dissertation, University of Miami, 1990). *Dissertation Abstracts International*, 56(06B), p. 2815.

Blanchard, D. (1996). The lived experience of intimacy: A study using Parse's theory and research methodology (Doctoral dissertation, Wayne State University, 1996). *Dissertation Abstracts International*, 57(12B), 7447.

Bournes, D. A. (in press). Having courage: A lived experience of human becoming. *Nursing Science Quarterly*.

Bunkers, S. S. (1998). Considering tomorrow: Parse's theory-guided research. *Nursing Science Quarterly*, 11, 56–63.

Cody, W. K. (1991). Grieving a personal loss. *Nursing Science Quarterly*, 4, 61–68.

Cody, W. K. (1995a). Of life immense in passion, pulse, and power: Dialoguing with Whitman and Parse—A hermeneutic study. In R. R. Parse (Ed.), *Illuminations: The human becoming theory in practice and research* (pp. 269–307). New York: National League for Nursing Press.

Cody, W. K. (1995b).The lived experience of grieving, for families living with AIDS. In R. R. Parse (Ed.), *Illuminations: The human becoming theory in practice and research* (pp. 197–242). New York: National League for Nursing Press.

Cody, W. K. (1995c). The meaning of grieving for families living with AIDS. *Nursing Science Quarterly*, 8, 104–114.

Daly, J. (1995). The lived experience of suffering. In R. R. Parse (Ed.), *Illuminations: The human becoming theory in practice and research* (pp. 243–268). New York: National League for Nursing Press.

Gadamer, H.-G. (1976). *Philosophical hermeneutics* (D. E. Linge, Ed. & Trans.). Berkeley: University of California Press.

Gadamer, H.-G. (1998). *Truth and method* (2nd rev. ed.) (J. Weinsheimer & D. G. Marshall, Trans.). New York: Continuum. (Original work published 1960).

Gouty, C. A. (1996). Feeling alone while with others (Doctoral dissertation, Loyola University Chicago, 1996). *Dissertation Abstracts International*, 57(03B), 1711.

Heidegger, M. (1962). *Being and time* (J. Macquarrie & E. Robinson, Trans.). New York: Harper & Row.

Jonas, C. M. (1995).Evaluation of the human becoming theory in family practice. In R. R. Parse (Ed.), *Illuminations: The human becoming theory in practice and research* (pp. 347–366). New York: National League for Nursing Press.

Jonas-Simpson, C. (1998). Feeling understood: A melody of human becoming. (Doctoral dissertation, Loyola University Chicago, 1998). *Dissertation Abstracts International*, 58(12B), 6488.

Kelley, L. S. (1991). Struggling with going along when you do not believe. *Nursing Science Quarterly*, 4, 123–129.

Kruse, B. G. (1999). The lived experience of serenity: Using Parse's research method. *Nursing Science Quarterly*, 12, 143–150.

Legault, F., & Ferguson-Paré, M. (1999). Advancing nursing practice: An evaluation study of Parse's theory of human becoming. *Canadian Journal of Nursing Leadership*, 12(1), 30–35.

Liu, S. L. (1994). The lived experience of health for hospitalized older women in Taiwan. *Journal of National Taipei College of Nursing*, 1, 1–84.

Milton, C. (1998). Making a promise (Doctoral dissertation, Loyola University Chicago, 1998). *Dissertation Abstracts International*, 59(06B), 2684.

Mitchell, G. J. (1990). The lived experience of taking life day-by-day in later life: Research guided by Parse's emergent method. *Nursing Science Quarterly*, 3, 29–36.

Mitchell, G. J. (1995a). Evaluation of the human becoming theory in practice in an acute care setting. In R. R. Parse (Ed.), *Illuminations: The human becoming theory in practice and research* (pp. 367–399). New York: National League for Nursing Press.

Mitchell, G. J. (1995b). The lived experience of restriction-freedom in later life. In R. R. Parse (Ed.), *Illuminations: The human becoming theory in practice and research* (pp. 159–195). New York: National League for Nursing Press.

Mitchell, G. J., & Heidt, P. (1994). The lived experience of wanting to help another: Research with Parse's method. *Nursing Science Quarterly*, 7, 119–127.

Mitchell, G. J., & Lawton, C. (2000). Living with the consequences of personal choices for person with diabetes: Implications for educators and practitioners. *Canadian Journal of Diabetes Care*, 24(2), 23–31.

Northrup, D. (1995). Exploring the experience of time passing for persons with HIV disease: Parse's theory-guided research. *Dissertation Abstracts International*, 56(06B), 3129. (University Microfilms International No. 9534912)

Northrup, D. T., & Cody, W. K. (1998). Evaluation of the human becoming theory in an acute care psychiatric setting. *Nursing Science Quarterly*, 11, 23–30.

Parse, R. R. (1981). *Man-living-health: A theory of nursing*. New York: Wiley.

Parse, R. R. (1987). *Nursing science: Major paradigms, theories, and critiques*. Philadelphia: Saunders.

Parse, R. R. (1989). Parse's man-living-health model and administration of nursing service. In B. Henry, C. Arndt, M. DiVincenti, & A. Marriner-Tomey (Eds.), *Dimensions of nursing administration: Theory, research, education, practice* (pp. 69–74). Boston: Blackwell Scientific.

Parse, R. R. (1990). Parse's research methodology with an illustration of the lived experience of hope. *Nursing Science Quarterly*, 3, 9–17.

Parse, R. R. (1992). Human becoming: Parse's theory of nursing. *Nursing Science Quarterly*, 5, 35–42.

Parse, R. R. (1994). Laughing and health: A study using Parse's research method. *Nursing Science Quarterly*, 7, 55–64.

Parse, R. R. (Ed.). (1995). *Illuminations: The human becoming theory in practice and research*. New York: National League for Nursing Press.

Parse, R. R. (1996a). Building knowledge through qualitative research: The road less traveled. *Nursing Science Quarterly*, 9, 10–16.

Parse, R. R. (1996b). The human becoming theory: Challenges in practice and research. *Nursing Science Quarterly*, 9, 55–60.

Parse, R. R. (1997a). The human becoming theory: The was, is, and will be. *Nursing Science Quarterly, 10,* 32–38.

Parse, R. R. (1997b). Joy-sorrow: A study using the Parse research method. *Nursing Science Quarterly, 10,* 80–87.

Parse, R. R. (1997c). Transforming research and practice with the human becoming theory. *Nursing Science Quarterly, 10,* 171–174.

Parse, R. R. (1998). *The human becoming school of thought: A perspective for nurses and other health professionals.* Thousand Oaks, CA: Sage.

Parse, R. R. (1999a). *Hope: An international human becoming perspective,* Sudbury, MA: Jones and Bartlett.

Parse, R. R. (1999b). Nursing science: The transformation of practice. *Journal of Advanced Nursing, 30*(6), 1383–1387.

Pilkington, F. B. (1993). The lived experience of grieving the loss of an important other. *Nursing Science Quarterly, 6,* 130–139.

Pilkington, F. B. (1997). Persisting while wanting to change: Research guided by Parse's theory (Doctoral dissertation, Loyola University Chicago, 1997). *Dissertation Abstracts International, 57*(12B), 7454.

Pilkington, F. B. (2000). Persisting while wanting to change: Women's lived experiences. *Health Care for Women International, 21*(6), 1–6.

Ricoeur, P. (1974). *The conflict of interpretations: Essays in hermeneutics* (W. Domingo et al., Trans.). Evanston, IL: Northwestern University Press.

Ricoeur, P. (1976). *Interpretation theory: Discourse and the surplus of meaning.* Fort Worth: Texas Christian University Press.

Ricoeur, P. (1981). *Hermeneutics and the human sciences.* New York: Cambridge University Press.

Ricoeur, P. (1984). *Time and narrative, Vol. 1* (K. McLaughlin & D. Pellauer, Trans.). Chicago: University of Chicago Press.

Ricoeur, P. (1985). *Time and narrative, Vol. 2* (K. McLaughlin & D. Pellauer, Trans.). Chicago: University of Chicago Press.

Ricoeur, P. (1992). *History and truth* (C. A. Kelbley, Trans.). Evanston, IL: Northwestern University Press.

Santopinto, M. D. A., & Smith, M. C. (1995). Evaluation of the human becoming theory in practice with adults and children. In R. R. Parse (Ed.), *Illuminations: The human becoming theory in practice and research* (pp. 309–346). New York: National League for Nursing Press.

Smith, M. C. (1990). Struggling through a difficult time for unemployed persons. *Nursing Science Quarterly, 3,* 18–28.

Thornburg, P. D. (1993). The meaning of hope in parents whose infants died from sudden infant death syndrome. *Dissertation Abstracts International, 54*(06B), 3000. (University Microfilms International No. 9329939)

Wang, C. E. H. (1997). Mending a torn fishnet: Parse's theory-guided research on the lived experience of hope (Doctoral dissertation, Loyola University Chicago, 1997). *Dissertation Abstracts International, 57*(12B), 7457.

CHAPTER 18

THE LIVED EXPERIENCE OF CONTENTMENT

A STUDY USING THE PARSE RESEARCH METHOD

Contentment is a human experience inextricably intertwined with feeling satisfied, tranquil, and happy (Pearsall & Trumble, 1995). It is a satisfaction, a chosen way of being with the moment that arises in the context of feeling satisfied–not satisfied with activities or endeavors that are cherished. Contentment "requires being who you are—no more and no less" (Johnson & Ruhl, 1999, p. 48). The experience of contentment is important to human health and quality of life. Knowing more about it will shed light on the meaning of quality of life for persons being served by health professionals—thus, the purpose of this research study was to answer the research question *What is the structure of the lived experience of contentment?* and, in so doing, provide new knowledge about contentment as an experience of health and quality of life to guide further research and practice.

The importance of contentment to persons' perspectives of their health and quality of life is clearly articulated in the literature. For instance, there are a number of sources in which the authors report that good health, active engagement in social activities (Carp & Christensen, 1986; Hegland, 1994; Jacob & Guarnaccia, 1997; Johnson & Barer, 1992; Markides & Martin, 1979; Meyers & Diener, 1995; Nilsson, Ekman, Ericsson, & Winblad, 1996), self-efficacy, subjective well-being, and life satisfaction (Jacob & Guarnaccia, 1997; Schmotkin & Hadari, 1996) are connected, and perhaps synonymous, with contentment (Jacob & Guarnaccia, 1997). As well, having "peace of mind" is thought to be important to retaining health (Nystrom & Andersson-Segesten, 1990) and achieving spiritual well-being and is believed to be characterized by an inner harmony and contentment with life (Young, 1993). The connection of contentment with *peace of mind* and *inner harmony* is similar to Johnson and Ruhl's (1999) view that contentment, an inner experience, is a way of feeling at home honoring what is. It is further supported by other theoretical literature that has associated contentment with serenity and tranquility (Glick, 1951), pleasure (Ekiken, 1913/1979), and financial security (Galbraith, 1992).

Recognition of the importance of contentment to health and quality of life also is evident if one considers the availability and frequent use of a wide variety of tools that include some measure of contentment in their assessment of quality of life, health, or life satisfaction (Darling & McKoy-Smith, 1993; McKoy, 1996; Schmotkin & Hadari, 1996; Tkachuk, 1995). Kane (1985) even suggests that contentment should be considered an ideal outcome for elderly people. Kane believes that older persons should be relatively content—stating that achieving contentment would diminish currently unacceptable rates of depression, suicide, loneliness, and anxiety among this age group. Kane's view is supported by many authors who have used level of contentment as a variable to assess positive affect in nursing home residents with Alzheimer's disease (Lawton, VanHaitsma, & Klapper, 1996); as a variable to address, when assessing marital relationships (Moroi, 1990); and as a measure of depression (see for example, Attala, Oetker, & McSweeney, 1995; Courts & Boyette, 1998; Demers & Lavoie, 1996). Kane's view is also supported by the work of Lerner and Gignac (1992), who contend that most elderly persons are content, since they "describe themselves as leading useful lives with surprisingly little anxiety or depression" (p. 322).

Only 11 studies were found in which the phenomenon of concern was contentment (Attala et al., 1995; Bylsma & Major, 1994; Courts & Boyette, 1998; Demers & Lavoie, 1996; Hirsch & Hirsch, 1995; Karaku, 1995; Kovacs, 1996; Kriedler, Campbell, Lanik, Gray, & Conrad, 1994; Lindgren, Svardsudd, & Tibblin, 1994; Lloyd-Cobb & Dixon, 1995; Pardeck & Chung, 1995). The findings of these various studies suggest that people's contentment with their health is related to life situation (Bylsma & Major, 1994; Lindgren et al., 1994), ability to live independently (Kriedler et al., 1994; Nilsson et al., 1996; Schmotkin & Hadari, 1996), and level of depression (Attala et al., 1995; Courts & Boyette, 1998; Demers & Lavoie, 1996; Hirsch & Hirsch, 1995; Kovacs, 1996; Lloyd-Cobb & Dixon, 1995; Pardeck & Chung, 1995).

To date, only one qualitative study of the phenomenon of contentment has been reported. Karaku (1995) used Giorgi's phenomenological method to increase understanding about and to develop a conceptualization of *psychological well-being*—defined for the study as the experience of *feeling exceptionally good*. Feeling exceptionally good was distinguished from ordinary well-being, which, from Karaku's view, is equivalent to contentment. The five participants were asked to write descriptions of one episode of exceptional well-being. One of the participants also was asked to write a contrasting description of feeling very content so that Karaku could contrast the situated structure of *feeling very content* with the situated structure of *feeling exceptionally good*. Although contrasting the situated structures of two different phenomena is not consistent with any phenomenological research method, Karaku was otherwise true to Giorgi's methodological specifications. Participants described their experience of feeling exceptionally good using phrases such as these: a relaxation of unnecessary effort and tension; a sense of rightness; a joyful pleasure; an unimagined ecstatic bliss; a deeply calm relaxation; a pleasurable responsiveness; a sense of unity with others and situation; a sense of flowing unity; a feeling of being at home; a noted absence of negative thinking; a sense of lightness and buoyancy; and a feeling of being able to relax. They also described being more spontaneous and peaceful and feeling a sense of wonder and profoundness.

Karaku (1995) said *feeling very content*, a similar but less intense experience than *feeling exceptionally good*, was described by one participant as a familiar friend—an ordinary and common experience grounded in a sense of trust and tolerance for uncertainty that is accompanied by the joy of being engaged in a situation in which one feels a sense of accomplishment while being connected to and supported by others. Referring to the participant's description, Karaku says:

> The episodes of contentment were always in the context of a project to teach Tai Chi. They were in situations of engaged action and involved a sense of accomplishment and completion. . . . True happiness is an underlying steady state of contentment. [Contentment] involves an easeful attunement to the present moment. [It involves] a contrast with . . . tensing and . . . struggling. (pp. 113–114)

Karaku's findings about contentment are similar to those that emerged in several studies guided by human becoming (Parse, 1981, 1998).

Contentment has been clearly illuminated in the findings of seven previous research studies in which human becoming was the nursing perspective guiding the investigation (Parse, 1993, 1994a, 1996, 1997b; Parse, Coyne, & Smith, 1985; Takahashi, 1999; Toikkanen & Muurinen, 1999). The findings of these qualitative research studies were descriptions of laughing your heart out (Parse, 1993), laughing and health (Parse, 1994a), quality of life (Parse, 1996), joy-sorrow (Parse, 1997b), health (Parse et al., 1985, pp. 27–37), and hope (Takahashi, 1999; Toikkanen & Muurinen, 1999). In all of these studies on lived experiences related to health, participants mentioned in some way the feeling of contentment.

For example, Parse (1993) conducted a phenomenological study to uncover a structural definition of laughing with 30 persons over age 65. The structural definition of laughing was this: *Laughing is a buoyant immersion in the presence of unanticipated glimpsings, prompting harmonious integrity which surfaces anew in contemplative visioning.* The common element, *harmonious integrity*, is related to contentment. *Harmonious integrity*

> is the sense of being in tune with others and the universe. It is the feeling of calm that arises through a satisfying experience. Laughing cocreates such an experience. . . . [It] is expressed by participants [in ideas] related to calmness, openness, and feeling more relaxed. (Parse, 1993, p. 42)

The descriptions of being in tune with others and the universe, and the idea of a "feeling of calm" arising with a satisfying experience are similar to the descriptions given by the participants in Parse's (1994a) investigation of *laughing and health*—descriptions that led to the extraction of the core concept *emerging with blissful contentment.*

In the Parse method study to uncover the structure of the lived experience of laughing and health with 20 men and women over 65 years of age, Parse (1994a) reported that the structure of the lived experience of laughing and health was this: *a potent buoyant vitality sparked through mirthful engagements prompting an unburdening delight deflecting disheartenments while emerging with blissful contentment.* The final concept of the structure, *blissful contentment,* is the "creating anew which tells and does not tell all-at-once about cherished beliefs. . . . The cherished beliefs lived in the contentment are the treasured meanings given to the situation" (Parse, 1994a, p. 61).

> Participants described clearly the desire to laugh, which they said lifted their spirits and made them feel good, peaceful, and satisfied with life. In the desire [to laugh] are the revealed and concealed cherished beliefs that arise in creating the contentment. (Parse, 1994a, p. 61)

These findings are similar to others reported by Parse (1996, 1997b).

Parse (1996) conducted a descriptive-exploratory study of the meaning of quality of life for persons with Alzheimer's disease. Twenty-five people with mild to moderate Alzheimer's disease were asked to describe their quality of life. They all spoke about quality of life in ways reflective of the peacefulness and satisfaction that accompanies contentment. The theme, *contentment with the remembered and now affiliations arises amidst the tedium of the commonplace,*

> surfaced in discussions with all participants as they talked about how their lives now compared to how they used to be. Their conversations reflected an appreciation for family and old and new friends as they described the humdrum of everyday by sharing the details about unchanging routines. (p. 130)

Parse (1997b) conducted a phenomenological-hermeneutic Parse method study on the lived experience of joy-sorrow with 11 women over age 65. The structure of the lived experience of joy-sorrow was found to be *pleasure amid adversity emerging in the cherished contentment of benevolent engagements.* Cherished contentment, the second core concept in the structure of the lived experience of joy-sorrow, was described as "the gladness that emerges in accomplishing something that is treasured" (p. 85). The contentedness for the participants in Parse's study was

> the lightness of satisfactions that arose in considering the cherished of the moment while living the joys and sorrows of everydayness. What was cherished was clear in the choosings of the participants as they

moved with activities that were fulfilling, confirming certain values and not confirming others. . . . The participants' descriptions reflected satisfactions with activities they chose. . . . [and] while all participants suggested that joys and sorrows arose together in situations, they turned to activities they cherished in reaching contentment. (p. 85)

Parse et al. (1985) reported a phenomenological investigation of the lived experience of health. Following analysis of the descriptions given by 400 subjects, a hypothetical definition of health was created: *health is harmony sparked by energy leading to plentitude*. The participants' descriptive expressions that led to the extraction of the common element *harmony* support that *harmony*, for the participants in this study, is similar to the concept contentment. Participants spoke about "feeling all is going well," "feeling relaxed," experiencing a "sense of well-being," and being "happy, relaxed, and relieved." They described "being at ease," "feeling peaceful," "feeling light inside," and having a "general sense of everything right . . . a certain serenity."

Finally, findings from two Parse method studies on the lived experience of hope (Takahashi, 1999; Toikkanen & Muurinen, 1999) shed light on the phenomenon of contentment. Takahashi (1999) reported that the structure of the lived experience of hope for 10 Japanese participants is *an anticipation of expanding possibilities, while liberation amid arduous restriction arises with the contentment of desired accomplishments*. The core concept *contentment of desired accomplishments* was said to incarnate the concept valuing. Similarly, Toikkanen and Muurinen (1999) reported that the lived experience of hope is *persistent anticipation of contentment arising with the promise of nurturing affiliations, while inspiration emerges amid easing the arduous*. The core concept *persistent anticipation of contentment* related to the interpretation that their 10 participants from Finland experienced hope in ways reflective of their actively seeking contentment—of wanting wishes to come true.

In summary, the phenomenon contentment was referred to in some way in each of the human becoming studies previously mentioned. There are similarities in how contentment is alluded to in each of the reports. For instance, in several investigations (Parse, 1993, 1994a, 1996, 1997b; Parse et al., 1985) contentment surfaced as feeling calm, relaxed, at ease, good, or satisfied. In others, peacefulness and serenity were associated with feeling content. In several of the studies, contentment was connected with participants' descriptions of the fulfillment and satisfaction arising with either achieving or striving for what they cherished (Parse, 1994a, 1997b; Takahashi, 1999; Toikkanen & Muurinen, 1999).

To date, there has been no work published that specifically studies contentment from a human becoming perspective and there is no evidence of research to uncover the meaning of the lived experience of contentment, or to describe a structure of contentment, even though the research literature clearly points to its importance for health and quality of life. The knowledge gained from this research expands the human becoming theory and may be used to guide the research and practice of health professionals with persons in their homes and in healthcare settings.

NURSING PERSPECTIVE

Human becoming is the nursing theory that guided this study (Parse, 1981, 1998). From this perspective, contentment is a feeling of peacefulness in the context of everyday struggles as meaning is structured with the cocreating rhythms of cotranscending with the possibles. Contentment is the speaking–being silent and moving–being still in the pushing-resisting of creating anew in light of the certainty-uncertainty of conforming–not conforming. The explicit-tacit of the familiar-unfamiliar is transformed through choosing tranquil ways of becoming in the moment that disclose-hide value priorities, as imaged projects affirm and do not affirm opportunities-restrictions. Contentment is a chosen way of being with the universe and important to health and quality of life.

Quality of life, from the human becoming perspective, is "what the person there living the life says it is" (Parse, 1994b, p. 17) and the individual and family are considered the experts on health (Parse, 1990, 1994b). Quality of life is what life is like for people. It is the "whatness . . . or the essence of life" (Parse, 1994b, p. 17). It is about meaning and values, desires and dreams, relationships and plans, concerns and fears. Persons' experiences of quality of life guide decisions about health (Parse, 1990, 1994b). .

The human becoming theory (Parse, 1981, 1998) posits the notion that each human being lives in unique ways. Contentment is the personal meaning that one gives to a situation in cocreating rhythms of relating while moving beyond the meaning moments of the now with the not-yet. Contentment is a universal lived experience that can be described by persons willing to share their experiences.

PARTICIPANT SELECTION AND PROTECTION OF PARTICIPANTS' RIGHTS

This study was approved by an institutional review board for the protection of human subjects. Participant selection involved inviting persons to participate in the study who were willing to speak about contentment—a universal lived experience of health that all individuals are able to describe. Ten women over age 65 agreed to participate. They were all persons who volunteer in community projects in a large metropolitan setting in North America. The participants met with the principal investigator in a convenient setting conducive to private discussion. They all signed a consent form, and standard measures were taken to protect their rights.

METHODOLOGY

The phenomenological-hermeneutic Parse research method (Parse, 1987, 1995, 1998) was used. This method is unique to the discipline of nursing and it evolves from the ontology of the human becoming school of thought (Parse, 1981, 1987, 1992, 1995, 1997a, 1998)—the nursing perspective that guided this study. The purpose of the Parse research method is to discover the structure of universal lived experiences of health, such as contentment, through the processes of dialogical engagement, extraction-synthesis, and heuristic interpretation.

Dialogical engagement is the unique researcher-participant dialogue that is not an interview but, rather, a true presence. The researcher, in true presence, engaged in a dialogue about contentment with each participant. The dialogues began with the researcher asking the participants to speak about their experiences of contentment. The researcher was then attentive to each participant's description. No other questions were asked, although participants were often encouraged to say more about some things or to speak about how something they said related to their experience of contentment. The dialogues lasted from 30 to 60 minutes. They were audiotaped and transcribed to typed format for the extraction-synthesis process.

Extraction-synthesis is the process of moving the descriptions from the language of the participants across levels of abstraction to the language of science (Parse, 1987, 1990, 1992, 1995, 1997a, 1998). These transformational shifts in levels of abstraction occur through dwelling with the transcribed dialogues. Dwelling with is a way of centering during which the researcher becomes fully immersed in the description that was shared by the participant. For this study, the researcher spent time contemplating the transcribed dialogues about contentment—which required both reading the transcribed dialogues and listening to the dialogues on tape all-at-once. The researcher was immersed with the dialogue in the extraction-synthesis process (Parse, 1987, 1995). The extraction-synthesis process includes the following:

1. Constructing a story that captures the core ideas about contentment from each participant's dialogue.
2. Extracting-synthesizing essences from transcribed descriptions in the participants' language. The essences are succinct expressions of the core ideas about contentment described by the participants.
3. Synthesizing-extracting essences in the researcher's language. These essences are expressions of the core ideas conceptualized by the researcher at a higher level of abstraction.
4. Formulating a proposition from each participant's description. A proposition is a non-directional statement conceptualized by the researcher joining the core ideas of the essences. The essences arise directly from the participants' descriptions.

5. Extracting-synthesizing core concepts from the formulated propositions of all participants. Core concepts are ideas (written in phrases) that capture the central meaning of the propositions.
6. Synthesizing a structure of the lived experience from the core concepts. A structure is a statement conceptualized by the researcher joining the core concepts. The structure as evolved answers the research question *What is the structure of this lived experience?* (Parse, 1998, p. 65).

Heuristic interpretation involves two processes: structural transposition and conceptual integration (Parse, 1987, 1998). Structural transposition is moving the structure of the lived experience up another level of abstraction. Conceptual integration further specifies the structure of the lived experience at the level of the theory. The finding of the study is the structure of the lived experience as discovered through the processes of dialogical engagement and extraction-synthesis (Parse, 1998).

In the next section, the stories of the 10 women participants, along with the extraction-synthesis for each, are presented. They are followed by the core concepts, the structure, and the heuristic interpretation.

Myra's Story

Myra, director of a nonprofit organization, is married to a man who was going blind during their courtship and is now legally blind. She says, "We lost his sight together—and then we got married." Her first husband of 46 years died what she describes as a tragic death. She says her daughter, who lives at a great distance, is angry about her marriage, but her son who recently remarried also is close to her. Myra says, "Contentment is feeling good about life. . . . It is being OK where you are, no matter where you are. Contentment can be what you make yourself to be, what you make of your surroundings." She says, "If you don't have pheasant under glass, enjoy peanut butter and jelly." She says she has "good things and bad things" but is very fortunate. She didn't realize how lonely she was until she was married again to a "dear and caring husband." She says, "To once again have somebody who cares, who knows when I come home, who cares when I come home—I feel that is contentment." Myra's 92-year-old mother is now in a nursing home and this is a "great stress" but "it is contentment because she is making this so easy. She talks about everything and cares about everything. Contentment is, I can handle it—what I have on my plate—and life is very lovely."

Essences: Participant's Language

1. Contentment is feeling good about life—being OK no matter where you are. It feels right; it is good to get up in the morning and go to sleep tired. It's what you make yourself to be. If you don't have pheasant under glass, enjoy peanut butter and jelly.
2. Contentment is having someone care about you, and caring about family and friends even though there are some stressful family situations.

Essences: Researcher's Language

1. Satisfaction arises with the fortifying liberty of appreciating everydayness.
2. Comfort emerges amid the arduous with benevolent affiliations.

Proposition.   Contentment is satisfaction arising with the fortifying liberty of appreciating everydayness, as comfort emerges amid the arduous with benevolent affiliations.

Joan's Story

Joan, who likes to keep busy with her church and community volunteer work, says contentment is a "good feeling," a "peaceful feeling." Even though she gets upset about things sometimes, she learns to handle things by telling herself to relax. She says she is "pretty well-adjusted, prays, and practices the Christian religion." Joan remembers a good friend who died. He cared about her and they enjoyed a good relationship in which she was very contented. Joan says she is happy and mostly does not confront but lets upsetness slide by, rather than fight. When Joan is upset, she relaxes, thinks of other things, and looks at pictures of family and friends that remind her of happy times. She says she has learned to accept a lot of things in life and enjoys a good social life with friends and their families. "I keep busy and I'm glad I have a place. . . . I'm just happy with what I do . . . and the way I lived my life."

Essences: Participant's Language

1. Contentment is a good peaceful feeling, keeping busy, and being able to handle things. In times of upsetness the participant lets things slide by and tells herself to relax. She says she is well-adjusted and happy with the way she has lived her life.
2. Contentment is thinking of pleasant relationships with friends, viewing family photographs, and praying.

Essences: Researcher's Language

1. Genuine calm amid the arduous emerges with the joy of resolute liberty.
2. Satisfaction arises with benevolent engagements.

Proposition.   Contentment is a genuine calm amid the arduous emerging with the joy of resolute liberty, as satisfaction arises with benevolent engagements.

Judith's Story

Judith has two children, her husband is dead, and she is now close to her brother and sister. Though she was sad about her husband's death and now about her daughter's depression, she is contented because she can keep on going. She says contentment "just runs through" her and she feels good and has a wonderful life. She believes that it is in the genes from her parents. She says contentment is exhilarating and gives her confidence to push away anything that is negative. She has many friends because she is a good listener. Judith says contentment is doing what she wants to do and she enjoys being alone but is not a loner. She is happy being an individual, not going along with what others do.

Essences: Participant's Language

1. Contentment is a good feeling about having a wonderful life. It is exhilarating and gives the participant confidence to push away anything negative and do what she wants to do.
2. Contentment is not going along with what others do, yet being close to friends and family.

Essences: Researcher's Language

1. Enlivening satisfaction emerges with resolute certitude in fortifying the now amid adversity.
2. Gladness arises with the prized liberty of intimate engagements.

Proposition.   Contentment is an enlivening satisfaction emerging with resolute certitude in fortifying the now amid adversity, as gladness arises with the prized liberty of intimate engagements.

Angela's Story

Angela, whose husband died 20 years ago, is retired but keeps active walking, doing volunteer work, going to church, and doing exercises. She likes to get out and meet people and has walked more than 800 miles with the Village Pacers. She exercises every day and prays a lot. She says contentment is a good feeling and she is happy and very contented even though there are difficult times along the way. She says she was "down in the dumps" after her husband died because they had a good life together traveling to many places in and out of the United States. Angela is contented in that she has grandchildren and a great-granddaughter. She is contented with her living arrangements in the same home with her daughter, but in a separate apartment with a garage. To be contented "you have to help yourself. To me the best contentment in the whole world is to be independent."

Essences: Participant's Language

1. Contentment is a good feeling of being very happy with life while being independent and busy with many activities, even though there are difficult times along the way.
2. Contentment comes with praying, meeting and helping people, and being with her grandchildren.

Essences: Researcher's Language

1. Uplifting satisfaction amid the arduous arises with liberating enterprises.
2. Gladness emerges with cherished engagements.

Proposition.   Contentment is an uplifting satisfaction amid the arduous arising with liberating enterprises, as gladness emerges with cherished engagements.

Marianne's Story

Marianne says contentment is waking up in the morning and being able to get out of bed without problems. She has had problems, a brain operation, and the death of her husband, but she has learned to be content on her own and fill her life. She takes care of her grandson, quilts, goes to the spa, line dances, attends classes given by a psychologist, and has taken some modeling classes so she can "get up and speak to people." She says, "Contentment to me is just being able to move around and do things you have to do and get your house cleaned and wash the dishes and get the clothes going and that is good." Contentment is "happiness that you have in your life and when your house is all nice and clean and sparkling." Marianne walks, watches TV, and listens to music. She likes to cook: "Chicken soup is contentment." She is contented that her grandson says that she is his life. She meets with her four sisters at least once a year for a celebration. She says she thinks positive thoughts and tries not to think negatively—and that is contentment. To do what you want to do is wonderful contentment according to Marianne. She likes to watch the sun set over the river near her mobile home—"that's contentment—just a piece of heaven. Contentment is when you make a birthday cake for your kids, and they come out and sing 'Happy Birthday.' "

Essences: Participant's Language

1. Contentment is waking up and being able to do the things you have to do and want to do and not thinking negatively. It is watching the sun set over the river and the happiness that comes when the house is clean and sparkling.
2. Contentment is celebrating with her sisters and taking care of a grandson. It's singing "Happy Birthday" with the kids after making a cake.

Essences: Researcher's Language

1. Enlivening satisfaction arises amid potential adversity with the wonderment of prized liberty.
2. Gladness emerges with joyful intimate engagements.

Proposition.   Contentment is an enlivening satisfaction arising amid potential adversity with the wonderment of prized liberty, as gladness emerges with joyful intimate engagements.

Janet's Story

Janet is a widow who lost her son several years ago. She lives alone but is close to her sisters. Contentment for Janet is a good feeling that she has most of the time. She says she is happy with all that she does; she loves company and likes to cook, be active, and participate in volunteer work. She says she buys gifts for herself and takes trips. There are not too many close family or friends to buy gifts for and sometimes she feels a bit guilty since some relations could use the money she spends on herself. Yet the gifts and trips bring her contentment.

Essences: Participant's Language

1. Contentment is feeling good and being happy with having company, volunteering, and keeping active.
2. Contentment is taking trips and buying gifts for herself and others, though the participant sometimes feels guilty buying for herself, when relatives need the money.

Essences: Researcher's Language

1. Joyful satisfaction emerges with enlivening engagements.
2. Gladness arises with the liberty of gratifying pleasures amid remorse.

Proposition.   Contentment is joyful satisfaction emerging with enlivening engagements, as gladness arises with the liberty of gratifying pleasures amid remorse.

Jeanine's Story

Jeanine is a widow who says contentment is feeling good while keeping busy with housework and volunteering. She is thinking that there may be a change in her relationship with a close friend who is going blind. She has been dating him for 20 years. They usually went dancing and to dinner several times every weekend. "I am content with that," she says. Jeanine is preparing herself by keeping extra, extra busy, anticipating that her companion will be moved to another state by his children. Jeanine does not know how she will be with this move. She says that contentment is peace of mind, and "I think I have peace of mind right now. I think being content is keeping very busy. It's just everything going smoothly." Jeanine has three daughters and two grandchildren whom she says "are all doing good." She says, "I'm great on the phone; that is my contentment, I have lots of friends."

Essences: Participant's Language

1. Contentment is feeling good with peace of mind while keeping extra busy and having everything run smoothly.
2. Contentment is dating a close friend and having lots of other friends, daughters, and grandchildren that are doing well. The participant

doesn't know how she will be if the friend she is dating leaves the state to be with his children.

Essences: Researcher's Language

1. Satisfaction emerges with the wholesome easiness of a liberating deliberateness.
2. Gratifying enjoyment arises with the pleasure of intimate engagements amid unsure possibilities.

Proposition.   Contentment is a satisfaction emerging with the wholesome easiness of a liberating deliberateness, as gratifying enjoyment arises with the pleasure of intimate engagements amid unsure possibilities.

Elizabeth's Story

Elizabeth is 77 years old, has been married to a "nice" husband for 36 years, and is very contented. She says contentment is feeling peaceful and not getting upset about things. She says that being upset doesn't make her feel good, so it is important to straighten things out to feel contentment. She line dances, plays cards, and does volunteer work. She says she feels content with these activities and helping others. She feels good about having helped her mother and her sister while they were dying. The feeling of contentment is knowing that she did all she could for them. "I think you live longer and healthier if you are content." Elizabeth says making others happy makes her feel contented, and keeping busy mingling with people is important to contentment.

Essences: Participant's Language

1. Contentment is feeling peaceful by straightening things out and not getting upset about things. It is keeping busy with line dancing, playing cards, and doing volunteer work.
2. Contentment for the participant is knowing that she does all she can to help her family, and she likes the feeling she gets when helping others to be happy.

Essences: Researcher's Language

1. Gratifying calm amid adversity arises with spirited enterprises.
2. Satisfaction emerges with the liberating benevolence of devoted engagements.

Proposition.   Contentment is a gratifying calm amid adversity arising with spirited enterprises, as satisfaction emerges with the liberating benevolence of devoted engagements.

Anna's Story

Anna says contentment is being able to do what she sets out to do, and it is accomplishing something worthwhile, such as shoveling the snow or doing things around the house. She also drives her niece's children to school when asked to do so, and that gives her a feeling of contentment. Anna says contentment is "a good feeling, a relaxing feeling." It is a "feeling of relief" that she can help people. She likes to stay in touch with her neighbors. "I feel relaxed and happy that I can do that and I feel cozy and comfortable." Contentment is "being in control of what I want to do and accomplishing that without obstacles."

Essences: Participant's Language

1. Contentment is being in control and able to accomplish something worthwhile such as helping others and staying in touch with her neighbors.
2. Contentment is a good feeling, a relaxing, happy, cozy, and comfortable feeling. It is a feeling of relief with no obstacles.

Essences: Researcher's Language

1. Calm satisfaction arises with the liberty of rewarding benevolent engagements.
2. Serene pleasure emerges with unencumbered ease.

Proposition.   Contentment is a calm satisfaction arising with the liberty of rewarding benevolent engagements, as serene pleasure emerges with unencumbered ease.

Julie's Story

Julie is 81 years old and she says that contentment is keeping busy with volunteer work and other activities. "I am contented because I work on tapestries and am learning to play the piano again. I am interested in music." She says contentment is achieving something you want, and she is challenged to play difficult music on the piano. "Sharing with other people is important" for contentment. Julie does not like to be put in the same category with other elders. She says she is different. For contentment, people have to make up their minds to be what they want to be and then succeed. She lets go of things that might get in the way of her happiness.

Essences: Participant's Language

1. Contentment is achieving something by keeping busy working on tapestries, learning to play the piano, and volunteering. The participant lets go of things that could make life difficult.
2. Contentment is sharing with other people in your own, different way.

Essences: Researcher's Language

1. Liberating satisfaction arises with enlivening enterprises amid potential adversity.
2. Calmness surfaces with unique benevolent engagements.

Proposition.   Contentment is the liberating satisfaction arising with enlivening enterprises amid potential adversity, as calm surfaces with unique benevolent engagements.

Propositions

Myra   Contentment is satisfaction arising with the fortifying liberty of appreciating everydayness, as comfort emerges amid the arduous with benevolent affiliations.

Joan   Contentment is a genuine calm amid the arduous emerging with the joy of resolute liberty, as satisfaction arises with benevolent engagements.

Judith   Contentment is an enlivening satisfaction emerging with resolute certitude in fortifying the now amid adversity, as gladness arises with the prized liberty of intimate engagements.

Angela   Contentment is an uplifting satisfaction amid the arduous arising with liberating enterprises, as gladness emerges with cherished engagements.

Marianne   Contentment is an enlivening satisfaction arising amid potential adversity with the wonderment of prized liberty, as gladness emerges with joyful intimate engagements.

Janet   Contentment is joyful satisfaction emerging with enlivening engagements, as gladness arises with the liberty of gratifying pleasures amid remorse.

Jeanine   Contentment is a satisfaction emerging with the wholesome easiness of a liberating deliberateness, as gratifying enjoyment arises with the pleasure of intimate engagements amid unsure possibilities.

Elizabeth   Contentment is a gratifying calm amid adversity arising with spirited enterprises, as satisfaction emerges with the liberating benevolence of devoted engagements.

Anna   Contentment is a calm satisfaction arising with the liberty of rewarding benevolent engagements, as serene pleasure emerges with unencumbered ease.

Julie   Contentment is the liberating satisfaction arising with enlivening enterprises amid potential adversity, as calm surfaces with unique benevolent engagements.

DISCUSSION OF FINDINGS

The finding of this study is the structure, *contentment is a satisfying calmness amid the arduous as resolute liberty arises with benevolent engagements.* The structural transposition is *contentment is a fulfilling tranquility amid the disquieting as an unwavering reliance arises with solicitous involvements*. The conceptual integration is *contentment is valuing the powering of connecting-separating* (see Table 18–1).

TABLE 18–1   Progressive Abstraction of the Core Concepts of the Lived Experience of Contentment

Core Concept	Structural Transposition	Conceptual Integration
Satisfying calmness amid the arduous	Fulfilling tranquility amid the disquieting	Valuing
Resolute liberty	Unwavering reliance	Powering
Benevolent engagements	Solicitous involvements	Connecting-Separating

Structure
Contentment is a satisfying calmness amid the arduous as resolute liberty arises with benevolent engagements.

Structural Transposition
Contentment is a fulfilling tranquility amid the disquieting as an unwavering reliance arises with solicitous involvements.

Conceptual Integration
Contentment is valuing the powering of connecting-separating.

Satisfying Calmness Amid the Arduous

The first core concept, *satisfying calmness amid the arduous*, arose as participants spoke of feeling good and peaceful, even though there are stressful situations in everyday life. One participant said, "Contentment is a peaceful feeling," but she says she gets upset about things sometimes. Another participant said she lets upsetness slide by and relaxes and thinks of things that do not bother her. Still another participant said she was content with her life, even when anticipating a drastic change in a relationship. Yet another participant said, "I am content . . . when everything is running smoothly." One person said being content is "accomplishing something worthwhile even if it may be difficult." Another illustration of *satisfying calmness amid the arduous* arose with one participant who said that contentment is exhilarating and gives her confidence to push away anything that is negative. These ideas from the participants' descriptions illustrate the structural transposition as a sense of fulfilling tranquility that arises amid disquieting situations in the confirming–not confirming of values. The conceptual integration of *satisfying calmness amid the arduous* as *valuing* sheds light on the meaning of choosing a cherished calmness even in the presence of obstacles. Valuing is a concept from the first principle of human becoming (Parse, 1998). It is the confirming–not confirming of cherished beliefs.

From among myriad options people make choices that incarnate value priorities. These priorities are the structured meaning that confirms contentment as a *satisfying calmness amid the arduous*. For participants in this study, this satisfying calmness arose with a resolute liberty, which is the second core concept surfacing in the participants' descriptions.

Resolute Liberty

Resolute liberty, a determined independence, surfaced in all participants' descriptions of contentment. Participants were unwavering in affirming their self-reliance. Statements such as "being able to do what I want to do" and "keeping busy on my own" were prevalent in the descriptions. One participant said, "I can handle it—what I have on my plate." Another participant said that being independent is most important to contentment. Yet another participant said she enjoys being alone and not going along with others. All of these statements show that for these participants independence is important for contentment and thus for health and quality of life.

Resolute liberty is structurally transposed to *unwavering reliance* and conceptually integrated as *powering*. Powering, a concept from the third principle of human becoming, is the pushing-resisting rhythm of affirming–not affirming being with nonbeing (Parse, 1998). Living being with nonbeing is incarnating the known of the now and the seeming unknown potential of the not-yet. The resolute liberty of contentment expressed by the participants in this study is affirming being through deliberately engaging in enterprises such as volunteer work, line dancing, cleaning, shoveling snow, playing cards, and other activities that illuminated their strong desire to promote their independence. The resolute liberty arose with benevolent engagements.

Benevolent Engagements

Benevolent engagements is the third core concept surfacing from the participants' descriptions. All participants described relationships with others when asked to talk about contentment. They told of being with their many friends, celebrating with sisters, taking care of their children, having loving and caring spouses or friends, helping family, and sharing with others. The participants' descriptions specified the engagements of contentment as benevolent, loving, and intimately close as they unfolded in day-to-day happenings with others. The core concept of benevolent engagements is structurally transposed as *solicitous involvements* and integrated conceptually as *connecting-separating*. Connecting-separating, a concept of the second principle of human becoming, is the paradoxical rhythm of being with and away from others, ideas, objects, and events (Parse, 1998). The participants spoke of being with and away from close others. Although they appreciated their time with others, they also liked being alone.

FINDINGS AND RELATED LITERATURE

The finding of this study, the structure, *contentment is a satisfying calmness amid the arduous as resolute liberty arises with benevolent engagements*, contributes knowledge about contentment to the extant literature. Two of the core concepts surfacing from the participants' descriptions in some way arose in the literature on contentment. *Satisfying calmness*, for example, is alluded to in the theoretical literature (Allestree, 1677; Glick, 1951; Nystrom & Andersson-Segesten, 1990; Pearsall & Trumble, 1995; Young, 1993) that connects contentment with being abundantly satisfied (Allestree, 1677), serenity and tranquility (Glick, 1951), peace of mind (Glick, 1951; Nystrom & Andersson-Segesten, 1990), and inner harmony (Young, 1993). Contentment also was connected with ideas similar to *satisfying calmness* in several recent studies (Bylsma & Major, 1994; Karaku, 1995; Lindgren et al., 1994; Parse, 1993, 1994a, 1996, 1997b; Parse et al., 1985; Takahashi, 1999; Toikkanen & Muurinen, 1999). No literature specified *amid the arduous*, but some authors (Attala et al., 1995; Courts & Boyette, 1998; Demers & Lavoie, 1996; Hirsch & Hirsch, 1995; Kane, 1985; Kovacs, 1996; Lawton et al., 1996; Lloyd-Cobb & Dixon, 1995; Pardeck & Chung, 1995) did say contentment is related to diminished chances of depression, loneliness, and anxiety.

The core concept *benevolent engagements* was alluded to in the theoretical literature on contentment (Hegland, 1994; Jacob & Guarnaccia, 1997; Markides & Martin, 1979; Meyers & Diener, 1995) and in some research studies (Johnson & Barer, 1992; Karaku, 1995; Kovacs, 1996) but not to the extent that it was described in this study. For example, in the Karaku (1995) study, participants described feeling exceptionally good as a sense of unity with others, which connects to some statements by participants in this study who talked about a sense of caring in relationships.

The concept *resolute liberty* was not explicitly found in the theoretical literature or the research literature on contentment. Three studies (Kriedler et al., 1994; Nilsson et al., 1996; Schmotkin & Hadari, 1996) did connect contentment with the *ability* to live independently; however, descriptions of contentment as the determination and resolve to live independently were not found. The participants in the present study strongly indicated in their descriptions the importance of independence. Their unwavering self-reliance was expressed in the determination they had for carrying out activities and living alone.

NEW KNOWLEDGE

The unique knowledge about contentment found in this study follows:

1. Contentment is a satisfying calmness, but it is lived amid potential or remembered adversity.
2. Contentment arises with benevolent engagements with family and friends.

3. Resolute liberty, as an unwavering determination to be independent, is integral to contentment.

RECOMMENDATIONS

From the new knowledge and to further the line of inquiry on contentment related to health and quality of life, studies may be conducted on several phenomena, for example, feeling calm, feeling peaceful, feeling independent, feeling dependent, and feeling alone. Research on these phenomena, and others, will expand understanding about human becoming.

SUMMARY

This study on contentment with 10 women over 65 years of age adds new knowledge to the general literature on contentment and its connection to health and quality of life, and expands understanding of human becoming. The findings lay the foundation for further research on the essences of contentment. New knowledge about human experiences offers nurses and other health processionals ways to understand and be with people living their health and quality of life (Parse, 1981, 1998).

REFERENCES

Allestree, R. (1677). *The art of contentment*. Oxford: At the Theater.

Attala, J. M., Oetker, D., & McSweeney, M. (1995). Partner abuse against female nursing students. *Journal of Psychosocial Nursing & Mental Health Services, 33*(1), 17–24.

Bylsma, W. H., & Major, B. (1994). Social comparisons and contentment: Exploring the psychological costs of the gender wage gap. *Psychology of Women Quarterly, 18*(2), 241–249.

Carp, F. M., & Christensen, D. L. (1986). Older women living alone: Technical environmental assessment of psychological well-being. *Research on Aging, 8*(3), 407–425.

Courts, N. F., & Boyette, B. G. (1998). Psychosocial adjustment of males on three types of dialysis. *Clinical Nursing Research, 7*(1), 47–63.

Darling, C. A., & McKoy-Smith, Y. M. (1993). Understanding hysterectomies: Sexual satisfaction and quality of life. *Journal of Sex Research, 30,* 324–335.

Demers, A., & Lavoie, J. P. (1996). Effect of support groups on family caregivers to the frail elderly. *Canadian Journal on Aging, 15*(1), 129–144.

Ekiken, K. (1979). *The way of contentment* (K. Hoshino, Trans.). Washington, DC: University Publications of America. (Original work published 1913)

Galbraith, J. K. (1992). *The culture of contentment*. New York: Houghton Mifflin.

Glick, C. (1951). *The secret of serenity*. New York: Thomas Y. Crowell.

Hegland, A. (1994). Power of pastimes: Even seemingly mundane activities for residents can yield therapeutic results. *Contemporary Long Term Care, 17*(3), 63–64.

Hirsch, A. M., & Hirsch, S. M. (1995). The long-term psychosocial effects of infertility. *Journal of Obstetric, Gynecologic, & Neonatal Nursing*, 24(6), 517–522.

Jacob, M., & Guarnaccia, V. (1997). Motivational and behavioral correlates of life satisfaction in an elderly sample. *Psychological Reports*, 80(3, Part 1), 811–818.

Johnson, C. L., & Barer, B. M. (1992). Patterns of engagement and disengagement among the oldest old. *Journal of Aging Studies*, 6(4), 351–364.

Johnson, R. A., & Ruhl, J. M. (1999). *Contentment: A way to true happiness*. San Francisco: HarperSanFrancisco.

Kane, R. A. (1985). Long term status quo untenable? What is more ideal for nation's elderly? *Perspective on Aging*, 14(5), 23–26.

Karaku, A. T. (1995). Psychological well-being as exemplified by adults' experiences of feeling exceptionally good: An empirical phenomenological study. *Dissertation Abstracts International*, 56(04B), 2310.

Kovacs, P. J. (1996). *Persons with AIDS receiving hospice services: Variables related to client satisfaction and generalized contentment*. Unpublished doctoral dissertation, Florida International University.

Kriedler, M. C., Campbell, J., Lanik, G., Gray, R., & Conrad, M. A. (1994). Community elderly: A nursing center's use of change theory as a model. *Journal of Gerontological Nursing*, 20(1), 25–30.

Lawton, M. P., VanHaitsma, K., & Klapper, J. (1996). Observed affect in nursing home residents with Alzheimer's disease. *Journals of Gerontology. Series B, Psychological Sciences & Social Sciences*, 51(1), P3–P14.

Lerner, M. J., & Gignac, M. A. M. (1992). Is it coping or is it growth? A cognitive-affective model of contentment in the elderly. In L. Montada, F. Sigrun-Heide, & M. J. Lerner (Eds.), *Life crises and experiences of loss in adulthood* (pp. 321–337). Hillsdale, NJ: Erlbaum.

Lindgren, A. M., Svardsudd, H., & Tibblin, G. (1994). Factors related to perceived health among elderly people: The Albertina project. *Age and Ageing*, 23, 328–333.

Lloyd-Cobb, P., & Dixon, D. R. (1995). A preliminary evaluation of the effects of a veteran's hospital domiciliary program for homeless persons. *Research on Social Work Practice*, 5, 309–316.

Markides, K. S., & Martin, H. W. (1979). A causal model of life satisfaction among the elderly. *Journal of Gerontology*, 34, 86–93.

McKoy, Y. D. (1996). An examination of marital stress, sexual satisfaction, marital satisfaction, and quality of life of myocardial infarction patients. *Dissertation Abstracts International*, 57(04A), 1633. (University Microfilms No. AAI9625986)

Meyers, D., & Diener, E. (1995). Who is happy? *Psychological Science*, 6, 10–19.

Moroi, K. (1990). Perceptions of equity and sex-role attitudes in married couples. *Japanese Journal of Family Psychology*, 4, 109–120.

Nilsson, M., Ekman, S. L., Ericsson, K., & Winblad, B. (1996). Some characteristics of the quality of life in old age illustrated by means of Allardt's concept. *Scandinavian Journal of Caring Sciences*, 10(2), 116–121.

Nystrom, A., & Andersson-Segesten, M. (1990). Peace of mind as an important aspect of old people's health. *European Journal of Caring Sciences*, 4, 55–62.

Pardeck, J. T., & Chung, W. S. (1995). An empirical analysis of the psychosocial well-being of undergraduate students majoring in social work. *Family Therapy*, 22 (2), 121–124.

Parse, R. R. (1981). *Man-living-health: A theory of nursing*. New York: Wiley.

Parse, R. R. (1987). *Nursing science: Major paradigms, theories, and critiques*. Philadelphia: Saunders.

Parse, R. R. (1990). Health: A personal commitment. *Nursing Science Quarterly*, 3, 136–140.

Parse, R. R. (1992). Human becoming: Parse's theory of nursing. *Nursing Science Quarterly*, 5, 35–42.

Parse, R. R. (1993). The experience of laughter: A phenomenological study. *Nursing Science Quarterly*, 6, 39–43.

Parse, R. R. (1994a). Laughing and health: A study using Parse's research method. *Nursing Science Quarterly*, 7, 55–64.

Parse, R. R. (1994b). Quality of life: Sciencing and living the art of human becoming. *Nursing Science Quarterly*, 7, 16–21.

Parse, R. R. (Ed.). (1995). *Illuminations: The human becoming theory in practice and research*. New York: National League for Nursing Press.

Parse, R. R. (1996). Quality of life for persons living with Alzheimer's disease: The human becoming perspective. *Nursing Science Quarterly*, 9, 126–133.

Parse, R. R. (1997a). The human becoming theory: The was, is, and will be. *Nursing Science Quarterly*, 10, 32–38.

Parse, R. R. (1997b). Joy-sorrow: A study using the Parse research method. *Nursing Science Quarterly*, 10, 80–87.

Parse, R. R. (1998). *The human becoming school of thought: A perspective for nurses and other health professionals*. Thousand Oaks, CA: Sage.

Parse, R. R., Coyne, A. B., & Smith, M. J. (1985). *Nursing research: Qualitative methods*. Bowie, MD: Brady.

Pearsall, J., & Trumble, B. (1995). *The Oxford English reference dictionary*. New York: Oxford University Press.

Schmotkin, D., & Hadari, G. (1996). An outlook on subjective well-being in older Israeli adults: A unified formulation. *International Journal of Aging & Human Development*, 42, 271–289.

Takahashi, T. (1999). Kibou: Hope for persons in Japan. In R. R. Parse, *Hope: An international human becoming perspective* (pp. 115–128). Sudbury, MA: Jones and Bartlett.

Tkachuk, B. P. (1995). Toward the development of a quality of life instrument for the chronically mentally ill. *Dissertation Abstracts International*, 34(02), 896.

Toikkanen, T., & Muurinen, E. (1999). Toivo: Hope for persons in Finland. In R. R. Parse, *Hope: An international human becoming perspective* (pp. 79–96). Sudbury, MA: Jones and Bartlett.

Young, C. (1993). Spirituality and the chronically ill Christian elderly. *Geriatric Nursing*, 14, 298–303.

CHAPTER 19

"MENDACITY" AS THE REFUSAL TO BEAR WITNESS

A HUMAN BECOMING HERMENEUTIC STUDY OF A THEME FROM TENNESSEE WILLIAMS' *CAT ON A HOT TIN ROOF*

William K. Cody, RN; PhD

Bearing witness to one another's experiences, our triumphs and tragedies, and our fundamental humanity, is one of the basic, central processes of human-to-human relating. To be fully present with another—to acknowledge the authenticity of her or his experience, to demonstrate respect for the truth of her or his life—forms the basis of friendship, camaraderie, affectionate partnerships, and lasting familial commitments. Bearing witness is at the foundation of all relationships grounded in mutual respect and all those in which one construes right action as demonstrating respect and honor for the achievement, talents, generosity, vulnerability, or, indeed, the simple human dignity of another. Bearing witness happens face to face in moment-to-moment living, but it also takes multidimensional forms and expressions, including established and emerging rituals, spontaneous and formal testimonies, documentation in public records and literature, and innumerable other permutations of attentive and lingering presence offered and experienced in an infinite variety of human situations (Parse, 1998).

Although many authors have written of this fundamental process of human life, there remain endless dimensions of meaning to be explored in the ways in which persons bear witness to the realities of one another's lives. Sartre (1943/1966) wrote about the relationship between the self and the other as innervated and shaped by "the look," the regard for one person that another demonstrates through the many connotations of the actual human gaze. Though his philosophy has been called solipsistic, he devoted roughly a third of *Being and Nothingness* to the relationship between the individual and others, of which "the look" is emblematic. Buber (1923/1958) wrote of the differences between the "I-It" relation, which is a relationship between an individual and an object, and the "I-Thou" relation, which is a relationship between an individual and a venerated being. Only in the latter does the human bear witness to the humanity of the other and thereby to her or his own humanity as well. Parse (1981, 1998) discusses bearing witness primarily in relation to *true presence*, which is the living of the human becoming theory in service to people. Parse describes bearing witness in this context as an interpersonal art, "an intentional reflective love," and "a free-flowing attentiveness" (1998, p. 71). She says

> Witnessing is beholding, an attending to with unconditional presence. It is a *dwelling with* incarnating availability. Witnessing is a non-intrusive gentle glimpsing in reaching beyond to honor the other as human dignity. The gentle glimpsing is a non-judgmental gaze embracing the other as a unique cocreation. Embracing is an unadorned intending acknowledging the significance of the other's choices; it is a standing with during a journey. Witnessing is living true presence. (Parse, 1999, p. 1)

Few authors have attempted to describe the phenomenon that in this chapter I will call *the refusal to bear witness*. It was Tennessee Williams who called my attention to the importance of the refusal to bear witness in the famous yet little-discussed theme of *mendacity* in his play *Cat on a Hot Tin Roof*. In this work, Williams examines myriad facets of what he calls mendacity throughout almost every page of the work. According to Williams, mendacity in everyday life is so pervasive and the consequences of its pervasiveness so tragic—mendacity is so insidiously and unavoidably threaded through every interpersonal encounter—that it leaves us profoundly challenged as to how to identify something like "truth" in our multidimensional interpersonal relating. As the character Brick says, "Mendacity is a system we live in" (Williams, 1955, p. 94).

THE HERMENEUTIC SITUATION FOR THE STUDY

Tennessee Williams is widely considered to be one of the preeminent playwrights of the 20th century. His plays, most of which richly exploit his Southern heritage in characterization and language, are known for their passion and endless layers of meaning. *Cat on a Hot Tin Roof* was written in the early 1950s and first performed publicly in 1954. In 1955, "*Cat*" opened on Broadway, it had a much celebrated run, and Tennessee Williams received both the Drama Critics' Award and the Pulitzer Prize for the play. Subsequently, the play was made into a successful Hollywood movie, which popularized some of the more memorable lines, including the scathing references to "mendacity."

The action in *"Cat"* (the original play) unfolds in one bedroom in a Mississippi delta plantation mansion, in real time, on a hot summer evening. All six major characters are members of an extended family, the patriarch of which is Big Daddy, who has been ill for some time. Big Daddy finally has been diagnosed with terminal cancer, while at the same time being told by those around him that he is cancer-free (as was the custom in the 1950s). The action of the play takes place on the evening of his birthday, and the family is gathered for that occasion. Big Daddy's wife, Big Mama, dotes on her husband, although he can barely conceal his contempt for her, a contempt that has festered for decades. The younger of their two sons, Brick, and his wife, Margaret ("Maggie the Cat"), are the focal point of much of the action and dialogue in the play, inasmuch as Brick is Big Daddy's favorite, although he is alcoholic and the second-born son, and his wife remains childless. Competing with Brick and Maggie for the favor and the estate of Big Daddy are Brick's older brother, Gooper, and his wife, Mae, who boast frequently about the five grandchildren (and one on the way) they have given Big Daddy.

Brick spends much of the play doggedly pursuing the numbing effect of alcohol and is thus somewhat removed, attitudinally, from this competition. Feeling it more keenly is his wife, Maggie, who appears initially, and very dramatically, as a truth-teller, insisting on the truth again and again as others attempt to cover it up. Maggie fears that Brick and she will receive no inheritance because of their childlessness. In this connection, it is revealed in the first few minutes of the play that Brick has refused to sleep with Maggie for some time, and there is great tension between them.

The tension arises in relation to Brick's former close friendship with his life-long pal and sports buddy, Skipper, who died some months before, prompting Brick to start drinking. As the story of Brick and Skipper's relationship and the way it was regarded by others is gradually revealed through Acts I and II of the play, it is made clear that Skipper was probably homosexual and was certainly in love with Brick. Although Brick profoundly bonded with Skipper in a way he considered almost sacred, and although people, including his father, thought he and Skipper were sexually involved, Brick could not reciprocate Skipper's affection. On Skipper's desperate telephone confession to Brick that he was gay and in love with him, Brick hung up, and that was the last time they spoke in life. It is implied that Skipper essentially committed suicide in the wake of his devastation over Brick's rejection. Act III shifts the focus to the question of the inheritance of Big Daddy's estate and pivots decisively on a calculated lie told, surprisingly, by Maggie. Every character has those aspects of his or her life to which they themselves and others do or do not bear witness, and all interact by bearing witness or refusing to bear witness throughout the play. The layers of truth, untruth, and half-truth, and one person's truth that is another person's lie, permeate the play from beginning to end.

The researcher is, like Williams, an American Southerner, so that many of the connotations and speech patterns reflected in the text are familiar to him. The year of the play's opening on Broadway was, coincidentally, the year of the researcher's birth. There is a specific significance to the different eras (the 1950s and the present) in that there is a theme of repressed homosexuality in the play, which would be somewhat, but not completely, anachronistic were the play produced today. The researcher also happens to be gay, with a gay man's unique vantage on the dynamics of concealing one's sexuality, "coming out," and other experiences common to gay people. Of overarching importance to the study is that the researcher is a nurse, grounded in the human becoming school of thought who seeks primarily to generate new knowledge for the discipline of nursing from a nursing perspective. Specifically, the perspective on the human-universe-health process is the human becoming school of thought.

NURSING PERSPECTIVE: THE HUMAN BECOMING SCHOOL OF THOUGHT AS THE HORIZON OF INQUIRY

Inasmuch as the human becoming school of thought (Parse, 1981, 1998) is described in chapter 17 of the present volume, only a brief explication of human becoming as the horizon of inquiry will be offered here. That the horizon of inquiry for the study is Parse's human becoming school of thought means that the researcher's understanding of what it is to be human and the meaning and significance of human experience is expressed in the body of work emanating from the human becoming theory. The researcher lives and works in this tradition and, therefore, seeks to reach an understanding of mendacity as the refusal to bear witness from this perspective. The human becoming theory as a horizon of inquiry is set forth in detail by Cody (1995) in the first human becoming hermeneutic study.

This belief system specifies that reality is cocreated as persons structure meaning from many realms of the universe in a nonlinear, acausal process that arises with human coexistence as self-interpreting yet interrelated agents who freely choose meaning and direction in life. Life is lived in patterns that ebb and flow with the opportunities and limitations found in being with and apart from others while disclosing and not disclosing aspects of self. All persons continuously propel themselves beyond the now moment with what is not-yet by choosing innovative ways of viewing themselves and their universe and carving out unique pathways for living. Bearing witness to one another's lived realities as we cocreate families and communities is an intrinsic element in this ontology. It is from this perspective that a new understanding of mendacity as the refusal to bear witness was sought. It is worth noting, however, that, as Gadamer (1960/1975) contends, a horizon of inquiry is *always open*, in that human life itself is experienced in such a fluid, paradoxical, and unpredictable way that one is never completely bound to any one standpoint.

SIGNIFICANCE FOR NURSING SCIENCE

The significance of this study for nursing science resides in its potential to enhance understanding of the refusal to bear witness, as experienced by those who choose this attitude and by those who suffer from the refusal. Bearing witness is a universal humanly lived experience. Choosing with whom to bear witness, how, when, to what extent, and for what reason is at the very crux of human coexistence. Absent a willingness to bear witness, both full-fledged family relations and genuine caregiving are ultimately impossible, though it is clear that efforts are not uncommonly made under precisely those conditions. The refusal to bear witness, although perhaps unavoidable at times, can be tragic; it can change lives irreversibly; it can eliminate (or create) possibilities; and it can diminish (or enhance) quality of life. It is toward an understanding of this important yet understudied phenomenon of interpersonal relating that this study aims.

METHODOLOGY

This study unfolded with the rhythms of the human becoming hermeneutic method as originated by Cody (1995), further specified by Parse (1998), and described in Chapter 17. The processes of the method are *discoursing with penetrating engaging, interpreting with quiescent beholding,* and *understanding with inspiring envisaging.* The researcher was moved to pursue the conceptualization of mendacity as the refusal to bear witness after having seen the film version of *Cat on a Hot Tin Roof* a number of times and having dwelled with the concept of *bearing witness* in previous empirical studies and in nursing practice with persons, families, and groups. No permission for the study was necessary, since both the play and the film version of *Cat on a Hot Tin Roof* are in the public domain.

As the crucial importance of bearing witness became clear, arising simultaneously was the question of the meaning and significance of *not* bearing witness, the neglect to do so, the ignorance of the need to do so, and ultimately the refusal to do so. The researcher's perspective, which includes a deeply held belief that persons freely choose meaning and direction from many realms of the universe all-at-once, led him to focus on *the refusal to bear witness* as the phenomenon of central concern. The treatment of mendacity in *Cat on a Hot Tin Roof*, an artistic "expression of life" (Dilthey, 1883/1988), emerged as an opportunity for discoursing with the intent of understanding mendacity as the refusal to bear witness. On examination, the exploration of the theme of mendacity in *Cat* can be seen to be remarkably extensive, with repeating patterns and rhythms and subtle variations throughout.

Interpreting occurred over a period of years in which the play was read a number of times, in whole and in part, and the film was viewed (on video) in whole and in part several times as well. This process was indeed, as Parse describes it, "a disciplined drifting with the rational-intuitive ebb and flow through the labyrinths of meanings in the researcher-text . . . dialogue" (p. 172, this volume). The researcher wished to apprehend the denotations and connotations of the play's text for the intended (1950s) audience and to appreciate the theme of mendacity as deliberately developed by Williams, yet also to dwell closely with the notion of mendacity as the refusal to bear witness. In successive readings, rich new meanings of the text emerged in a variety of rational-intuitive moments lived by the researcher.

Understanding as described by Parse happens with inspiring envisaging. It is coconstituting a unique vision with the text, enriching the researcher's explicit-tacit knowing of the phenomenon under study. It is this new knowledge that the researcher seeks to share in this chapter.

FINDINGS[1]

Although almost all the direct talk of "mendacity" is confined to one long scene between Big Daddy and Brick, the refusal or neglect to bear witness is evident from the very first action. Maggie enters the bedroom while Brick is showering just offstage (beyond an open door). She calls to Brick, and he answers, in only the second line of the play, "Wha'd you say, Maggie? Water was on s' loud I couldn't hearya . . ." (p. 15). One page later, Maggie says of her greedy in-laws, "It's so obvious what they're up to!" and Brick replies, "What are they up to, Maggie?" to which she in turn responds, "Why, you know what they're up to!" Brick then says, "No, I don't know what they're up to" (pp. 16–17). Less than one page later, Maggie introduces the topic of Big Daddy having cancer, in a phrase that goes, ". . . Now we know Big Daddy's dyin' of—*cancer.*" And Brick interjects, "Do we?" (p. 17). Shortly, after a "swift flood" of words from Maggie—more than 200 words, actually—delivered in an obvious flurry of emotion, Brick responds, "Did you *say* something, Maggie?" (p. 18). This series of exchanges offers many examples of one person being either unable or unwilling to bear witness to what is being held forth (or held back) by the other. From a human becoming perspective, these interactions strongly reflect the paradoxical rhythms of speaking–being silent and moving–being still, revealing-concealing, and connecting-separating. One person's self-expression, explicitly and implicitly evincing shared and unshared values, encounters the self-expression of the other, also explicitly and implicitly evincing shared and unshared values. What is not said, and what is not heard, is coconstitutive of the situation just as what is stated and what is heard are.

---

[1]All citations in the Findings section refer to the Signet edition as represented in the reference list. Italics are preserved from the original. Quotations from Act III are from the second version of Act III (New York performance version) in the Signet edition, since this was believed by Williams at the time of publication to be an improvement on his original.

Later in the first act, as Maggie and Brick are having a one-sided conversation (Maggie doing most of the talking), Maggie "catches sight of him in the mirror, gasps slightly, wheels about to face him," and there is a long pause before she finally asks, "Why are you looking at me like that?" To this Brick replies, "I wasn't conscious of lookin' at you, Maggie" (p. 22). She then says, "Well, I was conscious of it! What were you thinkin'?" And Brick says, "I don't remember thinking anything, Maggie" (p. 22). During a long soliloquy in which Maggie laments how lonely she is and how much she loves Brick and wishes he loved her, while Brick is plainly doing his best to ignore her, Maggie says

> Oh, excuse me, forgive me, but laws of silence don't work! No, laws of silence don't work. . . . Laws of silence don't work. . . . When something is festering in your memory or your imagination, laws of silence don't work, it's just like shutting a door and locking it on a house on fire in hope of forgetting that the house is burning. But not facing a fire doesn't put it out. Silence about a thing just magnifies it. It grows and festers in silence, becomes malignant. (p. 25)

It is no stretch of the imagination to consider this speech as an indictment of Brick for the refusal to bear witness to Maggie's reality as well as his own. From a human becoming perspective, what is languaged with self and others contributes to the structuring of meaning that is cocreating reality. What one languages expresses one's value priorities in one way or another. When the value priorities languaged are not acknowledged, not heard, or not respected, one experiences a sense of the diminution of one's presence as experienced and acknowledged by the other. When the value priorities languaged by another *negate* or *cancel* the value priorities one is languaging, one's being/becoming as *who one is* is threatened. In this sense, seeking to enforce "laws of silence" is a form of a refusal to bear witness that undermines quality of life. In this case, Maggie rejects and refutes "laws of silence." Indeed, she goes on to forcefully breach the silence, affirming her right to be (and express herself as) who she is.

In a later scene, Brick and Maggie discuss Big Daddy's cancer. Brick says, "Big Mama just said he *wasn't* [dying of cancer], that the report was okay." To this, Maggie replies

> That's what she thinks because she got the same story that they gave Big Daddy. And was just as taken in by it as he was, poor ole things. . . . But tonight they're going to tell her the truth about it. When Big Daddy goes to bed, they're going to tell her that he is dying of cancer. [*She slams the dresser drawer.*] — It's malignant and it's terminal.

Brick asks, "Does Big Daddy know it?" And Maggie answers, "Hell, do they *ever* know it? Nobody says, 'You're dying.' You have to fool them. They have to fool *themselves*" (p. 40). This scene reflects one of the "norms" of healthcare culture of the 1950s—not informing persons dying of cancer of their true diagnosis. This was a withholding of information, a misguided attempt to enhance quality of life by not allowing the person to see her- or himself as dying. As such, the practice reflected a certain use of professional privilege and power. It is important to remember even now that the power of professional privilege can, at times, be reality-shaping. The refusal to bear witness to the truth of a person's life is equally as dishonest, a breach of professional ethics, as deliberately withholding specific information, as seen in the play.

The power of silence is again explored in a later scene when Maggie tries to broach the subject of Skipper. Maggie also happens to be discussing truth-telling, which, she says, was in this instance a mistake. Maggie says, "I've thought a whole lot about it and now I know when I made my mistake. Yes, I made my mistake when I told you the truth about that thing with Skipper. Never should have confessed it, a fatal error, tellin' you about that thing with Skipper." And Brick's reply could not be more direct: "Maggie, shut up about Skipper. I mean it, Maggie; you got to shut up about Skipper" (p. 43). Here Maggie is referring to her confession of having slept with Skipper, at his behest, to prove that he was not homosexual—which didn't succeed. It is not so much the fact that Maggie and Skipper slept together as the context—the desperate attempt of Skipper (with whom Brick is more sympathetic) to disavow his homosexuality—that disturbs Brick. Bearing witness to one thing may mean bearing witness to another thing even more difficult to face than that which has been ostensibly avoided. Williams masterfully explores the varied lies, truths, innuendoes, enforced silences, shallow conventions, half-truths, and shocking proclamations that make up day-to-day life.

In a later scene, Maggie describes a time when she confronted Skipper about his relationship with Brick. "In this way I destroyed him, by telling him truth that he and his world which he was born and raised in, your and his world, had told him could not be told." Later in the same stretch of dialogue, she says, "I'm not tryin' to whitewash my behavior, Christ, no! Brick, I'm not good. I don't know why people have to pretend to be good, nobody's good. The rich or the well-to-do can afford to respect moral patterns, conventional moral patterns, but I could never afford to, yeah, but—I'm honest! Give me credit for just that, will you *please*?"(p. 45). Here the notion of bearing witness to what *is*, for Maggie, is even seen to outweigh *goodness*. Of course, to what end are "conventional moral patterns" in a world in which it is so rare to bear witness to the truth?

In the focal scene involving mendacity, Big Daddy is trying to find out why his favorite son has become an alcoholic. It has been apparent throughout the play that Brick is seeking to anesthetize himself with alcohol for some intensely personal reason. After much bullying from Big Daddy, Brick relents only enough to reveal that he drinks because of "disgust." When Big Daddy refuses to be quiet or let him go until Brick tells him disgust with *what*, Brick finally introduces the topic with the line, "You ever heard the word 'mendacity'?" His father answers yes, and Brick asks, "You know what it means?" To this Big Daddy replies, "Don't it mean lying and liars?" and a moment later he demands, "Who's been lying to you, and what about?" Brick says, "No one single person and no one lie. . . . The whole, the whole—thing . . ." (p. 80).

At this point, Big Daddy furiously launches into a tirade:

> I could write a book on it! . . . Think of all the lies I got to put up with!—
> Pretenses! Ain't that mendacity? Having to pretend stuff you don't
> think or feel or have any idea of? Having for instance to act like I care
> for Big Mama!—I haven't been able to stand the sight, sound, or smell
> of that woman for forty years now! . . . Pretend to love that son of a
> bitch of a Gooper and his wife Mae . . . Jesus! Can't stand to look at
> 'em! Church!—it bores the Bejesus out of me but I go! . . . Clubs!—
> Elks! Masons! Rotary!—*crap*! . . . I've lived with mendacity! Why can't
> *you* live with it? Hell, you *got* to live with it, there's nothing *else* to *live*
> with except mendacity, is there? (pp. 80–81)

Cat is generally seen as a tragedy, even though there is only one death, months previously, of a character never seen in the play, and the impending death of Big Daddy, who is elderly, wealthy, and accomplished. The real tragedy in the play is the astonishing array of denial, negation, pretense, enforced silence, shallow conventions, and half-truths that seemingly permeates the characters' whole lives—and by extension, characterizes life itself. Williams wrote, in an unusually wordy stage direction:

> *The bird that I hope to catch in the net of this play is not the solution of one man's
> psychological problem. I'm trying to catch the true quality of experience in a group of
> people, that cloudy, flickering, evanescent—fiercely charged!—interplay of live hu-
> man beings in the thundercloud of a common crisis. Some mystery should be left in
> the revelation of character in a play, just as a great deal of mystery is always left in
> the revelation of character in life, even in one's own character to himself.* (p. 85)

Parse would concur with this characterization of mystery in life, which is highly consistent with the human becoming school of thought. In knowing, there is always the unnamable that resides in the tacit dimension. In telling, one can never disclose all there is to know about oneself, yet even in silent stillness a very great deal may become known. In choosing a path in life, much is always uncertain and outcomes can never be fully known in advance. Exploration of the notion of mendacity as the refusal to bear witness projects a faint ray of light into the darkest recesses of everyday living. Bearing witness is an intersubjective process that says, at a minimum, "What is real for you *matters* to me." Bearing witness in many forms (testimony, publication, and so forth) is an expression of a commitment to stand for the truth as one understands it. It also can be seen as the most respectful response to existential aloneness, the sense that ultimate meaning in life is uniquely personal, that one goes through the greatest crises and transitions of life profoundly alone in the realm of deepest personal meaning. Although one cannot by definition "be there" with another in regard to existential aloneness, one can certainly bear witness to her or his experience if it is made evident. The refusal to bear witness, in a very real sense, then, emerges as an abandonment of the other, a negation of her or his value, and an assertion of some greater priority than acknowledging or standing for the truth of the other's experience.

In the climactic scene between Brick and Big Daddy, the "truth" about Skipper is revealed at last. Or at least enough has been said—from several different viewpoints—that the audience becomes aware of several competing contentions that converge on some intersubjective agreements. Brick finally has revealed his version of events, at least as much as he wants to, concluding with the ill-fated tryst between Maggie and Skipper, which Skipper undertook to prove he wasn't gay but which ended disastrously. Big Daddy, a street-smart and worldly man, insists that there has to be more to the story, asserting, "Something's left out of that story. What did you leave out?" A fortuitous phone ringing reminds Brick: "Yes!—I left out a long-distance call which I had from Skipper, in which he made a drunken confession to me and on which I hung up!—last time we spoke to each other in our lives . . ." (p. 92).

Thus it is revealed that Brick—heretofore ostensibly outraged by the others' belief that Skipper and he were lovers, perhaps wanting to believe it was they who destroyed his friend—actually rejected Skipper himself on the occasion of Skipper's confession to him. He refused to hear or to bear witness to this painful truth that was tormenting Skipper: He was in love with Brick. Big Daddy responds assertively to this crucial revelation. He cries out

> Anyhow now!—we have tracked down the lie with which you're disgusted and which you are drinking to kill your disgust with, Brick. You been passing the buck. This disgust with mendacity is disgust with yourself. You!—dug the grave of your friend and kicked him in it!—before you'd face truth with him! (p. 92)

Brick cries out in response, "His truth, not *mine*!" to which Big Daddy replies knowingly, "His truth, okay! But you wouldn't face it with him!" Brick counterpunches, "Who *can* face the truth? Can *you*?" (p. 92). And at this point, Brick reveals to Big Daddy in short order that he (Big Daddy) does have cancer and he is dying. Big Daddy is extremely shocked and the pace of the scene slows from rage to pathos. Big Daddy seems almost equally shocked that he is dying and that all those around him have methodically lied to him. Brick exits, then reenters and says

> I'm sorry, Big Daddy. My head don't work any more and it's hard for me to understand how anybody could care if he lived or died . . . or cared about anything but whether or not there was liquor left in the bottle and so I said what I said without thinking. In some ways I'm no better than the others, in some ways worse because I'm less alive. Maybe it's being alive that makes them lie, and being almost *not* alive that makes me sort of accidentally truthful—I don't know but—anyway—we've been friends. . . .—and being friends is telling each other the truth. . . . [*There is a pause.*] You told *me*! I told *you*! (pp. 94–95)

Here, then, condensed into one remarkably complex and passionate scene, are two instances of bearing witness arising from prior refusals to bear witness. All dimensions of the interactions (the reluctant truth-tellings and the prior refusals) are shot through with suffering and confusion on the parts of all those involved. This chaotic anguish characterizes the experience of the refusal to bear witness, for both the refuser and the one who suffers the refusal. Clearly, as shown eloquently by Williams, the essence of crucial relationships in one's life may turn on the willingness or unwillingness to bear witness. To have one's truth witnessed by others is all-at-once as vital for living as who one is, yet also potentially devastating.

The trajectories of the plot lines in *Cat on a Hot Tin Roof*, through to the last four or five pages, seem to suggest that mendacity is harmful and exceedingly undesirable. Ironically, however, one key plotline is resolved sympathetically in favor of Maggie and Brick by a crucial and well-timed *lie* told by Maggie—the truth-teller!—that she is pregnant by Brick, thereby ensuring Brick's inheritance (as well as hers and their as-yet-unconceived child's). In response to this unexpected announcement, Big Daddy assesses his daughter-in-law's appearance and pronounces, "*Uh-huh, this girl has life in her body, that's no lie!*" (p. 153). Gooper and Mae, however, having eavesdropped to learn of Brick's conjugal rejection of Maggie, attack the two of them, calling the lie. Brick responds, "You heard what Big Daddy said. This girl has life in her body" (p. 156). Mae cries out, "That is a lie!" To this Brick says calmly

> No, truth is something desperate, an' she's got it. Believe me, it's somethin' desperate, an' she's got it. . . . An' now if you will stop actin' as if Brick Pollitt was dead an' buried, invisible, not heard, an go on back to your peep-hole in the wall—I'm drunk, and sleepy—not as alive as Maggie, but still alive. (p. 156)

In addition to adding the concluding ironic touch of triumph through a form of mendacity, Williams seems to want to link the essence of *truth* with the essence of *life* here in a radical way, having little to do with "objective" truth or "biological" life. By implication, then, bearing witness can be seen as life-affirming. What would be the usefulness of a concept of truth in human affairs that was not life-affirming? Bearing witness to another's professed (or confessed) experiences and truths is bearing witness to the person's "living of value priorities" (Parse, 1998, p. 71). "It is being with the rhythms of the sounds *and silences* [italics added], the visions *and blindnesses* [italics added] of the human-universe process" (p. 71). It does not require an element of objective truth, nor does it necessarily require a precise understanding of the details of the person's experience. What it requires is respect and attention, a nonjudgmental regard and unconditional love rooted in a profound respect for human dignity.

The meaning of mendacity, then, as the refusal to bear witness, is a turning-away-from. It is a *not*-being-with that devalues the other by devaluing that which is dismissed as not real or unimportant. It is an unloving, judgmental way of being/becoming (with regard to those who suffer the refusal) that serves to alienate others and engender mistrust. This is not to say that the refusal to bear witness is not at times necessary, honorable, or even, in the broadest sense, inevitable. One may refuse to bear witness with a deep intention of beneficence, as when a spouse refuses to testify in court against her or his partner. (However, if the partner has participated in harming another person, certainly such a refusal to bear witness is unloving and devaluing toward that person.) The refusal to bear witness surfaces in many ways in everyday lived experience as the permutations of this universal human lived experience multiply with the complexity of human relations. Perhaps it is instructive to recall how Williams (1955) characterized his goal in this play, as thoroughly inundated with examples of mendacity and the refusal to bear witness as it is. His goal was to portray *"the true quality of experience in a group of people, that cloudy, flickering, evanescent—fiercely charged!—interplay of live human beings in the thundercloud of a common crisis"* (p. 85).

DISCUSSION

The refusal to bear witness surfaces when we believe we cannot bear witness to our own reality with those around us. It surfaces when we demur from bearing witness to the reality of others around us. This is similar to what Irving Goffman (1959) writes about in *The Presentation of Self in Everyday Life*. People live frontstage realities and backstage realities. Unfortunately, the frontstage reality—which is artificial and may serve to hide important truths—is often the face that professionals put on for the public. As previously stated, this is not to say that the refusal to bear witness may not be necessary, honorable, or inevitable in situations, but even these considerations *do not* mitigate against the fact that the refusal to bear witness *is* an unloving, judgmental way of being/becoming that serves to alienate others and engender mistrust. If this is not the face that professionals, or a profession, wish to present to the public they serve, it would behoove them to consider ways of more closely and meaningfully attending to the lived realities of the people they serve.

Perhaps the apparent pervasiveness of mendacity and the refusal to bear witness is linked to what Edward T. Hall (1973) calls the illusiveness of "isolates," the meaningful units of experienced social life that specific words and categories are created to represent. Hall contends that these entities, which, as part of the fabric of social life, exist *to be perceived*, are paradoxically so mercurial as to be instantly fragmented almost beyond recognition by the very act of inspection. Just holding onto that to which one might be willing to bear witness may be beyond one's capacity. As we are with multiple persons in day-to-day living, that to which one may wish to bear witness may fall apart before one's gaze in kaleidoscopic fashion, while all-at-once other "isolates" emerge unbeckoned, multiplying possibilities and undermining what sense of certainty one may have had.

In recent years, many authors have appropriated the concept of *bearing witness* in relation to specific causes. Some have sought to document the atrocities committed by the Nazis in the 1930s and 1940s and the suffering experienced by Jewish persons and others against whom were carried out the atrocities. For example, Schindler, Spiegel, and Malachi (1992) state plainly, "The need to share with others becomes urgent; to bear witness is vital" (p. 243). Wiesel (1970) discusses the foibles of taking too straightforward a tack on bearing witness: "[The Holocaust survivors] were afraid of saying what must now be said, of attempting to communicate with language what eludes language, of falling into traps of half truths. The truer the tale the more factitious it appears" (p. 16). Laub and Auerhahn (1989) discuss how the perpetrators of the atrocities inflicted on Holocaust survivors so blatantly denied the humanity of those against whom the atrocities were committed that they destroyed their "representational matrix of interpersonal relatedness," resulting in "vulnerability and loneliness . . . which is the sine qua non of man-made trauma" (p. 377).

Some nurse scholars have discussed nurses bearing witness to the suffering of their clients. Apart from the human becoming literature, which includes bearing witness as a prescribed component of "true presence" (Parse, 1998), the meaning of bearing witness and the meaning of the nurse's presence with the client are considered separately. For example, in Kahn and Steeves' (1994) article, based on interviews with 26 nurses, the genuinely beneficent, effective quality of the presence of the nurses with their clients is assumed and is given no particular or special characterization. The nurses were asked "what suffering, caring, and coping meant to them within the context of their clinical practices" (p. 261). Witnessing suffering, among the nurses, is compared in general to the experiences of "witnesses to natural and other kinds of disasters" (p. 263) in that "they seem to need to speak about what they have seen and usually do so readily" (p. 263). The authors conclude that "a witness is a special kind of moral agent, one with an obligation to speak out about that which is witnessed" (p. 263), and frame four ways in which this obligation is carried out—in firsthand observation, in a ceremonial role, in serving as expert witness, and in bearing witness as "visionary" to "testify to one's faith in a collective vision of the future" (p. 264).

The pandemic human immunodeficiency virus (HIV), which has been a central feature in the lives of several broadly defined communities (gay men, African Americans, Hispanics and Latinos, injection drug users, sex workers) in the 1980s and 1990s, has prompted a growing body of literature on aspects of bearing witness (Chambre, 1988; Garfield, 1995; Kayal, 1993; Verghese, 1994). "AIDS is such a shattering human event," writes Kayal (1993), "that it is only possible to capture its horror in a direct face-to-face encounter—by living in a relationship with a PWA" (p. xv). The theological concept of bearing witness, she writes, "is quite appropriate to an analysis of gay/AIDS volunteerism. In its basic form, bearing witness means taking on the cross or the suffering of others as if it were one's own" (p. xviii).

Garfield (1995) provides numerous examples of the (multidisciplinary) practice widely discussed as being "fully present" that seems to have evolved organically with the growth in human understanding emanating from the complexities of the HIV pandemic. He quotes one caregiver as saying

> The first word that comes to my mind when I think of being with people who are in the dying process is the word "witness." I've always had this very strong feeling that as we suffer we need a witness—there has to be someone there who really sees how we suffer, and how much we suffer. (p. 195)

Caregiver "Micaela" concurs and adds, on the subject of having someone bear witness to her own experience, "If you're going to be in my life, you're going to have to deal with the intensity. I'm not going to talk to you about trivia" (p. 273).

The concept of bearing witness has been central in other discourses as well. For example, Price (1989), a renowned community psychologist, urges readers to take sides, to bear witness, and to tell the truth. Taking sides means deciding *whose* views to represent: for professionals, if not the people we serve, then whose? Bearing witness involves speaking out, and telling the truth means telling the truth "about what we do not know as well as what we do" (p. 162).

Glassman (1994) proposes that bearing witness to "the wholeness of life" is the essential core of the spiritual practice of Zen peacemaking, which he characterizes as follows:

> When we really listen, when we really pay attention to the sounds of joy and suffering in the universe, then we are not separate from them, we become them. Because in reality we are not separate from those who suffer. We are them; they are us. It is our suffering, and it is our joy. When we don't listen, we are shutting ourselves off—not from others but from ourselves.
>
> We can't do any of this from a place of knowing. When we think we know something, we don't listen. We have to empty ourselves over and over, return to unknowing, and just listen. And listen. And listen. (p. 78)

EMERGENT MEANINGS

Emergent meanings surfaced while living the human becoming hermeneutic method in studying Tennessee Williams' *Cat on a Hot Tin Roof*. The processes of *discoursing with penetrating engaging, interpreting with quiescent beholding,* and *understanding with inspiring envisaging* were effective in bringing to light the meaning of the universal lived experience *mendacity as the refusal to bear witness*. The new knowledge about this humanly lived experience is reflected in the emergent meanings discussed here.

Mendacity and the refusal to bear witness stand as obstacles to genuine human-to-human relating, to caring ways in both personal and professional dimensions, and to the expansion of one's own possibilities, knowledge of self, and quality of life. As such, the refusal to bear witness represents an impediment to many highly valuable human services. The refusal to bear witness surfaces in working with sexual and relationship issues, as professionals refuse to bear witness to the variety of human sexual experiences (which may be positive and contribute to quality of life) or to the interpersonal crimes that occur in families, for example, the rape and abuse of women and children carried out predominantly by known intimates and family members. The refusal to bear witness surfaces also as the refusal to acknowledge the reality of the lives of poverty and degradation that many citizens lead. It surfaces when we see healthcare and education policies, methods, and standards that really are not working for the good of people, yet, because powerful vested interests claim that objective science and "the bottom line" support continuation of these ways, we allow the status quo to persist to the detriment of people. The refusal to bear witness, then—as explored in the theme of mendacity in Tennessee Williams' *Cat on a Hot Tin Roof*—clearly contributes dangerously to experiences of devastation, horror, and misery in individuals, families, and communities.

Parse (1981, 1987, 1998) already has explicated thoroughly the notion that bearing witness is a vital component of high-quality nursing practice and has provided guidance for nurses who wish to bear witness by living true presence with persons in their work. If we as nurses seek to objectify and judge the people with whom we work, rather than seeking to understand and value their lives as they are lived, rather than being open to the reality that they experience everyday, this *is* the refusal to bear witness. Our knowledge base already has produced an awareness that reality as experienced by different people in different situations rarely conforms completely to objective knowledge, strict logic, or societal norms. Rather, life as it is lived varies immensely and is unpredictable, paradoxical, and infinitely complex. Works of art such as "*Cat*" offer many eloquent examples. Not to acknowledge life as such in the fullness of its subtleties, its extremities, its contradictions and impenetrably personal dimensions is not to acknowledge life as it is lived at all. Reflecting on the interpretation of mendacity as the refusal to bear witness in *Cat on a Hot Tin Roof*, then, leads directly to the suggestion that bearing witness to the reality of people's lives is an indispensable foundation for the genuine, lasting enhancement of the quality of life for the people we serve.

REFERENCES

Buber, M. (1958). *I and thou* (R. G. Smith, Trans.). New York: Collier Books. (Original work published 1923)

Chambre, S. (1988). *Responding to uncertainty by bearing witness: Volunteering as collective behavior in the* AIDS *epidemic, 1981–1988.* (Unpublished monograph.) Center for the Study of Philanthropy, City University of New York.

Cody, W. K. (1995). Of life immense in passion, pulse, and power: Dialoguing with Whitman and Parse—A hermeneutic study. In R. R. Parse (Ed.), *Illuminations: The human becoming theory in practice and research* (pp. 269–307). New York: National League for Nursing Press.

Dilthey, W. (1988). *Introduction to the human sciences* (R. J. Betanzos, Trans.). Detroit: Wayne State University Press. (Original work published 1883)

Gadamer, H.-G. (1975). *Truth and method* (2nd rev. ed.) (J. Weinsheimer & D. G. Marshall, Trans.). New York: Crossroad. (Original work published 1960)

Garfield, C. (1995). *Sometimes my heart goes numb: Love and caregiving in a time of* AIDS. San Francisco: Jossey-Bass.

Glassman, B. (1994). *Bearing witness: A Zen master's lessons in making peace.* New York: Bell Tower.

Goffman, E. (1959). *The presentation of self in everyday life.* Garden City, NY: Doubleday.

Hall, E. T. (1973). *The silent language.* Garden City, NY: Anchor Press/Doubleday.

Kahn, D. L., & Steeves, D. L. (1994). Witnesses to suffering: Nursing knowledge, voice, and vision. *Nursing Outlook, 42*(6), 260–264.

Kayal, P. M. (1993). *Bearing witness: Gay men's health crisis and the politics of* AIDS. Boulder, CO: Westview Press.

Laub, D., & Auerhahn, N. C. (1989). Failed empathy—A central theme in the survivor's Holocaust experience. *Psychoanalytic Psychology, 6*(4), 377–400.

Parse, R. R. (1981). *Man-living-health: A theory of nursing.* New York: Wiley.

Parse, R. R. (1987). *Nursing science: Major paradigms, theories, and critiques.* Philadelphia: Saunders.

Parse, R. R. (1998). *The human becoming school of thought: A perspective for nurses and other health professionals.* Thousand Oaks, CA: Sage.

Parse, R. R. (1999). Witnessing as true presence. *Illuminations: Newsletter for the International Consortium of Parse Scholars, 8*(3), 1.

Price, R. H. (1989). Bearing witness. *American Journal of Community Psychology, 17*(2), 151–167.

Sartre, J.-P. (1966). *Being and nothingness* (H. E. Barnes, Trans.). New York: Washington Square Press. (Original work published 1943)

Schindler, R., Spiegel, C., & Malachi, E. (1992). Silences: Helping elderly Holocaust victims deal with the past. *International Journal of Aging and Human Development, 35*(4), 243–252.

Verghese, A. (1994). *My own country: A doctor's story.* New York: Vintage/Random House.

Wiesel, E. (1970). *One generation after.* New York: Simon & Schuster.

Williams, T. (1955). *Cat on a hot tin roof.* New York: Signet.

CHAPTER 20

EVALUATION OF THE HUMAN BECOMING THEORY IN PRACTICE IN AN ACUTE CARE PSYCHIATRIC SETTING[1]

Deborah Thoun Northrup, RN; PhD
William K. Cody, RN; PhD

Using a descriptive evaluation research method, this study evaluated Parse's theory of human becoming in practice in the psychiatric setting. A pre- mid- post-implementation design served to generate qualitative data from nurses, patients, unit nurse managers, hospital nurse supervisors, and nurse documentation that illuminated changes in the quality of nursing care on three diverse pilot units. Major themes of change supported by all data sources were *shifting views of human beings, altered ways of listening, altered foci of nurse-person discussions, and personal transformations*. Identified themes surfaced strikingly different qualities of change for each pilot unit. Recommendations related to the successful implementation of Parse theory–based practice are presented.

Support for nursing theory–based practice abounds in the literature (Chinn & Kramer, 1991; Fawcett, 1980; Parse, 1981, 1995; Walker & Avant, 1983). Benefits claimed for nursing theory–based practice include professional identity and autonomy, coherence of purpose, and professional communication. As Chinn and Kramer (1991) contend, "Deliberate application of theory is the essence

[1]Deborah Thoun Northrup & William K. Cody, Evaluation of the human becoming theory in practice in an acute care psychiatric setting, *Nursing Science Quarterly*, 11, 23–30, copyright © 1998 by Chestnut House Publications. Reprinted by permission of Sage Publications, Inc.

of the theory-practice relationship" (p. 167). Despite these repeated claims, a paucity of research on the outcomes of theory implementation exists. Such research is needed to document the usefulness of nursing theory in ensuring quality of care. Accordingly, an evaluation of Parse's (1981, 1992) human becoming theory in practice was conducted to determine its value for nursing practice in a psychiatric setting.

Selecting Parse's Theory of Human Becoming

Within the 200-bed acute-care psychiatric hospital in Canada, where this study took place, the decision to implement nursing theory–based practice was related to a change from the traditional structure of hospital management to a program management model. This process involved the dissolution of discipline-specific departments and the development of programs comprising various services maintained in medical specialties. Administrative authority was assigned to clinical and service directors (physicians) and to administrative directors hired for their administrative acumen irrespective of their discipline. This model introduced new roles, responsibilities, leadership, and channels of communication. Further, the multidisciplinary team approach demanded that all professionals clearly articulate their unique contribution to the team. Hence, nursing theory–based practice surfaced as a necessary yet deficient component of autonomous professional practice required to confirm nursing's uniqueness and illuminate its disciplinary purpose, direction, and boundaries.

Based on the understanding that different nursing theories structure knowledge representing different values and beliefs about human beings and health, choosing a nursing theory began with a process of reflection and exploration. Literature on nursing theory–based practice was circulated to all units and a series of forums was held to clarify nurses' values and beliefs. Over time, a philosophy of individual wholeness, human freedom, individual choice and responsibility, and a desire to "be with" patients was articulated. The essence of nursing practice explicated by the nurses was clearly aligned with a human science perspective. As such, the nursing theory chosen as the basis for guiding and ultimately improving nursing practice was Parse's (1981, 1992) theory of human becoming.

Purposes of the Study

There were three purposes of the study:

1. To describe the changes that occur for nurses and patients with the initiation of a theory of nursing as a guide to practice on selected units of an acute-care psychiatric institution.

2. To describe the perceptions of the unit manager and hospital supervisor (all of whom were nurses) of nursing care pre- and post-implementation of nursing theory–based practice.
3. To contribute to the knowledge base of nursing theory application in practice settings.

The research question was this: What happens to nurses' beliefs and actions and patients' health experiences when Parse's theory is used as the basis for practice?

METHOD AND PROCEDURES

As with all research, the purpose of the study and the nature of the question indicate the appropriate methodological approach. Since the purpose of this investigation was evaluation of a theory in practice, a descriptive evaluation research method was used. Support for qualitative evaluation research is increasingly prevalent in the literature (Guba & Lincoln, 1985; Patton, 1980), as scholars and practitioners call for evaluation studies that include the extensive, detailed, qualitative data needed to more fully understand the situation under study.

The descriptive qualitative method used in this study includes pre-, mid-, and post-implementation data gathered by a nurse researcher not affiliated with the study site. The processes involved in this method are (a) written questionnaires and taped interviews with nurses regarding beliefs about human beings, health, and nursing; (b) written questionnaires and taped interviews with nurse managers and supervisors regarding differences in nursing care following implementation of Parse's theory; (c) taped interviews with patients regarding their experiences with nursing care; and (d) examination of nursing documentation of patient care (Parse, 1995).

Setting and Sample Selection

Three settings were chosen for inclusion in this study. For purposes of anonymity, these settings were randomly assigned the code descriptors, "Unit One," "Unit Two," or "Unit Three." The settings that were used included a 16-bed minimally secure forensic in-patient unit to which persons were admitted to receive treatment and detailed multidisciplinary medical-legal evaluation during pre-trial or pre-sentencing periods; a 9-bed neuropsychiatric in-patient unit to which persons who were living with progressive disorders of the nervous system such as Parkinson's or Huntington's disease were admitted; and, a 24-bed geriatric psychiatry in-patient unit to which persons 65 and older were admitted primarily for assessment and treatment of symptoms related to affective disorders or dementia.

Selection of units for the project was made on the basis of apparent congruence between the values underlying Parse's theory and those of the nurses. In addition, the participation of the clinical nurse specialist associated with the unit and the support of the managers and supervisors were viewed as essential to such a process of fundamental change.

Study participants included 54 patients, 4 unit managers, 3 supervisors, and varying numbers of nurses over the duration of the project. Of the 39 nurses who were eligible to participate, 2 refused. Pre-implementation questionnaires were completed by 37 nurses. The questionnaire return rates and interview participation declined during the study on all three units. Reasons for this included the withdrawal of four nurses, scheduling difficulty for interview purposes, illness of nurses, the attrition of five nurse participants, and the resignation of one supervisor related to intercity transfer.

Protection of Participants' Rights

The protection of participants' rights was ensured in accordance with ethical guidelines for confidentiality, disclosure of risks and benefits, parameters of participation, and provision for withdrawal. After participants' involvement was explained and their questions answered, all participants signed a consent form. All data were coded to provide the maximum possible anonymity, and the usual confidentiality and security measures were maintained.

Data Collection

Data were collected through taped interviews with nurses, patients, unit managers, and hospital supervisors; written questionnaires by nurses, unit managers, and hospital supervisors; and chart audits conducted pre-implementation (May 1993), mid-implementation (May 1994), and post-implementation (September 1994). All taped interviews were guided by the same set of open-ended questions. Charts were examined for the content and style of nurses' charting. At the end of the study, all nurses participating in the project were asked to share their thoughts in writing about the way nursing practice had changed since using Parse's theory.

INTRODUCING PARSE'S THEORY-BASED PRACTICE

Parse's (1981, 1987, 1992) theory has been presented extensively in the literature. The essence of the Parse practice method is to be truly present with clients as they freely explore the meaning of their life situations and choose ways of becoming.

Seven one-hour formal Parse theory learning sessions were held weekly on pilot units during the day and evening shifts to accommodate as many nurses as possible. Initial discussion and instruction focused on the values and beliefs of Parse's theory as lived by nurses in relationships with patients and families. Learning modules developed for an earlier implementation project were used as a basis for the discussions (Jonas, Pilkington, Lyon, & MacDonald, 1992). Over time, small group discussions were focused on enhancing understanding of the assumptions, principles, and concepts of the theory and the dimensions of the practice method.

Informal learning took place on a day-to-day basis since nurses were often accompanied by the principal investigator as they were with patients throughout the study. Two educational consultants having post-graduate experience with Parse's theory made monthly visits to the institution to assist nurses in their learning. Dr. Parse made two site visits, and an educational consultant held two all-day workshops. Nursing functions, procedures, and charting continued on the pilot units in keeping with hospital policies and standards.

PRESENTATION OF FINDINGS

Pre-, mid-, and post-implementation evaluation generated qualitative data related to nurse changes, patient changes, manager and supervisor perceptions, and changes in documentation, which were strikingly different for each unit. While every effort was made to interview the same patients at each data collection period, the admission of patients for purposes of this research was not a viable option. Nonetheless, three patients, each from a different unit, were interviewed twice.

Pre-implementation data from nurse-participants on all three pilot units are considered collectively and presented first. Next, themes of change during mid- and post-implementation are presented with supporting data from each pilot unit. Major findings related to patient, manager, and supervisor perceptions about change follow. Finally, changes in nurse charting are reported.

Nurse Descriptions

Pre-Implementation: All Units.   Data analyzed from 18 pre-implementation interviews and 37 questionnaires revealed a predominant mechanistic perspective of human beings that focused on the individual as the object of biomedical and behaviorist interventions. This view was evident in nurses' comments about "techniques of care" that centered on the "state" and "functioning" of the individual. Assessment was oriented toward finding, labelling, and fixing irregularities, undesirable behaviors, and broken parts. "Therapeutic intervention" was aimed at shaping more desirable behaviors and exerting a controlling influence over the pathology or problem located primarily in the individual.

Care appeared to be guided by assumptions and unspoken causal theories about human beings, who were seen as being in the institution in order to be taught, managed, influenced, and regulated. Topics of nurse-patient discussions were identified as problem solving, methods of coping, and managing patients' illnesses. The approaches to care in use were exemplified by such nursing activities as "setting realistic goals," providing reality orientation, giving reassurance, providing health teaching accompanied by encouragement to accept and follow recommended treatment regimens, and "allowing" patients to express their feelings.

When describing their nursing practice pre-implementation, participants said:

Unit One.   [Nursing practice is] looking at patient problems . . . it's nursing looking at what we see their concerns are. . . . They're not functioning, but how can we best meet their needs. . . . A lot of our patients are experiencing grieving and sometimes they don't realize that they are, so we talk about their feelings, about their illness . . . your concerns about them and help them to ventilate.

Unit Two.   I spend the majority of the day discussing the patient's illness . . . what causes it . . . ways of coping with it, medications. . . . When they start complaining about somatic complaints and not wanting to get out of bed, etc., explaining that to them . . . trying to achieve the highest level of functioning.

Unit Three.   [We] give people medications, we document . . . care plan, do our progress notes. . . . Probably the thing we talk about most is [patient] medication. A lot of our patients are reluctant to take them. A lot of them have a lot of complaints about side effects . . . [and] have a long history of noncompliance.

Themes in the Change Process: Mid- and Post-Implementation.   Analysis of mid- and post-implementation data from interviews and questionnaires revealed five themes: (a) shifting views of human beings; (b) altered ways of listening; (c) altered focus of nurse-person discussions; (d) altered job satisfaction; and (e) personal transformations.

The most common theme was *shifting views of human beings*. Embedded within this theme were shifts from problem- to person-focused care, from nurse-identified to patient-identified priorities, and from a belief in the nurse as expert in health to a belief in the patient as expert in his/her personal health. Mid- and post-implementation data which typify this theme for each unit were as follows.

Unit One.   There used to be a lot of rules and restrictions with consequences for people who did not "obey our rules". . . . There is far less rigidity now. I don't label people anymore. We used to say things such as noncompliant and disruptive behavior or ineffective individual coping. . . . Now I think, "How could I have said that about people?" I could never go back to the other way.

Unit Two.   [With persons considered to be psychotic, confused, or demented], I go with them and talk about it [their reality]. It is important to them. . . . It doesn't matter to me, being confused or disoriented or psychotic. I used to use those labels a lot and. . . Now it is more important to find out what that person is saying [and] feeling. . . . The labels don't mean anything.

Unit Three.   Sometimes I feel I have to make decisions for people or certainly guide people into making decisions. That is just a belief I have; I haven't changed it. But it [learning Parse's theory] has probably made me more aware of giving people time to make their own decisions instead of . . . [tending] to do it for them.

The second theme was *altered ways of listening*. This theme was linked with the quality of the nurse-person interrelationship. Rather than wishing to control conversations, or give unsolicited advice and/or teach, which were all highly valued pre-implementation, nurses developed a comfort in being with patients who set the tone, tempo, pitch, and direction of interactions.

Unit One.   I go with my patients as they speak about their health, what brings them quality of life, what is important to them. I feel comfortable . . . if they are happy or sad or angry, seeking the meaning of their situation, and going with them, as opposed to telling them what would be best for them or what they should be doing.

Unit Two.   Instead of [having] sessions where I gather information according to my agenda, the patients now decide if they want to talk, about what, and for how long. I have gone from spending about 1.5 hours per shift talking to my patients to now spending at least 3 hours per shift being with my patients.

Unit Three.   I tend to be a person who needs to be in control or I get very anxious. . . . I want to fix things and I know the right way to do it, my way. . . . But I have found that I have been able to listen more to my patients . . . instead of offering suggestions constantly.

The third theme was *altered focus of nurse-person discussions*. Intricately interwoven with altered ways of listening were the changes in discussion topics described by nurses on all units.

Unit One.   [We discuss] what is important to them, what brings them quality of life, what their hopes and dreams are, their goals, who they are close to . . . what health means to them. . . .

Unit Two.   In the past . . . I didn't have the answers so we didn't discuss it. Our conversations consisted mostly of taking medications, side effects, signs and symptoms of depression, and assessing orientation. This theory has allowed me to share with my patients their struggles of wanting to live and wanting to die, loneliness, death and what it means to them, growing old, and placement issues. I no longer have to have the answers for them.

Unit Three.   [We discuss] what they want to discuss at the time, unless I feel there is something that I need to find out about, and then I have my own agenda.

The fourth theme was *altered job satisfaction*. This theme was associated with nurses' commitment to and passion for nursing practice as well as a new understanding of nursing as a scientific discipline and learned profession. Many nurses expressed a heightened sense of job satisfaction with adoption of the theory, while others reported doubts associated with the adequacy of the theory to guide their chosen way of being with people.

Unit One.   The theory has given meaning back to my practice. . . . It has just been one of the most gratifying experiences I have ever had in my life. . . . This has allowed me to nurse the way I hoped and dreamed I would when I went to school. I had become hard and cold . . . with the judgment and labelling.

Unit Two.   Using Parse's theory as a scientific base for my nursing practice has allowed me to practice in the way I always wanted. . . . Being able to state that I practice according to Parse's theory has given me much confidence to . . . present my patient's point of view. I have grown as a person and especially as a nurse.

Unit Three.   In some ways I feel better about my practice. . . . My nursing practice has definitely changed since my involvement in this project. Unfortunately, I find myself with one foot in two very different camps. I'm uncomfortable with the old way . . . but feel that I lack sufficient knowledge and skill to practice Parse's theory effectively.

The fifth theme was *personal transformations*. This theme was linked to the nurses' doubts, struggles, and feelings of inadequacy, as well as their growth, aspirations, reflections, and triumphs associated with learning Parse's theory and practice methodology.

Unit One.   Learning the theory has been uplifting and painful. When you are with people you feel their pain. . . . I have lost friends, people who do not like the theory. The theory has made me softer, more human and more aware that I do not have to wield power. I am able . . . to practice the way I want. . . . Patients are not different; I am different.

Unit Two.   I do know that since being exposed to Parse, I will never be the same person again. . . . Initially, we, the Parse nurses, were criticized, ridiculed, and attacked as we struggled to articulate our practice. By continuing on, however, the other nurses were able to see through our examples . . . how we are different with the patients, and the impact this has had on the patients.

Unit Three.   I have enjoyed learning about this theory. . . . I have found it has given me a lot to think about in the way I interact with patients. I don't know that it has made any really significant changes. . . . I believe I have always related to my patients in a caring, humane way. I continue to address "problems" in a non-Parse way.

Changes Described by Patients

Unit One.   Data were gathered from samples of 5 to 6 patients pre-, mid-, and post-implementation. Evidence of patient changes over the course of the study surfaced from the comments offered by patients. For example, when patients were asked to describe the *quality of nursing care*, pre- and post-implementation statements included such expressions as "excellent," "friendly," "great," and "fun." During a pre-implementation interview, however, one patient added:

> I ask them questions but . . . I don't like to take up too much of their time; they have their own work to do and there are other patients.

Another recounted his experience with a nurse who would not allow him to take a shower prior to 6 o'clock, citing hospital policy. Conversely, a common statement post-implementation was "The nurses are always around when we need them and they always show concern. . . . The nurses are definitely compassionate."

When asked to identify nurse-patient *discussion topics*, the majority of patients spoke of relationship issues, such as marital difficulties or the death of a parent, living with memory loss, headaches, seizures, and "private things." A shift in perspectives from the nurse as expert to the patient as expert was reflected. One patient, pre-implementation, said, "They [nurses] can help you see other points of view. . . . You get a very different outlook from each [nurse]." In contrast, another patient, mid-implementation, stated, "They make a point of coming to visit me, [taking] some time to talk. . . . They are asking and trying to get my views on things." Most of the patients on Unit One affirmed that the nurse spoke with them of their hopes and plans for the future during mid- and post-implementation interviews. Patients revealed greater detail about these discussions after nurse learning had taken place. For example, one patient, mid-implementation, reported,

> The nurses asked about the future, how I would like to see things, how my life would be, and actually had me doing some visualization or you know, pretend what I would be doing now if I was feeling better.

When asked who influenced their *quality of life* during hospitalization, mid- and post-implementation data revealed that 10 of 11 patients reported that the nurses did. One patient said, "The nurses are open . . . always smiling. . . . It is like . . . a small family here . . . I feel safer here."

Unit Two.   Data were gathered from samples of 6 to 7 patients pre-, mid-, and post-implementation. Little change in the descriptions of *nursing care* was evident during the study. Patients described the care as "excellent," "efficient, kind, and caring," "very good," or "no complaints." One patient, pre-implementation, stated, "I think some of the nurses could be, not all but a few, could be more compassionate towards us. . . ." When patients hinted at deficiencies in the nursing care, they followed it with a defense of the care, such as, "I think they're very capable girls, [but] they're busy . . . all busy all the time."

Discussion topics identified by patients over the duration of the study included diet, sleep, aches and pains, sadness, and depression. Patients spoke of seeking and receiving reassurance. The primary consideration of nursing reported by the majority of patients was medication. The majority of patients spoke of having close relationships with their primary nurses but only superficial interactions with other nurses. Patients said they discussed their hopes and plans with their physicians but seldom if ever with the nurses. When asked how nurses influenced their *quality of life*, the majority of patients on Unit Two reported no nurse impact. During mid- and post-implementation, three patients identified a small number of nurses who had made a difference in their lives, making the following comments:

> I feel at home with her . . . she is a wonderful nurse . . . she is overly good. You have the feeling that she is not just in this work for the money but that she is in it because she cares for people.

Unit Three.   Data were gathered from 5 to 6 patients pre-, mid- and post-implementation. Patient comments revealed minimal to no changes over the duration of the study. The most noted change was evident in the descriptions of the *quality of nursing care* on the unit. Pre-implementation comments included, "I wouldn't speak very highly of the nursing care," "it's OK," "they're very ignorant," "very good," and "excellent." Mid- and post-implementation data, however, contained positive descriptors only. One person commented, "This time around I found it pretty good. I found them not condescending and . . . friendly."

As to *discussion topics* and *planning for the future*, the majority of patients on Unit Three over the duration of the study commented that little or no discussion took place between themselves and the nurses. Help was received from the nurses in the form of suggestions, advice, and medication teaching. Essentially, patients reported that nurses had minimal to no impact on the quality of their lives while in hospital.

Manager and Supervisor Perceptions

Managers from all three units participated in the study, albeit with some personnel changes during the course of the study. Supervisors provided a unique, comparative view of practice across the three units and various shifts not offered by any other data source. Two supervisors provided only mid- and post-implementation data; therefore, only mid- and post-implementation supervisor data are presented.

Unit One.   Pre-implementation manager data revealed that issues most discussed with the manager were patient safety, behavioral aspects of diagnosis, and medical areas of responsibility. Additionally, the manager wanted to see work satisfaction based on nursing rather than medical expectations. Key points identified by the manager during mid-implementation were changes in nursing practice related to shifting views of human beings, enhanced job satisfaction, and a growing respect for the uniqueness of nursing by other professionals. Supervisors described the strengths of the nurses in this way:

> I think the nursing staff are very accepting of their patients' values and beliefs and their choices. . . . They don't label people anymore. . . .
> They spend a lot of time with their patients . . . and with the families.

> The nurses have a much more caring attitude or much more clear concept of the person's perspective of things. . . . My impression of nursing care is [that it] is much happier, both for the patient and for the nurses. . . . There's much less restraint [physical and chemical] used [and] much less extra staff required. . . .

Topics of nurse-supervisor discussions were quality of life for patients, patients who were dying, patients needing much assistance to move, and aggression. When asked what they thought contributed to the satisfaction of nurses on Unit One, one supervisor wrote the following:

> The nursing staff are satisfied with their work because they are practicing from Parse's theory. They have a certain calmness and joy which is more apparent since practicing from Parse's theory.

Unit Two.   Pre-implementation data revealed that Unit Two nurses were seen by the manager as having a caring attitude toward patients and a strong commitment to their jobs. The predominant foci of nurse-manager discussions were safety issues, physical problems, behavior problems, and legal matters. Documentation was seen as requiring "too much time." Job satisfaction was linked to respect from other disciplines, particularly physicians, support of co-workers, and enjoyment of the patient population. Key points addressed by the unit managers mid- and post-implementation were shifting perspectives of human beings and changes in charting with the person as the focus rather than the problem, along with nurse-physician relationships continuously undermining nursing autonomy and nursing's uniqueness.

During mid- and post-implementation evaluation, the strengths identified by supervisors of Unit Two nurses were a caring attitude, a warmth in approach in which nurses "discuss patients as if they are people," experience with the patient population, and a willingness to learn. One change was described in this way:

> There's much more consideration given for what really is going on from the person's perspective. Even if the nurse doesn't really understand what's going on, there's a lot more searching and seeking to try and find that out. . . .

The supervisors believed that job satisfaction for Unit Two nurses was related to a feeling that they were being heard, to visible client comfort, to nurse-client interaction, and to a great measure, learning Parse's theory. As one supervisor said:

> Those who have been exposed to the Parse teaching . . . are expressing a lot more satisfaction with their work. . . . They see the difference it makes in people they work with; they seem much happier with their work situation.

For the most part, topics of nurse-supervisor discussions remained the same. One added topic was staff conflict arising from different philosophical perspectives on issues such as the use of restraints. When asked what changes were needed on the unit, one supervisor said:

> I would change the arguing between nurses . . . the Parse versus the non-Parse . . . approach . . . but that's slowly developing anyway. . . . [Further], I would like to change . . . the dependent relationship on the physician that the nurses have which tends to influence their thinking . . . unduly.

Unit Three.   Pre-, mid-, and post-implementation data revealed very little change in manager perceptions of nursing care over the duration of the study on Unit Three. Key points addressed by the manager pre-, mid-, and post-implementation were a lack of professional identity and understanding about the uniqueness of nursing practice, the limited focus of patient care (behavior control), and a sustained reliance on other disciplines for job satisfaction.

When asked how the nurses talked about patients, supervisor comments changed slightly, from "patients . . . [are perceived] as being major problems, and a less than respectful attitude is evident" to "a respectful manner mostly with a degree of condescension in relation to the [reasons for their hospitalization]." Strengths of the nurses identified in mid- and post-implementation data were experience in nursing and knowledge of the patient population, consistency in approach to patient management, and good communication in terms of unit policies. One supervisor commented:

> On [Unit Three] . . . control is the major issue and there's this idea that you're dealing predominantly with people who have to be managed. . . . It's a strength in the sense that the system seems to reward it; it's not something I particularly find positive. . . . There's no particular change on that unit.

Very little change in nurse-supervisor topics of discussion was revealed. In addition to previous topics, nurses discussed with the supervisors their difficulties in learning Parse's theory. Aspects of nursing that, pre-implementation, supervisors desired to see change resurfaced mid- and post-implementation. These were a change in attitude from patient as problem to patient as person and a change in approach from custodial to caring. It was believed that nurses on Unit Three associated job satisfaction with communication, the feeling that they were being heard, following routines, and maintaining control. One supervisor commented, "I'm not sure that the nurses are very satisfied with their work."

Changes in Documentation

The introduction of documentation congruent with Parse's theory, based on learner readiness and desire to learn, occurred at varying times among the three units. When appropriate, traditional nursing care plans using a problem-based process with nursing diagnoses were replaced with *personal health descriptions*. These descriptions focused on the meaning of experience from the person's perspective; the person's values, beliefs, hopes, dreams, and goals; actualizing the person's plans; and nurse-person activities.

Evaluation of documentation was based on the use or non-use of nursing diagnoses, psychiatric jargon, and evaluative patient descriptions; the charting of PRN medication and patient responses to same; differences in documentation by type of patient; the use of statements of support and reassurance; frequency of references to routine practices and institutional expectations; and nurses' preoccupation with the location and activities of patients. Changes associated with documentation varied among units. Mid-implementation findings for Unit One showed that documentation was in the process of change consistent with Parse's theory (using the personal health descriptions) and moved toward being wholly consistent at post-implementation evaluation. On Unit Two, the documentation changed somewhat for the nurses who were involved in the learning over the duration of the project. Unit Three showed no change in documentation patterns.

CONCLUSIONS

Unit One.   The use of Parse's theory in practice on Unit One brought about explicit and dramatic change as all nurses on Unit One adopted the theory. The nurses, manager, and supervisors reported these changes: nurses viewed patients as people rather than psychiatric problems in need of repair, eliminated use of labels for patients, minimized their judgments of patient views and behavior, and became more flexible. Nurses changed their ways of listening and the foci of discussions. No longer directed by their own agendas, nurses sought the patients' perspectives, valuing them as the experts in their own health. Patients revealed pre and post differences in nursing practice related to nurse availability and respect for patient views. The majority of patients interviewed reported that Unit One nurses influenced the quality of their lives. Nurses also spoke of their struggle in learning Parse's theory. Letting go of old ways brought pain and frustration as well as joy and triumph. Learning and practicing from Parse's theory enhanced nurse job satisfaction. The nurses' commitment to ongoing practice with Parse's method was evidenced by the creation of a format for documentation congruent with the theory.

Unit Two.   While nurse changes were not as extensive as on Unit One, the nurses who did embrace the Parse method revealed similar changes. Shifts in perspectives about human beings, the adoption of new ways of being with people, enhanced job satisfaction, and personal transformations were evident throughout these data. Additional support for these findings came from the patient, manager, supervisor, and documentation data.

Unit Three.   Parse's method was not used post-implementation to guide nursing practice on Unit Three. The principal focus of nursing practice on Unit Three before and after implementation remained the same—the assessment, diagnosis, and control of patient behaviors. Subtle differences related to changes in nurse perspectives about human beings, ways of listening, and topics of nurse-patient discussions were evident in some nurse and patient data. Supervisors and manager suggested that Unit Three nurses were not satisfied with their jobs and that these nurses gained job satisfaction through recognition from other disciplines, notably medicine. Learning Parse's theory made it difficult for them to work with patients who they did not consider capable of making decisions. Learning the theory, however, did provide nurses an opportunity to examine their practice and explore or reaffirm their own values and beliefs.

DISCUSSION

Similarities and differences related to this and other evaluation studies (Jonas, 1995; Mitchell, 1995; Santopinto & Smith, 1995) of Parse's theory as a guide to practice exist. While space limitations do not permit a lengthy discussion of each, a few nurse changes warrant comment. The most common theme which surfaced for nurses in this study, *shifting views of human beings*, bore a profound similarity to Mitchell's (1995) *"thinking of patients as persons and having closer relationships"* (p. 376), the *"heightened awareness of the person's perspective"* proffered by Jonas (1995, p. 356), and *"looking beyond the labels"* identified by Santopinto and Smith (1995, p. 336). Each of the four themes identified above reveals that knowledge of and practice within Parse's perspective inspires an enhanced respect for and concern with people as self-determining human beings that pursue and create their chosen way of being with the world. Additionally, *altered ways of listening* and *altered focus of nurse-person discussions*, found within the present study, further substantiate the change in nurse actions reported by Mitchell (1995) that nurses *"spend more time talking and listening to patients"* (p. 390). Another theme which bears similarity to previous studies is *personal transformations*. The struggle and pain related to learning and living new values and beliefs in practice conveyed in this study are similar to the patterns of comfort-discomfort in *"changing patterns of practice"* noted by Santopinto and Smith (1995, p. 337) and the intense struggle lived by nurses in their letting go of old beliefs identified by Mitchell (1995) and Jonas (1995).

One different theme in this project that commands attention is *altered job satisfaction*. While some nurses did enjoy "enhanced satisfaction and meaningfulness in practice" (Jonas, 1995, p. 354) or "feeling freed, relaxed, and more satisfied in practice" (Mitchell, 1995, p. 375), other nurses rejected Parse's practice methodology and spoke of it as inadequate as a guide for their practice within the psychiatric setting. Accordingly, some nurses expressed anger and outrage at the difference necessitated by a new perspective. One nurse revealed her difficulty in this way:

> I find a lot of difficulty working in Parse with really psychotic people. . . . Sometimes you have to separate yourself from the conversation because mentally you can't handle it. It has nothing to do with listening to the patient, but when they're talking absolute garbage [and] you can't put three words together to make a sentence, it's very difficult to listen to. So, sometimes you just say, okay, okay, talk to me later. . . .

While one can speculate on the myriad reasons nurses choose or fail to choose Parse's theory as a guide for practice, it behooves nursing to conduct further studies that capture the value of nursing theory–based practice for the discipline.

RECOMMENDATIONS

Study findings as well as insights gained throughout the process of program implementation gave rise to recommendations for future implementation projects. Requirements essential to implementation of Parse theory–based practice in comparable settings include (a) the presence of a consistent, on-site, master's or doctorally prepared facilitator knowledgeable in the theory; (b) the allocation of resources necessary for learning; (c) the endorsement of Parse theory–based practice by management personnel; and (d) administrative support for continued educational opportunities related to Parse's theory of human becoming.

REFERENCES

Chinn, P., & Kramer, M. (1991). *Theory and nursing: A systematic approach.* St. Louis: Mosby.

Fawcett, J. (1980). A declaration of nursing independence: The relation of theory and research to nursing practice. *The Journal of Nursing Administration,* 10, 36–39.

Guba, E., & Lincoln, Y. (1985). *Effective evaluation.* San Francisco: Jossey-Bass.

Jonas, C., Pilkington, B., Lyon, P., & MacDonald, G. E. (1992). *Parse's theory of human becoming learning modules.* Toronto: St. Michael's Hospital.

Jonas, C. M. (1995). Evaluation of the human becoming theory in family practice. In R. R. Parse (Ed.), *Illuminations: The human becoming theory in practice and research* (pp. 347–366). New York: National League for Nursing Press.

Mitchell, G. J. (1995). Evaluation of the human becoming theory in practice in an acute care setting. In R. R. Parse (Ed.), *Illuminations: The human becoming theory in practice and research* (pp. 367–399). New York: National League for Nursing Press.

Parse, R. R. (1981). *Man-living-health: A theory of nursing.* New York: Wiley.

Parse, R. R. (1987). *Nursing science: Major paradigms, theories, and critiques.* Philadelphia: Saunders.

Parse, R. R. (1992). Human becoming: Parse's theory of nursing. *Nursing Science Quarterly,* 5, 35–42.

Parse, R. R. (1995). Research with the human becoming theory. In R. R. Parse (Ed.), *Illuminations: The human becoming theory in practice and research* (pp. 151–157). New York: National League for Nursing Press.

Patton, M. Q. (1980). *Qualitative evaluation methods.* Beverly Hills, CA: Sage.

Santopinto, M. D. A., & Smith, M. C. (1995). Evaluation of the human becoming theory in practice with adults and children. In R. R. Parse (Ed.), *Illuminations: The human becoming theory in practice and research* (pp. 309–346). New York: National League for Nursing Press.

Walker, L., & Avant, K. (1983). *Strategies for theory construction in nursing.* Norwalk: Appleton-Century-Crofts.

CHAPTER 21

EMERGING QUALITATIVE METHODS OF THE SCIENCE OF UNITARY HUMAN BEINGS

This chapter explicates the ontology, epistemology, and methodologies of the emerging qualitative methods of the science of unitary human beings (Butcher, 1994, 1996, 1998; Carboni, 1995; Cowling, 1998).

ONTOLOGY

The science of unitary human beings was created by Martha E. Rogers and first published in 1970. Rogers set forth a new paradigm specifying nursing as a science and an art (Rogers, 1970, 1986, 1990, 1992, 1983/1994a, 1980/1994b, 1994c). The science of unitary human beings is an acausal framework in which Rogers (1970, 1986, 1990, 1992, 1983/1994a, 1980/1994b, 1994c) purports that the pandimensional human energy field in mutual process with the pandimensional environmental energy field is the central focus of nursing. The postulates of the science as described by Rogers (1986, 1992) follow:

Energy Fields: "*Field* is a unifying concept. *Energy* signifies the dynamic nature of the field. *Energy fields* are infinite. Two energy fields are identified: the human field and the environmental field. Specifically, human beings and environment *are* energy fields. They do not have them. Moreover, human and environmental fields are *not* biological fields or physical fields, or social or psychological fields. Neither are human and environmental fields a summation of biological, physical, social, and psychological fields. This is not

237

	a denial of other fields. Rather, it is to make clear that human and environmental fields have their own identity and are not to be confused with parts" (Rogers, 1986, pp. 4–5).
Openness:	"In a universe of open systems, causality is not an option. . . . Energy fields are open—not a little bit or sometimes, but continuously. The human and environmental fields are integral with one another" (Rogers, 1986, p. 5).
Pattern:	"Pattern is an abstraction. It gives identity to the field. The nature of the pattern changes continuously. Each human field pattern is unique and is integral with its own unique environmental field pattern. The term 'pattern' is used only to refer to an energy field. Manifestations of field pattern emerge out of the human and environmental field mutual process" (Rogers, 1986, p. 5).
Pandimensionality:	Pandimensional is a "non-linear domain without spatial or temporal attributes" (Rogers, 1992, p. 29).

These postulates described by Rogers (1986, 1992) underpin the three principles of the science, which follow:

1. *Helicy* is the "continuous, innovative, unpredictable, increasing diversity of human and environmental field patterns" (Rogers, 1992, p. 31).
2. *Resonancy* is the "continuous change from lower to higher frequency wave patterns in human and environmental fields" (Rogers, 1992, p. 31).
3. *Integrality* is the "continuous mutual human field and environmental field process" (Rogers, 1992, p. 31).

EPISTEMOLOGY

The nature of nursing research for the emerging qualitative methods of the science of unitary human beings focuses on human-environment pattern manifestations. Entities for study have been dispiritedness (Butcher, 1996), despair (Cowling, 1998), and nurse-client relationships (Carboni, 1995) (see Table 1–2). There have been no published research studies guided by these methods except the original research introducing the methods (Butcher, 1996, 1998; Carboni, 1995; Cowling, 1998). Other entities will evolve as the methods are used and refined.

EMERGING QUALITATIVE METHODOLOGIES

There are three published emerging qualitative methodologies basically congruent with the science of unitary human beings (Rogers, 1970, 1986, 1990, 1992, 1983/1994a, 1980/1994b, 1994c). These methods are in keeping with the acausal nature of the ontology. They are relatively new and require further use and refinement. The procedures for each of the methods are presented here in the order of their publication.

Rogerian Process of Inquiry Method

Judith T. Carboni (1995) designed the research method called the Rogerian process of inquiry method to answer research questions such as *What is the pandimensional unitary field process in a nurse-client relationship?* Carboni (1995) says that the purpose of research using the Rogerian process of inquiry method is discovery. Further, there is no need for representative sampling, since the method is designed to allow the researcher to capture manifestations of the energy field through shared descriptions and understanding between researcher and participants—who are protected by ethical standards of inquiry (Carboni, 1995). (See Chapter 2 of this book.) There is no limit to the number of participants with this method. The assumptions underpinning the method follow:

1. Dynamic energy fields are integral and unpredictable.
2. The researcher-researched relationship is evolutionary, integral, and open to unconstrained mutual discovery (Carboni, 1995, p. 23).

Processes of the Method.   The processes include the following:

1. Initial shared description is the beginning phase, which entails a general orientation to participant and setting, that is the human-environmental field pattern.
2. Mutual exploration and discovery is the phase that begins the "focused aspect of the study" (Carboni, 1995, p. 30). The envisioned evolutionary change process and the emergence of inductive data are consistent with the ontology and arise in multiple nonpredictable possibilities (Carboni, 1995).
3. Enfoldment of evolutionary change is the recognition of pattern configurations for unitary knowing that is arrived at through unitary instrumentation, immersion in the field, and shared descriptions (Carboni, 1995).
4. Creative induction and deduction data synthesis is the pulling together of descriptive data from field notes and unitary instrumentation. Synthesized data is examined and refined by researcher and

participant to arrive at a shared mutual understanding. This phase
leads to the pandimensional unitary process report from which theory
is born and refined and application is made to practice (Carboni, 1995).

For further details on this method see Carboni (1995).

Unitary Field Pattern Portrait Method

Howard K. Butcher (1996, 1998) created the unitary field pattern portrait
method to answer research questions such as *What is the unitary field pattern portrait of dispiritedness?* The method was "designed to create a unitary understanding of the dynamic kaleidoscopic and symphonic pattern manifestations
emerging from the pandimensional human/environment mutual process to
enhance understanding of significant phenomena related to human well being" (Butcher, 1998, p. 13). The assumptions underpinning the method follow:

1. The researcher and researched-into are integral and engaged in mutual
   process;
2. Human beings can describe their own experiences, perceptions, and
   expressions in ways that uncover an understanding of a particular
   phenomenon;
3. Experiences, perceptions, and expressions are unitary pattern
   manifestations emerging from the human/environmental energy field
   mutual process; and
4. The unitary field pattern portrait of an experience related to human
   betterment reflects the dynamic kaleidoscopic and symphonic
   human/environmental field mutual process. (Butcher, 1998, p. 14)

Processes of the Method.   The processes of the unitary field pattern portrait
research method (Butcher, 1998) are as follows:

1. Initial engagements with any number of participants, who are
   protected by the ethical standards of inquiry (see Chapter 2 of this
   book), focus on a phenomenon relevant to well-being.
2. A *priori* nursing science.
3. Immersion (intensity sampling and selection of the natural setting).
4. Pattern appraisal through indepth interviews (experiences,
   perceptions, expressions), field notes (observational, theoretical,
   methodological), and reflective journals.
5. Unitary field pattern profile construction through creative pattern
   synthesis.
6. Mutual unitary field pattern profile construction through mutual processing.
7. Unitary field pattern portrait construction through
   immersion/crystallization.
8. Theoretical unitary field pattern portrait construction through evolutionary interpretation.

For a detailed explanation of the Unitary Field Pattern Portrait method, with
refinements, see Butcher (1994, 1996, 1998).

Unitary Pattern Appreciation Case Method

W. Richard Cowling (1998) described the unitary pattern appreciation case method. It was designed to answer research questions such as *What is the pattern of a person experiencing despair as the dominant sensation of the person's experience?* The unitary pattern appreciation case method focuses on the "individual or group human and environmental energy fields," or "on phenomena conceptualized within a unitary context" (Cowling, 1998, p. 139), to gain understanding of the human-environment mutual process. The purpose of the method is to provide a "conceptualization of unitary case inquiry that transcends the typical social science notion of a case as a bounded system situated in a context that is physical, social, and/or historic with temporal and spatial qualities" (Cowling, 1998, p. 139). The assumptions underpinning the method follow:

1. The pandimensional human energy field is unitary and in mutual process with the pandimensional environmental energy field.
2. The principles of helicy, resonancy, and integrality from the science of unitary human beings (see Rogers 1970, 1986, 1994c) form the underpinning beliefs.

Processes of the Method. The processes of the unitary pattern appreciation case method (Cowling, 1998) are as follows:

1. Discussing intention with participant after ensuring ethical standards of inquiry (see Chapter 2).
2. Engaging in pattern appreciation through interviewing, observing, and creative expression.
3. Documenting experiences, perceptions, and expressions through journaling, audio and video recording, photography, musical recordings, or drawing.
4. Comprehending the pattern of the whole.
5. Recognizing features as an ensemble reflecting pattern and wholeness.
6. Developing a pattern profile.
7. Verifying the pattern profile with the participant.

Unitary pattern appreciation focuses on an orientation to the wholeness of the case through a process for comprehending a pattern leading to an approach for constructing a unitary profile. The processes of the method may be peer reviewed at the request of the researcher or participant. For further details of the method see Cowling (1998).

CONTRIBUTIONS OF THE METHODS

Findings from all three of these methods are connected to the science of unitary human beings (Rogers, 1970, 1986, 1990, 1992, 1983/1994a, 1980/1994b, 1994c) and shed light on pattern manifestations of the human-environment mutual process. These three emerging qualitative nursing methods derived from the science of unitary human beings are continually being refined by their authors. Other seasoned and budding scholars with congruent beliefs may use them to enhance nursing science from the simultaneity paradigm (Parse, 1987).

REFERENCES

Butcher, H. K. (1994). The unitary field pattern portrait method: Development of research method within Rogers' science of unitary human beings. In M. Madrid & E. A. M. Barrett (Eds.), *Rogers' scientific art of nursing practice* (pp. 397–429). New York: National League for Nursing Press.

Butcher, H. K. (1996). A unitary field pattern portrait of dispiritedness in later life. *Visions: The Journal of Rogerian Nursing Science*, 4(1), 41–58.

Butcher, H. K. (1998). Crystallizing the processes of the unitary field pattern portrait research method. *Visions: The Journal of Rogerian Nursing Science*, 6(1), 13–26.

Carboni, J. T. (1995). A Rogerian process of inquiry. *Nursing Science Quarterly*, 8, 22–37.

Cowling, W. R. (1998). Unitary case inquiry. *Nursing Science Quarterly*, 11, 139–141.

Parse, R. R. (1987). *Nursing science: Major paradigms, theories, and critiques*. Philadelphia: Saunders.

Rogers, M. E. (1970). *An introduction to the theoretical basis of nursing*. Philadelphia: Davis.

Rogers, M. E. (1986). Science of unitary human beings. In V. M. Malinski (Ed.), *Explorations on Martha Rogers' science of unitary human beings* (pp. 3–8). Norwalk, CT: Appleton-Century-Crofts.

Rogers, M. E. (1990). Nursing: Science of unitary, irreducible, human beings: Update 1990. In E. A. M. Barrett (Ed.), *Visions of Rogers' science-based nursing* (pp. 5–11). New York: National League for Nursing Press.

Rogers, M. E. (1992). Nursing science and the space age. *Nursing Science Quarterly*, 5, 27–34.

Rogers, M. E. (1994a). Beyond the horizon. In V. M. Malinski & E. A. M. Barrett (Eds.), *Martha E. Rogers: Her life and her work* (pp. 282–287). Philadelphia: Davis. (Reprinted from *The nursing profession: A time to speak*, pp. 795–801, by N. L. Chaska, Ed., 1983, New York: McGraw-Hill)

Rogers, M. E. (1994b). Nursing: A science of unitary man. In V. M. Malinski & E. A. M. Barrett (Eds.), *Martha E. Rogers: Her life and her work* (pp. 225–232). Philadelphia: Davis. (Reprinted from *Conceptual models for nursing practice*, 2nd ed., pp. 329–331, by J. P. Riehl & C. Roy, Eds., 1980, New York: Appleton-Century-Crofts)

Rogers, M. E. (1994c). The science of unitary human beings: Current perspectives. *Nursing Science Quarterly*, 7, 33–35.

CHAPTER 22

CRITERIA FOR CRITICAL APPRAISAL OF QUALITATIVE RESEARCH

Critical appraisal, a vital dimension of scholarly dialogue, is "the art of analyzing and judging the worth of a work in light of a set of criteria related to correspondence and logical coherence" (Parse, 1993, p. 163). This art is essential to the advancement of science in all disciplines. Critical appraisal clarifies meanings and refines ideas. It is responsible judgment undertaken by qualified scholars on works by other qualified scholars. Criteria for critical appraisal of qualitative research have been described in numerous ways in varying detail (see, for example, Altheide & Johnson, 1994; Beck, 1993; Burns, 1989; Dreher, 1994; Hinds, Scandrett-Hibden, & McAuley, 1990; Knafl & Howard, 1984; Lincoln & Guba, 1985; Mays & Pope, 1995; Morse, 1989, 1999; Parse, Coyne, & Smith, 1985; Rempusheski, 1999; Rose & Webb, 1998; Sandelowski, 1986, 1993, 1995, 1997). The purpose of this chapter is to set forth and describe a definitive set of criteria that may be used to examine the substance and clarity of published qualitative research reports.

Substance refers to the soundness and comprehensiveness of presentation of the phenomenon under study, accuracy of the supporting evidence, and semantic consistency in levels of discourse (see Chapter 1 for a discussion of levels of discourse). *Clarity* refers to logical flow of ideas, appropriate grammatical expressions, and technical precision. Evidence of substance and clarity should flow through the dimensions of the research process and may be determined through a dialogue with the text of a report during which the reviewers read, reread, and dwell with what is written while thinking about what the researcher is saying about the essence of what the participants, the text, or the artform communicated about the phenomenon of concern. The dialogue between the reviewer and the text of the report is guided by specific criteria.

Specific criteria for appraisal of qualitative research (see Table 22–1) correspond with the four dimensions of the research process: conceptual, ethical, methodological, and interpretive. A description of the dimensions of the research process is provided in Chapter 2. Each dimension of critical appraisal of qualitative research is described in the following sections.

CONCEPTUAL

The criteria for appraisal of the conceptual dimension of qualitative research are substance and clarity in presentation of the phenomenon under study, the frame of reference, and the research question. The phenomenon under study should be stated clearly and comprehensively, specifically related to the phenomenon of concern to the discipline of the researcher, and precisely connected with a discipline-specific frame of reference. The frame of reference is the discipline-specific theoretical perspective, or the ontology (underlying values and beliefs), with which the researcher approaches the phenomenon under study and which underpins the research question. What researchers believe about the phenomenon of concern circumscribes what they want to know about it. Reviewers of qualitative research studies should search for a discipline-specific frame of reference that makes explicit the researcher's ontological perspective, comprehensively describes the phenomenon under study in light of that perspective, and shows how the frame of reference led to the research question. The research question should be stated clearly in an interrogatory sentence, and it should be ontologically and epistemologically consistent with the frame of reference.

ETHICAL

The criteria for appraisal of the ethical dimension of qualitative research are substance and clarity related to the scientific merit of the study, the protection of participants' rights, and the accuracy and authenticity of the ways the researcher handles the data. To meet standards of scientific merit, the published report should present the entire research process in a way that is semantically consistent and logically coherent—from the description of the frame of reference right through the synthesis of data and discussion of the findings. In addition, the phenomenon under study should be consistent with a frame of reference relevant to the discipline of the researcher; there should be articulation of a focus on discipline-specific knowledge acquisition; the language of the discipline should be used throughout the research process; and semantic consistency should be preserved with appropriate use of levels of discourse.

The research report also should reflect clearly the measures the researcher took to protect the rights of the participants. It should indicate that the study

TABLE 22–1	CRITERIA FOR APPRAISAL OF QUALITATIVE RESEARCH: CONCEPTUAL, ETHICAL, METHODOLOGICAL, AND INTERPRETIVE DIMENSIONS
Conceptual	How does the phenomenon under study relate to the phenomenon of concern to the discipline?
	How does discipline-specific knowledge underpin the frame of reference?
	How does the research question flow from the frame of reference?
Ethical	How does the plan of study meet standards of scientific merit?
	How does the study contribute to unique discipline-specific knowledge?
	How are participants' rights protected?
	How does the researcher treat the data in light of accuracy and authenticity?
	Are the credentials and experience of the researcher adequate for conduction of the study?
Methodological	Is the method identified correctly?
	Are participants, the text, or the artforms appropriate for the method?
	Is the participant selection process appropriate for the method?
	Is the data-gathering process appropriate for the method?
	Is the data analysis-synthesis process appropriate for the method?
	How does the researcher show conceptual shifts in levels of abstraction?
	How do the abstract statements evolve from the participants' descriptions, the text, or the artforms?
	Is the path of inquiry easily identifiable?
	Is the path of inquiry logical from question to findings?
Interpretive	How do the interpretive statements correspond to the findings?
	To what extent are the findings interpreted in light of the conceptualization of the study?
	How do heuristic implications reflect an accurate interpretation of the findings?
	How are the interpretations woven with theory, research, and, when appropriate, practice?

was approved by an institutional review board for the protection of human subjects; the process for recruiting participants and obtaining their consent; and whether or not standard measures were taken to ensure the participants' knowledge of the research project, safety, privacy, confidentiality, and anonymity. Finally, it should be evident that the researcher preserved scientific merit by precisely and accurately reporting all details of the research process. The reviewer should be able to recognize, for example, how the findings of the study arose from the participants' descriptions, what was written in the text, or what was portrayed by the artform. There should be examples of data in the participants' language, the language of the text, or from the artform that show the reviewer that the findings in the language of the researcher actually did emerge from the data.

METHODOLOGICAL

The criteria for appraisal of the methodological dimension of qualitative research are substance and clarity relative to the data-gathering and analysis-synthesis phases of the research process. The method should be clearly and correctly identified as appropriate to answer the research question consistent with the frame of reference underpinning the study. The data-gathering processes—including the techniques and the nature and number of participants, texts, or artforms used—and the analysis-synthesis processes should be appropriate for the method. As well, the report should show how the researcher made conceptual shifts in levels of abstraction—from the language of the participants, the text, or the artform, to the language of science—and the ways any abstract statements evolved from the participants' descriptions, the text, or the artforms. The transformations in levels of abstraction of the descriptions, text, or artforms should be vivid, precise, and comprehensively presented in a clear, semantically consistent fashion. The path of inquiry should be logical and easily identifiable.

INTERPRETIVE

The criteria for appraisal of the interpretive dimension of qualitative research are substance and clarity in relation to the description of findings in light of disciplinary knowledge that demonstrates the value of the research for theory development, further research, and, when applicable, practice. Interpretive statements made by the researcher must correspond logically and semantically with the findings of the study. The findings must have heuristic relevance, that is, they must be recognized by readers as a valuable contribution to the literature. The accuracy of the heuristic implications drawn from the findings must be reflected in the logical flow and semantic consistency from (a) the presentation of the phenomenon under study to the interpretation of the data; (b) the participants' descriptions, the text, or the artforms that support the interpretive statements; and (c) the ease with which the reviewer can follow the interpretive decisions made by the researcher. The findings of the study should be discussed clearly and comprehensively in light of the initial conceptualization of the study, since this is what enhances understanding and builds disciplinary knowledge. Interpretations of the findings should be woven with the new ideas for theory development and further research.

An example of a qualitative nursing research study (Bunkers, 1998) is provided in the next chapter. It is followed, in Chapter 24, by a critical appraisal using the criteria set forth in this chapter.

REFERENCES

Altheide, D. L., & Johnson, J. M. (1994). Criteria for assessing interpretive validity in qualitative research. In N. K. Denzin, & Y. S. Lincoln (Eds.), *Handbook of qualitative research* (pp. 485–499). Thousand Oaks, CA: Sage.

Beck, C. T. (1993). Qualitative research: The evaluation of its credibility, fittingness, and auditability. *Western Journal of Nursing Research*, 15(2), 263–266.

Bunkers, S. S. (1998). Considering tomorrow: Parse's theory-guided research. *Nursing Science Quarterly*, 11, 56–63.

Burns, N. (1989). Standards for qualitative research. *Nursing Science Quarterly*, 2, 44–52.

Dreher, M. (1994). Qualitative research methods from the reviewer's perspective. In J. M. Morse (Ed.), *Critical issues in qualitative research methods* (pp. 281–297). Thousand Oaks, CA: Sage.

Hinds, P. S., Scandrett-Hibden, S., & McAuley, L. S. (1990). Further assessment of a method to estimate reliability and validity of qualitative research findings. *Journal of Advanced Nursing*, 15, 430–435.

Knafl, K. A., & Howard, M. J. (1984). Interpreting, reporting, and evaluating qualitative research. *Research in Nursing & Health*, 7, 17–24.

Lincoln, Y. S., & Guba, E. G. (1985). *Naturalistic inquiry*. Beverly Hills, CA: Sage.

Mays, N., & Pope, C. (1995). Rigour and qualitative research. *British Medical Journal*, 311, 109–112.

Morse, J. M. (1989). Qualitative nursing research: A free-for-all? In J. M. Morse (Ed.), *Qualitative nursing research: A contemporary dialogue* (pp. 3–10). Rockville, MD: Aspen.

Morse, J. M. (1999). Silent debates in qualitative inquiry. *Qualitative Health Research*, 9(2), 163–165.

Parse, R. R. (1993). Critical appraisal: Risking to challenge. *Nursing Science Quarterly*, 6, 163.

Parse, R. R., Coyne, A. B., & Smith, M. J. (1985). *Nursing research: Qualitative methods*. Bowie, MD: Brady.

Rempusheski, V. F. (1999). Qualitative research and Alzheimer disease. *Alzheimer Disease and Associated Disorders*, 13(Suppl. 1), S45–S49.

Rose, K., & Webb, C. (1998). Analyzing data: Maintaining rigor in a qualitative study. *Qualitative Health Research*, 8(4), 556–562.

Sandelowski, M. (1986). The problem of rigor in qualitative research. *Advances in Nursing Science*, 8(3), 27–37.

Sandelowski, M. (1993). Rigor or rigor mortis: The problem of rigor in qualitative research revisited. *Advances in Nursing Science*, 16(2), 1–8.

Sandelowski, M. (1995). On the aesthetics of qualitative research. *Image: Journal of Nursing Scholarship*, 27(3), 205–209.

Sandelowski, M. (1997). "To be of use": Enhancing the utility of qualitative research. *Nursing Outlook*, 45(3), 125–132.

CHAPTER 23

CONSIDERING TOMORROW: PARSE'S THEORY-GUIDED RESEARCH[1]

Sandra Schmidt Bunkers, RN; PhD

The purpose of this nursing study, guided by Parse's human becoming theory and research methodology, was to investigate the meaning of considering tomorrow for women who are homeless. This is the first study to explore the newly conceptualized health phenomenon of considering tomorrow; thus, this research provides new knowledge for nursing and expands Parse's theory in relation to considering tomorrow, health, and quality of life. Through dialogical engagements with 10 women who were homeless and the process of extraction-synthesis, the researcher generated the structure of considering tomorrow as *contemplating desired endeavors in longing for the cherished, while intimate alliances with isolating distance emerge, as resilient endurance surfaces amid disturbing unsureness.* Conceptual integration led to a theoretical structure in which considering tomorrow is imaging the valuing in the connecting-separating of originating.

The woman stood in the doorway of the homeless shelter in Chicago. What brought her to see the midwife was the need for AIDS testing, since she had discovered that her boyfriend was bisexual. Her statement to this author was "I want to be tested as often as necessary for AIDS. I'm not very big and if I

---

[1]Sandra Schmidt Bunkers, Considering tomorrow: Parse's theory-guided research, *Nursing Science Quarterly*, 11, 56–63, copyright © 1998 by Chestnut House Publications. Adapted and reprinted by permission of Sage Publications, Inc.

know right away that I have it, I can get treatment. Then I will have a better chance of surviving." That statement was the beginning of a conversation in which many episodes in her life were discussed. This woman was seeking assistance because of possible exposure to a life-threatening disease. Through all of this difficulty, this woman was hoping for survival; she was considering tomorrow. Toward the end of the conversation the woman pondered, "People don't understand what survival is for us street people. Do you know what I mean?"

This woman's question is relevant not only for this researcher, but for all of nursing. Her question also denotes a desire to have her lived experience understood; it indicates a pushing toward tomorrow.

The purpose of this study was to advance nursing science by gaining an understanding of the lived experience of considering tomorrow for persons living the phenomenon. Through the theoretical lens of Parse's human becoming theory, this study investigated the meaning of considering tomorrow for women who are homeless.

SIGNIFICANCE AND RESEARCH QUESTION

The significance of this study is threefold. Understanding this lived experience through the lens of Parse's theory of human becoming advances nursing science. It expands the human becoming theory, providing nurses with new insights concerning how individuals move on in the face of profound and unique life experiences. Secondly, new understandings concerning how individuals move on through considering tomorrow can lead to new ways for nurses "to interrelate with persons in practice" (Mitchell & Heidt, 1994, p. 119). Understanding sheds light on the importance of respect for human diversity and poses different nurse-person patterns of cocreating quality of life.

And, finally, gaining insight into the lived experience of considering tomorrow helps to explicate unique ways of becoming, thus uncovering unique and diverse ways of living health. The fact that there are multiple ways of living health is a crucial consideration for nurses if they value the person's own perspective. The research question was "What is the structure of the lived experience of considering tomorrow?"

NURSING PERSPECTIVE

Parse's human becoming theory (Parse, 1981, 1992, 1995a) is the nursing perspective through which the lived experience of considering tomorrow was studied. Three major themes emerge from the philosophical assumptions of the human becoming theory: meaning, rhythmicity, and cotranscendence

(Parse, 1981, 1987, 1992, 1995a). These themes are explicated in the following three principles of the theory.

Principle 1: "Structuring meaning multidimensionally is cocreating reality through the languaging of valuing and imaging" (Parse, 1992, p. 37). This principle means human beings cocreate meaning with the universe. Imaging, valuing and languaging emerge with diversity within individuals, and considering tomorrow is lived through these unitary processes. Considering tomorrow involves envisioning hopes, dreams, and new possibilities through reflection and prereflection as cherished beliefs are examined, confirmed and not confirmed, and lived out in speaking–being silent and moving–being still.

Principle 2: "Cocreating rhythmical patterns of relating is living the paradoxical unity of revealing-concealing, enabling-limiting while connecting-separating" (Parse, 1992, p. 37). This principle relates to how the human-universe-health process emerges through cocreated paradoxical rhythms. Experiencing contradiction in opposites opens one to unlimited choices that can be lived through imagining the "journey to the not-yet" (Mitchell, 1993, p. 51). Considering tomorrow can thus be viewed as involving these paradoxes of lived experiences in the process of connecting-separating in the struggle to decide what is next. Every choice facilitates and hinders the individual in some way, revealing and concealing value priorities simultaneously, and showing the paradoxical nature of the situation and of considering tomorrow.

Principle 3: "Cotranscending with the possibles is powering unique ways of originating in the process of transforming" (Parse, 1992, p. 38). This principle describes moving beyond with hopes and dreams through creating new ways of viewing what is familiar. Powering, originating, and transforming imply a movement beyond what is with what is not-yet. Thus, considering tomorrow is linked to powering and is a movement involving contemplation of possibilities for transforming arising out of imagining and hoping. Considering tomorrow is contemplating what might be while living moment to moment in the now as striving to be unique and like others all-at-once sheds light on the uncertainty embedded in the not-yet. It is not a human experience that can be managed, avoided, coped with, or manipulated. It is essential to one's becoming. All of an individual's imagined possibilities are interwoven in the processes of choosing a path in life.

RESEARCH METHOD AND FINDINGS

The Parse research method was utilized to uncover the structure of the lived experience of considering tomorrow. This is a phenomenological-hermeneutic method congruent with the philosophy and principles of the nursing theory of human becoming. The method is "generically phenomenological in that the entities for study are experiences as described by people who have lived them" (Parse, 1995b, p. 153). It is a hermeneutic method in that the inquiry focuses on uncovering the meanings of lived experiences of health (Parse,

1995b). The method is composed of several processes: participant selection, dialogical engagement, extraction-synthesis, and heuristic interpretation. These processes occur simultaneously as the study emerges, as has been discussed in detail in previous works (Parse, 1987, 1990b, 1992, 1993, 1995b).

Participants and Setting

Ten women who were homeless, 18 years of age and over, and with the knowledge and desire to participate were invited to take part in this study. These participants were recruited through a large metropolitan health outreach center for the homeless. Community outreach workers assisted the researcher in informing and recruiting women who were interested in volunteering to participate in the study. The final explanation of the study and obtaining informed consent was conducted by this researcher. A university review board for the protection of human subjects approved the study. Potential participants were informed that refusal to participate in the study would not affect the services they received from the outreach program. Participants were able to understand, read, and speak English and were able to focus on and describe the lived experience of considering tomorrow. The sessions took place in a small room at the outreach center. The discussions were tape recorded, and varied in length from about 30 to 60 minutes.

Processes of the Method and Findings

Dialogical engagement is a discussion between the researcher and participant. The researcher listened in true presence as each participant described the experience of considering tomorrow. The dialogical engagement began with the researcher making the following statement: "Tell me what it is like for you to consider tomorrow . . . to think about tomorrow."

The extraction-synthesis process occurred as the researcher "dwelled with" the dialogical engagement, both the audiotape and the typed dialogue. Essences were first written in the language of the participant and then taken up levels of abstraction and written in the language of science (researcher's language). (See Table 23–1.)

A proposition was formulated from each participant's extracted-synthesized essences. The proposition captured the participant's experience in "a nondirectional statement conceptualized by the researcher" (Parse, 1987, p. 177). (See Table 23–2.) Core concepts were then drawn from all participants' propositions; these concepts were synthesized into a structure, which is the answer to the research question: *Considering tomorrow is contemplating desired endeavors in longing for the cherished, while intimate alliances with isolating distance emerge, as resilient endurance surfaces amid disturbing unsureness.* (See Table 23–3.)

Heuristic interpretation, the final process of the research method, is interpreting the structure of the lived experience in the language of the human becoming theory. At the structural transposition level of theory *the lived experience*

(continued on p. 256)

TABLE 23–1   EXTRACTION-SYNTHESIS PROCESS WITH RELATED PROPOSITIONS

ESSENCES—PARTICIPANT 6

Participant's Language	*Researcher's Language*
1. Stating that it not wise to plan for tomorrow because you never know where you will be or what is going to happen to you, the participant still hopes for a better life. She is working on preparing a way to get an apartment, start her own typing business, and make some money.	1. Disturbing unsureness emerges with deliberations on desired endeavors.
2. Expressing a lack of trust in others because she believes her home, belongings, and children were taken from her and that she has been used by others, the participant still wants to be reunited with her children and be around and talk to people at the airport. She does not want to get involved with many people but believes meeting others may help her, and she refuses to be defeated.	2. Longing for the cherished amid disillusioning estrangement surfaces a renewed vigor for launching new alliances.
3. Stating that she thinks people look down on her like a piece of dirt and wanting to hide her homelessness, the participant is disappointed in herself in areas of her life. However, at the same time she says she wants to maintain what dignity she has, is not ashamed of herself, is not a bad person, and is a person with a conscience.	3. Resilient integrity arises with the simultaneous presence of pride and disgrace.

Proposition

The lived experience of considering tomorrow is longing for the cherished amid a disillusioning estrangement that surfaces with renewed vigor for launching new alliances, while deliberations on desired endeavors emerge with disturbing unsureness, as resilient integrity arises with the simultaneous presence of pride and disgrace.

TABLE 23–1   EXTRACTION-SYNTHESIS PROCESS WITH RELATED PROPOSITIONS (CONTINUED)

ESSENCES—PARTICIPANT 8

Participant's Language	*Researcher's Language*
1. Stating that at one time all her tomorrows were dark and feeling like she didn't have a tomorrow, the participant had given up on life. However, now in a treatment house, she sees tomorrow as a blessing and as a time for her to learn about herself and build her self-esteem. She looks toward having her children living with her.	1. Disillusioning unsureness emerges with contemplating the gift of launching ahead with what is cherished.
2. Indicating that she feels like everyone else has turned their backs on her and that she is getting the dirt back that she had done to others, the participant sees Jesus as the only one who has not forsaken her. However, she is thankful to her mother for being there to care for her children.	2. Alienating isolation emerges amid gratefulness for nurturing solemn alliances.
3. Stating she is ashamed and scared of saying things in a group, the participant is now building herself up, depending on her own self-esteem, and learning to talk to and share herself with others.	3. Innovative engagements arise with the dread of potential humiliation in intimacy.

Proposition

The lived experience of considering tomorrow is contemplating the gift of launching ahead with what is cherished, while disillusioning unsureness with alienating isolation emerges amid gratefulness for nurturing solemn alliances, as innovative engagements arise with the dread of potential humiliation in intimacy.

TABLE 23–2   Propositional Statements of Participants

1. The lived experience of considering tomorrow is ardent anticipation of initiating alliances anew, while disillusioning disengagement arises amid intentional holding, as the presence of disturbing impatience emerges with deliberate resolve in longing for the cherished, when frightening unsureness surfaces with contemplation of desired undertakings.

2. The lived experience of considering tomorrow is contemplation of launching desired undertakings with intimate alliances emerging with disillusioning anguish amid the isolating estrangement of longing for the cherished, while the tormenting despair of disturbing unsureness surfaces with solemn anticipation in the persevering steadfastness of the immediate.

3. The lived experience of considering tomorrow is contented deliberate anticipation of undertakings amid striving with multiple encumbrances, while reflections of isolating estrangement arise with a pleasurable longing for nurturing cherished intimate affiliations, as threatening unsureness surfaces with faithfully envisioning endurance.

4. The lived experience of considering tomorrow is the puzzling deliberations of desired endeavors which shift with the ease of routinizing the immediate, while a longing for the remembered cherished surfaces with grateful solemn alliances amid a frightening unsureness of estrangement, as enthused vigor for moving on arises with the disquieting forebodings of deliberate contemplation.

5. The lived experience of considering tomorrow is anticipating new likelihoods amid troubling reflections of alienation, while longing for nurturing the cherished surfaces in mediating on solemn alliances, as frightening unsureness in contemplation eases with routinizing undertakings.

6. The lived experience of considering tomorrow is longing for the cherished amid a disillusioning estrangement that surfaces with renewed vigor for launching new alliances, while deliberations on desired endeavors emerge with disturbing unsureness, as resilient integrity arises with the simultaneous presence of pride and disgrace.

TABLE 23–2 PROPOSITIONAL STATEMENTS OF PARTICIPANTS (CONTINUED)	
7. The lived experience of considering tomorrow is contemplating significant strivings amid threatening doubts of unsureness, while forging ahead with the cherished in solemn confidence surfaces with the solitary aloofness of disillusionment with the desired calmness of harmonious alliances, as resisting nurturing yields to gradual acceptance.	9. The lived experience of considering tomorrow is contemplating desired endeavors with remorse for the remembered, while disturbing unsureness emerges with aspiring for a stability with what is cherished in the immediate, as turbulent distancing arises amid longing for attentive joyous alliances.
8. The lived experience of considering tomorrow is contemplating the gift of launching ahead with what is cherished, while disillusioning unsureness with alienating isolation emerges amid gratefulness for nurturing solemn alliances, as innovative engagements arise with the dread of potential humiliation in intimacy.	10. The lived experience of considering tomorrow is concentrating on the immediate strivings of longing for the cherished amid disillusioning unsureness, while rueful adversity emerges with the contented prosperity of a tolerant resolute integrity, as stubborn distancing yields to sustaining solemn alliances.

of considering tomorrow is pondering the possibles, while yearning for the treasured, as communion-aloneness emerges with certainty-uncertainty. At the conceptual integration level of theory *considering tomorrow is imaging the valuing in the connecting-separating of originating.* (See Tables 23–3 and 23–4.)

DISCUSSION OF FINDINGS

The first core concept, *contemplating desired endeavors*, describes the hopes and dreams that all participants held for moving beyond what was by thinking about acquiring education, a job or some type of income, and a place to call home. One participant said, "All I want is a little room for me and a little kitten and my own typing business. I don't need a lot of luxury and fancy stuff. . . . Now I've got to find a way to restructure my existence, my being, so that even if I don't get everything back that I lost, at least I can have some comfort and peace of mind." Another woman said, "I just want to go to school, I want to get

TABLE 23–3   THE LIVED EXPERIENCE OF CONSIDERING TOMORROW

Core Concepts

- Contemplating desired endeavors
- Longing for the cherished
- Intimate alliances with isolating distance
- Resilient endurance and disturbing unsureness

Structure of the Lived Experience

The lived experience of considering tomorrow is contemplating desired endeavors in longing for the cherished, while intimate alliances with isolating distance emerge, as resilient endurance surfaces amid disturbing unsureness.

Heuristic Interpretation

Structural Transposition. The lived experience of considering tomorrow is pondering the possibles, while yearning for the treasured, as communion-aloneness emerges with certainty-uncertainty.

Conceptual Integration. The lived experience of considering tomorrow is imaging the valuing in the connecting-separating of originating.

TABLE 23–4   HEURISTIC INTERPRETATION: PROGRESSIVE ABSTRACTION OF CORE CONCEPTS OF CONSIDERING TOMORROW

Core Concept	Structural Transposition	Conceptual Integration
Contemplating desired endeavors	⟶ Pondering the possibles	⟶ Imaging
Longing for the cherished	⟶ Yearning for the treasured	⟶ Valuing
Intimate alliances with isolating distance	⟶ Communion-aloneness	⟶ Connecting-separating
Resilient endurance amid disturbing unsureness	⟶ Certainty-uncertainty	⟶ Originating

---

a shop, I want something of my own. I want something of my own that I can show to my children and say, 'This is ours.' "

The core concept of *contemplating desired endeavors* was structurally transposed at a higher level of abstraction as pondering the possibles. At the conceptual integration level, pondering the possibles is imaging. Imaging is a way of structuring meaning and cocreating reality (Parse, 1981, 1995a) and is

connected to the first principle of the human becoming theory. All participants in the study described the imaging process involved in contemplating
desired endeavors by statements such as "My days were dark from the drugs
and alcohol, you know. I just gave up on life. . . . Now I can say tomorrow is a
blessing. . . . I can live tomorrow better. I can smell the grass. I can hear birds
whistle."

Contemplating desired endeavors is creating actuality out of possibility in living
the now with hopes and dreams of the not-yet. The women in this study described envisioning new ways of living, and these new ways created new
meanings in the lived experience of considering tomorrow.

The second core concept, longing for the cherished, was described by the participants as wanting to be rejoined with loved ones and wanting life to be different from now or the way it was before. One woman's description of longing
for the cherished was the following: "You know, you see these people on TV where
they are reunited with their families. Maybe one day something like that
might happen. It may not be as glamorous. Something like that might come up
where I'm reunited with my children." Another woman spoke about praying for
survival so she could do something with her life. She stated, "Lord, please let
me live to see tomorrow . . . because I have three beautiful, lovely children
that I always will love and want to be back in their world with them." Another
said, "It's going to take a lot of work, a lot of hard work, a lot of time, a lot of pa-
tience to mend the relationship that I broke with my kids. But, I'm going to.
And I'm going to be there for them."

This core concept of longing for the cherished was structurally transposed to the
concept of yearning for the treasured. Yearning for the treasured involves living patterns of preference in affirming self (Parse, 1990a). Thus, at the conceptual integration level, yearning for the treasured is valuing and is connected to the first principle of the theory of human becoming (Parse, 1981,
1995a).

Meaning-giving and the shaping of reality through the valuing process is
clear in all participants' descriptions and is portrayed in the following statement by one participant: "I hope God walks with me tomorrow the same as He
does today. I know with His power and my determination, I'm sure tomorrow
will be OK. . . . I got to have something to show for my life." Another woman
said, "After I get myself together and settle down, maybe I can start looking for
my kids. At least I want them to know that I'm not a bad person and that I did-
n't give them away; they were actually stolen from me. . . . I would like to make
it up to my kids. . . . And, I would like them to have respect for me and understanding." The participants in this study on considering tomorrow created
meaning in their lived situations in longing for the treasured and focusing on de-
riving from life's transitoriness an incentive to be connected with what they
yearned for and treasured.

The third core concept, intimate alliances with isolating distance, was described
by the women in this study as day-to-day struggles in relationships (alienation from others and connectedness to those loved). Many of the women

also described connectedness to a higher power most often identified as God or Jesus.

The dialogues surfaced intense feelings concerning how the participants viewed belonging in community with others. One woman described the paradoxical relational pattern of intimate alliances with isolating distance as follows: "It's not that I dislike people; it's that I see what they have done to me. They don't know what honesty is. . . . It's just like, 'Let me dig my claws in you until you bleed and, hey, then I'm satisfied.' And then when there is no more blood, throw you away." At the same time, however, this woman indicated she looked forward to being associated with others by saying, "I like to go out to the airport. You meet a lot of positive people out there. You know, I leave there at night and say, 'Well, I'll be back tomorrow.'" The paradoxical rhythm of engaging and distancing is present in this woman's message. Another woman said, "I just thank my Higher Power because He is the only one that never turned His back on me. If it weren't for Jesus, I'd be gone."

The core concept of *intimate alliances with isolating distance* was structurally transposed as communion-aloneness. Communion-aloneness portrays a paradoxical lived pattern of moving toward and away from persons, ideas, places, and events as one considers tomorrow. It involves the languaging of closeness and distancing all-at-once.

Communion-aloneness at the conceptual integration level is connecting-separating. Connecting-separating is a coming together with others and various phenomena while simultaneously separating from other possibilities (Parse, 1981). This connecting-separating is related to the second principle of the theory of human becoming.

The final core concept, *resilient endurance amid disturbing unsureness*, was characterized by the participants as a knowing of unique ways of moving with the not-yet in particular patterns of relating to others, planning activities, and diverse ways of structuring their treasured possibles. Coexisting with the resilient endurance was a pervasive feeling of not knowing what tomorrow would bring or whether or not one would live to see tomorrow. This paradoxical pattern of being sure and unsure, of knowing and not knowing was noted in the participants' stories. One woman said, "I just keep hoping that the future will be better than it is. . . . As long as I keep faith and keep on hoping and praying, things will improve and life will go on." However, she also stated, "You don't know what to expect anymore. You go out to the store and somebody can mug you. It's rough. Life is getting worse."

The tension of *resilient endurance amid disturbing unsureness* present in the descriptions of the women in this study involved actively imaging that things would get better. Knowles (1987) suggests that this type of believing, which is related to imaging, is "a particular way of moving in the world" (p. 61).

One participant remarked, "You see, I got to hold on to the little bit of sanity I have, the little bit of dignity that I have. . . . At least tomorrow I can push myself a little closer to getting to that goal . . . search for ways to put yourself in the best position to meet people who can help get to that position."

This woman depicts in her statements the search for possibilities emerging as part of her response to the lived paradox of *resilient endurance amid disturbing unsureness*.

The core concept of *resilient endurance amid disturbing unsureness* was structurally transposed as certainty-uncertainty. Certainty-uncertainty is lived "in human encounters as individuals make concrete or clear their choices in situation yet, simultaneously, live the ambiguity of the unknown outcomes" (Parse, 1981, p. 60).

At conceptual integration, certainty-uncertainty is originating. Originating is a process of mutual unfolding, of choosing unique individual ways of living (Parse, 1981), and is connected to the third principle of the human becoming theory.

Resilient endurance amid disturbing unsureness involves novel ways of struggling with what-is and what-is-not-yet. It involves knowing and not-knowing one's possibilities and moving with the not-yet in confidence while pausing with the realization of unpredictability.

CONSIDERING TOMORROW, HEALTH, AND QUALITY OF LIFE

The theory of human becoming (Parse, 1981, 1987, 1990b, 1992, 1995a) posits that health is a process of unfolding, a personal commitment to a lived value system. Women who were homeless in this study shared their unique ways of emerging lived patterns of health as they moved with the not-yet. These patterns were described by them and interpreted in the language of science as the four core concepts of contemplating desired endeavors, longing for the cherished, intimate alliances with isolating distance, and resilient endurance amid disturbing unsureness.

Quality of life, in the human becoming theory, is defined as "what the person there living the life says it is" (Parse, 1994b, p. 17). The women in this study described and defined their own quality of life as they related the meanings of considering tomorrow through describing the struggles and joys of their day-to-day patterns of moving with the now and the not-yet.

CORE CONCEPTS AND RELATED LITERATURE

In contemplating desired endeavors through pondering the possibles, the women depicted unique stances toward creating anew. The cocreation of the new arose in imaging what could be. These considerations shaped the emerging health patterns of these women. Studies conducted by Brunsman (1987),

Parse (1990b), Smith (1990a), Stanley (1978), and Thornburg (1993) also uncovered the notion of an envisioning or orientation toward the future. For example, Parse (1990b) studied hope with 10 persons and found hope to include "anticipating possibilities through envisioning the not-yet" and linked it to "imaging the will-be" (Parse, 1990b, p. 17).

All participants described a longing for the cherished related to considering tomorrow as an experience of health. Longing for the cherished as a way of living health relates to the theory of human becoming's concept of valuing. Valuing as a yearning for the treasured is shown in Pilkington's (1993) study of the lived experience of grieving the loss of an important other. Cody (1991) and Smith (1990b) also identify valuing as integral to grieving a prized personal loss. The findings from these Parse studies raise the question of whether or not the participants in this study, in yearning for the treasured, are not also grieving a loss. Further research could explore such a possibility.

The third core concept, *intimate alliances with isolating distance*, was manifest in all participant descriptions of relationships. The paradoxical nature of this connecting-separating experience described by the participants is shown in findings of other Parse studies (Cody, 1991, 1995; Pilkington, 1993). Cody (1995) identifies a communion-solitude of "bearing witness to aloneness with togetherness" (p. 222). Pilkington (1993) describes an engaging and disengaging with the absent presence and others.

The fourth core concept, *resilient endurance amid disturbing unsureness*, is an expression of the life pattern of certainty-uncertainty. The paradox of certainty-uncertainty is linked to Parse's concept of originating. Although originating has been identified as a core concept in other Parse studies (Brunsman, 1987; Cody, 1995; Mitchell, 1994, 1995; Mitchell & Heidt, 1994; Parse, 1994a), this is the first study to identify resilient endurance amid disturbing unsureness as a changing health process of living the rhythm of certainty-uncertainty.

Resilient endurance amid disturbing unsureness stands in direct contrast to the findings of the studies conducted by Newman (1993), who found the core concept emerging from data in a study of abused homeless women was "giving up" and Baumann (1993), who used the metaphor of "a whirlpool of poverty and powerlessness" to describe the experience of homeless women.

However, consistent with *resilient endurance amid disturbing unsureness* are Hodnicki and Horner's (1993) findings of the core theme of "one step at a time" for homeless mothers caring for children in a shelter and Montgomery's (1994) synthesis of the metaphor of "swimming upstream" to describe homeless women's experiences of courage and strength. Fromm (1968), Frankl (1984), and Marcel (1962, 1965) in their writings on hope also relate the human phenomenon of moving on with fortitude in times of trial and uncertainty.

In light of considering tomorrow, *health is the process of envisioning what will be while living cherished personal commitments.* The meaning given to this health process of considering tomorrow emerges as one's quality of life. Considering tomorrow is a way persons create themselves in the now.

IMPLICATIONS FOR RESEARCH

Considering tomorrow is a new formulation of a health phenomenon providing new information for nursing and for the literature on homeless women. Future studies of considering tomorrow conducted with different persons in a variety of settings across the life span may surface new knowledge of envisioning the not-yet and health. In addition, the core concepts of the structure could be further explored as related lived experiences. The significance of these core concepts in generating future research is immense.

REFLECTIONS

Understanding the meaning of the lived experience of another is the essence of coming to know another and valuing the other as a unique human being. Dialoguing with these women in true presence shed light on the difficulty, the pain and suffering, and the promise of the meaning of considering tomorrow when access to resources such as money, property, and significant others poses a challenge. And, although all core concepts of the human becoming theory are present in human experiences, at the conceptual integration level of theory, considering tomorrow for these women brings to the foreground the imaging of valuing in the connecting-separating of originating.

In dialogue, opportunities were cocreated with these women to lift their voices and uncover personal truths for others to hear and understand. Kearney (1987) suggests that a critical-poetic-hermeneutic imagination "bids us to tell and retell the story of ourselves . . . out of fidelity to the other. It is above all the other who demands that I remain responsible to myself. For if there is no longer a self to abide by its promises or covenants, there is no ethical relation to the other possible" (p. 55).

REFERENCES

Baumann, S. (1993). The meaning of being homeless. *Scholarly Inquiry for Nursing Practice: An International Journal*, 7(1), 59–70.

Brunsman, C. (1987). *A phenomenological study of the lived experience of hope in families with a chronically ill child*. Unpublished master's thesis, Michigan State University, Ann Arbor, MI.

Cody, W. (1991). Grieving a personal loss. *Nursing Science Quarterly*, 4, 61–68.

Cody, W. (1995). The lived experience of grieving, for families living with AIDS. In R. R. Parse (Ed.), *Illuminations: The human becoming theory in practice and research* (pp. 197–242). New York: National League for Nursing Press.

Frankl, V. (1984). *Man's search for meaning*. New York: Simon & Schuster.

Fromm, E. (1968). *The revolution of hope*. New York: Harper & Row.

Hodnicki, D., & Horner, S. (1993). Homeless mothers caring for children in a shelter. *Issues in Mental Health Nursing*, 14, 349–356.

Kearney, R. (1987). Ethics and the postmodern imagination. *Thought*, 62(244), 39–58.

Knowles, R. (1987). Fantasy and imagination. *Studies in Formative Spirituality*, VI(1), 53–63.

Marcel, G. (1962). *Homo viator: A metaphysics of hope*. New York: Harper & Row.

Marcel, G. (1965). *Being and having*. New York: Harper & Row.

Mitchell, G. (1993). Living paradox in Parse's theory. *Nursing Science Quarterly*, 6, 44–51.

Mitchell, G. (1994). Discipline-specific inquiry: The hermeneutics of theory-guided nursing research. *Nursing Outlook*, 42(5), 224–228.

Mitchell, G., & Heidt, P. (1994). The lived experience of wanting to help another: Research with Parse's method. *Nursing Science Quarterly*, 7, 119–127.

Mitchell, G. J. (1995). The lived experience of restriction-freedom in later life. In R. R. Parse (Ed.), *Illuminations: The human becoming theory in practice and research* (pp. 159–195). New York: National League for Nursing Press.

Montgomery, C. (1994). Swimming upstream: The strengths of women who survive homelessness. *Advances in Nursing Science*, 16(3), 34–45.

Newman, K. (1993). Giving up: Shelter experiences of battered women. *Public Health Nursing*, 10(2), 108–113.

Parse, R. R. (1981). *Man-living-health: A theory of nursing*. New York: Delmar.

Parse, R. R. (1987). *Nursing science: Major paradigms, theories, and critiques*. Philadelphia: Saunders.

Parse, R. R. (1990a). Health: A personal commitment. *Nursing Science Quarterly*, 3, 136–140.

Parse, R. R. (1990b). Parse's research methodology with an illustration of the lived experience of hope. *Nursing Science Quarterly*, 3, 9–17.

Parse, R. R. (1992). Human becoming: Parse's theory of nursing. *Nursing Science Quarterly*, 5, 35–42.

Parse, R. R. (1993). The experience of laughter: A phenomenological study. *Nursing Science Quarterly*, 6, 39–43.

Parse, R. R. (1994a). Laughing and health. A study using Parse's research method. *Nursing Science Quarterly*, 7, 55–64.

Parse, R. R. (1994b). Quality of life: Sciencing and living the art of human becoming. *Nursing Science Quarterly*, 7, 16–21.

Parse, R. R. (1995a). The human becoming theory. In R. R. Parse (Ed.), *Illuminations: The human becoming theory in practice and research* (pp. 5–8). New York: National League for Nursing Press.

Parse, R. R. (1995b). Research with the human becoming theory. In R. R. Parse (Ed.), *Illuminations: The human becoming theory in practice and research* (pp. 151–157). New York: National League for Nursing Press.

Pilkington, F. B. (1993). The lived experience of grieving the loss of an important other. *Nursing Science Quarterly*, 6, 130–139.

Smith, M. C. (1990a). *The lived experience of hope in families with critically ill persons*. Paper presented at UCLA National Nursing Theory Conference, Los Angeles.

Smith, M. C. (1990b). Struggling through a difficult time for unemployed persons. *Nursing Science Quarterly, 3,* 18–28.

Stanley, A. T. (1978). *The lived experience of hope: The isolation of discreet descriptive elements common to the experience of hope in healthy adults.* Unpublished doctoral dissertation, Catholic University of America, Washington, DC.

Thornburg, P. D. (1993). *The meaning of hope in parents whose infants died from sudden infant death syndrome.* Unpublished doctoral dissertation, University of Cincinnati, Cincinnati, OH.

CHAPTER 24

CRITICAL APPRAISAL OF "CONSIDERING TOMORROW: PARSE'S THEORY-GUIDED RESEARCH"

The purpose of this chapter is to provide an example of a critical appraisal of a qualitative research study using the conceptual, ethical, methodological, and interpretive criteria set forth in Chapter 22 (see Table 22–1). The criteria are used to critique Sandra Schmidt Bunkers' (1998) study (reprinted in Chapter 23 of this book) of the phenomenon *considering tomorrow*.

CONCEPTUAL

Bunkers introduces the phenomenon of concern, the lived experience of considering tomorrow, with a poignant vignette about a woman in a homeless shelter who was pregnant and seeking assistance after being exposed to AIDS. Bunkers shares that the woman spoke about many aspects of her life and was hoping to survive. Bunkers then conceptualizes this "hoping to survive" as considering tomorrow. In the abstract, the author defines considering tomorrow as a "health phenomenon" and further explicates this connection in the nursing perspective section where she skillfully and comprehensively discusses the experience of considering tomorrow in light of the three principles of human becoming (Parse, 1981, 1998) and elaborates clearly on the importance of the phenomenon for human becoming—the process of humans living health. Considering tomorrow, then, is directly connected with the human-universe-health process—the phenomenon of concern for nursing (Parse, 1997).

The purpose of this study was to advance nursing science by gaining an understanding of the experience of considering tomorrow. In order to achieve this purpose, Bunkers used human becoming, a nursing-specific frame of reference, to guide the study from inception to completion. Universal lived experiences of health, such as considering tomorrow, are the phenomena for study with the human becoming school of thought (Parse, 1981, 1998). The research question, *What is the structure of the lived experience of considering tomorrow?*, flows from the frame of reference and is consistent with human becoming and appropriate for the Parse research method—the research method used for this study—which provided Bunkers with a theoretically consistent process for data gathering and analysis-synthesis.

The substance and clarity of the conceptual dimension of this research report generally is excellent but would have been strengthened if Bunkers had presented, even briefly, some literature on hope that supported her conceptualization of the woman's story of "hoping to survive" as considering tomorrow—especially since the discussion of findings at the end of the report connects the findings with other literature on hope. In addition, Bunkers' explication of considering tomorrow in the nursing perspective section is, at times, written at different levels of discourse. For example, when discussing considering tomorrow in light of the second principle of human becoming, Bunkers writes:

> Considering tomorrow can thus be viewed as involving . . . paradoxes of lived experiences in the process of connecting-separating in the struggle to decide what is next. Every choice facilitates and hinders the individual in some way, revealing and concealing value priorities simultaneously. (1998/2001, p. 251)

In the same sentence, Bunkers uses language at and below the theoretical level to describe the paradoxes connected with the principle "cocreating rhythmical patterns of relating" (Parse, 1998, p. 34). Perhaps enabling-limiting would have expressed her "facilitates and hinders" (Bunkers, 1998/2001, p. 251) in a more semantically consistent way.

ETHICAL

The substance and clarity of the ethical dimension of Bunkers' (1998/2001) study is excellent. Bunkers presents the research process in a way that is logically coherent—from the introduction of the phenomenon, to the statement of the significance of the study, to the nursing perspective, to the description of the research method, and the presentation and discussion of the findings. The phenomenon of concern is consistent with human becoming, and Bunkers clearly articulates that the purpose of the study is to enhance understanding of nursing knowledge—specifically the human becoming theory. Accordingly, she uses the ontology, epistemology, and research methodology of human becoming to guide her entire study. This ontological-epistemological-methodological connection with human becoming is reflected in the language Bunkers uses throughout her research report. This study does in fact expand unique nursing knowledge, since Bunkers describes and interprets the findings of the study in light of the specific concepts of the human becoming theory—thereby expanding understanding of the findings as well as of the theoretical concepts. This study is semantically sound.

Bunkers' (1998/2001) report comprehensively addresses the measures she took to protect the rights of the participants. Her study was approved by an institutional review board (IRB) for the protection of human subjects; the participants signed consents and were told that refusal to participate would have no effect on services they receive. The data gathering took place in a private room, and the reader can assume that other standard measures to protect confidentiality and anonymity were used, since the study was approved by an IRB.

Bunkers clearly presents examples from two of the participants that demonstrate, using participants' own words, that the findings of the study are accurate and reflective of the ways the participants described their experiences of considering tomorrow. Table 23–1 shows how what these two participants said about their experiences of considering tomorrow was captured, conceptualized at a higher level of abstraction, and formulated into propositions. The propositions developed for all of the participants are presented in Table 23–2 so that the reader can evaluate how well the findings are supported by data gathered from each and every participant. Careful examination of the propositions of all participants shows that there is logical support for each of the core concepts. Bunkers also uses examples from the participants' descriptions to support the findings throughout the discussion section. Thus, one can be relatively certain that Bunkers has treated the data accurately and authentically. Also, Bunkers is a well-known, well-published Parse scholar. This study was her doctoral dissertation, and it was guided by Rosemarie Rizzo Parse—the creator of the human becoming school of thought and an expert in qualitative research, particularly the Parse research method. Thus, it is reasonable to assume that Bunkers had the knowledge, experience, and guidance necessary to conduct this study.

METHODOLOGICAL

Bunkers clearly identifies the Parse research method to study the lived experience of considering tomorrow (Parse, 1987, 1998). She correctly identifies it as a phenomenological-hermeneutic method but could have described more clearly what hermeneutic means. In the article, Bunkers (1998/2001) says, "It is a hermeneutic method in that the inquiry focuses on uncovering the meanings of lived experiences of health" (p. 251). Substantively, it might have been better to have explained that the method is hermeneutic in that the findings are interpreted in light of the principles and concepts of human becoming.

Participants for this study were recruited through a metropolitan health outreach center. Ten women who were homeless agreed to participate. According to Parse (1998, 1999), this is an adequate sample size. There have been numerous studies that have discovered structures of lived experiences with this number of participants. Although the participants in this particular study were all homeless, it is not necessary to have a particular participant group to use the Parse method. The purpose of the method is to discover the meaning of universal lived experiences through a study of persons' original descriptions. The only criterion for participation in a Parse method study is that potential participants be willing and able to describe the lived experience under study in a way that the researcher can understand.

Bunkers (1998/2001) followed the processes of the Parse research method appropriately. She lists and clearly describes the dialogical engagement, extraction-synthesis, and heuristic interpretation processes in ways consistent with the way Parse describes them (Parse, 1987, 1998). In this book (see Chapter 17), Parse includes constructing a story of essential ideas about the phenomenon from each participant's dialogue using the extraction-synthesis process. Since this is a very recent addition to the Parse method, Bunkers' study does not include examples of participants' stories.

Bunkers (1998/2001) uses a series of tables to show conceptual shifts in levels of abstraction, moving logically from the language of the participants to the language of the researcher. As discussed previously, the tables show the ways the more abstract conceptualizations of the findings evolved from the participants' descriptions. In Table 23–1, the examples are generally clear and the transformations of the essences from the participants' to the researcher's language can, for the most part, be followed. The first essence in the researcher's language for participant 6, *"disturbing unsureness emerges with deliberations on desired endeavors"* (Bunkers, 1998/2001, p. 253), is not clearly connected with the ideas in the corresponding essence in the participant's language. In addition, the essences in the language of participant 8 are not mutually exclusive. For example, both the first and the third essences in the language of participant 8 include references to "building herself up," "learning," and "self-esteem" (p. 254). Semantic consistency would have been adhered to more precisely with further synthesis of these two essences.

Tables 23–2, 23–3, and 23–4 (Bunkers, 1998/2001) show the path of inquiry from the level of the propositions to the core concepts, the structure of the lived experience of considering tomorrow, and the heuristic interpretation level. In Table 23–4, the four core concepts—*contemplating desired endeavors, longing for the cherished, intimate alliances with isolating distance,* and *resilient endurance amid disturbing unsureness*—are structurally transposed to the level of the theory. The reader is able to follow the logical flow of the shifts Bunkers makes in the levels of abstraction of the findings but wonders whether the first two core concepts, *contemplating desired endeavors* and *longing for the cherished*, might have been synthesized further into one. The notion of contemplating something desired is very similar to longing for something cherished. This critique is supported further if one examines the similar examples Bunkers uses in the discussion section to support the two concepts. For instance, in describing the meaning of the core concept *contemplating desired endeavors*, Bunkers (1998/2001) writes,

"The women in this study described envisioning new ways of living" (p. 258). Similarly, Bunkers says *longing for the cherished* "was described by the participants as a wanting to be rejoined with loved ones and wanting life to be different from now" (p. 258). In both instances, the participants' descriptions are used to support the notion that considering tomorrow is thinking about and yearning for something treasured. At the conceptual integration level, the synthesized core concept could be interpreted as the construct imaging valuing.

The third core concept, *resilient endurance amid disturbing unsureness*, was structurally transposed by Bunkers (1998/2001) as certainty-uncertainty and conceptually integrated with human becoming as originating. Substantively, perhaps this could have been powering originating, inasmuch as resilient endurance suggests a pushing-resisting rhythm consistent with powering, and Bunkers, describing the "tension of resilient endurance" (p. 259) in the discussion section, says this core concept "involves novel ways of struggling with what-is and what-is-not-yet" (p. 260), and quotes a participant who said, "You see, I got to hold on to the little bit of sanity that I have, the little bit of dignity that I have. . . . At least tomorrow I can push myself a little closer to getting to that goal" (p. 259). The notion of *affirming being* in spite of the possibility of *nonbeing*, which is inherent in powering, surfaced in this participant's description of "push[ing] . . . a little closer to . . . that goal" in spite of the possibility of losing "the little bit of dignity" (p. 259) she has left. Bunkers' path of inquiry is logically consistent and easy to follow.

INTERPRETIVE

Bunkers (1998/2001) presents a thoroughly substantive discussion of the major findings of this study. Each of the four core concepts is described clearly, supported with examples from the participants' descriptions, and connected with the principles of human becoming and the related literature. The clarity of the interpretive dimension of this study is very good—though in at least one instance it was not entirely clear how interpretive statements were connected with the findings. For example, in discussing the core concept *yearning for the cherished* in light of other literature, Bunkers notes that other authors reported similar core concepts in their studies on the phenomenon *grieving a loss*. Bunkers suggests that perhaps the participants in her study, who gave descriptions that led to the notion of *yearning for the treasured*, also might be grieving a loss (p. 261). This seems to be an interpretive leap in that it is unsubstantiated by the portion of the data that Bunkers presents in this particular study.

In the discussion portion, Bunkers (1998/2001) includes a section in which she connects *considering tomorrow* with health and quality of life—thus supporting her initial conceptualization of this phenomenon. The findings are discussed comprehensively. Bunkers states that there is "immense" (p. 262) potential for guiding future knowledge development; however, the substance of this piece of the study could have been enhanced by one or two examples of the universal lived experiences that Bunkers gleaned from the core concepts that could be studied in the future.

CONCLUSION

Bunkers' (1998/2001) study on the phenomenon *considering tomorrow* is a significant contribution to disciplinary nursing knowledge. There are very few aspects of this report that could be further clarified and substantiated. The findings of this Parse method study expand understanding of the human experience of considering tomorrow, enhance understanding of human becoming, and add to a growing body of knowledge about human lived experiences of health and quality of life.

In Bunkers' (1998/2001) "Reflections" at the end of the study, she refers to the experience of living true presence with the participants and calls attention to the way the experience of true presence in research is woven into the researcher's life (p. 262). She quotes Kearney (1987), who suggests that qualitative research "bids us to tell and retell the story of ourselves . . . out of fidelity to the other" (p. 55).

REFERENCES

Bunkers, S. S. (2001). Considering tomorrow: Parse's theory-guided research. In R. R. Parse, *Qualitative inquiry: The path of sciencing*. (Reprinted from *Nursing Science Quarterly*, 11, 56–63, 1998).

Kearney, R. (1987). Ethics and the postmodern imagination. *Thought*, 62(244), 39–58.

Parse, R. R. (1981). *Man-living-health: A theory of nursing*. New York: Wiley.

Parse, R. R. (1987). *Nursing science: Major paradigms, theories, and critiques*. Philadelphia: Saunders.

Parse, R. R. (1997). The language of nursing knowledge: Saying what we mean. In I. M. King, & J. Fawcett (Eds.), *The language of nursing theory and metatheory* (pp. 73–77). Indianapolis, IN: Sigma Theta Tau International, Center Nursing Press.

Parse, R. R. (1998). *The human becoming school of thought: A perspective for nurses and other health professionals*. Thousand Oaks, CA: Sage.

Parse, R. R. (1999). *Hope: An international human becoming perspective*, Sudbury, MA: Jones and Bartlett.

Chapter 25

EXAMPLE OF A QUALITATIVE RESEARCH GRANT PROPOSAL

The purpose of this chapter is to provide an example of a qualitative research grant proposal. *The Lived Experience of Contentment: A Proposal for a Study Using the Parse Research Method* is presented.

ABSTRACT

The purpose of this study is to answer the research question *What is the structure of the lived experience of contentment?* Twenty volunteers will be sought to engage in dialogue about their experience of contentment, since according to earlier research by the principal investigator, contentment is essential to health and quality of life. The participants will be recruited from groups of persons over age 65 who volunteer in community projects in several large metropolitan settings. The Parse research method, a phenomenological-hermeneutic method, will be used to discover the structure of contentment. The findings will provide new knowledge about contentment and its connection to health and quality of life, which will guide future research and practice of health professionals.

BACKGROUND

The purpose of this research study is to discover the structure of the lived experience of contentment for persons living in a variety of situations and, in so doing, to provide new knowledge about persons' perspectives of health and quality of life to guide further research. Investigations aimed at increasing understanding about issues related to health and quality of life, such as the experience of contentment for persons over age 65, are crucial since, according to the United States Census Bureau's projections, the elderly population will more than double between now and the year 2050. By the year 2050, as many as one in five Americans could be elderly (U.S. Census Bureau, 1998). As a result, increased knowledge about persons' perspectives of contentment as an experience of health and quality of life will become even more essential to providing healthcare (Parse, 1981, 1998).

Nursing Perspective

Human becoming is the nursing theory that will guide this study (Parse, 1981, 1998). From this perspective, contentment is a feeling of peacefulness in the context of everyday struggles as meaning is structured with the cocreating rhythms of cotranscending with the possibles. Contentment is the speaking–being silent and moving–being still in the pushing-resisting of creating anew in light of the certainty-uncertainty of conforming–not conforming. The explicit-tacit of the familiar-unfamiliar is transformed through choosing tranquil ways of becoming in the moment that disclose-hide value priorities, as imaged projects affirm and do not affirm opportunities-restrictions. Contentment is a chosen way of being with the universe and is important to health and quality of life.

Quality of life, from the human becoming perspective, is "what the person there living the life says it is" (Parse, 1994b, p. 17), and the individual and family are considered the experts on health (Parse, 1990, 1994b). Quality of life is what life is like for people. It is the "whatness . . . or the essence of life" (Parse, 1994b, p. 17). It is about meaning and values, desires and dreams, relationships and plans, concerns and fears. Persons' experiences of quality of life guide decisions about health (Parse, 1990, 1994b).

The human becoming theory (Parse, 1981, 1998) posits the notion that each human being lives in unique ways. Contentment is the personal meaning that one gives to a situation in cocreating rhythms of relating while moving beyond the meaning moments of the now with the not-yet. Contentment is a universal lived experience that can be described by persons willing to share their experiences. Knowing more about contentment will shed light on the meaning of quality of life for persons being served by health professionals. The knowledge base of health-related disciplines, such as nursing, can be enhanced by qualitative research on phenomena such as contentment (Mitchell, 1993; Parse, 1981, 1990, 1992, 1996a), since health professionals whose practice is guided by the human becoming school of thought (Parse, 1981, 1998) focus on the meaning of the experience of health and quality of life with persons in their care. Therefore the aims of this study are

1. To enhance understanding of human becoming in relation to the lived experience of contentment.
2. To provide new knowledge about health and quality of life related to contentment for health professionals to use as a guide in future research and practice.
3. To further explicate the importance of contentment for elders.

RELATED RESEARCH: PREVIOUS WORK OF PRINCIPAL INVESTIGATOR

Contentment has been clearly illuminated in the findings of five previous research studies conducted by the principal investigator (Parse, 1993, 1994a, 1996b, 1997a; Parse, Coyne, & Smith, 1985). The findings of these qualitative research studies were descriptions of health (Parse, Coyne, & Smith, 1985, pp. 27–37), laughing your heart out (Parse, 1993), laughing and health (Parse, 1994a), quality of life (Parse, 1996b), and joy-sorrow (Parse, 1997a). In all of these studies on lived experiences related to health, participants mentioned in some way the feeling of contentment.

OTHER RELATED LITERATURE

Contentment is a human experience inextricably intertwined with feeling satisfied, tranquil, and happy (Pearsall & Trumble, 1995). It is a satisfaction, a chosen way of being with the moment that arises in the context of feeling satisfied–not satisfied with activities or endeavors that are cherished. Contentment "requires being who you are—no more and no less" (Johnson & Ruhl, 1999, p. 48). Many authors focus on aspects of the phenomenon of contentment as it is related to health and quality of life (see, for example, Argyle, 1987; Bernstein, 1990; Burroughs, 1650; Darling & McKoy-Smith, 1993; Ekiken, 1913/1979; Galbraith, 1992; Glick, 1951; Hollan & Wellencamp, 1994; Hudson, 1996; Lindgren, Svardsudd, & Tibblin, 1994; McKoy, 1996; Meyers, 1992; Nilsson, Ekman, Ericsson, & Winblad, 1996; Nystrom & Andersson-Segesten, 1990; Sheen, 1967; Tkachuk, 1995; Young, 1993). Recognition of the importance of contentment to health and quality of life is evident if one considers the availability and frequent use of a wide variety of tools that include some measure of contentment in their assessment of quality of life, health, or life satisfaction (see, for example, Darling & McKoy-Smith, 1993; McKoy, 1996; Schmotkin & Hadari, 1996; Tkachuk, 1995). One author, Kane (1985), even suggests that contentment should be considered an ideal outcome for elderly people. Kane believes that older persons should be relatively content—stating that achieving contentment would diminish currently unacceptable rates of depression, suicide, loneliness, and anxiety among this age group. Kane's view is supported by many authors who have used level of contentment as a variable to assess positive affect in nursing home residents with Alzheimer's disease (Lawton, VanHaitsma, & Klapper, 1996), as a variable to address when assessing marital relationships (Moroi, 1990), and as a measure of depression (see, for example, Attala, Hudson, & McSweeney, 1994; Attala, Oetker, & McSweeney, 1995; Courts & Boyette, 1998; Demers & Lavoie, 1996).

The importance of contentment to persons' perspectives of their health and quality of life is clearly articulated in the literature. Participants in a variety of investigations indicated that having "peace of mind" is important to retaining health (Nystrom & Andersson-Segesten, 1990); feeling exceptionally good is equated with contentment (Karaku, 1995); and achieving spiritual well-being is characterized by an inner harmony and contentment in life (Young, 1993). In one study (Nilsson et al., 1996), 87 elderly people were asked what quality of life means to them. In summing up the characteristics of quality of life reported by the participants, the authors state that the emphasis is not on material things, but on independence and health—which are considered a resource for contentment and a peaceful life. This is similar to the findings reported in a study by Schmotkin and Hadari (1996) that supports the premise that older persons generally report contentment if living independently.

In another instance, Lindgren, Svardsudd, and Tibblin (1994) conducted a study with 706 persons 75 years and older. The purpose of their study was to measure the prevalence of poor eyesight, hearing problems, sleeping problems, mobility problems, loneliness, and discontentment and to analyze the extent to which these conditions affect well-being. Among other measures, participants were asked to indicate their contentment with their situation on a verbal scale ranging from "very contented" to "very discontented" and to grade their perceived health on a visual analogue scale. A series of multivariate analyses indicated that contentment and perceived health were highly intercorrelated. Next to their level of activity score, level of contentment explained the highest amount of variation in the participants' perceived health scores. Conversely, perceived health, activity score, and loneliness, together, explained 44% of the variance in level of contentment. The authors suggest that perhaps these results indicate that more attention should be focused on efforts to improve people's satisfaction with their life situations.

The results of the Lindgren et al. (1994) study are congruent with a number of other sources in which the authors report that good health, active engagement in social activities (Johnson & Barer, 1992; Markides & Martin, 1979; Meyers & Diener, 1995), good physical and social resources (Johnson & Barer, 1992), and life satisfaction (Jacob & Guarnaccia, 1997) are connected with contentment. Even though there have been a number of studies, as is evident from the preceding discussion, none in any age group have focused on the lived experience of contentment.

Participant Selection and Protection of Participants' Rights

Participants for this study will be 20 persons over age 65 recruited from groups of persons who volunteer in community projects in several large metropolitan settings in North America. Previous experience has shown that recruiting participants from a variety of settings is not problematic. The principal investigator recently coordinated the recruitment of 130 participants from nine countries to participate in a study on the lived experience of hope (Parse, 1999). There is no set number of participants necessary for the Parse method; however, studies with four or more participants have discovered structures of lived experiences using the Parse method.

This study has been approved by an institutional review board for the protection of human subjects. Once the persons have agreed to participate, they will meet with the principal investigator, or a doctorally prepared consultant with expertise in the research method, in a convenient setting conducive to private discussion. Participants will sign a consent form (see the example of a consent form in Chapter 2). They will be informed about the purpose of the research, that it will take about 20 to 60 minutes or longer depending on how long they wish to discuss contentment, that the discussion will be recorded on audiotape and videotape, that they may withdraw at any time, that confidentiality will be maintained, that their names will not be associated with the information shared, that there are no known risks, and that they may contact the researcher should they have uncomfortable feelings after the discussion. All audiotapes and videotapes will be kept in a locked file drawer to protect confidentiality. Only code numbers (no names) will be used to identify participants during the research process and in publications. Audiotapes and videotapes will be erased and transcriptions shredded after completion of the study to protect the anonymity of the participants.

Methodology

The Parse research method, a phenomenological-hermeneutic method, has been used to study a number of lived experiences of health and quality of life (see, for example, Allchin-Petardi, 1998; Baumann, 1996; Cody, 1991, 1995; Kelley, 1991; Kruse, 1999; Mitchell, 1990, 1995; Mitchell & Lawton, 2000; Parse, 1990, 1994a, 1997a, 1999; Pilkington, 1993, 2000; Smith, 1990; and many others) and will be used to answer the research question *What is the structure of the lived experience of contentment?* This method is unique to the discipline of nursing, yet it is much like other human science methods (Gadamer, 1975, 1976; Giorgi, 1985; Parse, 1987, 1992, 1996a, 1998). The Parse research method evolves from the ontology of the human becoming school of thought (Parse, 1981, 1987, 1992, 1995, 1997b, 1998), and its purpose is to discover the structure of lived experiences of health through dialogical engagement, extraction-synthesis, and heuristic interpretation.

Dialogical engagement (data gathering) is a true presence of the researcher with the participant. It is not an interview. Dialogical engagement focuses on the phenomenon under study as it is described by the participant. In this study, participants will be asked to describe their experience of contentment. The researcher, in true presence, will then be attentive to each participant's description. No other questions will be asked. Participants may be encouraged to say more about something, or to speak about how something they say relates to their experience of contentment. This method of asking participants to describe their lived experience has led more than 500 participants to give detailed descriptions of universal lived experiences in previous Parse method research studies. The dialogical engagements, which are usually 30 to 60 minutes in length, will be audiotaped and videotaped, and then transcribed to a typed format for the extraction-synthesis process.

Extraction-synthesis (analysis-synthesis) is the process of moving the descriptions from the language of the participants across levels of abstraction to the language of science (Parse, 1987, 1990, 1992, 1995, 1997b, 1998). These transformational shifts in levels of abstraction occur through dwelling with the transcribed dialogues. Dwelling with is a way of centering during which the researcher becomes fully immersed in the description shared by the participant. The researcher spends time contemplating the transcribed discussions, which for this particular method requires both reading the transcribed dialogue and listening to it on tape all-at-once. If the dialogical engagement has been videotaped, the researcher also views the situation after reading about it and while listening to it so that the researcher is immersed with the dialogue in the extraction-synthesis process (Parse, 1987, 1995). The extraction-synthesis process includes the following:

1. Constructing a story that captures the core ideas about the phenomenon of concern from each participant's dialogue.
2. Extracting-synthesizing essences in the participant's language from recorded and transcribed descriptions. The essences are succinct expressions of the core ideas about the phenomenon of concern as described by the participants.
3. Synthesizing-extracting essences in the researcher's language. These essences are expressions of the core ideas conceptualized by the researcher at a higher level of abstraction.
4. Formulating a proposition from each participant's essences. A proposition is a nondirectional statement conceptualized by the researcher joining the core ideas of the essences in the researcher's language. The essences arise directly from the participants' descriptions.
5. Extracting-synthesizing core concepts from the formulated propositions of all participants. Core concepts are ideas (written in phrases) that capture the central meaning of the propositions.

6. Synthesizing a structure of the lived experience from the core concepts. A structure is a statement conceptualized by the researcher joining the core concepts. The structure as evolved answers the research question.

Heuristic interpretation involves two processes: structural transposition and conceptual integration (Parse, 1987, 1998). Structural transposition is moving the structure of the lived experience up another level of abstraction. Conceptual integration further specifies the structure of the lived experience at the level of the theory. The finding of the study is the structure of the lived experience as discovered through the processes of dialogical engagement and extraction-synthesis. The structure of contentment that emerges from this study will be related to health and quality of life to guide health professionals in future research and practice.

SIGNIFICANCE TO NURSING AND OTHER HEALTH DISCIPLINES

To date, there has been no work published that focuses on contentment from a human becoming perspective, and no evidence of research to discover the meaning of the lived experience of contentment, or to describe the essences of contentment, even though the research literature clearly points to its importance for health and quality of life. The knowledge gained from this research will expand the human becoming theory and be used to guide the practice of health professionals with persons in their homes and in healthcare settings. It will also lead to further research on health experiences.

EVALUATION

A report of the study will be published in a health-related refereed journal. The findings from this investigation will be new knowledge to enhance understanding of people's experiences of contentment, and thus they will enhance understanding of what people say is important to health and quality of life. The findings will provide health professionals with an opportunity to use the knowledge to change their ways of practicing. The findings also will offer insights into other relevant research questions in the ongoing quest for quality of life for people.

TIMETABLE

July 1, 2001–July 31, 2001	➤ Hire consultants.
	➤ Recruit participants.
	➤ Purchase equipment.
August 1, 2001–November 30, 2001	➤ Conduct dialogical engagements (data gathering).
December 1, 2001–February 29, 2002	➤ Transcribe all 20 audiotapes.
March 1, 2002–May 31, 2002	➤ Extract and synthesize essences from all descriptions (data analysis-synthesis).
June 1, 2002–July 1, 2002	➤ Prepare manuscript for publication.

BUDGET WITH JUSTIFICATION

Personnel

➤ Consultants—two doctorally prepared researchers who work with the Parse research method and can gather data from 10 participants. The intricacies of the data-gathering and analysis processes require persons with experience and will require at least 15 hours per participant.	$50.00/hour for 150 hours for each of the two consultants	$15,000.00
➤ Transcriptionist (20 1-hour tapes take 4-5 hours each to transcribe)	90 hours at $30.00/hour	$2,700.00

Equipment

➤ Tape recorder and transcription machine to record dialogues (data-gathering procedure)	*	$1,200.00
➤ Videotape recorder and tripod to visually record dialogues	*Estimate from Best Buy Camcorder: $800.00 Tripod: $80.00	$880.00
➤ Lap-top computer to manage large amounts of qualitative data	*	$4,500.00
➤ NVivo (software and license extension for qualitative data analysis)	*Price obtained from Scolari Software Web site	$1,265.00

Supplies

➢ Audiotapes	20 tapes at $10.00/tape	$200.00
➢ Videotapes to record dialogues (see data-gathering procedure)	20 camcorder tapes at $10.00 per tape	$200.00
	20 VHS videotapes at $5.00 per tape	$100.00
➢ Two printer cartridges	$80.00 each	$160.00
➢ Paper (500 sheets × 3)	$5.00 each	$15.00
➢ 12 AAA batteries for tape recorder	$2.00 each	$24.00

Miscellaneous Expenses

➢ Photocopying, postage, phone bills		$750.00

Mileage

➢ Travel to meet participants	Average of 20 miles round trip per participant (for data gathering) = 400 miles @ 32.5 cents/mile	$130.00

TOTAL:	$27, 124.00

*Include documentation of price quotes and/or invoices.

REFERENCES

Allchin-Petardi, L. (1998). Weathering the storm: Persevering through a difficult time. *Nursing Science Quarterly, 11,* 172–177.

Argyle, M. (1987). *The psychology of happiness.* New York: Methuen.

Attala, J. M., Hudson, W. W., & McSweeney, M. (1994). A partial validation of two short-form partner abuse scales. *Women and Health, 21*(2–3), 125–139.

Attala, J. M., Oetker, D., & McSweeney, M. (1995). Partner abuse against female nursing students. *Journal of Psychosocial Nursing & Mental Health Services, 33*(1), 17–24.

Baumann, S. (1996). Children in families with no place of their own. *Nursing Science Quarterly, 9,* 152–159.

Bernstein, H. E. (1990). *Being human: The art of feeling alive.* New York: Gardner Press.

Burroughs, J. (1650). *The rare jewel of Christian contentment.* London: P. Cole.

Cody, W. K. (1991). Grieving a personal loss. *Nursing Science Quarterly, 4,* 61–68.

Cody, W. K. (1995). The lived experience of grieving, for families living with AIDS. In R. R. Parse (Ed.), *Illuminations: The human becoming theory in practice and research* (pp. 197–242). New York: National League for Nursing Press.

Courts, N. F., & Boyette, B. G. (1998). Psychosocial adjustment of males on three types of dialysis. *Clinical Nursing Research, 7*(1), 47–63.

Darling, C. A., & McKoy-Smith, Y. M. (1993). Understanding hysterectomies: Sexual satisfaction and quality of life. *Journal of Sex Research, 30,* 324–335.

Demers, A., & Lavoie, J. P. (1996). Effect of support groups on family caregivers to the frail elderly. *Canadian Journal on Aging*, 15(1), 129–144.

Ekiken, K. (1979). *The way of contentment* (K. Hoshino, Trans.). Washington, DC: University Publications of America. (Original work published 1913)

Gadamer, H. G. (1975). *Truth and method* (2nd rev. ed.) (J. Weinsheimer & D. G. Marshall, Trans.). New York: Continuum.

Gadamer, H. G. (1976). *Philosophical hermeneutics* (D. E. Linge, Ed. & Trans.). Berkeley: University of California Press.

Galbraith, J. K. (1992). *The culture of contentment*. New York: Houghton Mifflin.

Giorgi, A. (1985). Sketch of a psychological phenomenological method. In A. Giorgi (Ed.), *Phenomenology and psychological research* (pp. 8–22). Pittsburgh, PA: Duquesne University Press.

Glick, C. (1951). *The secret of serenity*. New York: Thomas Y. Crowell.

Hollan, D. W., & Wellenkamp, J. C. (1994). *Contentment and suffering: Culture and experience in Toraja*. New York: Columbia University Press.

Hudson, D. W. (1996). *Happiness and the limits of satisfaction*. Lanham, MD: Rowman and Littlefield.

Jacob, M., & Guarnaccia, V. (1997). Motivational and behavioral correlates of life satisfaction in an elderly sample. *Psychological Reports*, 80(3 Pt. 1), 811–818.

Johnson, C. L., & Barer, B. M. (1992). Patterns of engagement and disengagement among the oldest old. *Journal of Aging Studies*, 6(4), 351–364.

Johnson, R. A., & Ruhl, J. M. (1999). *Contentment: A way to true happiness*. San Francisco: HarperSanFrancisco.

Kane, R. A. (1985). Long term status quo untenable? What is more ideal for nation's elderly? *Perspective on Aging*, 14(5), 23–26.

Karaku, A. T. (1995). Psychological well-being as exemplified by adults' experiences of feeling exceptionally good: An empirical phenomenological study. *Dissertation Abstracts International*, 56(04B), 2310.

Kelley, L. S. (1991). Struggling with going along when you do not believe. *Nursing Science Quarterly*, 4, 123–129.

Kruse, B. G. (1999). The lived experience of serenity: Using Parse's research method. *Nursing Science Quarterly*, 12, 143–150.

Lawton, M. P., VanHaitsma, K., & Klapper, J. (1996). Observed affect in nursing home residents with Alzheimer's disease. *Journals of Gerontology. Series B, Psychological Sciences & Social Sciences*, 51(1), P3–P14.

Lindgren, A. M., Svardsudd, H., & Tibblin, G. (1994). Factors related to perceived health among elderly people: The Albertina project. *Age and Ageing*, 23, 328–333.

Markides, K. S., & Martin, H. W. (1979). A causal model of life satisfaction among the elderly. *Journal of Gerontology*, 34, 86–93.

McKoy, Y. D. (1996). An examination of marital stress, sexual satisfaction, marital satisfaction, and quality of life of myocardial infarction patients. (Doctoral dissertation, Florida State University, 1996). *Dissertation Abstracts International*, 57(04A), p. 1633. (AAI9625986)

Meyers, D., & Diener, E. (1995). Who is happy? *Psychological Science, 6,* 10–19.

Meyers, D. G. (1992). *The pursuit of happiness: Who is happy and why.* New York: William Morrow.

Mitchell, G. J. (1990). The lived experience of taking life day-by-day in later life: Research guided by Parse's emergent method. *Nursing Science Quarterly, 3,* 29–36.

Mitchell, G. J. (1993). Living paradox in Parse's theory. *Nursing Science Quarterly, 6,* 44–51.

Mitchell, G. J. (1995). The lived experience of restriction-freedom in later life. In R. R. Parse (Ed.), *Illuminations: The human becoming theory in practice and research* (pp. 159–195). New York: National League for Nursing Press.

Mitchell, G. J., & Lawton, C. (2000). Living with the consequences of personal choices for persons with diabetes: Implications for educators and practitioners. *Canadian Journal of Diabetes Care, 24*(2), 23–31.

Moroi, K. (1990). Perceptions of equity and sex-role attitudes in married couples. *Japanese Journal of Family Psychology, 4,* 109–120.

Nilsson, M., Ekman, S. L., Ericsson, K., & Winblad, B. (1996). Some characteristics of the quality of life in old age illustrated by means of Allardt's concept. *Scandinavian Journal of Caring Sciences, 10*(2), 116–121.

Nystrom, A., & Andersson-Segesten, M. (1990). Peace of mind as an important aspect of old people's health. *European Journal of Caring Sciences, 4,* 55–62.

Parse, R. R. (1981). *Man-living-health: A theory of nursing.* New York: Wiley.

Parse, R. R. (1987). *Nursing science: Major paradigms, theories, and critiques.* Philadelphia: Saunders.

Parse, R. R. (1990). Health: A personal commitment. *Nursing Science Quarterly, 3,* 136–140.

Parse, R. R. (1992). Human becoming: Parse's theory of nursing. *Nursing Science Quarterly, 5,* 35–42.

Parse, R. R. (1993). The experience of laughter: A phenomenological study. *Nursing Science Quarterly, 6,* 39–43.

Parse, R. R. (1994a). Laughing and health: A study using Parse's research method. *Nursing Science Quarterly, 7,* 55–64.

Parse, R. R. (1994b). Quality of life: Sciencing and living the art of human becoming. *Nursing Science Quarterly, 7,* 16–21.

Parse, R. R. (Ed.). (1995). *Illuminations: The human becoming theory in practice and research.* New York: National League for Nursing Press.

Parse, R. R. (1996a). Building knowledge through qualitative research: The road less traveled. *Nursing Science Quarterly, 9,* 10–16.

Parse, R. R. (1996b). Quality of life for persons living with Alzheimer's disease: The human becoming perspective. *Nursing Science Quarterly, 9,* 126–133.

Parse, R. R. (1997a). Joy-sorrow: A study using the Parse research method. *Nursing Science Quarterly, 10,* 80–87.

Parse, R. R. (1997b). The human becoming theory: The was, is, and will be. *Nursing Science Quarterly, 10,* 32–38.

Parse, R. R. (1998). *The human becoming school of thought: A perspective for nurses and other health professionals.* Thousand Oaks, CA: Sage.

Parse, R. R. (1999). *Hope: An international human becoming perspective.* Sudbury, MA: Jones and Bartlett.

Parse, R. R., Coyne, A. B., & Smith, M. J. (1985). *Nursing research: Qualitative methods.* Bowie, MD: Brady.

Pearsall, J., & Trumble, B. (1995). *The Oxford English reference dictionary.* New York: Oxford University Press.

Pilkington, F. B. (1993). The lived experience of grieving the loss of an important other. *Nursing Science Quarterly, 6,* 130–139.

Pilkington, F. B. (2000). Persisting while wanting to change: Women's lived experiences. *Health Care for Women International, 21*(6), 1–6.

Schmotkin, D., & Hadari, G. (1996). An outlook on subjective well-being in older Israeli adults: A unified formulation. *International Journal of Aging & Human Development, 42,* 271–289.

Sheen, F. J. (1967). *Guide to contentment.* New York: Simon & Schuster.

Smith, M. C. (1990). Struggling through a difficult time for unemployed persons. *Nursing Science Quarterly, 3,* 18–28.

Tkachuk, B. P. (1995). Toward the development of a quality of life instrument for the chronically mentally ill. (Masters thesis, University of Regina, 1995). *Dissertation Abstracts International, 34*(02), p. 896.

U.S. Census Bureau. (1998). *Statistical brief: Sixty-five plus in the United States.* [Online.] Available: http://blue.census.gov/socdemo/www/agebrief.html.

Young, C. (1993). Spirituality and the chronically ill Christian elderly. *Geriatric Nursing, 14,* 298–303.

CHAPTER 26

QUALITATIVE RESEARCH AND THE USE OF COMPUTERS

Debra A. Bournes, RN; PhD

Software programs that can assist the researcher in organizing qualitative data have been available since the early 1980s (Brent, 1984; Tesch, 1991). Since then, the field has grown exponentially. The age of the computer has reached qualitative researchers. Whether to use a computer to aid with qualitative research in some way is no longer an issue. It is probable that all qualitative researchers, at some stage of their projects, will use computers to collect and store some kind of information. The more relevant questions are "How *can* the computer be used?" and "How *will* the computer be used?" The possibilities are infinite—restricted only by the researcher's imagination and the technological development of any given moment. Computer capabilities that were once mere possibilities are now expected, even taken for granted, in qualitative research circles. Indeed, computer programs that can assist with qualitative research are created and upgraded almost daily. This chapter then, is not about specific programs—that would be out-of-date before the book was in print—rather, it is about the current terminology, the possible functions a computer can perform on qualitative data, and the resources that qualitative researchers must be familiar with in order to decide how best they can use a computer to assist them with their projects.

The purposes of this chapter are to provide readers with information about a variety of computer program functions (including word processing, data management, and specialized qualitative analysis), an examination of several concerns about using computers to assist with qualitative research, and criteria for choosing the optimum program for a project.

THE POSSIBILITIES

Ultimately, all methods of qualitative data analysis require hermeneutical interpretation and synthesis of key information culled from rich, in-depth descriptions of the phenomenon of interest. Data analysis-synthesis is a process that entails concentrated contemplation and creative interpretation by the researcher (Parse, 1996). Computers cannot perform the actual analysis-synthesis (Kelle, 1997; Richards, 1997, 1999; Richards & Richards, 1994; Sandelowski, 1995; Tesch, 1991; Walker, 1993). This process is the responsibility of the qualitative researcher. Computer programs can assist the researcher by providing data management mechanisms that support the researcher's insights and discoveries; organize and archive entire texts; store individual ideas and descriptions of ideas; maintain easily accessible links between original data and interpretive statements, themes, and categories; and facilitate some forms of theory construction and hypothesis testing (Kelle, 1997; Richards, 1997, 1999; Richards & Richards, 1991, 1994; Tesch, 1991; Weitzman, 1999, 2000; Weitzman & Miles, 1995).

Specific data management functions that are currently available in various computer programs include facilities for storing, handling, and finding multiple documents simultaneously; searching text; coding and retrieving data; setting up hyperlinks; indexing, graphing, and modeling information; handling external data; annotating data; displaying and developing data in rich text format; facilitating the use of data in multiple programs using extensible markup language (XML); and supporting teamwork (Baker, 1988; BSSMedia, 1999; Coffey, Holbrook, & Atkinson, 1996; Gerson, 1984; Kelle, 1997; Morison & Moir, 1998; Pilkington, 1996; Qualis Research, 1999; Researchware, 1999; Richards, 1998, 1999; Richards & Richards, 1994; Scientific Software Development, 1999; Taft, 1993; Tesch, 1991; Walker, 1993; Webb, 1999; Weitzman, 1999, 2000; Weitzman & Miles, 1995).

Storing, Handling, and Finding Multiple Documents Simultaneously

The earliest literature on qualitative computing indicates that in the early 1980s the computer was primarily used as a filing cabinet. Qualitative data were transcribed into text format and stored on the computer—which served as a clerk for organizing, indexing, and retrieving data (Baker, 1988; Gerson, 1984). At that time, concerns about using the computer to store information focused on the limitations on the maximum size of the files that could be stored. Today, most qualitative researchers continue to use computers, in some way, to record, organize, and store information—though the size of a file is no longer a concern.

Multiple large-size documents can be stored, opened, viewed, and manipulated simultaneously. Increasingly efficient central processing units, combined with enormous hard drives and an explosion in the amount of random access memory (RAM) available on personal computers, allow instantaneous access to multiple documents. It is possible to view several files on the screen at the same time and to move data from one document to another with the simple drag and drop, or cut, copy, and paste functions that are standardized computer functions. It also is possible to search for and retrieve particular documents, or even pieces of text, from open and unopened files from any location on a personal computer, a local area network, or the Internet. Computers are able to search for and locate document files if they are given one or more of the following: the name and location of the file, the approximate size of the file, the approximate date the file was created or modified, or specific pieces of text contained in the file. Specific text searches are enhanced by several text-search functions.

Searching Text

The ability to search for particular words, phrases, or strings of characters is basic to most general word processing and specialized qualitative research programs. In addition, some programs will conduct semantic thesaurus searches to look not only for the word the researcher has specified, but also for all of the other words that mean approximately the same thing. As mentioned previously, the files that the computer searches for words, phrases, or strings of characters do not necessarily have to be open (Richards & Richards, 1994). Programs that facilitate such searches often have the capability of providing the results statistically, since in many instances they are capable of interfacing with statistical and other database programs and they can report the frequency of occurrence of specific items, perform frequency distributions and cross-tabulations, display data in matrices, and/or give simple correlational data about the co-occurrence of items (Richards & Richards, 1994; Pilkington, 1996).

Co-occurrences of specific items can be searched for in a variety of ways. The simplest method is a Boolean search for co-occurrences of items. A Boolean search for co-occurrence refers to a computer function that facilitates looking for all co-occurrences of items using, for example, "*and, or,* and *not*" or "*yes* and *no*" criteria (Richards & Richards, 1994). For instance, the researcher may ask the computer to look for all occurrences of X and Y together. This would yield a different result than asking it for all occurrences of either X *or* Y, or for all instances when Y occurs but X does *not.*

Researchers also can search for co-occurrences of specific items using either proximity (BSSMedia, 1999; Scientific Software Development, 1999) or "if-then" commands (Researchware, 1999). A proximity search means that the computer will look for items that, for example, may be "before," "after," or "followed by" another particular item. If-then rules also can be constructed and used to search, retrieve, or add coding to specific portions of data. For instance, the researcher may ask the program to look for cases where A, B, and

C occur. An "if-then" rule then might be constructed to say, "If A, B, and C," then "add D" (Researchware, 1999). In general, the results of any type of search can be displayed and used as data in new searches.

An important feature of a qualitative research program is the ability to retain search results in the system (Richards & Richards, 1994). In some programs, search results can be built into the database and used as additional data for future queries (Richards, 1999; Weitzman, 1999, 2000; Weitzman & Miles, 1995). This feature, called *system closure* (Richards, 1998, 1999; Richards & Richards, 1994), means that "results obtained about the system, [and] analytic techniques used on the system, become part of the system" (Richards & Richards, 1994, p. 449). This is considered an important feature for some qualitative research methods, since it "allows the iterative building of inquiry that is central to theorizing" (Richards, 1999, p. 420).

System closure is closely related to, and supports, another important computer function called *data-theory bootstrapping* (Richards & Richards, 1994). According to Richards and Richards, *data-theory bootstrapping* is the

> building of relationships between data and theory. . . . Providing direct conceptual-level support for this process puts some interesting demands on software design. . . . Researchers . . . want to hold their growing nets of hierarchies of concepts, evidence links, groupings of ideas, and so on that make up the explanatory structure in an accessible way that will help them see where they have been and [where they are going]. The software systems that . . . help with this [do] not hold just the data and tools for manipulating it, but also in some sense the growing analysis and explanation system. (p. 449)

Coding, or marking, data so that it can be retrieved and indexed is central to *data-theory bootstrapping* and, thus, to supporting and recording conceptual level interpretation of qualitative data. Any search functions that can be performed on raw text also can be used to search for, group, and make inquiries about the codes the researcher used to mark data sources.

Coding and Retrieving Data

Coding and retrieving data is a function that is supported readily by computer programs. It has become the basis on which most specialized qualitative research software has been developed (Richards & Richards, 1994; Weitzman, 1999, 2000; Weitzman & Miles, 1995). Coding simply means assigning labels to data. The label identifies a piece of data that the researcher interprets as having a particular meaning (Webb, 1999). The ability to code data is one way that computers support conceptual-level qualitative data analysis—since the act of assigning a code to a portion of data is in itself theoretical and guided by the particular perspective of the researcher (Kelle, 1997; Richards & Richards, 1994; Webb, 1999).

Codes also can be used to group and sort data in multiple ways according to the researcher's theoretical hunches. They can be used as the subject of further searches to identify patterns or themes in the data. Patterns in the data can be supported by demonstrating the presence or absence of specific codes and by demonstrating specific relationships among the codes (Richards & Richards, 1994; Weitzman & Miles, 1995). For instance, a researcher may want to support a particular theme as a major finding of a qualitative study by showing the co-occurrence of several codes in the interview data from all participants. If they are using programs that enable them to specify different attributes or values of individual codes, researchers also may be interested in search procedures that can, for example, look for positive or negative instances of a particular code (BSSMedia, 1999; Richards, 1999; Richards & Richards, 1994; Webb, 1999). Some programs even will calculate the textual distance between codes (Richards & Richards, 1994; Weitzman & Miles, 1995).

Software designed for coding and retrieving data allows researchers to select and code specific sections of data on-screen (BSSMedia, 1999; Qualis Research, 1999; Researchware, 1999; Richards, 1999; Scientific Software Development, 1999; Webb, 1999). Some programs have specific criteria about what can be coded and how it can be done; however, in most instances a code can be assigned to as little or as much data as desired (BSSMedia, 1999; Qualis Research, 1999; Researchware, 1999; Richards, 1999; Scientific Software Development, 1999). Researchers may choose to code one character or an entire paragraph of data. Most programs also allow complex data to be interpreted and coded for multiple meanings and make provisions that facilitate editing, deleting, or adding coding at any time during the project (BSSMedia, 1999; Qualis Research, 1999; Researchware, 1999; Richards, 1999; Richards & Richards, 1994; Scientific Software Development, 1999; Tesch, 1991; Webb, 1999). Once a researcher has coded data, the computer is able to extract, assemble, and display sections that have been marked by the same code without changing the form of the original text (Coffey et al., 1996; Kelle, 1997; Richards & Richards, 1991, 1994; Tesch, 1991; Weitzman & Miles, 1995). The most recent advances in coding and retrieval functions provide options to access data using specific "information about cases, sites, and so forth, or by a topic or pattern of topics in order to display and interpret patterns, interrogate coding, and question and test interpretation" (Richards, 1999, p. 415). Recent advances in qualitative research software also have paid particular attention to facilitating rapid and easy transitions between coded and original data so that researchers can return to the source of their ideas to ensure that their interpretation remains true to and supported by the data (BSSMedia, 1999; Qualis Research, 1999; Researchware, 1999; Richards, 1999; Scientific Software Development, 1999; Webb, 1999). One way this is made possible is through the use of hyperlinks.

Links Between Objects [Hyperlinks]

Qualitative researchers must be able to move back and forth between all material associated with the project. This may mean moving from one code to another; from a code to the original data; from one data segment to others sharing the same code; from data segments to memos; from data documents to other supporting documents or literature; or to audio, video, and pictorial data sources (Researchware, 1999; Richards, 1999; Scientific Software Development, 1999). Qualitative researchers even may need the option to "integrate sounds and pictures . . . not only as more codeable documents, but also with the sound or image woven as more threads in the fabric of interpretation" (Richards, 1999, p. 419). Computers are able to support interactive and instantaneous links among any parts of one or more files through the use of hyperlink facilities.

A hyperlink joins " 'nodes' and the analyst can create dense webs or networks of . . . links, which can then be 'navigated' in various explorations of the data" (Coffey et al., 1996, paragraph 8.6). Hyperlinks are based on the idea of a "button which marks a point in the text (or other data) at which various functions can be performed. A 'link button' allows the user to go to another point in the data in order to make a suitable cross-reference, to pick up another instance of 'the same' occurrence, and so on" (Coffey et al., 1996, paragraph 8.6). In some qualitative research programs, hyperlinks not only take the reader to a particular destination, they also allow the reader to return to the original location (Richards, 1999).

The terminology used to describe hyperlink functions varies among the different qualitative analysis software programs—but regardless of what they are called, they perform similar tasks. For instance, John Seidel, the developer of *The Ethnograph* (Qualis Research, 1999), does not use the term hyperlink. He says they are simply a link between one object and another. The objective of any link is to be able to click on something and go somewhere else that is related—thus, code words can be set up to link data segments that share the same code, segments can be linked to memos, and so on. Seidel (personal communication, December 13, 1999) notes that hyperlinks usually only take the reader to one destination. He believes that a goal for future software development is to create ways to click on code words in text and *automatically* initiate a search that will find all segments related to that code word.

Using terminology different from that used by the developers of *The Ethnograph* (Qualis Research, 1999), Richards (1999) describes three types of hyperlinks that are used in the program called NVivo—*databites*, *doclinks*, and *nodelinks*. A *databite* is a hyperlink to annotations, other texts, HTML files, sounds, images, spreadsheets, and others. A *doclink* takes the reader from any document, text, or node to any other document. Doclinks may be used, for example, if the researcher wants to mark a connection between a particular interpretation of a piece of data and another document that supports the interpretation. A *nodelink*, however, goes from documents or nodes to existing nodes and/or text extracts with the supporting data for a particular node (Richards, 1999). Nodes are like containers. They are used to store ideas, categories, codes, search results, memos, definitions, and descriptions that emerge throughout the course of a qualitative research project (Richards, 1998, 1999; Richards & Richards, 1994). Nodes can be used to form the basis of an indexing system.

Indexing, Graphing, or Modeling Information

Any information associated with a qualitative research project can be kept in an index system that allows the researcher to "create and manipulate concepts and store and explore emerging ideas" (Richards & Richards, 1994, p. 457). In programs that use an index-based approach, nodes are "optionally organized into hierarchies, or *trees*, to represent the organization of concepts into categories and subcategories" (Richards & Richards, 1994, p. 457). The history of each node can be documented in order to assist with auditing the research process at a later time. The trees themselves can be represented visually and easily manipulated on the computer screen. The software that facilitates indexing has been designed to reflect the progress of the researcher's interpretive thinking by allowing the system to grow and change as his or her thinking about a project grows and changes (Morison & Moir, 1998; Richards, 1999).

Researchers might prefer programs that assist with creating other kinds of visual representations of their project. For instance, they may want the ability to construct conceptual diagrams, models, or graphs to document, represent, and display the insights and ideas that emerge with qualitative data analysis-synthesis (Richards & Richards, 1994). Several programs are available that offer these options, which are variously referred to as functions that support concept diagrams, conceptual graphs, semantic nets, conceptual networks (Richards & Richards, 1994), or models (Richards, 1999). Most software programs fully support and record changes in any models, diagrams, or graphs that are created.

Handling External Data

External data are any data that are not in the computer. These can be just about anything that a researcher used as a source of information about the phenomenon of concern—from nontranscribed audiotapes and videotapes, to pieces of artwork, to newspaper clippings, to a particular rock in the park where data was gathered. Qualitative data analysis programs handle the storage and retrieval of information about external data in different ways—but generally those programs that make allowances for external data enable the researcher to create some kind of document that stores information pertaining to the data and allows that information to be coded and annotated.

Annotating Data

Computer functions that help researchers annotate their data are standard in specialized qualitative research software packages (BSSMedia, 1999; Coffey et al., 1996; Qualis Research, 1999; Researchware, 1999; Richards, 1999; Richards & Richards, 1994; Scientific Software Development, 1999; Weitzman, 1999, 2000; Weitzman & Miles,1995). Annotation facilities allow qualitative researchers to insert, create, and read memos containing commentary about their project from any point within a document or node (Richards, 1999). In the most recent qualitative research software packages, memos can be treated as full-status documents that can be edited, coded, searched, and managed like any other document—even in rich text format (Richards, 1999).

Displaying and Developing Data in Rich Text Format

In general, data must be imported into specialized software systems in plain ASCII text format (Richards, 1999; Tesch, 1991; Walker, 1993; Webb, 1999); however, there are programs currently available—Atlas.ti (Scientific Software Development, 1999) and NVivo (Richards, 1999)—that allow researchers to use rich, fully-formatted, and colorful text to bring their data *alive* (Richards, 1999); that assist them to "differentiate themes and identify questions, voices, or researcher commentary" (Richards, 1999, p. 417); and that facilitate in-place editing and updating of embedded data from other programs (Scientific Software Development, 1999; T. Muhr, personal communication, December 13, 1999). Embedded data include graphs, tables, and spreadsheets from programs such as Microsoft Excel or PowerPoint, which can be altered using the menus and buttons from the originating program that automatically appear inside the qualitative analysis program (Scientific Software Development, 1999; T. Muhr, personal communication, December 13, 1999). Rich data can be imported and exported directly from these other programs (Scientific Software Development, 1999; T. Muhr, personal communication, December 13, 1999).

Facilitating Use of Data in Multiple Programs Using XML

Importing and exporting rich, complex data from one program to another—in a format that is recognizable and useable by any software program—is facilitated by the use of XML (Scientific Software Development, 1999). Data exported from one program in XML format can be transformed into any format needed by the importing software package. This feature is useful for researchers who might want to process their data in a variety of ways that require using more than one software program (Scientific Software Development, 1999).

Supporting Teamwork

Specialized qualitative research software also has the ability to support multiple users who are working on the same project—even at multiple sites (Richards & Richards, 1991). The programs can be set up so that different users can have varying abilities to access and alter data (BSSMedia, 1999; Scientific Software Development, 1999; Richards & Richards, 1991; Taft, 1993).

As this chapter shows, there are many computer functions that can assist qualitative researchers with organizing, recording, and managing their projects. It is important, however, to be aware of some of the potential concerns associated with computer-assisted qualitative research.

USING COMPUTERS IN QUALITATIVE RESEARCH: AREAS OF CONCERN

There are several substantive areas of concern that qualitative researchers should consider when making decisions about how they will use a computer to assist with their projects (see, for example, Coffey et al., 1996; Kelle, 1997; Lee & Fielding, 1996; Morison & Moir, 1998; Richards, 1997, 1998; Richards & Richards, 1991, 1994; Sandelowski, 1995; Taft, 1993; Tallerico, 1991; Tesch, 1991; Webb, 1999). Concerns include the perception that using a computer automatically adds rigor to a project (Morison & Moir, 1998; Webb, 1999); the possibility that the computer will routinize data analysis-synthesis (Morison & Moir, 1998; Richards & Richards, 1991, 1994); and the tendency to use a computer to guide the researcher by performing *all* of the functions that it is capable of performing (Kelle, 1997; Morison & Moir, 1998; Sandelowski, 1995; Taft, 1993; Tesch, 1991).

The belief that one's project is more rigorous if one uses a computer to assist with data analysis-synthesis emerges from the perception that computers generate objective, systematic, and thorough analyses (Webb, 1999)—which are thought to be indicators of "good science." Researchers should be cautious about embracing this assumption, since "good science" is not the equivalent of being objective, systematic, and thorough. Rather, "good science" surfaces when researchers design qualitative studies that are based on an ontology and adhere to a specific, consistent qualitative research methodology. Being able to locate rapidly and accurately each and every instance when participants use a particular phrase does not constitute "good science" if the process of analysis specified by the qualitative method does not require such information in order to answer the original research question.

Conducting computerized analytic processes that are unrelated to the research methodology being used is one practice that could lead to the routinizing of data analysis. Routinization of data analysis-synthesis is an issue when researchers use the same computerized processes to analyze whatever qualitative data they collect—regardless of their stated research methodology, or perhaps *as* their methodology. This potential for routinization relates to the concern that qualitative research projects will be designed to fit the capabilities of computers and that researchers will be tempted to use whatever computer programs are available, rather than searching for the ones that are most appropriate for their project. Sandelowski (1995) cautions that qualitative researchers using technology "must have a clear idea of the kind of analysis their work demands and their data permit" (Sandelowski, 1995, p. 208). That clear understanding will help them to choose the most appropriate, as opposed to the most convenient, computerized tools for their projects.

CHOOSING THE RIGHT TOOL(S): ONTOLOGICAL-EPISTEMOLOGICAL-METHODOLOGICAL CONGRUENCE

Researchers' values and beliefs about the overarching phenomenon of concern to their discipline emerge from their commitment to a specific theoretical perspective, or school of thought. These values and beliefs, called ontological assumptions, have particular epistemological and methodological consequences. That is, they lead researchers to be interested in studying certain phenomena, to ask questions about those phenomena in particular ways, and to choose methods of inquiry that provide theoretically consistent processes for data gathering and analysis-synthesis.

A variety of qualitative methods of inquiry have been specified in this book. Each method has emerged from a specific disciplinary and theoretical perspective and each specifies precise processes for data gathering and analysis-synthesis. To conduct a rigorous qualitative study, researchers must choose and adhere to a method of inquiry that is consistent with the ontological and epistemological beliefs underpinning their work (Denzin & Lincoln, 1994, 2000; Guba & Lincoln, 1994; Parse, 1996). Once the phenomenon, the research question, and the research method have been determined, researchers can investigate the possible ways a computer can be used to support their project.

In some instances, computer support may begin by providing researchers with ways to record and archive ideas and resources that further explicate the original question that prompted designing the study. In fact, Richards (1999) challenges qualitative researchers to imagine using software to support and record a project beginning with "the original question or puzzlement and perhaps links to grant applications and research design memos" (p. 425). Richards (1999) asks qualitative researchers to imagine software that creates a file that

> grows as the project does, from a hunch or a curiosity and is constructed, as the project is, by links to other documents and ideas. In

this model, for some time there may be no data . . . rather the project document joins others in a thread and tells a story—with databites to spreadsheets of sample characteristics, correspondence with other researchers, links to literature, [and] early ideas expressed in nodes. . . . As [ideas] change in light of developments, the document is edited and annotated to express what is seen and [to] record the journey taken. (p. 425)

Computers then, may be integral to archiving and managing one's entire project, or they may be used only for certain aspects of a project. Knowing what computers are capable of and what functions one would like them to perform helps one to make decisions about what general word processing and/or specialized qualitative research software package, or packages, might be the most helpful. Consideration should be given to how a computer will support researchers with organizing, storing, and presenting data during each process of their chosen research method. It is the research method that should circumscribe the functions a computer is asked to perform. A computer's capabilities should not dictate how data is managed, analyzed, and synthesized (Morison & Moir, 1998; Richards, 1997; Richards & Richards, 1994; Sandelowski, 1995; Taft, 1993; Tesch, 1991; Walker, 1993; Weitzman & Miles, 1995). For example, although a program may have the ability to count the number of times each participant uses a specific phrase and to correlate it with the number of times participants talk about a particular topic, a researcher conducting any type of a phenomenological study would not look for or use this capability, since none of the phenomenological methods call for this type of analysis. Table 26–1 illustrates, using the Parse research method as an example, what functions researchers might look for when choosing appropriate software to support their project.

Once researchers have determined what they would like to be able to do with a computer, they must determine which, if any, software program(s) will support them. For some researchers, capitalizing on the increasingly sophisticated capabilities of general word processing and database programs will suffice. Other researchers will be interested in the unique functions offered by a variety of specialized qualitative research software programs. Information about specialized software that can be used to support qualitative research is changing constantly. To assist readers in learning about and choosing a suitable program for their projects, Table 26–2 provides general information about the major functions of six of the most well-known programs. Listing all of the software available and giving a detailed account of what each program is capable of would be futile—since such a list would be out-of-date before this book were even in print. Instead, readers are encouraged to use Table 26–2 as a place to begin, and to explore the most current information on specialized qualitative research software on the Internet. Table 26–3 provides a list of Web sites that are useful. Readers also are encouraged to download the free demonstration versions of the various programs from their respective

TABLE 26–1 USING A COMPUTER TO ASSIST WITH ORGANIZING A PARSE METHOD STUDY

PROCESS	INFORMATION TO BE MANAGED	COMPUTER FUNCTIONS THAT MAY BE HELPFUL	LOOK FOR SOFTWARE THAT SUPPORTS
Dialogical Engagement (*Data Gathering*) A dialogue in true presence between the researcher and participant. The dialogue focuses on the participant's description of the phenomenon under study using words, symbols, metaphors, music, photographs, poetry, drawings, or movements (Parse, 1987, 1995, 1997, 1998).	Audio- and videotaped data Photographs Music Drawings Artwork	Transcribe audiotaped data. Store transcribed data. Store segments of videotaped data. Store photographs, drawings, or music. Store information about external data.	Importing scanned items Links with audio, video, and pictorial data External data handling
Extraction-Synthesis (*Data Analysis-Synthesis*) The process of moving the descriptions from the language of the participants across levels of abstraction to the language of science (Parse, 1987, 1995, 1997, 1998).	Data transcripts Photographs, music, or drawings used to describe the phenomenon All excerpts specifically describing the phenomenon of interest	Maintain integrity of original transcript. Allow researcher to mark and retrieve all data specifically describing the phenomenon of interest. Support retrieval of original transcript at any time.	Code and retrieval Text searches Hyperlinks Indexing Automatic grouping and extracting of similarly marked data Rich text

	Participant stories (a synthesis of what they say about the phenomenon)	Allow researcher to retrieve, refer to, and/or insert drawings, photos, music, or video clips.
	Extracted essences in participants' language	Allow researcher to link stories with quotations in original transcript.
	Essences in the researcher's language	Allow researcher to link essences with supporting data from stories and transcripts.
	Propositions	Allow researcher to link propositions with supporting data from essences, stories, and transcripts.
	Core concepts	Allow researcher to link core concepts with supporting data from propositions, essences, stories, and transcripts.
		Allow researcher to color code parts of propositions that support each core concept.
Heuristic Interpretation The process of integrating the core concepts with the human becoming theory (Parse, 1987, 1995, 1997, 1998).	Multiple theoretical concepts	Allow researcher to set up and maintain links with original transcripts, stories, essences, and core concepts.

TABLE 26–2 General Capabilities of Well-Known Qualitative Software Packages

	Atlas.ti	Ethnograph v.5	HyperRESEARCH	NVivo	NUD*IST4	winMAX
Runs simple text searches	X	X	X	X	X	X
Runs Boolean searches	X	X	X	X	X	X
Runs semantic searches	X					
Runs proximity searches	X		X	X	X	X
Supports other types of search strategies	X		X	X	X	X
Supports simple statistical calculations	X	X		X	X	X
Includes statistical packages links	X	X	X	X	X	X
Includes coding and retrieval tools	X	X	X	X	X	X
Allows easy review and modification of codes	X	X	X	X	X	X
Supports creation of annotations and memos	X	X	X	X	X	X

	1	2	3	4	5	6
Allows specification of attributes of data	X	X		X	X	X
Includes hyperlink functions	X	X	X	X	X	
Uses system closure	X	X	X	X	X	X
Uses data display tools (indexing, graphing, or modeling)	X		X	X	X	
Supports conceptual/theory-building work	X		X	X	X	
Supports teamwork	X	X	X	X	X	X
Handles external data	X	X	X	X	X	X
Embeds pictorial, audio, video, or spreadsheet data	X		X	X		
Supports rich text	X			X		
Uses XML files to support in-place editing and updating of embedded documents (i.e., Excel, PowerPoint, and Bitmap documents)	X					

TABLE 26–3   ONLINE RESOURCES WITH UP-TO-DATE INFORMATION ABOUT
QUALITATIVE RESEARCH SOFTWARE

GENERAL RESOURCES	
Computer Assisted Qualitative Data Analysis Networking Project (CAQDAS)	http://www.soc.surrey.ac.uk/caqdas/
Judy Norris' Qual Page	http://www.ualberta.ca/jrnorris/qda.html
Qualitative Research	http://www.uvm.edu/People/brodg/ qualres.html
Qualitative Research Consulting	http://www.quarc.de/body_overview.html
SCOLARI	http://www.scolari.co.uk/
RESOURCES ABOUT SPECIFIC SOFTWARE	
Atlas.ti	http://www.atlasti.de
Ethnograph v.5.0	http://www.qualisresearch.com
HyperRESEARCH	http://www.researchware.com
NVivo	http://www.qsr.com.au/software/nvivo/ nvivo.htm
QSR NUD*IST 4	http://www.qsr.com.au/software/n4/n4.htm
WinMAX	http://www.winmax.de/
SOFTWARE FOR CONCEPT MAPPING	
Decision Explorer	http://www.banxia.co.uk/demain.html
Inspiration	http://www.inspiration.com/

Web sites (Table 26–2), to read Weitzman's (2000) assessment as well as Weitz-man and Miles' (1995) book *Computer Programs for Qualitative Data Analysis* (look for the new edition of this classic source by spring 2001), and to talk to colleagues who have experience using the different software packages.

REFERENCES

Baker, C. A. (1988). Computer applications in qualitative research. *Computers in Nursing*, 6(5), 211–214.

Brent, E. (1984). Qualitative computing: Issues and answers. *Qualitative Sociology*, 7(1/2), 34–59.

BSSMedia. (1999, October 8). *WinMax*. [Online.] Available: http://www.winmax.de/.

Coffey, A. B., Holbrook, P., & Atkinson, P. (1996). Qualitative data analysis: Technologies and representations. *Sociological Research Online*, 1(1). [Online.] Available: http://www.socresonline.org.uk/socresonline/1/1/4.html.

Denzin, N. K., & Lincoln, Y. S. (Eds.). (1994). *Handbook of qualitative research*. Thousand Oaks, CA: Sage.

Denzin, N. K., & Lincoln, Y. S. (Eds.). (2000). *Handbook of qualitative research* (2nd ed.). Thousand Oaks, CA: Sage.

Gerson, E. (1984). Qualitative research and the computer. *Qualitative Sociology,* 7(1/2), 61–74.

Guba, E. G., & Lincoln, Y. S. (1994). Competing paradigms in qualitative research. In N. K. Denzin & Y. S. Lincoln (Eds.), *Handbook of qualitative research* (pp. 105–117). Thousand Oaks, CA: Sage.

Kelle, U. (1997). Theory building in qualitative research and computer programs for the management of textual data. *Sociological Research Online,* 2(2). [Online.] Available: http://www.socresonline.org.uk/socresonline/2/2/1.html.

Lee, R. M., & Fielding, N. (1996). Qualitative data analysis: Representations of a technology: A comment on Coffey, Holbrook and Atkinson. *Sociological Research Online,* 1(4). [Online.] Available: http://www.socresonline.org.uk/socresonline/1/4/1f.html.

Morison, M., & Moir, J. (1998). The role of computer software in the analysis of qualitative data: Efficient clerk, research assistant, or Trojan horse? *Journal of Advanced Nursing,* 28(1), 106–116.

Parse, R. R. (1987). Nursing science: *Major paradigms, theories, and critiques*. Philadelphia: Saunders.

Parse, R. R. (Ed.). (1995). *Illuminations: The human becoming theory in practice and research*. New York: National League for Nursing Press.

Parse, R. R. (1996). Building knowledge through qualitative research: The road less traveled. *Nursing Science Quarterly,* 9, 10–16.

Parse, R. R. (1997). The human becoming theory: The was, is, and will be. *Nursing Science Quarterly,* 10, 32–38.

Parse, R. R. (1998). *The human becoming school of thought: A perspective for nurses and other health professionals*. Thousand Oaks, CA: Sage.

Pilkington, F. B. (1996). The use of computers in qualitative research. *Nursing Science Quarterly,* 9, 5–7.

Qualis Research. (1999, October 8). *Text based qualitative data analysis software: The Ethnograph v5.0*. [Online.] Available: http://www.qualisresearch.com/main.htm.

Researchware. (1999, October 8). *HyperRESEARCH*. [Online.] Available: http://www.researchware.com.

Richards, L. (1997). User's mistake as developer's challenge: Designing the new NUD*IST. *Qualitative Health Research,* 7(3), 425–433.

Richards, L. (1998). Closeness to data: The changing goals of qualitative data handling. *Qualitative Health Research,* 8(3), 319–328.

Richards, L. (1999). Data alive! The thinking behind NVivo. *Qualitative Health Research,* 9(3), 412–428.

Richards, L., & Richards, T. (1991). Computing in qualitative analysis: A healthy development? *Qualitative Health Research,* 1(2), 234–262.

Richards, T. J., & Richards, L. (1994). Using computers in qualitative research. In N. K. Denzin & Y. S. Lincoln (Eds.), *Handbook of qualitative research* (pp. 445–462). Thousand Oaks, CA: Sage.

Sandelowski, M. (1995). On the aesthetics of qualitative research. *Image: Journal of Nursing Scholarship,* 27(3), 205–209.

Scientific Software Development. (1999, October 8). *Atlas.ti The knowledge workbench.* [Online.] Available: http://www.atlasti.de/.

Taft, L. B. (1993). Computer-assisted qualitative research. *Research in Nursing & Health,* 16(5), 379–383.

Tallerico, M. (1991). Applications of qualitative analysis software: A view from the field. *Qualitative Sociology,* 14, 275–285.

Tesch, R. (1991). Computer programs that assist in the analysis of qualitative data: An overview. *Qualitative Health Research,* 1, 309–325.

Walker, B. L. (1993). Computer analysis of qualitative data: A comparison of three packages. *Qualitative Health Research,* 3(1), 91–111.

Webb, C. (1999). Analysing qualitative data: Computerized and other approaches. *Journal of Advanced Nursing,* 29(2), 323–330.

Weitzman, E. A. (1999). Analyzing qualitative data with computer software. *Health Services Research,* 34(5, part II), 1241–1263.

Weitzman, E. A. (2000). Software and qualitative research. In N. K. Denzin & Y. Lincoln (Eds.), *Handbook of qualitative research* (2nd ed.), pp. 803–820). Thousand Oaks, CA: Sage.

Weitzman, E. A., & Miles, M. B. (1995). *Computer programs for qualitative data analysis.* Thousand Oaks, CA: Sage.

CODA

This book was born out of a personal desire to contribute to knowledge building through qualitative inquiry. The goal is to set forth a logically congruent work as a standard for the conduction of qualitative research. The specific qualitative methods selected for inclusion are ones most frequently used by those scholars concerned with discovering the meaning of humanly lived experiences. Each method is embedded in an ontology, is epistemologically appropriate for the study of specific phenomena, and has a specific methodology with unique processes; thus, the ontology, epistemology, and methodology are shown for each chosen method. Some examples of methods appearing in well-written studies from the nursing literature are included to show complete published reports in the format for publication in a refereed journal. Two original research studies are also included. In addition, this volume contains a chapter on critical appraisal, an example of a research critique, and a grant proposal. A chapter on using computers in qualitative research and a list of selected references are also presented.

This work is set forth to promote scholarly dialogue as more scholars of all disciplines are becoming concerned with lived experiences that cannot be studied using quantitative methods. As scholars embrace questions that lead to qualitative inquiry, there will be a shift in the mainstream of science to sciencing humanly lived experiences.

"Do not block the way of inquiry."
—*Charles Sanders Peirce*
1839–1914

SELECTED REFERENCES

BOOKS

Abdellah, F. G. (1994). *Preparing nursing research for the 21st century: Evolution, methodologies, challenges*. New York: Springer.

Alasuutari, P. (1995). *Researching culture: Qualitative method and cultural studies*. Thousand Oaks, CA: Sage.

Alvesson, M., & Skoldberg, K. (1999). *Reflexive methodology: Interpretation and research*. Thousand Oaks, CA: Sage.

Atkinson, R. (1998). *The life story interview*. Thousand Oaks, CA: Sage.

Barbour, R. S., & Kitzinger, J. (Eds.). (1999). *Developing focus group research: Politics, theory, and practice*. Thousand Oaks, CA: Sage.

Benner, P. (Ed.). (1994). *Interpretive phenomenology: Embodiment, caring, and ethics in health and illness*. Thousand Oaks, CA: Sage.

Bishop, A. H., & Scudder, J. R., Jr. (1990). *The practical, moral, and personal sense of nursing: A phenomenological philosophy of practice*. Albany: State University of New York Press.

Bleicher, J. (1980). *Contemporary hermeneutics: Hermeneutics as method, philosophy and critique*. London: Routledge & Kegan Paul.

Bleicher, J. (1982). *The hermeneutic imagination*. London: Routledge & Kegan Paul.

Blumer, H. (1969). *Symbolic interactionism*. Englewood Cliffs, NJ: Prentice-Hall.

Bogdan, R., & Bilken, S. (1982). *Qualitative research for education*. Boston: Allyn & Bacon.

Bogdan, R., & Taylor, S. J. (1975). *Introduction to qualitative research methods: A phenomenological approach to the social sciences*. New York: Wiley.

Boyatzis, R. E. (1998). *Transforming qualitative information: Thematic analysis and code development*. Thousand Oaks, CA: Sage.

Braud, W., & Anderson, R. (1998). *Transpersonal research methods for the social sciences: Honoring human experience*. Thousand Oaks, CA: Sage.

Briggs, J. (1988). *Fire in the crucible: The alchemy of creative genius*. New York: St. Martin's Press.

Briggs, J. P., & Peat, F. D. (1984). *Looking glass universe: The emerging science of wholeness*. New York: Simon & Schuster.

Bruteau, B. (1979). *The psychic grid: How we create the world we know*. Wheaton, IL: Theosophical Publishing.

Bryman, A., & Burgess, R. (Eds.). (1999). *Qualitative research volume* I: *Fundamental issues in qualitative research*. Thousand Oaks, CA: Sage.

Bryman, A., & Burgess, R. (Eds.). (1999). *Qualitative research volume* II: *Methods of qualitative research*. Thousand Oaks, CA: Sage.

Bryman, A., & Burgess, R. (Eds.). (1999). *Qualitative research volume* III: *Analysis and interpretation of qualitative data*. Thousand Oaks, CA: Sage.

Bryman, A., & Burgess, R. (Eds.). (1999). *Qualitative research volume* IV: *Issues in qualitative research*. Thousand Oaks, CA: Sage.

Buber, M. (1958). I *and thou* (R. G. Smith, Trans.). New York: Collier Books. (Original work published 1923)

Buber, M. (1965). *The knowledge of man*. New York: Harper & Row.

Burgess, R. G. (Ed.). (1995). *Studies in qualitative methodology*: *Computing and qualitative research*: *Volume* 5. London: JAI Press.

Campbell, J., & Moyers, B. (1988). *The power of myth*. New York: Doubleday.

Cantor, N., & Schneider, R. (1967). *How to study history*. Arlington Heights, IL: Harlan Davidson.

Carr, E. (1961). *What is history*? New York: Vintage.

Chenitz, W. C., & Swanson, J. M. (1986). *From practice to grounded theory*: *Qualitative research in nursing*. Menlo Park, CA: Addison-Wesley.

Coffey, A. (1999). *The ethnographic self*: *Fieldwork and the representation of identity*. Thousand Oaks, CA: Sage.

Coffey, A., & Atkinson, P. (1996). *Making sense of qualitative data*: *Complementary research strategies*. Thousand Oaks, CA: Sage.

Cohen, M. Z., Kahn, D. L., & Steeves, R. H. (2000). *Hermeneutic phenomenological research*: *A practical guide for nurse researchers*. Thousand Oaks, CA: Sage.

Colaizzi, P. F. (1973). *Reflection and research in psychology*: *A phenomenological study of learning*. Dubuque, IA: Kendall/Hunt.

Crabtree, B. F., & Miller, W. L. (Eds.). (1992). *Doing qualitative research*. Newbury Park, CA: Sage.

Crabtree, B. F., & Miller, W. L. (Eds.). (1999). *Doing qualitative research* (2nd ed.). Thousand Oaks, CA: Sage.

Creswell, J. W. (1994). *Research design*: *Qualitative and quantitative approaches*. Thousand Oaks, CA: Sage.

Creswell, J. W. (1997). *Qualitative inquiry and research design*: *Choosing among five traditions*. Thousand Oaks, CA: Sage.

Czarniawska, B. (1997). *A narrative approach to organization studies*. Thousand Oaks, CA: Sage.

Davidson, J., & Lytle, M. (1986). *After the fact*: *The art of historical detection*. New York: Knopf.

Denzin, N. K. (1996). *Interpretive ethnography*: *Ethnographic practices for the 21st century*. Thousand Oaks, CA: Sage.

Denzin, N. K., & Lincoln, Y. S. (Eds.). (1994). *Handbook of qualitative research*. Thousand Oaks, CA: Sage.

Denzin, N. K., & Lincoln, Y. S. (Eds.). (1998). *Handbook of qualitative research*: *Collecting and interpreting qualitative materials*. Thousand Oaks, CA: Sage.

Denzin, N. K., & Lincoln, Y. S. (Eds.). (1998). *Handbook of qualitative research: The landscape of qualitative research*. Thousand Oaks, CA: Sage.

Denzin, N. K., & Lincoln, Y. S. (Eds.). (1998). *Handbook of qualitative research: Strategies of qualitative inquiry*. Thousand Oaks, CA: Sage.

Denzin, N. K., & Lincoln, Y. (Eds.). (2000). *Handbook of qualitative research* (2nd ed.). Thousand Oaks, CA: Sage.

Dufrenne, M. (1973). *The phenomenology of aesthetic experience*. Evanston, IL: Northwestern University Press.

Ellis, C., & Bochner, A. P. (Eds.). (1996). *Composing ethnography: Alternative forms of qualitative writing*. London: Altamira Press.

Erickson, K., & Stull, D. (1997). *Doing team ethnography: Warnings and advice*. Thousand Oaks, CA: Sage.

Fetterman, D. M. (1989). *Ethnography: Step by step*. Thousand Oaks, CA: Sage.

Fetterman, D. M. (1998). *Ethnography: Step by step* (2nd ed.). Thousand Oaks, CA: Sage.

Fetterman, D. M., Kaftarian, S. J., & Wandersman, A. (Eds.). (1996). *Empowerment evaluation: Knowledge and tools for self-assessment and accountability*. Thousand Oaks, CA: Sage.

Feyerabend, P. (1990). *Against method* (Rev. ed.). London: Verso. (Original work published 1975)

Field, P. A., & Morse, J. M. (1985). *Nursing research: The application of qualitative approaches*. Rockville, MD: Aspen Systems.

Fielding, N. G., & Lee, R. M. (Eds.). (1991). *Using computers in qualitative research*. Newbury Park, CA: Sage.

Fielding, N. G., & Lee, R. M. (1998). *Computer analysis and qualitative research*. Thousand Oaks, CA: Sage.

Filstead, W. (Ed.). (1970). *Qualitative methodology*. Chicago: Rand McNally.

Fischer, D. H. (1970). *Historian's fallacies: Toward a logic of historical thought*. New York: Harper & Row.

Fitzpatrick, M. (1977). *Historical studies in nursing*. New York: Teachers College Press.

Flick, U. (1998). *An introduction to qualitative research*. Thousand Oaks, CA: Sage.

Foucault, M. (1994). *The order of things: An archeology of the human sciences*. New York: Vintage Books.

Gadamer, H.-G. (1975). *Truth and method* (G. Barden & J. Cumming, Ed. & Trans.). New York: Seabury.

Gadamer, H.-G. (1976). *Philosophical hermeneutics* (D. E. Linge, Ed. & Trans.). Berkeley: University of California Press.

Gadamer, H.-G. (1980). *Dialogue and dialectic: Eight hermeneutical studies on Plato* (P. C. Smith, Trans.). New Haven: Yale University Press.

Gahan, C., & Hannibal, M. (1998). *Doing qualitative research using QSR NUD.IST*. Thousand Oaks, CA: Sage.

Gephart, R. P. (1988). *Ethnostatistics: Qualitative foundations for quantitative research*. Newbury Park: Sage.

Giorgi, A. (1970). *Psychology as a human science: A phenomenologically based approach*. New York: Harper & Row.

Giorgi, A. (Ed.). (1985). *Phenomenology and psychological research*. Pittsburgh, PA: Duquesne University Press.

Giorgi, A., Fischer, C. L., & Murray, E. L. (1975). *Duquesne studies in phenomenological psychology*. Pittsburgh, PA: Duquesne University Press.

Glaser, B. G. (1978). *Theoretical sensitivity: Advances in methodology or grounded theory*. Mill Valley, CA: Sociology Press.

Glaser, B. G., & Strauss, A. L. (1967). *The discovery of grounded theory: Strategies for qualitative research*. New York: Aldine.

Glassner, B., & Hertz, R. (1999). *Qualitative sociology as everyday life*. Thousand Oaks, CA: Sage.

Goffman, E. (1959). *The presentation of self in everyday life*. Garden City, NY: Doubleday Anchor.

Goldberg, P. (1983). *The intuitive edge: Understanding and developing intuition*. Los Angeles: Tarcher.

Golden-Biddle, K., & Locke, K. D. (1997). *Composing qualitative research*. Thousand Oaks, CA: Sage.

Graue, M. E., & Walsh, D. J. (1998). *Studying children in context: Theories, methods, and ethics of studying children*. Thousand Oaks, CA: Sage.

Grbich, C. (1999). *Qualitative research in health: An introduction*. Thousand Oaks, CA: Sage.

Greenbaum, T. L. (1997). *The handbook for focus group research* (2nd ed.). Thousand Oaks, CA: Sage.

Greig, A., & Taylor, J. (1998). *Doing research with children*. Thousand Oaks, CA: Sage.

Grills, S. (Ed.). (1998). *Doing ethnographic research*. Thousand Oaks, CA: Sage.

Guba, E. G. (Ed.). (1990). *The paradigm dialogue*. Newbury Park, CA: Sage.

Guba, E. G., & Lincoln, Y. S. (1989). *Fourth generation evaluation*. Newbury Park, CA: Sage.

Gubrium, J. F., & Sankar, A. (Eds.). (1994). *Qualitative methods in aging research*. Thousand Oaks, CA: Sage.

Gurwitsh, A. (1974). *Phenomenology and the theory of science* (L. Embree, Ed.). Evanston, IL: Northwestern University Press.

Habermas, J. (1968). *Knowledge and human interests* (J. Shapiro, Trans.). Boston: Beacon.

Hamel, J. (1993). *Case study methods*. Thousand Oaks, CA: Sage.

Harris, M. (1968). *The rise of anthropological theory*. New York: Thomas & Crowell.

Heron, J. (1996). *Co-operative inquiry: Research into the human condition*. Thousand Oaks, CA: Sage.

Hertz, R. (1997). *Reflexivity and voice*. Thousand Oaks, CA: Sage.

Holmes, R. M. (1998). *Fieldwork with children*. Thousand Oaks, CA: Sage.

Holstein, J. A., & Gubrium, J. F. (1995). *The active interview*. Thousand Oaks, CA: Sage.

Husserl, E. (1962). *Ideas: General introduction to pure phenomenology*. (W. R. Boyce Gibson, Trans.). New York: Collier Books. (Original work published 1913).

Janesick, V. (1998). *Stretching exercises for qualitative researchers*. Thousand Oaks, CA: Sage.

Johnson, J. (1975). *Doing field research*. Englewood Cliffs, NJ: Prentice-Hall.

Jorgensen, D. L. (1989). *Participant observation: A methodology for human studies*. Thousand Oaks, CA: Sage.

Josselson, R., & Lieblich, A. (1999). *Making meaning of narratives* (6th ed.). Thousand Oaks, CA: Sage.

Josselson, R., Lieblich, A., Sharabany, R., & Wiseman, H. (1997). *Conversation as method: Analyzing the effects of growing up communally on later relationships.* Thousand Oaks, CA: Sage.

Kelle, U. (Ed.). (1995). *Computer-aided qualitative data analysis: Theory, methods, and practice.* Thousand Oaks, CA: Sage.

Kikuchi, J. F., & Simmons, H. (Eds.). (1992). *Philosophic inquiry in nursing.* Newbury Park, CA: Sage.

Kirk, J. (1987). *Reliability and validity in qualitative research.* Beverly Hills, CA: Sage.

Kopala, M., & Suzuki, L. A. (1999). *Using qualitative methods in psychology.* Thousand Oaks, CA: Sage.

Krueger, R. A. (1994). *Focus groups: A practical guide for applied research* (2nd ed.). Thousand Oaks, CA: Sage.

Kvale, S. (1996). *Interviews: An introduction to qualitative research interviewing.* Thousand Oaks, CA: Sage.

Lambert, E., Ashery, R. S., & Needle, R. H. (Eds.). (1995). *Qualitative methods in drug abuse and HIV research,* Rockville, MD: U.S. Department of Health and Human Services, National Institute of Health.

Lee, T. W. (1998). *Using qualitative methods in organizational research.* Thousand Oaks, CA: Sage.

Leininger, M. (1970). *Nursing and anthropology: Two worlds to blend.* New York: Wiley.

Leininger, M. (1981). *Caring: An essential human need.* Thorofare, NJ: Slack.

Leininger, M. M. (Ed.). (1985). *Qualitative research methods in nursing.* Orlando, FL: Grune & Stratton.

Lieblich, A., & Josselson, R. (Eds.). (1997). *The narrative study of lives.* Thousand Oaks, CA: Sage.

Lieblich, A., Tval-Mashiach, R., & Zilber, T. (1998). *Narrative research: Reading, analysis, and interpretation.* Thousand Oaks, CA: Sage.

Lincoln, Y. S., & Guba, E. G. (1985). *Naturalistic inquiry.* Beverly Hills, CA: Sage.

Lofland, J., & Lofland, L. H. (1984). *Analyzing social settings: A guide to qualitative observation and analysis* (2nd ed.). Belmont, CA: Wadsworth.

Lujpen, W. A. (1960). *Existential phenomenology.* New York: Humanities Press.

Lujpen, W. A., & Koren, H. J. (1969). *A first introduction to existential phenomenology.* Pittsburgh, PA: Duquesne University Press.

Madison, G. B. (1990). *The hermeneutics of postmodernity: Figures and themes.* Bloomington: Indiana University Press.

Makkreel, R. A., & Rodi, F. (Eds.). (1989). *Wilhelm Dilthey selected works/volume 1: Introduction to the human sciences.* Princeton, NJ: Princeton University Press.

Marcel, G. (1956). *The philosophy of existentialism.* Secaucus, NJ: Citadel.

Marshall, C., & Rossman, G. B. (1989). *Designing qualitative research.* Newbury Park, CA: Sage.

Marshall, C., & Rossman, G. B. (1994). *Designing qualitative research* (2nd ed.). Thousand Oaks, CA: Sage.

Marshall, C., & Rossman, G. B. (1998). *Designing qualitative research* (3rd ed.). Thousand Oaks, CA: Sage.

Mason, J. (1996). *Qualitative researching*. Thousand Oaks, CA: Sage.

Maxwell, J. A. (1996). *Qualitative research design: An interactive approach*. Thousand Oaks, CA: Sage.

McCall, G., & Simmons, J. (1969). *Issues in participant observation: A text and reader*. Reading, MA: Addison Wesley.

McCracken, G. (1988). *The long interview*. Thousand Oaks, CA: Sage.

McLoughlin, Q. (1991). *Relativistic naturalism: A cross-cultural approach to human science*. New York: Praeger.

Merleau-Ponty, M. (1964). *The primacy of perception*. Evanston, IL: Northwestern University Press.

Mertens, D. M. (1997). *Research methods in education and psychology: Integrating diversity with qualitative and quantitative approaches*. Thousand Oaks, CA: Sage.

Miles, M., & Huberman, A. (1984). *Qualitative data analysis*. Beverly Hills, CA: Sage.

Miles, M. B., & Huberman, A. M. (1994). *Qualitative data analysis: An expanded source book* (2nd ed.). Thousand Oaks, CA: Sage.

Miller, G. (1997). *Context and method in qualitative research*. Thousand Oaks, CA: Sage.

Moch, S. D. (1995). *Breast cancer. Twenty women's stories: Becoming more alive through the experience*. New York: National League for Nursing Press.

Moch, S. D., & Gates, M. F. (Eds.). (1999). *The researcher experience in qualitative research*. Thousand Oaks, CA: Sage.

Moody, L. E. (Ed.). (1990). *Advancing nursing science through research* (Vol. 1). Newbury Park, CA: Sage.

Moody, L. E. (Ed.). (1990). *Advancing nursing science through research* (Vol. 2). Newbury Park, CA: Sage.

Morgan, D. L. (1997). *Focus groups as qualitative research* (2nd ed.). Thousand Oaks, CA: Sage.

Morgan, D. L., & Krueger, R. A. (Eds.). (1997). *Focus group kit*. Thousand Oaks, CA: Sage.

Morse, J. M. (Ed.). (1991). *Qualitative nursing research: A contemporary dialogue* (Rev. ed.). Newbury Park, CA: Sage. (Original work published 1989).

Morse, J. M. (Ed.). (1992). *Qualitative health research*. Rockville, MD: Aspen.

Morse, J. M. (Ed.) (1993). *Critical issues in qualitative research methods*. Thousand Oaks, CA: Sage.

Morse, J. M. (1997). *Completing a qualitative project*. Thousand Oaks, CA: Sage.

Morse, J. M., & Field, P. A. (1995). *Qualitative research methods for health professionals* (2nd ed.). Thousand Oaks, CA: Sage.

Moustakas, C. E. (1967). *Creativity and conformity*. Princeton, NJ: Van Nostrand.

Moustakas, C. E. (1990). *Heuristic research: Design, methodology, and application*. Newbury Park, CA: Sage.

Moustakas, C. E. (1994). *Phenomenological research methods*. Thousand Oaks, CA: Sage.

Munhall, P., & Boyd, C. O. (Eds.). (1993). *Nursing research: A qualitative perspective* (2nd ed.). New York: National League for Nursing Press.

Munhall, P. L., & Oiler, C. J. (1986). *Nursing research: A qualitative perspective*. Norwalk, CT: Appleton-Century-Crofts.

Murray, M., & Chamberlain, K. (Eds.). (1999). *Qualitative health psychology: Theories and methods*. Thousand Oaks, CA: Sage.

Naumes, W., & Naumes, M. (Eds.). (1999). *The art and craft of case writing*. Thousand Oaks, CA: Sage.

Omery, A., Kasper, C. E., & Page, G. G. (1995). *In search of nursing science*. Thousand Oaks, CA: Sage.

Parse, R. R. (1987). *Nursing science: Major paradigms, theories, and critiques*. Philadelphia: Saunders.

Parse, R. R. (Ed.). (1995). *Illuminations: The human becoming theory in practice and research*. New York: National League for Nursing Press.

Parse, R. R. (1998). *The human becoming school of thought: A perspective for nurses and other health professionals*. Thousand Oaks, CA: Sage.

Parse, R. R. (1999). *Hope: An international human becoming perspective*. Sudbury, MA: Jones and Bartlett.

Parse, R. R., Coyne, A. B., & Smith, M. J. (1985). *Nursing research: Qualitative methods*. Bowie, MD: Brady.

Patton, M. Q. (1980). *Qualitative evaluation methods*. Beverly Hills, CA: Sage.

Patton, M. Q. (1990). *Qualitative evaluation and research methods* (2nd ed.). Newbury Park, CA: Sage.

Pelto, P. J., & Pelto, G. H. (1981). *Anthropological research: The structure of inquiry*. Cambridge, MA: Cambridge University Press.

Polanyi, M., & Prosch, H. (1975). *Meaning*. Chicago: University of Chicago Press.

Polkinghorne, D. (1983). *Methodology for the human sciences: Systems of inquiry*. Albany: State University of New York Press.

Polkinghorne, D. E. (1988). *Narrative knowing and the human sciences*. Albany: State University of New York Press.

Powers, B. A., & Knapp, T. R. (1990). *A dictionary of nursing theory and research*. Newbury Park, CA: Sage.

Progoff, I. (1983). *Life-study: Experiencing creative lives by the intensive journal method*. New York: Dialogue House Library.

Reason, P., & Rowan, J. (Eds.). (1981). *Human inquiry: A sourcebook of new paradigm research*. New York: Wiley.

Rheingold, H. (1991). *Virtual reality*. New York: Summit.

Ricoeur, P. (1981). *Hermeneutics and the human sciences*. New York: Cambridge University Press.

Riessman, C. K. (1993). *Narrative analysis*. Thousand Oaks, CA: Sage.

Roberts, C. A. (1989). *Nursing research: A quantitative and qualitative approach*. Boston: Jones and Bartlett.

Roper, J. M., & Shapira, J. (1999). *Ethnography in nursing research*. Thousand Oaks, CA: Sage.

Rossman, G. B., & Rallis, S. F. (1998). *Learning in the field: An introduction to qualitative research*. Thousand Oaks, CA: Sage.

Rubin, H. J., & Rubin, I. S. (1995). Qualitative interviewing: The art of hearing data. Thousand Oaks, CA: Sage.

Rykiewick, M., & Spradley, J. (Eds.). (1977). Ethics and anthropology: Dilemma in fieldwork. New York: Wiley.

Salisbury, J., & Delamont, S. (Eds.). (1995). Qualitative studies in education. Brookfield, VT: Ashgate.

Sapsford, R., & Jupp, V. (1996). Data collection and analysis. Thousand Oaks, CA: Sage.

Sarter, B. (Ed.). (1988). Paths to knowledge: Innovative research methods for nursing. New York: National League for Nursing Press.

Saunders, W. B., & Pinney, T. K. (1983). The conduct of social research. New York: Holt, Rinehart, & Winston.

Schatzman, L., & Strauss, A. (1973). Field research. Englewood Cliffs, NJ: Prentice-Hall.

Schulberg, H., Sheldon, A., & Baker, F. (1969). Program evaluation in the health fields. New York: Behavioral Publications.

Schutz, A. (1967). The phenomenology of the social world. Evanston, IL: Northwestern University Press.

Schwandt, T. A. (1997). Qualitative inquiry: A dictionary of terms. Thousand Oaks, CA: Sage.

Segall, M. (1979). Human behavior in cross-cultural psychology: Global perspective. Monterey, CA: Brooks/Cole.

Seung, T. (1982). Semiotics and thematics in hermeneutics. New York: Columbia University Press.

Shaffir, W. B., Stebbins, R. A., & Turozitz, A. (Eds.). (1980). Fieldwork experience: Qualitative approaches to social research. New York: St. Martin's.

Shofer, R. (1980). A guide to historical method. Chicago: Dorsey.

Silverman, D. (Ed.). (1993). Interpreting qualitative data: Methods for analyzing talk, text, and interaction. Thousand Oaks, CA: Sage.

Silverman, D. (Ed.). (1997). Qualitative research: Theory, method, and practice. Thousand Oaks, CA: Sage.

Silverman, D. (1999). Doing qualitative research: A practical handbook. Thousand Oaks, CA: Sage.

Skinner, Q. (Ed.). (1990). The return of grand theory in the human sciences. Cambridge, Great Britain: Cambridge University Press. (Original work published 1985)

Spiegelberg, H. (1975). Doing phenomenology: Essays on and in phenomenology. The Hague: Martinus Nijhoff.

Spiegelberg, H. (1981). The context of the phenomenological movement. Boston: Martinus Nijhoff.

Spiegelberg, H. (1982). The phenomenological movement: A historical introduction (3rd rev. and enlarged ed.). The Hague: Martinus Nijhoff. (Original work published 1960)

Spradley, J. P. (1979). The ethnographic interview. New York: Holt, Rinehart & Winston.

Spradley, J. P. (1980). Participant observation. New York: Holt, Rinehart & Winston.

Stake, R. E. (1995). The art of case study research. Thousand Oaks, CA: Sage.

Stewart, D. W., & Shamdasani, P. N. (1990). Focus groups: Theory and practice. Thousand Oaks, CA: Sage.

Strasser, S. (1963). *Phenomenology and the human sciences*. Pittsburgh, PA: Duquesne University Press.

Strauss, A. L. (1987). *Qualitative analysis for social scientists*. Cambridge: Cambridge University Press.

Strauss, A., & Corbin, J. (1990). *Basics of qualitative research: Grounded theory procedures and techniques*. Newbury Park, CA: Sage.

Strauss, A., & Corbin, J. (1997). *Grounded theory in practice*. Thousand Oaks, CA: Sage.

Strauss, A., & Corbin, J. (1998). *Basics of qualitative research: Techniques and procedures for developing grounded theory* (2nd ed.). Thousand Oaks, CA: Sage.

Stringer, E. T. (1996). *Action research: A handbook for practitioners*. Thousand Oaks, CA: Sage.

Struebert, H. J., & Carpenter, D. R. (1995). *Qualitative research in nursing: Advancing the humanistic imperative*. Philadelphia: Lippincott.

Symon, G., & Cassell, C. (1998). *Qualitative methods and analysis in organizational research: A practical guide*. Thousand Oaks, CA: Sage.

Tashakkori, A., & Teddlie, C. (1998). *Mixed methodology: Combining qualitative and quantitative approaches*. Thousand Oaks, CA: Sage.

Taylor, C. (1985). *Human agency and language*. New York: Cambridge University Press.

Taylor, C. (1985). *Philosophy and the human sciences*. New York: Cambridge University Press.

Taylor, S. J., & Bogdon, R. (1984). *Introduction to qualitative methods: The search for meaning* (2nd ed.). New York: Wiley.

ten Have, P. (1999). *Doing conversation analysis: A practical guide*. Thousand Oaks, CA: Sage.

Tesch, R. (1990). *Qualitative research: Analysis types and software tools*. New York: Falmer.

Thomas, B. S. (1990). *Nursing research: An experimental approach*. St. Louis: Mosby.

Thorne, S. E., & Hayes, V. E. (Eds.). (1997). *Nursing praxis: Knowledge and action*. Thousand Oaks, CA: Sage.

van Kaam, A. (1969). *Existential foundation of psychology*. New York: Doubleday.

Van Maanen, J. (1982). *Varieties of qualitative research*. Beverly Hills, CA: Sage.

Van Maanen, J. (Ed.). (1983). *Qualitative methodology*. Beverly Hills, CA: Sage. (Original work published 1979)

Van Maanen, J. (Ed.). (1995). *Representation in ethnography*. Beverly Hills, CA: Sage.

Van Maanen, J. (Ed.). (1998). *Qualitative studies in organizations*. Thousand Oaks, CA: Sage.

Van Manen, M. (1990). *Researching lived experience: Human science for an action sensitive pedagogy*. Albany: State University of New York Press.

Vaz, K. M. (1997). *Oral narrative research with black women*. Thousand Oaks, CA: Sage.

Walker, R. (1985). *Applied qualitative research*. Brookfield, IL: Gower.

Watson, J. (1988). *Nursing: Human science and human care. A theory of nursing*. New York: National League for Nursing Press.

Weitzman, E. A., & Miles, M. B. (1995). *Computer programs for qualitative data analysis*. Thousand Oaks, CA: Sage.

Wolcott, H. F. (1994). *Transforming qualitative data: Description, analysis, and interpretation*. Thousand Oaks, CA: Sage.

Wolf, R. M. (1979). *Evaluation in education: Foundations of competency assessment and program review*. New York: Praeger.

Yin, R. K. (1993). *Applications of case study research*. Thousand Oaks, CA: Sage.

Yin, R. K. (1994). *Case study research: Design and methods*. Thousand Oaks, CA: Sage.

Yow, V. R. (1994). *Recording oral history: A practical guide for social scientists*. Thousand Oaks, CA: Sage.

ARTICLES AND BOOK CHAPTERS

Aamodt, A. M. (1983). Problems in doing nursing research: Developing a criteria for evaluating qualitative research. *Western Journal of Nursing Research, 5*(4), 398–410.

Aanstoos, C. M. (1985). Psychology as a human science. *American Psychologist, 40,* 1417–1418.

Addison, R. B. (1997). Interviews: An introduction to qualitative research interviewing by Steiner K. Vale. *Qualitative Health Research, 7,* 434.

Agar, M. (1991). The right brain strikes back. In N. G. Fielding & R. M. Lee (Eds.), *Using computers in qualitative research* (pp. 181–194). London: Sage.

Allchin-Petardi, L. (1998). Weathering the storm: Persevering through a difficult time. *Nursing Science Quarterly, 11,* 172–177.

Allen, D. (1985). Nursing research and social control: Alternative models of science that emphasize understanding and emancipation. *Image: Journal of Nursing Scholarship, 17*(2), 58–64.

Allen, D., Benner, P., & Diekelman, N. (1986). Three paradigms for nursing research: Methodological implications. In P. L. Chinn (Ed.), *Nursing research methodology: Issues and implementations*. Rockville, MD: Aspen.

Andershed, B., & Ternestedt, B. M. (1999). Involvement of relatives in care of the dying in different care cultures: Development of a theoretical understanding. *Nursing Science Quarterly, 12,* 45–51.

Anderson, J., & Eppard, J. (1998). van Kaam's method revisited. *Qualitative Health Research, 8*(3), 399–403.

Artinian, B. M. (1998). Grounded theory research: Its value for nursing. *Nursing Science Quarterly, 11,* 5–6.

Asbury, J. (1995). Overview of focus group research. *Qualitative Health Research, 5,* 414–420.

Atkinson, P. (1992). Understanding ethnographic texts. In J. Van Maanen (Ed.), *Qualitative research methods* (Vol. 25), Newbury Park, CA: Sage.

Atkinson, P. (1997). Narrative turn or blind alley? *Qualitative Health Research, 7,* 325–344.

Ayres, L., & Poirier, S. (1996). Focus on qualitative methods: Virtual text and the growth of meaning in qualitative analysis. *Research in Nursing & Health, 19,* 163–169.

Bailey, P. H. (1996). Assuring quality in narrative analysis. *Western Journal of Nursing Research, 18,* 186–194.

Bailey, P. H. (1997). Finding your way around qualitative methods in nursing research. *Journal of Advanced Nursing, 25*(1), 18–22.

Baker, C. A. (1988). Computer applications in qualitative research. *Computers in Nursing*, 6(5), 211–214.

Banonis, B. C. (1989). The lived experience of recovering from addiction: A phenomenological study. *Nursing Science Quarterly*, 2, 37–43.

Barbour, R. S. (1998). Mixing qualitative methods: Quality assurance or qualitative quagmire? *Qualitative Health Research*, 8(3), 352–361.

Barrett, E. A. M. (1998). Unique nursing research methods: The diversity chant of pioneers. *Nursing Science Quarterly*, 11, 94–96.

Barry, C. (1998). Choosing qualitative data analysis software: Atlas/ti and Nudist compared. *Sociological Research Online*, 3(3). [Online]. Available: http://www.socresonline.org.uk/socresonline/3/3/4.html.

Barry, C. A., Britten, N., Barber, N., Bradley, C., & Stevenson, F. (1999). Using reflexivity to optimize teamwork in qualitative research. *Qualitative Health Research*, 9(1), 26–44.

Baumann, S. L. (1994). No place of their own: An exploratory study. *Nursing Science Quarterly*, 7, 162–169.

Baumann, S. L. (1995). Two views of homeless children's art: Psychoanalysis and Parse's human becoming theory. *Nursing Science Quarterly*, 8, 65–70.

Baumann, S. L. (1996). Feeling uncomfortable: Children in families with no place of their own. *Nursing Science Quarterly*, 9, 152–159.

Baumann, S. L. (1996). Parse's research methodology and the nurse researcher-child process. *Nursing Science Quarterly*, 9, 27–32.

Baumann, S. L. (1999). Art as a path of inquiry. *Nursing Science Quarterly*, 12, 106–110.

Bazeley, P. (1999). The *bricoleur* with a computer: Piecing together qualitative and quantitative data. *Qualitative Health Research*, 9(2), 279–287.

Beaudin, C. L., & Pelletier, L. R. (1996). Consumer-based research: Using focus groups as a method for evaluating quality of care. *Journal of Nursing Care Quality*, 10(3), 28–33.

Beck, C. T. (1993). Caring among nursing students. *Nurse Educator*, 17, 22–27.

Beck, C. T. (1993). Qualitative research: The evaluation of its credibility, fittingness, and auditability. *Western Journal of Nursing Research*, 15(2), 263–266.

Beck, C. T. (1994). Phenomenology: Its use in nursing research. *International Journal of Nursing Studies*, 31, 499–510.

Beck, C. T. (1994). Reliability and validity issues in phenomenology. *Western Journal of Nursing Research*, 16, 254–267.

Begley, C. M. (1996). Triangulation of communication skills in qualitative research instruments. *Journal of Advanced Nursing*, 24, 688–693.

Bennett, L. (1991). Adolescent girls' experience of witnessing marital violence: A phenomenological study. *Journal of Advanced Nursing*, 16, 431–438.

Bournes, D. A. (2000). Concept inventing: A process for creating a unitary definition of having courage. *Nursing Science Quarterly*, 13, 143–149.

Bournes, D. A. (in press). Having courage: A lived experience of human becoming. *Nursing Science Quarterly*.

Boyd, C. O. (1989). Dialogue on a research issue: Phenomenological research in nursing. Response: Clarifying the issues. *Nursing Science Quarterly*, 2, 16–19.

Boyd, C. O. (1990). Critical appraisal of developing nursing research methods. *Nursing Science Quarterly*, 3, 42–43.

Boyle, J. (1981). An application of the structure-functional method of the phenomenon of caring. In M. Leininger (Ed.), *Caring: An essential human need* (pp. 37–47). Thorofare, NJ: Slack.

Brennan, P. F., & Hays, B. J. (1992). The kappa statistic for establishing interrater reliability in the secondary analysis of qualitative clinical data. *Research in Nursing & Health*, 15, 153–158.

Brent, E. (1984). Qualitative computing: Issues and answers. *Qualitative Sociology*, 7(1/2), 34–59.

Brink, P. J. (1989). Issues in reliability and validity. In J. M. Morse (Ed.), *Qualitative nursing research: A contemporary dialogue* (pp. 151–168). Rockville, MD: Aspen.

Broome, M. E., & Stieglitz, K. A. (1992). The consent process and children. *Research in Nursing & Health*, 15, 147–152.

Bryder, T. (1981). Actor-reliability: Some methodological problems. In K. Rosgren (Ed.), *Advances in content analysis*. Beverly Hills, CA: Sage.

Bryman, A. (1984). The debate about quantitative and qualitative research: A question of method or epistemology? *The British Journal of Sociology*, 35, 75–92.

Buchanan, D. R. (1992). An uneasy alliance: Combining qualitative and quantitative research methods. *Health Education Quarterly*, 19(1), 117–135.

Bunkers, S. S. (1998). Considering tomorrow: Parse's theory-guided research. *Nursing Science Quarterly*, 11, 56–63.

Bunkers, S. S., Petardi, L. A., Pilkington, F. B., & Walls, P. A. (1996). Challenging the myths surrounding qualitative research in nursing. *Nursing Science Quarterly*, 9, 33–37.

Burns, N. (1989). Standards for qualitative research. *Nursing Science Quarterly*, 2, 44–52.

Buston, K. (1997). NUD.IST in action: Its use and its usefulness in a study of chronic illness in young people. *Sociological Research Online*, 2(3). [Online]. Available: http://www.socresonline.org.uk/socresonline/2/3/6.html.

Butcher, H. K. (1996). A unitary field pattern portrait of dispiritedness in later life. *Visions: The Journal of Rogerian Nursing Science*, 4(1), 41–58.

Butcher, H. K. (1998). Crystallizing the processes of the unitary field pattern portrait research method. *Visions: The Journal of Rogerian Nursing Science*, 6(1), 13–26.

Carboni, J. T. (1995). A Rogerian process of inquiry. *Nursing Science Quarterly*, 8, 22–37.

Carey, M. A. (1995). Concerns in the analysis of focus group data. *Qualitative Health Research*, 5, 487–495.

Carr, J. M. (1998). Vigilance as a caring expression and Leininger's theory of cultural care diversity and universality. *Nursing Science Quarterly*, 11, 74–78.

Carr, L. T. (1994). The strengths and weaknesses of quantitative and qualitative research: What method for nursing? *Journal of Advanced Nursing*, 20(4), 716–721.

Carson, M. G., & Mitchell, G. J. (1998). The experience of living with persistent pain. *Journal of Advanced Nursing*, 28(6), 1242–1248.

Cartwright, J. C., Archbold, P. G., Stewart, B. J., & Limandri, B. (1994). Enrichment processes in family caregiving to frail elders. *Advances in Nursing Science*, 17(1), 31–43.

Catterall, M., & MacLaren, P. (1997). Focus group data and qualitative analysis programs: Coding the moving picture as well as the snapshots. *Sociological Research*

Online, 2(1). [Online]. Available: http://www.socresonline.org.uk/
socresonline/2/1/6.html.

Chesla, C. (1992). When qualitative and quantitative findings do not converge. *Western Journal of Nursing Research*, 14(5), 681–685.

Clark, A. M. (1998). The qualitative-quantitative debate: Moving from positivism and confrontation to post-positivism and reconciliation. *Journal of Advanced Nursing*, 27(6), 1242–1249.

Clark, A. M., & Jack, B. (1998). Research in practice 2: The benefits of using qualitative research. *Professional Nurse*, 13(12), 845–847.

Clark, L. (1995). Nursing research: Science, vision and telling stories. *Journal of Advanced Nursing Science*, 21, 584–593.

Clark. P. N. (1998). Nursing theory as a guide for inquiry in family and community health nursing. *Nursing Science Quarterly*, 11, 47–48.

Cody, W. K. (1991). Grieving a personal loss. *Nursing Science Quarterly*, 4, 61–68.

Cody, W. K. (1995). Of life immense in passion, pulse, and power: Dialoguing with Whitman and Parse—A hermeneutic study. In R. R. Parse (Ed.), *Illuminations: The human becoming theory in practice and research* (pp. 269–307). New York: National League for Nursing Press.

Cody, W. K. (1995). The lived experience of grieving, for families living with AIDS. In R. R. Parse (Ed.), *Illuminations: The human becoming theory in practice and research* (pp. 197–242). New York: National League for Nursing Press.

Cody, W. K., & Mitchell, G. J. (1996). [Review of the book *Interpretive phenomenology: Embodiment, caring, and ethics in health and illness*]. *Nursing Science Quarterly*, 9, 44–46.

Coffey, A. B., Holbrook, P., & Atkinson, P. (1996). Qualitative data analysis: Technologies and representations. *Sociological Research Online*, 1(1). [Online]. Available: http://www.socresonline.org.uk/socresonline/1/1/4.html.

Cohen, M. Z. (1987). A historical overview of the phenomenologic movement. *Image: Journal of Nursing Scholarship*, 19(1), 31–34.

Cohen, M. Z., Knafl, K., & Dzurec, L. C. (1993). Grant writing for qualitative research. *Image: Journal of Nursing Scholarship*, 25(2), 151–156.

Cohen, R. (1999, March 14). Pity for the plagiarist. *New York Times Magazine*, 22.

Connor, M. J. (1998). Expanding the dialogue on praxis in nursing research and practice. *Nursing Science Quarterly*, 11, 51–55.

Corbin, J., & Strauss, A. (1990). Grounded theory research: Procedures, canons, and evaluative criteria. *Qualitative Sociology*, 13, 3–21.

Corner, J. (1991). In search of more complete answers to research questions. Quantitative versus qualitative research methods: Is there a way forward? *Journal of Advanced Nursing*, 16, 718–727.

Costello-Nickitas, D. M. (1994). Choosing life goals: A phenomemological study. *Nursing Science Quarterly*, 7, 87–92.

Coward, D. D. (1990). The lived experience of self-transcendence in women with advanced breast cancer. *Nursing Science Quarterly*, 3, 162–169.

Cowling, W. R. (1993). Unitary knowing in nursing practice. *Nursing Science Quarterly*, 6, 201–207.

Cowling, W. R. (1998). Unitary case inquiry. *Nursing Science Quarterly*, 11, 139–141.

Cowling, W. R. (1999). A unitary-transformative nursing science: Potentials for transcending dichotomies. *Nursing Science Quarterly,* 12, 132–135.

Cowman, S. (1993). Triangulation: A means of reconciliation in nursing research. *Journal of Advanced Nursing,* 18(5), 788–792.

Crothers, J. E., & Dokecki, P. R. (1989). Human science inquiry into the person: Methodological issues and an illustration. *Person-Centered Review,* 4(4), 446–464.

Crowe, M. (1998). The power of the word: Some post-structural considerations of qualitative approaches in nursing research. *Journal of Advanced Nursing,* 28(2), 339–344.

Cushing, A. (1994). Historical and epistemological perspectives on research and nursing. *Journal of Advanced Nursing,* 20(3), 406–411.

Dahlberg, K., & Drew, N. (1997). A lifeworld paradigm for nursing research. *Journal of Holistic Nursing,* 15, 303–317.

Daly, J. (1995). The lived experience of suffering. In R. R. Parse (Ed.), *Illuminations: The human becoming theory in practice and research* (pp. 243–268). New York: National League for Nursing Press.

David, A. (1978). The phenomenological approach in nursing research. In N. Chaska (Ed.), *The nursing profession: Views through the mist* (pp. 186–197). New York: McGraw-Hill.

Davis, D. K., & Cannava, E. (1995). The meaning of retirement for communally-living retired performing artists. *Nursing Science Quarterly,* 8, 8–16.

Davis, L. L., & Grant, J. S. (1994). Constructing the reality of recovery: Family home care management strategies. *Advances in Nursing Science,* 17(2), 66–76.

Dickoff, J., & James, P. (1968). A theory of theories: A position paper. *Nursing Research,* 17(3), 197–203.

Dombrowski, D. A. (1995). "Being is power." *American Journal of Theology & Philosophy,* 299–314.

Drew, N. (1989). The interviewer's experience as data in phenomenological research. *Western Journal of Nursing Research,* 11, 431–439.

Duffy, M. E. (1985). Designing nursing research: The qualitative-quantitative debate. *Journal of Advanced Nursing,* 10(3), 225–232.

Duffy, M. E. (1987). Methodological triangulation: A vehicle for merging quantitative and qualitative research methods. *Image: Journal of Nursing Scholarship,* 19, 130–134.

Duffy, M. E. (1987). Quantitative and qualitative research: Antagonistic or complementary. *Nursing & Health Care,* 8, 356–357.

Dzurec, L. C., & Abraham, I. L. (1993). The nature of inquiry: Linking quantitative and qualitative research. *Advances in Nursing Science,* 16(1), 73–79.

Endo, E. (1998). Pattern recognition as a nursing intervention with Japanese women with ovarian cancer. *Advances in Nursing Science,* 20(4), 49–61.

Fahlberg, L. L., & Fahlberg, L. A. (1994). A human science for health: An overview. *Health Values,* 18(5), 3–12.

Finfgeld, D. L. (1998). Courage in middle-aged adults with long-term health concerns. *Canadian Journal of Nursing Research,* 30(1), 153–169.

Fisher, M. A., & Mitchell, G. J. (1998). Patients' views of quality of life: Transforming the knowledge base of nursing. *Clinical Nurse Specialist*, 12(3), 99–105.

Fleitas, J. (1998). Spinning tales from the world wide web: Qualitative research in an electronic environment. *Qualitative Health Research*, 8(2), 283–292.

Fleury, J. (1993). Preserving qualitative meaning in instrument development. *Journal of Nursing Measurement*, 1(2), 135–144.

Fraser, C. (1999). The experience of transition for a daughter caregiver of a stroke survivor. *Journal of Neuroscience Nursing*, 31(1), 9–16.

Frybach, P. B. (1993). Health for people with a terminal diagnosis. *Nursing Science Quarterly*, 6, 147–159.

Frye, B. A., & D'Avanzo, C. D. (1993). Cultural themes in family stress and violence among Cambodian refugee women in the inner city. *Advances in Nursing Science*, 16(3), 64–77.

Futrell, M., Wondolowski, C., & Mitchell, G. J. (1993). Aging in the oldest old living in Scotland: A phenomenological study. *Nursing Science Quarterly*, 4, 189–194.

Gadamer, H.-G. (1975). Hermeneutics and social science. *Cultural Hermeneutics*, 2, 312.

Gardner, K. G., & Wheeler, E. (1981). Patient and staff perceptions of supportive nursing behaviors. In M. Leininger (Ed.), *Caring: An essential human need* (pp. 69–80). Thorofare, NJ: Slack.

Germain, C. (1986). Ethnography: The method. In P. Munhall & C. Oiler (Eds.), *Nursing research: A qualitative perspective* (pp. 147–162). Norwalk, CT: Appleton-Century-Crofts.

Gerson, E. (1984). Qualitative research and the computer. *Qualitative Sociology*, 7(1/2), 61–74.

Giorgi, A. (1968). Existential phenomenology and the psychology of the human person. *Review of Existential Psychology & Psychiatry*, 8(2), 102–116.

Giorgi, A. (1986). The "context of discovery/context of verification" distinction and descriptive human science. *Journal of Phenomenological Psychology*, 17(2), 151–166.

Giorgi, A. (1989). One type of analysis of descriptive data: Procedures involved in following a systematic phenomenological method. *Annual Edition of Methods: A Journal for Human Science*, 39–61.

Giorgi, A. (1989). Some theoretical and practical issues regarding the psychological phenomenological method. *Saybrook Review*, 7, 71–85.

Giorgi, A. (1992). Description versus interpretation: Competing alternative strategies for qualitative research. *Journal of Phenomenological Psychology*, 23(2), 119–135.

Goering, P. N., & Streiner, D. L. (1996). Reconcilable differences: The marriage of qualitative and quantitative methods. *Canadian Journal of Psychiatry*, 41, 491–497.

Goodwin, L. D., & Goodwin, W. L. (1984). Qualitative vs. quantitative research or qualitative and quantitative research? *Nursing Research*, 33, 378–380.

Gortner, S. R., & Schultz, P. R. (1988). Approaches to nursing science methods. *Image: Journal of Nursing Scholarship*, 20(1), 22–24.

Goss, G. L. (1998). Focus group interviews: A methodology for socially sensitive research. *Clinical Excellence for Nurse Practitioners*, 2(1), 30–34.

Gregory, D., Russell, C. K., & Phillips, L. R. (1997). Beyond textual perfection: Transcribers as vulnerable persons. *Qualitative Health Research*, 7, 294–300.

Guba, E. G., & Lincoln, Y. S. (1990). Can there be a human science? Constructivism as an alternative. *Person Centered Review*, 5(2), 130–154.

Hagendorn, M. (1994). Hermeneutic photography: An innovative esthetic technique for generating data in nursing research. *Advances in Nursing Science*, 17(1), 44–50.

Hall, J. M. (1993). How lesbians recognize and respond to alcohol problems: A theoretical model of problematization. *Advances in Nursing Science*, 16(3), 46–63.

Hamel, J. (1994). Case study methods. In J. Van Maanen (Ed.), *Qualitative research methods* (Vol. 32). Newbury Park, CA: Sage.

Heath, H. (1998). Paradigm dialogues and dogma: Finding a place for research, nursing models and reflective practice. *Journal of Advanced Nursing*, 28(2), 288–294.

Helmreich, R. (1974). The evaluation of environments: Behavioral observations in an undersea habitat. In J. Lang et al. (Eds.), *Designing for human behavior* (pp. 274–285). Stroudsbury, PA: Dowden, Hutchinson & Ross.

Henderson, D. J. (1994). Consciousness raising in participatory research: Method and methodology for emancipatory nursing inquiry. *Advances in Nursing Science*, 17(3), 58–69.

Higgins, I. (1998). Reflections on conducting qualitative research with elderly people. *Qualitative Health Research*, 8(6), 858–866.

Higgins, J. W. (1998). Social marketing and MARTIN: Tools for organizing, analyzing, and interpreting qualitative data. *Qualitative Health Research*, 8(6), 867–876.

Hinds, P. S., Vogel, R. J., & Clarke-Steffen, L. (1997). The possibilities and pitfalls of doing a secondary analysis of a qualitative data set. *Qualitative Health Research*, 7, 408–424.

Holloway, I., & Wheeler, S. (1995). Ethical issues in qualitative nursing research. *Nursing Ethics*, 2, 223–232.

Huber, G. L., & Garcia, C. M. (1991). Computer assistance for testing hypotheses about qualitative data: The software package AQUAD 3.0. *Qualitative Sociology*, 14, 325–348.

Hultgren, F. H. (1995). The phenomenology of "doing" phenomenology: The experience of teaching and learning together. *Human Studies*, 18, 371–388.

Hummelvoll, J. K., & Barbosa da Silva, A. (1998). The use of the qualitative research interview to uncover the essence of community psychiatric nursing. *Journal of Holistic Nursing*, 16(4), 453–478.

Jacobson, G. A. (1999). Parenting processes: A descriptive-exploratory study using Peplau's theory. *Nursing Science Quarterly*, 12, 240–244.

Janusic, V. J. (1994). The dance of qualitative research design: Metaphor, methodolotry, and meaning. In N. K. Denzin, & Y. S. Lincoln (Eds.), *Handbook of Qualitative Research* (pp. 209–219). Thousand Oaks, CA: Sage.

Jensen, K. P., Bäck-Pettersson, S. R., & Segesten, K. M. (1993). The caring moment and the green-thumb phenomenon among Swedish nurses. *Nursing Science Quarterly*, 6, 98–104.

Johansson, F., & Wiklund, D. (1981). Competition and newspaper content Sweden, 1912–1972. In K. E. Rosengren (Ed.), *Advances in content analysis*. Beverly Hills, CA: Sage.

Jonas, C. M. (1992). The meaning of being an elder in Nepal. *Nursing Science Quarterly*, 5, 171–175.

Jonas, C. M. (1995). Evaluation of the human becoming theory in family practice. In R. R. Parse (Ed.), *Illuminations: The human becoming theory in practice and research* (pp. 347–366). New York: National League for Nursing Press.

Jonas-Simpson, C. (1997). The Parse research method through music. *Nursing Science Quarterly*, 10, 112–114.

Jonsdottir, H. (1998). Life patterns of people with chronic obstructive pulmonary disease: Isolation and being closed in. *Nursing Science Quarterly*, 11, 160–166.

Kelle, U. (1997). Theory building in qualitative research and computer programs for the management of textual data. *Sociological Research Online*, 2(2). [Online.] Available: http://www.socresonline.org.uk/socresonline/2/2/1.html.

Kelley, L. S. (1991). Struggling with going along when you do not believe. *Nursing Science Quarterly*, 4, 123–129.

Kim, H. S. (1993). Identifying alternative linkages among philosophy, theory and method in nursing science. *Journal of Advanced Nursing*, 18, 793–800.

Kim, H. S. (1999). Critical reflective inquiry for knowledge development in nursing. *Journal of Advanced Nursing*, 29(5), 1205–1212.

Kim, M. S., Shin, K. R., & Shin, S. R. (1998). Korean adolescents' experiences of smoking cessation: A prelude to research with the human becoming perspective. *Nursing Science Quarterly*, 11, 105–109.

Kitzinger, J. (1995). Qualitative research. Introducing focus groups. *British Medical Journal*, 311(2000), 299–302.

Knafl, K. A., & Howard, M. J. (1984). Interpreting, reporting, and evaluating qualitative research. *Research in Nursing & Health*, 7, 17–24.

Knafl, K. A., & Webster, D. C. (1988). Managing and analyzing qualitative data: A description of tasks, techniques, and materials. *Western Journal of Nursing Research*, 10, 195–210.

Koch, T. (1998). Story telling: Is it really research? *Journal of Advanced Nursing*, 28(6), 1182–1190.

Koch, T., & Harrington, A. (1998). Reconceptualizing rigor: The case for reflexivity. *Journal of Advanced Nursing*, 28(4), 882–890.

Kremer, J. W. (1986). The human science approach as discourse. *Saybrook Review*, 6(1), 65–105.

Kruger, D. (1988). In search of a human science psychology. *South African Journal of Psychology*, 18(1), 1–9.

Kruse, B. G. (1999). The lived experience of serenity: Using Parse's research method. *Nursing Science Quarterly*, 12, 143–150.

Lamendola, F. P., & Newman, M. A. (1993). The paradox of HIV/AIDS as expanding consciousness. *Advances in Nursing Science*, 16(2), 13–21.

Lee, R. M., & Fielding, N. G. (1991). Computing for qualitative research: Options, problems, and potential. In N. G. Fielding & R. M. Lee (Eds.), *Using computers in qualitative research* (pp. 1–13). London: Sage.

Lee, R. M., & Fielding, N. (1996). Qualitative data analysis: Representations of a technology: A comment on Coffey, Holbrook and Atkinson. *Sociological Research Online*, 1(4). [Online]. Available: http://www.socresonline.org.uk/socresonline/1/4/1f.html.

Legault, F., & Ferguson-Paré, M. (1999). Advancing nursing practice: An evaluation study of Parse's theory of human becoming. *Canadian Journal of Nursing Leadership*, 12(1), 30–35.

Leininger, M. (1977). Caring: The essence and central focus of nursing. *American Nurses' Foundation Nursing Research Report*, 12(1).

Leininger, M. (1984). Editorial. *Western Journal of Nursing Research*, 6(2), 151–152.

Leininger, M. (1994). Quality of life from a transcultural nursing perspective. *Nursing Science Quarterly*, 7, 22–28.

Loehle, C. (1990). A guide to increased creativity in research: Inspiration or perspiration? *Bioscience*, 40, 123–129.

Lowenberg, J. S. (1993). Interpretive research methodology: Broadening the dialogue. *Advances in Nursing Science*, 16(2), 57–69.

Malinski, V. M. (1991). The experience of laughing at oneself in older couples. *Nursing Science Quarterly*, 4, 69–75.

Mathieson, C. M., & Barrie, C. M. (1998). Probing the prime narrative: Illness, interviewing, and identity. *Qualitative Health Research*, 8(5), 581–601.

Maunsbach, M., & Deholm-Lambertsen, B. (1997). Qualitative methods in empirical health research. *Nord Med*, 112(2), 63–65.

May, C. (1996). More semi than structured? Some problems with qualitative research methods. *Nurse Education Today*, 16, 189–192.

Mays, N., & Pope, C. (1995). Rigour and qualitative research. *British Medical Journal*, 311, 109–112.

McDaniel, R. W., & Bach, C. A. (1994). Focus groups: A data-gathering strategy for nursing research. *Nursing Science Quarterly*, 7, 4–5.

Meleis, A. I., Arruda, E. N., Lane, S., & Bernal, P. (1994). Veiled, voluminous, and devalued: Narrative stories about low-income women from Brazil, Egypt, and Columbia. *Advances in Nursing Science*, 17(2), 1–15.

Merleau-Ponty, M. (1956). What is phenomenology? *Cross Currents*, 6, 59–70.

Mitchell, G. J. (1990). The lived experience of taking life day-by-day in later life: Research guided by Parse's emergent method. *Nursing Science Quarterly*, 3, 29–36.

Mitchell, G. J. (1994). Discipline-specific inquiry: The hermeneutics of theory-guided nursing research. *Nursing Outlook*, 42(5), 224–228.

Mitchell, G. J. (1994). The meaning of being a senior: Phenomenological research and interpretation with Parse's theory of nursing. *Nursing Science Quarterly*, 7, 70–79.

Mitchell, G. J. (1995). Evaluation of the human becoming theory in practice in an acute care setting. In R. R. Parse (Ed.), *Illuminations: The human becoming theory in practice and research* (pp. 367–399). New York: National League for Nursing Press.

Mitchell, G. J. (1995). The lived experience of restriction-freedom in later life. In R. R. Parse (Ed.), *Illuminations: The human becoming theory in practice and research* (pp. 159–195). New York: National League for Nursing Press.

Mitchell, G. J. (1996). Clarifying contributions of qualitative research findings. *Nursing Science Quarterly*, 10, 143–144.

Mitchell, G. J. (1997). Questioning evidence-based practice for nursing. *Nursing Science Quarterly*, 10, 154–155.

Mitchell, G. J., & Cody, W. (1992). Nursing knowledge and human science: Ontological and epistemological considerations. *Nursing Science Quarterly*, 5, 54–61.

Mitchell, G. J., & Cody, W. K. (1993). The role of theory in qualitative research. *Nursing Science Quarterly*, 6, 170–178.

Mitchell, G. J., & Heidt, P. (1994). The lived experience of wanting to help another: Research with Parse's method. *Nursing Science Quarterly*, 7, 119–127.

Mitchell, G. J., & Lawton, C. (2000). Living with the consequences of personal choices for person with diabetes: Implications for educators and practitioners. *Canadian Journal of Diabetes Care*, 24(2), 23–31.

Mitchell, G. J., & Pilkington, F. B. (1999). A dialogue on the comparability of research paradigms—and other theoretical things. *Nursing Science Quarterly*, 12, 283–289.

Moccia, P. (1988). A critique of compromise: Beyond the methods debate. *Advances in Nursing Science*, 10(4), 1–9.

Montgomery, C. (1994). Swimming upstream: The strengths of women who survive homelessness. *Advances in Nursing Science*, 16(3), 34–45.

Morgan, D. L. (1995). Why things (sometimes) go wrong in focus groups. *Qualitative Health Research*, 5, 516–523.

Morison, M., & Moir, J. (1998). The role of computer software in the analysis of qualitative data: Efficient clerk, research assistant, or Trojan horse? *Journal of Advanced Nursing*, 28(1), 106–116.

Morse, J. (1991). Approaches to qualitative and quantitative methodological triangulation. *Nursing Research*, 40(1), 120–123.

Morse, J. M. (1989). Qualitative nursing research: A free-for-all? In J. M. Morse (Ed.), *Qualitative nursing research: A contemporary dialogue* (pp. 3–10). Rockville, MD: Aspen.

Morse, J. M. (1999). Qualitative generalizability. *Qualitative Health Research*, 9(1), 5–6.

Morse, J. M. (1999). Silent debates in qualitative inquiry. *Qualitative Health Research*, 9(2), 163–165.

Morse, J. M., Hutchinson, S. A., & Penrod, J. (1998). From theory to practice: The development of assessment guides from qualitatively derived theory. *Qualitative Health Research*, 8(3), 329–340.

Munhall, P. (1989). Philosophical ponderings on qualitative research methods in nursing. *Nursing Science Quarterly*, 2, 20–28.

Munhall, P. (1993). Unknowing: Toward another pattern of knowing in nursing. *Nursing Outlook*, 41, 125–128.

Newman, M. A. (1990). Newman's theory of health as praxis. *Nursing Science Quarterly*, 3, 37–41.

Newman, M. A. (1997). Experiencing the whole. *Advances in Nursing Science*, 20(1), 34–39.

Newman, M. A., & Moch, S. D. (1991). Life patterns of persons with coronary heart disease. *Nursing Science Quarterly*, 4, 161–167.

Niska, K. J. (1999). Mexican American family processes: Nurturing, support, and socialization. *Nursing Science Quarterly*, 12, 138–142.

Nokes, K. M., & Carver, K. (1991). The meaning of living with AIDS: A study using Parse's theory of man-living-health. *Nursing Science Quarterly*, 4, 175–179.

Norman, E. M. (1989). How to use word processing software to conduct content analysis. *Computers in Nursing*, 7(3), 127–128.

Norris, J. R. (1999). The internet: Extending our capacity for scholarly inquiry in nursing. *Nursing Science Quarterly*, 12, 197–201.

Northrup, D. T., & Cody, W. K. (1998). Evaluation of the human becoming theory in practice in an acute care psychiatric setting. *Nursing Science Quarterly*, 11, 23–30.

Nyman, C. S., & Lutzen, K. (1999). Caring needs of patients with rheumatoid arthritis. *Nursing Science Quarterly*, 12, 164–169.

Oberst, M. (1993). Possibilities and pitfalls in triangulation. *Research in Nursing & Health*, 16, 393–394.

Omery, A. (1983). Phenomenology: A method for nursing research. *Advances in Nursing Science*, 5(2), 49–63.

Osborne, J. W. (1994). Some similarities and differences among phenomenological and other methods of psychological qualitative research. *Canadian Psychology*, 35(2), 167–189.

Parse, R. R. (1988). The mainstream of science: Framing the issue. *Nursing Science Quarterly*, 1, 93.

Parse, R. R. (1989). Making more out of less. *Nursing Science Quarterly*, 2, p.155.

Parse, R. R. (1989). The phenomenological research method: Its value for management science. In B. Henry, C. Arndt, M. DiVincenti, & A. Marriner-Tomey (Eds.), *Dimensions of nursing administration: Theory, research, education, and practice*. Cambridge, MA: Blackwell Scientific.

Parse, R. R. (1989). Qualitative research: Publishing and funding. *Nursing Science Quarterly*, 2, 1.

Parse, R. R. (1990). Parse's research methodology with an illustration of the lived experience of hope. *Nursing Science Quarterly*, 3, 9–17.

Parse, R. R . (1991). Phenomenology and nursing. *Japanese Journal of Nursing*, 17 (2), 261–269.

Parse, R. R. (1992). Human becoming: Parse's theory of nursing. *Nursing Science Quarterly*, 5, 35–42.

Parse, R. R. (1992). Nursing knowledge for the 21st century: An international commitment. *Nursing Science Quarterly*, 5, 8–12.

Parse, R. R. (1993). Critical appraisal: Risking to challenge. *Nursing Science Quarterly*, 6, 163.

Parse, R. R. (1993). The experience of laughter: A phenomenological study. *Nursing Science Quarterly*, 6, 39–43.

Parse, R. R. (1993). Parse's human becoming theory: Its research and practice implications. In M. E. Parker (Ed.), *Patterns of nursing theories in practice* (pp. 49–61). New York: National League for Nursing Press.

Parse, R. R. (1993). Scholarly dialogue: Theory guides research and practice. *Nursing Science Quarterly*, 6, 12.

Parse, R. R. (1994). Laughing and health: A study using Parse's research method. *Nursing Science Quarterly*, 7, 55–64.

Parse, R. R. (1994). Quality of life: Sciencing and living the art of human becoming. *Nursing Science Quarterly*, 7, 16–21.

Parse, R. R. (1995). Research with the human becoming theory. In R. R. Parse (Ed.), *Illuminations: The human becoming theory in practice and research* (pp. 151–157). New York: National League for Nursing Press.

Parse, R. R. (1996). Building knowledge through qualitative research: The road less traveled. *Nursing Science Quarterly*, 9, 10–16.

Parse, R. R. (1996). The human becoming theory: Challenges in practice and research. *Nursing Science Quarterly*, 9, 55–60.

Parse, R. R. (1996). Quality of life for persons living with Alzheimer's disease: The human becoming perspective. *Nursing Science Quarterly*, 9, 126–133.

Parse, R. R. (1997). Concept inventing: Unitary creations. *Nursing Science Quarterly*, 10, 63–64.

Parse, R. R. (1997). Joy-sorrow: A study using the Parse research method. *Nursing Science Quarterly*, 10, 80–87.

Parse, R. R. (1997). The language of nursing knowledge: Saying what we mean. In I. M. King & J. Fawcett (Eds.), *The language of nursing theory and metatheory* (pp. 73–77). Indianapolis, IN: Sigma Theta Tau International, Center Nursing Press.

Parse, R. R. (1997). Transforming research and practice with the human becoming theory. *Nursing Science Quarterly*, 10, 171–174.

Parse, R. R. (1998). The art of criticism. *Nursing Science Quarterly*, 11, 43.

Parse, R. R. (1999). Authorship: Whose responsibility? *Nursing Science Quarterly*, 12, 99.

Parse, R. R. (1999). Expanding the vision: Tilling the field of nursing knowledge. *Nursing Science Quarterly*, 12, 3.

Parse, R. R. (1999). Integrity and the advancement of nursing knowledge. *Nursing Science Quarterly*, 12, 187.

Parse, R. R. (2000). Human becoming school of thought in research and practice. In M. E. Parker, *Nursing theories and nursing practice* (pp. 227–238). Philadelphia: F. A. Davis.

Parse, R. R. (2000). Language: Words reflect and cocreate meaning. *Nursing Science Quarterly*, 13, 187.

Pateman, B. (1998). Issues in research. Computer-aided qualitative data analysis: The value of NUD*IST and other programs. *Nurse Researcher*, 5(3), 77–89.

Peden, A. R. (1993). Recovering in depressed women: Research with Peplau's theory. *Nursing Science Quarterly*, 6, 140–146.

Phillips, J. R. (1988). Research blenders. *Nursing Science Quarterly*, 1, 4–5.

Phillips, J. R. (1989). Qualitative research: A process of discovery. *Nursing Science Quarterly*, 2, 5–6.

Phillips, J. R. (1993). Researching the lived experience: Visions of the whole experience. *Nursing Science Quarterly*, 6, 166–167.

Phillips, J. R. (1994). Martha E. Rogers' clarion call for global nursing research. *Nursing Science Quarterly*, 7, 100–101.

Phillips, J. R. (1994). A vision of nursing research priorities. *Nursing Science Quarterly*, 7, 52.

Pickens, J. M. (1999). Living with serious mental illness: The desire for normalcy. *Nursing Science Quarterly*, 12, 233–239.

Pilkington, F. B. (1993). The lived experience of grieving the loss of an important other. *Nursing Science Quarterly*, 6, 130–139.

Pilkington, F. B. (1996). The use of computers in qualitative research. *Nursing Science Quarterly*, 9, 5–7.

Pilkington, F. B. (1999). A qualitative study of life after stroke. *Journal of Neuroscience Nursing*, 31(6), 336–347.

Pilkington, F. B. (2000). Persisting while wanting to change: Women's lived experiences. *Health Care for Women International*, 21(6), 1–6.

Polkinghorne, D. E. (1986). Changing conversations about human science. *Saybrook Review*, 6(1), 1–32.

Polkinghorne, D. E. (1986). Conceptual validity in nontheoretical human science. *Journal of Phenomenological Psychology*, 17(2), 129–149.

Popay, J., Rogers, A., & Williams, G. (1998). Rationale and standards for the systematic review of qualitative literature in health services research. *Qualitative Health Research*, 8(3), 341–351.

Pope, C., & Mays, N. (1995). Reaching the parts other methods cannot reach: An introduction to qualitative methods in health and health services research. *British Medical Journal*, 311(6996), 42–45.

Porter, E. J. (1994). "Reducing my risks": A phenomenon of older widows' lived experience. *Advances in Nursing Science*, 17(2), 51–65.

Powell, R. A., Single, H. M., & Lloyd, K. R. (1996). Focus groups in mental health research: Enhancing the validity of user and provider questionnaires. *International Journal of Social Psychiatry*, 42, 193–206.

Powers, B. A. (1987). Taking sides: A response to Goodwin and Goodwin. *Nursing Research*, 36, 122–126.

Price, P. J. (1993). Parents' perceptions of the meaning of quality nursing care. *Advances in Nursing Science*, 16(1), 33–41.

Rappoport, L., & Kren, G. (1996). The holocaust and the postmodern trend in human science. In C. W. Tolman & F. Cherry (Eds.), *Problems of theoretical psychology* (pp. 274–279). North York, Ontario: Captus Press.

Rawnsley, M. M. (1998). Ontology, epistemology, and methodology: A clarification. *Nursing Science Quarterly*, 11, 2–4.

Rawnsley, M. M. (1999). Response to Cowling's unitary-transformative nursing science. *Nursing Science Quarterly*, 12, 135–137.

Ray, M. A. (1985). A philosophical method to study nursing phenomena. In M. Leininger (Ed.), *Qualitative research methods in nursing* (pp. 81–92). Orlando, FL: Grune & Stratton.

Ray, M. A. (1990). Critical reflective analysis of Parse's and Newman's research methodologies. *Nursing Science Quarterly*, 3, 44–46.

Reeder, F. (1987). The phenomenological movement. *Image: Journal of Nursing Scholarship*, 19(3),150–152.

Reeder, F. (1993). The science of unitary human beings and interpretive human science. *Nursing Science Quarterly*, 6, 13–24.

Rehorick, D. A., & Taylor, G. (1995). Thoughtful incoherence: First encounters with the phenomenological-hermeneutical domain. *Human Studies*, 18, 389–414.

Rendon, D. C., Sales, R., Leal, I., & Pique, J. (1995). The lived experience of aging in community-dwelling elders in Valencia, Spain: A phenomenological study. *Nursing Science Quarterly*, 8, 152–157.

Reswick, J. B. (1994). What constitutes valid research? Qualitative vs. quantitative research [editorial]. *Journal of Rehabilitation Research Development*, 31(2), vii–ix.

Rew, L., Bechtel, D., & Sapp, A. (1993). Self-as-instrument in qualitative research. *Nursing Research*, 42, 300–301.

Richards, L. (1997). User's mistake as developer's challenge: Designing the new NUD*IST. *Qualitative Health Research*, 7(3), 425–433.

Richards, L. (1998). Closeness to data: The changing goals of qualitative data handling. *Qualitative Health Research*, 8(3), 319–328.

Richards, L. (1999). Data alive! The thinking behind NVivo. *Qualitative Health Research*, 9(3), 412–428.

Richards, L. (1999). Qualitative teamwork: Making it work. *Qualitative Health Research*, 9(1), 7–10.

Richards, L., & Richards, T. (1991). Computing in qualitative analysis: A healthy development? *Qualitative Health Research*, 1(2), 234–262.

Richards, T., & Richards, L. (1995). Using hierarchical categories in qualitative data analysis. In U. Kelle (Ed.), *Computer-aided qualitative data analysis: Theory, methods and practice* (pp. 80–95). Thousand Oaks, CA: Sage.

Richards, T. J., & Richards, L. (1994). Using computers in qualitative research. In N. K. Denzin & Y. S. Lincoln (Eds.), *Handbook of qualitative research* (pp. 445–462). Thousand Oaks, CA: Sage.

Riessman, C. K. (1993). Narrative analysis. In J. Van Maanen (Ed.), *Qualitative research methods*, (Vol. 30). Newbury Park, CA: Sage.

Robertson-Malt, S. (1999). Listening to them and reading me: A hermeneutic approach to understanding the experience of illness. *Journal of Advanced Nursing*, 29, 290–297.

Rodgers, B. L., & Cowles, K. V. (1993). The qualitative research audit trail: A complex collection of documentation. *Research in Nursing & Health*, 16(3), 219–226.

Rose, K., & Webb, C. (1998). Analyzing data: Maintaining rigor in a qualitative study. *Qualitative Health Research*, 8(4), 556–562.

Ross, B. A. (1994). Use of a database for managing qualitative research data. *Computers in Nursing*, 12(3), 154–159.

Salner, M. (1986). Validity in human science research. *Saybrook Review*, 6(1), 107–130.

Salsberry, P. J. (1989). Dialogue on a research issue: Phenomenological research in nursing. Commentary: Fundamental issues. *Nursing Science Quarterly*, 2, 9–13.

Sandelowski, M. (1986). The problem of rigor in qualitative research. *Advances in Nursing Science*, 8(3), 27–37.

Sandelowski, M. (1989). Artful design: Writing the proposal for research in the naturalist paradigm. *Research in Nursing & Health*, 12, 77–84.

Sandelowski, M. (1991). Telling stories: Narrative approaches in qualitative research. *Image: Journal of Nursing Scholarship*, 23(3), 161–166.

Sandelowski, M. (1993). Rigor or rigor mortis: The problem of rigor in qualitative research revisited. *Advances in Nursing Science*, 16(2), 1–8.

Sandelowski, M. (1993). Theory unmasked: The uses and guises of theory in qualitative research. *Research in Nursing & Health*, 16(3), 213–218.

Sandelowski, M. (1994). Notes on transcription. *Research in Nursing & Health*, 17, 311–314.

Sandelowski, M. (1994). The use of quotes in qualitative research. *Research in Nursing & Health*, 17, 479–482.

Sandelowski, M. (1994). We are the stories we tell: Narrative knowing in nursing practice. *Journal of Holistic Nursing*, 12(1), 23–33.

Sandelowski, M. (1995). On the aesthetics of qualitative research. *Image: Journal of Nursing Scholarship*, 27(3), 205–209.

Sandelowski, M. (1995). Qualitative analysis: What is it and how to begin. *Research in Nursing & Health*, 18, 371–375.

Sandelowski, M. (1995). Sample size in qualitative research. *Research in Nursing & Health*, 18, 179–183.

Sandelowski, M. (1995). Triangles and crystals: On the geometry of qualitative research. *Research in Nursing & Health*, 18, 569–574.

Sandelowski, M. (1996). One is the liveliest number: The case orientation of qualitative research. *Research in Nursing & Health*, 19, 525–529.

Sandelowski, M. (1996). Using qualitative methods in intervention studies. *Research in Nursing & Health*, 19, 359–364.

Sandelowski, M. (1997). "To be of use": Enhancing the utility of qualitative research. *Nursing Outlook*, 45(3), 125–132.

Sandelowski, M. (1998). The call to experts in qualitative research. *Research in Nursing & Health*, 21(5), 467–471.

Sandelowski, M. (1998). Writing a good read: Strategies for re-presenting qualitative data. *Research in Nursing & Health*, 21(4), 375–382.

Sandelowski, M., Davis, D. H., & Harris, B. G. (1989). Artful design: Writing the proposal for research in the naturalist paradigm. *Research in Nursing & Health*, 12(2), 77–84.

Sandelowski, M., Docherty, S., & Emden, C. (1997). Qualitative metasynthesis: Issues and techniques. *Research in Nursing & Health*, 20, 365–371.

Santopinto, M. D. (1989). The relentless drive to be ever thinner: A study using the phenomenological method. *Nursing Science Quarterly*, 2, 29–36.

Santopinto, M. D. A, & Smith, M. C. (1995). Evaluation of the human becoming theory in practice with adults and children. In R. R. Parse (Ed.), *Illuminations: The human becoming theory in practice and research* (pp. 309–346). New York: National League for Nursing Press.

Schrum, L. (1995). Framing the debate: Ethical research in the information age. *Qualitative Inquiry*, 1(3), 311–326.

Schutz, S. E. (1994). Exploring the benefits of a subjective approach in qualitative nursing research. *Journal of Advanced Nursing*, 20(3), 412–417.

Schwartzman, H. B. (1992). Ethnography in organizations. In J. Van Maanen (Ed.), *Qualitative research methods* (Vol. 27). Newbury Park, CA: Sage.

Secord, P. (1990). The need for a radically new human science. In D. N. Robinson & P. L. Mos (Eds.), *Annals of theoretical psychology volume 6* (pp. 75–87). New York: Plenum Press.

Seidel, J. (1991). Method and madness in the application of computer technology to qualitative data analysis. In N. G. Fielding & R. M. Lee (Eds.), *Using computers in qualitative research* (pp.101–116). London: Sage.

Sharp, K. (1998). The case for case studies in nursing research: The problem of generalization. *Journal of Advanced Nursing, 27*(4), 785–789.

Shepard, K. F., Jensen, G. M., Schmoll, B. J., Hack, L. M., & Gwyer, J. (1993). Alternative approaches to research in physical therapy: Positivism and phenomenology. *Physical Therapy, 73*(2), 88–97.

Shih, F. (1998). Triangulation in nursing research: Issues of conceptual clarity and purpose. *Journal of Advanced Nursing, 28*(3), 631–641.

Sim, J. (1998). Collecting and analyzing qualitative data: Issues raised by the focus group. *Journal of Advanced Nursing, 28*(2), 345–352.

Smith, C. A. (1995). The lived experience of staying healthy in rural African American families. *Nursing Science Quarterly, 8,* 17–21.

Smith, M. C. (1989). Dialogue on a research issue: Phenomenological research in nursing. Response: Facts about phenomenology in nursing. *Nursing Science Quarterly, 2,* 13–16.

Smith, M. C. (1990). Struggling through a difficult time for unemployed persons. *Nursing Science Quarterly, 3,* 18–28.

Smith, M. C., & Santopinto, M. D. (1995). Evaluation of the human becoming theory in practice with adults and children. In R. R. Parse (Ed.), *Illuminations: The human becoming theory in practice and research* (pp. 309–346). New York: National League for Nursing Press.

Smithbattle, L. (1995). Teenage mothers' narratives of self: An examination of risking the future. *Advances in Nursing Science, 17*(4), 22–36.

Sorrell, J. M., & Redmond, G. M. (1995). Interviews in qualitative nursing research: Differing approaches for ethnographic and phenomenological studies. *Journal of Advanced Nursing, 21,* 1117–1122.

Stevens, P. E. (1993). Marginalized women's access to health care: A feminist narrative analysis. *Advances in Nursing Science, 16*(2), 39–56.

Stevenson, C., & Beech, I. (1998). Playing the power game for qualitative researchers: The possibility of a post-modern approach. *Journal of Advanced Nursing, 27*(4), 790–797.

Stuhlmiller, C. M., & Thorsen, R. (1997). Narrative picturing: A new strategy for qualitative data collection. *Qualitative Health Research, 7,* 140–149.

Sturtevant, W. V. (1968). Studies in ethnoscience in theory in anthropology. In R. Manners & D. Kaplan (Eds.), *Theory in anthropology: A sourcebook* (pp. 475–499). Chicago: Aldine-Atherton.

Swenson, M. M. (1996). Essential elements in a qualitative dissertation proposal. *Journal of Nursing Education, 35,* 188–190.

Sword, W. (1999). Accounting for presence of self: Reflections on doing qualitative research. *Qualitative Health Research, 9*(2), 270–278.

Taft, L. B. (1993). Computer-assisted qualitative research. *Research in Nursing & Health, 16*(5), 379–383.

Tallerico, M. (1991). Applications of qualitative analysis software: A view from the field. *Qualitative Sociology*, 14, 275–285.

Tesch, R. (1991). Computer programs that assist in the analysis of qualitative data: An overview. *Qualitative Health Research*, 1, 309–325.

Thomas, J. (1992). Doing critical ethnography. In J. Van Maanen (Ed.), *Qualitative research methods* (Vol. 26). Newbury Park, CA: Sage.

Thorne, S. (1998). Ethical and representational issues in qualitative secondary analysis. *Qualitative Health Research*, 8(4), 547–555.

Thorne, S. E. (1997). Phenomenological positivism and other problematic trends in health science research. *Qualitative Health Research*, 7, 287–293.

Tinkle, M. B., & Beaton, J. L. (1983). Toward a new view of science: Implications for nursing research. *Advances in Nursing Science*, 5(2), 27–36.

Todres, L. (1998). The qualitative description of human experience: The aesthetic dimension. *Qualitative Health Research*, 8(1), 121–127.

Twinn, S. (1998). An analysis of the effectiveness of focus groups as a method of qualitative data collection with Chinese populations in nursing research. *Journal of Advanced Nursing*, 28(3), 654–661.

Usher, K., & Holmes, C. (1997). Ethical aspects of phenomenological research with mentally ill people. *Nursing Ethics*, 4(1), 49–56.

van Kaam, A. (1993). Psychology as a human science and the human science of transcendent formation. *Studies in Formative Spirituality*, 14(2), 247–270.

Van Manen, M. (1997). From meaning to method. *Qualitative Health Research*, 7, 345–369.

Walker, B. L. (1993). Computer analysis of qualitative data: A comparison of three packages. *Qualitative Health Research*, 3(1), 91–111.

Wang, C. E. H. (2000). Developing a concept of hope from a human science perspective. *Nursing Science Quarterly*, 13, 248–251.

Webb, C. (1999). Analysing qualitative data: Computerized and other approaches. *Journal of Advanced Nursing*, 29,(2) 323–330.

Whitley, G. G., & Oddi, L. F. (1998). Graduate student-faculty collaboration in research and publication. *Western Journal of Nursing Research*, 20, 572–583.

Wondolowski, C., & Davis, D. K. (1988). The lived experience of aging in the oldest old: A phenomenological study. *The American Journal of Psychoanalysis*, 48, 261–270.

Wondolowski, C., & Davis, D. K. (1991). The lived experience of health in the oldest old: A phenomenological study. *Nursing Science Quarterly*, 4, 113–118.

Yamashita, M. (1998). Newman's theory of health as expanding consciousness: Research on family caregiving in mental illness in Japan. *Nursing Science Quarterly*, 11, 110–115.

Yamashita, M. (1999). Newman's theory of health applied in family caregiving in Canada. *Nursing Science Quarterly*, 12, 73–79.

THESES AND DISSERTATIONS

Beauchamp, C. (1990). *The lived experience of struggling with making a decision in a critical life situation*. (Doctoral dissertation, University of Miami, 1990). *Dissertation Abstracts International*, 56(06B), p. 2815.

Bournes, D. A. (1997). Quality of life: Exploring the perspective of patients with congestive heart failure. *Masters Abstracts International*, 36(06), 1583.

Brunsman, C. S. (1988). *A phenomenological study of the lived experience of hope in families with chronically ill children*. Unpublished master's thesis, Michigan State University, Lansing.

Bunkers, S. (1995). *Considering tomorrow*. Unpublished doctoral dissertation, Loyola University Chicago.

Chen, C. T. (1997). *The lived experience of suffering for persons living with spinal cord injury*: Parse's theory-guided research. Unpublished master's thesis, National Yang-Ming University Institute of Clinical Nursing, Taiwan.

Cody, W. K. (1989). *Grieving a personal loss: A preliminary investigation of Parse's man-living-health methodology*. Unpublished master's thesis, Hunter College, The City University of New York.

Cody, W. K. (1992). *Grieving in families with* AIDS. Unpublished doctoral dissertation, University of South Carolina, Columbia.

Costello-Nickitas, D. M. (1989). The lived experience of choosing among life goals: A phenomenological study. *Dissertation Abstracts International*, 50(09B), 3916. (University Microfilms International No. 9004353)

Dowling, T. C. (1987). *Sharing who you really are with another: A phenomenological inquiry*. Unpublished master's thesis, Hunter College, The City University of New York.

Gouty, C. A. (1996). *Feeling alone while with others*. (Doctoral dissertation, Loyola University Chicago, 1996.) *Dissertation Abstracts International*, 57(03B), 1711.

Huckshorn, K. A. (1988). *The lived experience of creating a new way of being*, Unpublished master's thesis, Florida State University, Tallahassee.

Jonas-Simpson, C. (1998). *Feeling understood: A melody of human becoming*. (Doctoral dissertation, Loyola University Chicago, 1998). *Dissertations Abstracts International*, 58(12B), 6488.

Lui, S.-L. (1993). *The meaning of health in hospitalized older women in Taiwan*. Unpublished doctoral dissertation, University of Colorado Health Sciences Center, Denver.

Milton, C. (1998). *Making a promise*. (Doctoral dissertation, Loyola University Chicago, 1998). *Dissertation Abstracts International*, 59(06B) 2684.

Mitchell, G. J. (1992). *Exploring the paradoxical experience of restriction-freedom in later life*: Parse's theory-guided research. Unpublished doctoral dissertation, University of South Carolina, Columbia.

Nellett, G. H. (1998). The caregiver's experience of deliberative mutual patterning with pain-ridden substance users. *Dissertation Abstracts International*, 59(06B), 2685.

Northrup, D. (1995). Exploring the experience of time passing for persons with HIV disease: Parse' theory-guided research. *Dissertation Abstracts International*, 56(06B), 3129. (University Microfilms International No. 9534912)

Petardi, L. A. (1995). Weathering the storm. Persevering through a difficult time. Unpublished doctoral dissertation, Loyola University Chicago.

Petras, E. M. (1986). The lived experience of sharing a painful moment with someone close: A phenomenological study. Unpublished master's thesis, Hunter College, The City University of New York.

Pilkington, F. B. (1997). Persisting while wanting to change: Research guided by Parse's theory. (Doctoral dissertation, Loyola University Chicago, 1997). Dissertation Abstracts International, 57(12B), 7454.

Santopinto, M. D. A. (1987). The relentless drive to be ever thinner: A phenomenological study. Unpublished master's thesis, The University of Western Ontario, London, Ontario.

Sklar, M. B. (1985). Qualitative investigation of the health patterns lived in an intergenerational family lifestyle. Unpublished master's thesis, Hunter College, The City University of New York.

Tambini, D. (1993). Attentive presence: A phenomenological study. Unpublished master's thesis, Hunter College, The City University of New York.

Thornburg, P. D. (1993). The meaning of hope in parents whose infants died from sudden infant death syndrome. Dissertation Abstracts International, 54(06B), 3000. (University Microfilms International No. 9329939)

Wang, C. E. H. (1997). Mending a torn fishnet: Parse's theory-guided research on the lived experience of hope. (Doctoral dissertation, Loyola University Chicago, 1997). Dissertation Abstracts International, 57(12B), 7457.

Author Index

Agar, M., 44, 45
Allchin-Petardi, L., 171, 179, 275, 279
Allen, D., 53, 54
Aller, L. J., 62, 70, 75
Allestree, R., 200, 201
Altheide, D. L., 243, 247
Andersson-Segesten, M., 183, 200, 202, 273, 274, 281
Argyle, M., 273, 279
Artinian, B. M., 16, 30, 35, 40
Atkinson, P., 127, 129, 131, 289
Attala, J. M., 184, 200, 201, 274, 279
Auerhahn, N. C., 217, 220
Avant, K., 221, 236
Avner, Z., 88, 94

Bacon, F., 2, 12
Bakemeier, R., 112, 125
Baker, C. A., 284, 298
Barer, B. M., 183, 200, 274, 280
Barnhart, R. K., 12
Barnhart, R. K., 1
Barrett, E. A. M., 15, 30
Baum, A., 73, 75
Baumann, S. L., 60, 171, 179, 261, 262, 275, 279
Beauchamp, C., 171, 179
Beck, C. T., 243, 247
Becker, H. S., 128, 131
Benner, P., 16, 30, 53, 54
Bernstein, H. E., 273, 279
Binswanger, L., 77, 83, 98, 99, 106, 107, 108
Bistodeau, J. A., 62, 70, 76
Blanchard, D., 171, 179
Bleicher, J., 51, 54
Blissett, S. E., 88, 95
Blumer, H., 35, 40
Bohm, D., 147, 149, 152, 162
Bortner, R. W., 156, 163

Bournes, D. A., 57, 60, 171, 179
Bowling, A., 62, 70, 75
Boyd, C. O., 57, 60
Boyette, B. G., 184, 200, 201, 274
Boyle, J. S., 127, 131
Bredin, K., 75
Brent, E., 283, 298
Broadhead, R., 35, 40
Brooks, P., 44, 45
Buber, M., 112, 125, 206, 219
Bunkers, S. S., 171, 179, 247, 265, 266, 267, 268, 269, 270
Burgess, E., 35, 41
Burns, N., 243, 247
Burroughs, J., 273, 279
Butcher, H. K., 17, 30, 237, 238, 240, 241, 242
Butler, R. N., 18, 30
Bylsma, W. H., 184, 200, 201

Campbell, J., 184, 202
Camus, A., 77, 83
Cannava, E., 57, 60, 73, 75
Carboni, J. T., 17, 30, 237, 238, 239, 242
Carp, F. M., 183, 201
Carson, M. G., 57, 60
Carver, K., 57, 60
Caswell, R. J., 76
Chambre, S., 217, 220
Charmaz, K., 16, 30, 35, 40
Chenitz, W. C., 40
Christensen, D. L., 183, 201
Chung, W. S., 184, 200, 203
Clark, P. G., 62, 70, 75
Cody, W. K., 1, 15, 16, 17, 18, 30, 32, 53, 54, 73, 75, 127, 132, 171, 172, 175, 179, 180, 208, 209, 220, 261, 262, 275, 279
Coeling, H., 62, 70, 75
Coffey, A. B., 287, 288, 290, 291, 298

Cohen, M. Z., 62, 127, 131
Colaizzi, P. F., 8, 17, 18, 30, 78, 79, 81, 82, 83, 84, 114, 115, 118, 125
Corbin, J., 16, 18, 30, 34, 35, 36, 38, 39, 40, 41
Courts, N. F., 184, 200, 201, 274, 279
Cowling, W. R., 17, 30, 237, 238, 241, 242
Cox, C., 62, 70, 75
Crow, S. S., 127, 132

Daly, J., 73, 75, 171, 179
Danforth, A., 63, 70, 73, 75
Darling, C. A., 184, 201, 273, 279
Darwin, C., 88, 95
Davis, D. K., 57, 60, 73, 75
Demers, A., 184, 200, 201, 274, 280
Denzin, N. K., 15, 16, 30, 44, 45, 57, 60, 289, 292
Descartes, R., 2, 12
Dewey, J., 35, 40
Diekelman, N., 53, 54
Diener, E., 183, 200, 202, 274, 281
Dilthey, W., 1, 2, 12, 16, 30, 51, 52, 54, 209, 220
Dimsdale, J. E., 73, 75, 156, 162
Dixon, D. R., 184, 200, 202
Dossa, P. A., 62, 75
Dreher, M., 243, 247

Ekiken, K., 184, 201, 273, 280
Ekman, S. L., 183, 202, 273, 281
Endo, E., 148, 149
Ericsson, K., 183, 202, 273, 281
Erikson, E. H., 43, 44, 45
Ermath, M., 2, 12, 51, 54

Fahlberg, L. L., 1, 12
Ferguson-Pare', M., 175, 180
Field, P. A., 18, 30, 57, 60, 127, 131
Fielding, N., 289, 291
Finfgeld, D. L., 40
Fischer, C. T., 44, 45
Fisher, M. A., 57, 60
Foucault, M., 1, 12
Frake, C. O., 128, 131
Frankl, V., 93, 95, 112, 123, 125, 261, 262

Gadamer, H.-G., 1, 12, 16, 18, 30, 52, 53, 54, 55, 173, 179, 208, 220, 275, 280
Galbraith, J. K., 184, 201, 273, 280
Garfield, C., 217, 218, 220
Gerson, E., 284, 289
Gignac, M. A. M., 184, 202

Giorgi, A., 1, 8, 12, 17, 18, 31, 44, 45, 78, 79, 81, 82, 83, 84, 97, 100, 101, 104, 108, 114, 125, 275, 280
Glaser, B. G., 16, 18, 31, 35, 36, 40
Glassman, B., 218, 220
Glick, C., 184, 200, 201, 273, 280
Goffman, E., 216, 220
Goodwin, L. D., 15, 31
Goodwin, W. L., 15, 31
Gouty, C. A., 171, 179
Grant, N. K., 62, 70, 75
Guarnaccia, V., 183, 200, 202, 274, 280
Guba, E. G., 1, 12, 15, 18, 31, 44, 45, 99, 108, 223, 236, 243, 247, 289, 292
Gubrium, J. F., 16, 31, 57, 60

Hadari, G., 183, 184, 200, 203, 273, 274, 282
Hall, E. T., 163, 216, 220
Hammersley, M., 127, 129, 131
Heading, C., 62, 70, 76
Hegland, A., 183, 200, 201
Heidegger, M., 16, 18, 32, 51, 52, 53, 55, 77, 84, 99, 108, 173, 179
Heidt, P., 171, 180, 250, 261
Hinds, P. S., 243, 247
Hirsch, A. M., 184, 200, 202
Hirsch, S. M., 184, 200, 202
Hobbs, J. R., 44, 45
Holbrook, P., 289
Hollan, D. W., 273, 280
Holstein, J. A., 16, 31
Howard, M. J., 243, 247
Hudson, D. W., 273, 274, 279, 280
Hudson, W. W., 273, 274, 279, 280
Hughes, E., 35, 40
Hume, D., 2, 12
Husserl, E., 18, 32, 77, 81, 84

Jacob, M., 183, 200, 202, 274, 280
Johnson, A. M., 243
Johnson, C. L., 183, 200, 202, 274, 280
Johnson, R. A., 273, 280
Jonas, C. M., 60, 179, 234, 235, 236
Jonas-Simpson, C., 63, 73, 76, 171, 179
Jonsdottir, H., 148, 149

Kaeser, L., 62, 70, 75
Kafka, F., 77, 84
Kahn, D. L., 112, 126, 217, 220
Kane, R. A., 184, 200, 202, 273, 274, 280
Kant, I., 2, 12
Karaku, A. T., 184, 200, 202, 274, 280

Kayal, S. L., 217, 220
Kayser-Jones, J., 62, 70, 75
Kearney, R., 262, 270
Kelle, U., 284, 286, 289, 291
Keller, M. D., 76
Kelley, L. S., 171, 179, 275, 280
Kierkegaard, S., 77, 84
Kitwood, T., 62, 70, 75
Klapper, J., 184, 202, 274, 280
Klein, E., 1, 12
Knaack, P., 18, 32
Knafl, K. A., 243, 247
Kockelmans, J. J., 18, 32, 78, 84
Kovacs, P. J., 184, 200, 202
Kriedler, M. C., 184, 200, 202
Kruse, B. G., 171, 180, 275, 280

Labov, W., 44, 45
Lanik, M. P., 184, 202
Laub, D., 217, 220
Laudan, L., 2, 12
Lavoie, J. P., 184, 200, 201, 274, 280
Lawton, C., 171, 180
Lawton, M. P., 184, 200, 202, 274, 275, 280
Lee, R. M., 162, 289, 291
Legault, F., 175, 180
Leininger, M. M, 17, 18, 32, 127, 128, 131,
     132, 134, 135, 136, 137, 141, 142, 143,
     144, 145
Lerner, M. J., 184, 202
Lessor, R., 41
Lincoln, Y. S., 1, 15, 16, 31, 44, 45, 57, 60,
     99, 108, 223, 236, 243, 247, 289, 292
Lindgren, A. M., 184, 200, 202, 273, 274,
     280
Liu, S. L., 171, 180
Lloyd-Cobb, P., 184, 200, 202
Long, T., 76

Macquarrie, J., 19, 32
Major, B., 184, 200, 201
Malachi, E., 217, 220
Malinski, V. M., 57, 60, 88, 89, 93, 95
Malott, O. W., 62, 70, 75
Marcel, G., 77, 84, 261, 262
Marion, L., 62, 70, 75
Markides, K. S., 183, 200, 202, 274, 280
Marshall, C., 57, 60
Martin, H. W., 183, 200, 202, 274, 280
Mason, J., 57, 60
Maxwell, J. A., 57, 60
May, R., 93, 95, 112, 125
Mays, N., 243, 247

McAiney, C., 62, 70, 75
McAuley, L. S., 243, 247
McKoy, Y. D., 184, 202, 273, 280
McKoy-Smith, Y. M., 184, 201, 273, 279
McSweeney, M., 184, 201, 274, 279
Mead, G. H., 35, 41
Merleau-Ponty, M., 77, 85
Meyers, D., 183, 200, 202, 274, 281
Meyers, D. G., 273, 281
Miles, M. B., 284, 286, 287, 290, 293, 298,
     300
Milton, C., 171, 180
Minkler, M., 62, 70, 75
Mishler, E. G., 44, 45
Mitchell, G. J., 1, 12, 15, 18, 32, 57, 60, 63,
     73, 75, 76, 127, 132, 171, 175, 180,
     234, 235, 236, 250, 261, 262, 275, 281
Moir, J., 289, 291, 293
Morison, M., 289, 291, 293
Moroi, K., 184, 202, 274, 281
Morse, J. M., 18, 32, 57, 60, 127, 131, 132,
     243, 247
Moustakas, C. E., 16, 32, 47, 48, 49, 50
Munhall, P., 57, 60, 127, 132
Murray, E. L., 44, 45
Muurinen, E., 185, 187, 200, 203

Nellett, G. H., 60
Nesu, C. M., 95
Newman, M. A., 17, 18, 32, 147, 148, 150,
     151, 153, 156, 162, 163, 262
Nezu, A. M., 88, 95
Nickel, J. T., 62, 76
Nilsson, M., 183, 200, 202, 273, 274, 281
Nokes, K. M., 57, 60
Northrup, D. T., 171, 175, 180
Nystrom, A., 183, 200, 202, 273, 274, 281

O'Connell, M., 76
Oetker, D., 184, 201, 274, 279
Oiler, C. J., 127, 132
Olesen, V. L., 16, 32, 62, 70
Onions, C. T., 1, 13

Pardeck, J. T., 184, 200, 203
Park, R., 35, 41
Parse, R. R., 1, 5, 13, 15, 16, 17, 18, 20, 22,
     33, 35, 41, 43, 45, 51, 52, 53, 55, 57,
     60, 62, 63, 64, 73, 76, 91, 92, 93, 94,
     95, 97, 98, 99, 100, 101, 105, 106, 107,
     108, 112, 125, 127, 132, 165, 167, 170,
     171, 172, 173, 175, 180, 181, 185, 186,
     187, 188, 189, 190, 198, 199, 200, 203,

205, 208, 209, 217, 219, 220, 221, 222, 224, 236, 242, 243, 247, 250, 258, 260, 261, 262, 265, 266, 267, 268, 270, 272, 273, 275, 276, 277, 281, 282, 284, 289, 292
Pearsall, J., 183, 200, 203, 273, 282
Pelto, G. H., 17, 33, 44, 45, 127, 128, 131, 132
Pelto, P. J., 17, 33, 44, 45, 127, 128, 131, 132
Pilkington, F. B., 57, 60, 73, 76, 171, 181, 225, 236, 261, 262, 275, 282, 289
Polkinghorne, D. E., 1, 13, 43, 44, 45, 51, 55
Pope, C., 243, 247
Popper, K. R., 2, 13
Powers, B. A., 15, 33
Prigogine, I., 147, 150, 160, 163

Ragucci, A. T., 127, 132
Reeder, F., 18, 33
Rempusheski, V. F., 243, 247
Richards, L., 284, 285, 286, 287, 288, 289, 290, 291, 292, 293
Richards, T., 284, 285, 286, 287, 288, 289, 290, 291, 292
Ricoeur, P., 1, 13, 16, 18, 33, 34, 43, 44, 45, 46, 52, 53, 54, 55, 181
Robinson, R., 61, 76
Rogers, M. E., 147, 150, 237, 238, 239, 241, 242
Rose, K., 243, 247
Rossman, G. B., 57, 60
Ruhl, J. M., 183, 202, 273, 280

Salsberry, P. J., 76
Sandelowski, M., 98, 109, 243, 248, 284, 291, 292, 293, 300
Sandrett-Hibden, S., 243
Sankar, A., 57, 60
Santopinto, M. D. A., 175, 181, 234, 235, 236
Sarte, J.-P., 77, 85, 205, 220
Scandrett-Hibden, S., 247
Schindler, R., 217, 220
Schleiermacher, F., 16, 34, 51, 52, 55
Schmotkin, D., 183, 184, 200, 203, 273, 274, 282
Schutz, A., 78, 85
Secord, P., 1, 13
Shadick, K. M., 62, 70, 76
Sheen, F. J., 273, 282
Silverman, D., 16, 34
Smith, M. C., 73, 171, 175, 181, 234, 260, 261, 262, 263

Spiegel, C., 217, 220
Spiegelberg, H., 17, 34, 77, 78, 79, 80, 83, 85, 99, 102, 109
Spradley, J. P., 17, 34, 127, 129, 130, 131, 132
Steeves, D. L., 112, 126, 217, 220
Strauss, A. L., 16, 18, 34, 35, 36, 37, 38, 39, 40, 41
Sturtevant, W. C., 127, 132
Svardsudd, H., 184, 202, 273, 274, 280
Swanso, J. M., 40

Taft, L. B., 291, 293, 300
Takahashi, T., 185, 187, 200, 203
Tallerico, M., 291, 300
Tanner, C., 53, 54
Taylor, C., 1, 13, 100
Tedlock, T., 17, 34, 127, 129, 131, 132
Tesch, R., 283, 284, 287, 291, 293, 300
Thomas, W. I., 35, 41
Thompson, T., 127, 132
Thornburg, P. D., 171, 181, 261, 264
Tibblin, G., 184, 273, 274, 280
Tkachuk, B. P., 184, 203, 273, 282
Toikkanen, T., 185, 187, 200, 203
Tripp-Reimer, T., 127, 131
Trumble, B., 183, 200, 203, 273, 282

Van Haitsma, K., 184, 202, 274, 280
van Kaam, A. L., 1, 8, 13, 17, 18, 34, 78, 79, 81, 83, 85, 89, 90, 96, 114, 126
Van Manen, M., 1, 13, 17, 34
Verghese, A., 217, 220

Walker, B. L., 221, 236, 284, 290, 293, 300
Wang, C. E. H., 171, 181
Watson, J., 1, 13
Webb, C., 243, 247, 286, 287, 290, 291, 300
Weitzman, E. A., 284, 286, 287, 290, 293, 298, 300
Wellenkamp, J. C., 273, 280
White, L., 1, 13
Wiesel, E., 220
Williams, T., 220
Winblad, B., 183, 202, 273, 281
Wing, D. M., 127, 132
Winters-Miner, L. A., 70, 73, 76

Young, A. M., 147, 150, 156, 161, 163
Young, C., 150, 183, 200, 203, 273, 274, 282

Znaniecki, F., 35, 41

Subject Index

accuracy in reporting, 20
annotation, data, 290
anthropology, 127
appraisal, research
  considering tomorrow study
    conceptual criteria, 265, 266
    conclusions, 270
    ethical criteria, 266, 267
    interpretive criteria, 269
    methodological criteria, 267, 268,
      269
    purpose of study, 265
  qualitative research
    advancement of science, necessity
      for, 243
    conceptual criteria, 244
    dialogue, guidance of, 243
    dimensions, research process, 244
    ethical criteria, 244, 246
    interpretive criteria, 246, 247
    methodological criteria, 246
    presentation, 243
ASCII text format, 290
Atlas.ti program, 290
axial coding, 39

bearing witness. See also Cat on a Hot Tin
    Roof study
  demonstration, 205
  intersubjective process, as, 213
bracketing, 80
budget, study, 278

Cat on a Hot Tin Roof study
  bearing witness, demonstration of, 205
  discoursing with penetrating engaging,
    209
  human becoming hermeneutic
    methodology application, 209
  human becoming school of thought, 208
  inquiry of study, 208
  interpretation period, 209
  interpreting with quiescent beholding,
    209
  intersubjective process, bearing
    witness as, 213
  methodology, 209
  nursing significance of this study, 209,
    217
  paradoxical rhythm reflection in
    character interactions, 210, 211,
    212, 213
  processes, 209
  refusal to bear witness, 206, 209, 216
  researcher's perspective, 208, 209
  selection, study, 206, 207
  study findings, 210
  true presence in relation to bearing
    witness, 206
  understanding with inspiring
    envisaging, 209
causal relationships role in natural
    science methodology, 2
clarity in reporting, 20
co-researchers, 48
cocreated horizon of meaning, 4
coding
  computer use in qualitative research,
    286, 287
  relevance, 38
  theoretical, 38
coding, axial, 39
coding, open, 38
coding, selective, 39
Colaizzi's
  phenomenological research method,
    113, 114
  procedural modification, 82, 83

comparative analysis, method of, 37
componential analysis, application of, 130
computer use in qualitative research
    annotation of data, 290
    ASCII text format, 290
    Atlas.ti program, 290
    capabilities, software, 296, 297
    coding, application of, 286, 287
    conceptual-level qualitative data analysis support, 286
    concern, areas of, 291, 292
    data management techniques, 284
    data-theory bootstrapping, 286
    databite, 288
    doclink, 288
    embedded data, 290
    exporting capabilities, 290
    external data, support of, 289
    hierarchical organizations, 289
    hyperlink facilities, application of, 288
    importing capabilities, 290
    indexing approaches, 289
    inquiry congruence, method of, 292, 293
    modeling capabilities, 289
    nodelink, 288, 289
    NVivo program, 288, 290
    online resources, 298
    rich text format, 290
    search capabilities, 285
    search results, retainment, 286
    semantic thesaurus searches, 285
    storage, information, 284
    system-closure, 286
    tree organizations, 289
    user support, multiple, 291
    visual representative capabilities, 289
    XML facilitation, 290
conceptual criteria, 265, 266
conceptual dimension, 18, 19
conceptual integration, 199
conceptual-level qualitative data analysis support, 286
consent form, sample, 21
considering tomorrow study
    appraisal. See appraisal, research
    conceptual integration level, 256
    core concept development, 252, 257, 258
    dialogical engagement, 252
    extraction-synthesis process, 252, 253, 254
    findings, study, 256

future implications, 262
    health phenomen of considering tomorrow, conceptualization of, 249
    heuristic interpretation, 252, 257
    human becoming theory, 250, 251, 258, 259, 260
    nursing implications, 250
    originating, integration with Parse's concept of, 261
    paradoxical nature of study experience, 261
    participants, 252
    principles, theoretical, 251
    processes, 252
    proposition, formulation of, 252, 255, 256
    purpose, study, 249, 250
    research question, 250
    respect for human diversity, importance of, 250
    structural transpositional level, 252, 256, 257
    themes, identification of, 250
    valuing, integration with human becoming concept of, 261
content analysis, 16
contentment study
    abstraction levels, transformational shifts in, 189
    conceptual integration, 198, 199, 200
    core concepts, 198, 199, 200
    definition, 183
    dialogical engagement, 189
    extraction-synthesis, 189
    findings, 197
    future recommendations, 201
    heuristic interpretation processes, 190
    literature, allusion to theoretical, 200
    methodology, 189
    participant information, 188
    powering, conceptual integration as, 199
    purpose of study, 183
    research studies, previous, 184, 185
    setting, study, 188
    structural transposition, 197, 198
    structure, identification of, 197
    theoretical guide, 188
context, 4
conversational analysis, 16
core concept development, 252, 257, 258
cotranscendence, 69
criteria. See appraisal, research

cultural care theory
  accommodation or negotiation,
      cultural care, 142, 143
  assumptions, 134, 135
  data-gathering techniques, 135
  decision-making modes identification,
      141
  descriptor identification, 137, 138, 139,
      140
  domain of inquiry, 134
  emic view, application of, 135, 136
  ethnonursing method application, 133,
      135
  etic view, application of, 135, 136
  generic care pattern identification,
      137, 138, 139, 140
  institutional collective care, focus on,
      141
  Leininger's theory of culture care
      diversity and universality, 133
  participant selection, 136
  preservation or maintenance, cultural
      care, 141
  purpose of study, 133, 134
  repatterning or restructuring, cultural
      care, 143
  Sunrise Model, 135, 143, 144
  themes, formulation of, 137, 138, 139,
      140
  theoretical selection, 135

data-gathering process, 37
data-theory bootstrapping, 286
databite, 288
descriptive narrative, 44
descriptive questions, application of,
    129
dialogical engagement, 170, 189, 252, 276
dimension integration, 39
discipline-specific
  frame of reference, 6
  research, 4, 5
  theory, application of, 127
discourse, 4, 102
discoursing with penetrating engaging,
    172, 209
discrete passage identification, 101
doclink, 288
domain analysis, 129
domain analysis, application of, 129

embedded data, 290
emic view, 128, 129, 135
empowerment, 148

energy field. *See* pandimensional energy
    field
epistemology. *See* specific studies
ethical dimension, 19, 20
ethical standards. *See* participant
    information under specific studies
ethnography, 17
  analysis-synthesis, 129
  anthropology, 127
  assumptions, 128
  componential analysis, application of,
      130
  contrast questions, application of, 129
  data-gathering processes, 128
  descriptive questions, application of,
      129
  discipline-specific theory, application
      of, 127
  domain analysis, 129
  emic view, 128, 129
  epistemology, 128
  etic view, 128, 129
  free entry setting, 129
  informants, general, 129
  informants, key, 129
  inquiry, ethnographic, 128
  limited entry setting, 129
  methodologies, 128
  observation, participant, 128
  ontological base, original, 6
  purpose, 127
  restricted entry setting, 129
  scholarly differences, 127
  settings, 129
  structural questions, application of,
      129
  taxonomic analysis, application of,
      130
  theme analysis, application of, 130
ethnonursing method, 7, 17, 127, 130,
    133, 135. *See also* ethnography
etic view, 128, 129, 135, 136
explanatory narrative, 44
explication, 49
extraction-synthesis, 170, 171, 189, 252,
    253, 254, 276

false reporting of research findings, 20
feminist qualitative procedure, 16
free entry setting, 129

Gadamer's hermeneutics, 53
general informants, 129
generative questions, raising, 38

Giorgi's
  modification of phenomenological
      inquiry, 100
  phenomenological modification
      analysis, 97
  procedural modification, 82
grant proposal demonstration
  background of study, description of,
      271, 272
  budget, study, 278
  data-gathering techniques, 276
  dialogical engagement, 276
  extraction-synthesis, 276
  heuristic interpretation, 277
  journal publication, benefits of, 277
  literature, related, 273, 274
  methodology, application of, 275
  nursing significance, 272, 273, 277
  participant selection, 275
  protection, participant, 275
  purpose of study, 271, 277
  research work, description of previous,
      273
  timetable, study, 278
grounded theory method, 16
  analysis-synthesis process, 37
  assumptions, underlying, 36
  coding, 38, 39
  comparative analysis, method of, 37
  data-gathering process, 37
  development, 35
  dimension integration, 39
  disciplinary debates, 35, 36
  epistemology, 36
  generative questions, raising, 38
  guideline operational emphasis, 37
  hypothesis development, 40
  interactions impact, symbolic, 35
  interpretation, research, 40
  linkage verification, 39
  methodology, 36, 37
  ontological base, original, 6
  participation procedures, 37
  phenomenon of study, 35
  pragmatism, impact of, 35
  recommendations for further research,
      40
  theoretical sampling, 38

health as expanding consciousness. See
    life patterns; research as praxis
    method
Heideggerian hermeneutics, 53

hermeneutic method
  applications, 51, 52
  appropriation, 53, 54
  assumptions, 52
  conceptualizations, differing, 53
  development, 51
  distinction, 53, 54
  epistemology, 53
  Gadamer's hermeneutics, 53
  Heideggerian hermeneutics, 53
  interpretation, 53
  methodology, 53
  Ricoeur's hermeneutics, 53
  situatedness, 53
  views, alternate, 52
heuristic research method, 16
  application, 47
  assumptions, 47
  co-researchers, 48
  creative synthesis, 49
  development, 47
  discipline-specific frame of reference,
      6
  epistemology, 47
  explication, 49
  focusing, 49
  identification with focus of inquiry, 49
  illumination, 49
  immersion, 49
  incubation, 49
  indwelling, 49
  initial engaging, 49
  internal frame of reference, 49
  intuition, 49
  methodology, 48, 49
  ontological base, original, 6
  participant information, 48
  phases, 49
  research question characteristics, 48
  researcher requirements, 47
  self-dialogue, 49
  tacit knowing, 49
  validation of research findings, 49
human becoming hermeneutic method,
      17. See also Cat on a Hot Tin Roof study
  application, 209
  assumptions, 172
  development, 172
  discipline-specific frame of reference, 7
  discoursing with penetrating engaging,
      172
  interpreting with quiescent beholding,
      172

ontological base, original, 7
processes, 172
understanding with inspiring
    envisaging, 172
human becoming modes of inquiry
assumptions, 166
epistemology, 165
focus of inquiry, 165
human becoming hermeneutic method.
    See human becoming hermeneutic
    method

methodologies, 167
Parse research method, 167
    assumptions, 170
    conceptual integration, 171
    development, 167
    dialogical engagement, 170
    differences among other qualitative
        research methods, 169
    extraction-synthesis, 170, 171
    heuristic interpretation, 171
    processes, 170
    structural transposition, 171
principles, 166
qualitative descriptive preproject-
    process-postproject method
    assumptions, 174
    development, 174
    processes, 174, 175
human becoming school of thought,
    Parse's, 208
human becoming theory
advancement of nursing science with
    application of theory of human
    becoming, 250
benefits for nursing theory-based
    practice, 221
congruence demonstration, 251, 258,
    259, 260
data collection, 224
descriptive evaluation research
    method, 223
documentation, 233
ensuring quality of care, 222
evidence of patient change over study
    period, 229, 230, 231
findings, study, 225, 234
health phenomenon of considering
    tomorrow, conceptualization of,
    249
human becoming theory application,
    250

implementation recommendations,
    236
laughter study. *See* laughter study
methods, 223
mid-implementation nurse
    descriptions, 226
multidisciplinary team approach,
    222
participant selection, 224
participants' rights, protection of,
    224
post-implementation nurse
    descriptions, 226, 227, 228
pre-implementation nurse
    descriptions, 225, 226
processes, 223
psychiatric setting, value of
    application in, 222
purposes of study, 221, 222, 223
qualitative evaluation research,
    support for, 223
selection as guide for practice,
    theoretical, 235
setting selection, 223
study leader theoretical introduction,
    224, 225
supervisory perceptions of study, 231,
    232, 233
theme identification, 235
theoretical effect on respect and
    concern, 235
human sciences role within qualitative
    inquiry, 2
hyperlink facilities, application of, 288

illumination, 49
imaginative variation, 80
imaging concept, Parse's, 105
immersion, 49
incubation, 49
indexing approaches, 289
indwelling, 49
integrity, 20, 22
interactionism impact, symbolic, 35
Internet impact on preservation of
    integrity, 22
interpreting with quiescent beholding,
    172, 209
interpretive dimension, 22
interpretive phenomenology, 16

key informants, 129
knowledge, 4, 5

laughter study
  analysis, 89
  data gathering, 89
  element identification, 90, 93
  elimination of non-related
      expressions, 90
  findings, 90, 93
  goals, 87
  historical application, 87, 88
  human becoming theory, 87, 94
  participants, 89
  perspective of the researcher, 89
  qualitative listing of descriptions, 90
  quantitative and qualitative listing of
      descriptions, 90
  structural definition, 87, 90
  themes, emerging, 91, 92, 93
  van Kaam's procedural modification of
      the phenomenological method
      application, 89
levels of abstraction, 189
life patterns
  assumption of disease as
      manifestation of evolving pattern,
      151
  assumptive role of the pattern, 161
  binding stage, 157, 158
  centering stage, 157, 158
  choice stage, 157, 159, 160
  differences in individual patterns,
      identification of, 156
  disease as manifestation of the
      pattern, 161
  health as expanding consciousness,
      explication of, 151
  implicate order, and, 152
  interview procedures, 15
  nurse's connectiveness to patient, 161
  objectives, 152, 162
  paradoxical impact, 161
  participant selection, 152
  patterns, 152, 153, 161
  repetitious manner of patterns at sub-
      microscopic levels, 152
  spectrum of human development,
      Young's, 156, 157
  study significance, 152
  theme identification, 153, 154
  transcendent stage, 160
  transcript analysis, secondary, 153
  wholeness, Bohm's theory of, 152
limited entry setting, 129
linkage verification, 39

lived time perspective congruence with
      Parse's powering concept, 105

mendacity. *See Cat on a Hot Tin Roof* study
methodological dimension, 22
methods. *See* specific methods
modeling capabilities, 289

narrative research
  assumptions, 43
  demonstrative examples, 44
  descriptive narrative, 44
  development, 43
  discipline-specific frame of reference,
      6
  epistemology, 44
  explanatory narrative, 44
  forms, 44
  ontological base, original, 6
  participant information, 44
  presentation media, 43
  processes, 44
  theme, development of common, 44
nodelink, 288, 289
novelty, 4
NVivo program, 288, 290

online resources, 298
ontological-epistemological-
      methodological congruence, 292,
      293
open coding, 38
originating, integration with Parse's
      concept of, 261

pandimensional energy field, 237
paradoxical rhythms, 71, 210, 211, 212,
      213
Parse research method, 167. *See also*
      contentment study
  assumptions, 170
  comparison, qualitative research
      method, 169
  conceptual integration, 171
  development, 167
  dialogical engagement, 170
  discipline-specific frame of
      reference, 7
  extraction-synthesis, 170, 171
  heuristic interpretation, 171
  ontological base, original, 7
  processes, 170
  structural transposition, 171

person-environment patterns. *See* life patterns
phenomenological method
  analysis, 79, 81, 82, 83
  application, 77, 78
  assumptions, 78
  biases, personal, 77
  bracketing, 80
  Colaizzi's procedural modification, 82, 83
  concealed meanings, interpretation of, 81
  describing, 79, 81, 82, 83
  development, 77
  differences, philosophical, 78
  discipline-specific frame of reference, 6
  elements, identification of common, 81
  epistemology, 78
  essences, investigating general, 79, 80
  expressions, identification of descriptive, 81
  Giorgi's procedural modification, 82
  hypothetical definition, synthesis of, 82
  imaginative variation, 80
  intuiting, 79, 81, 82, 83
  investigation, 79
  laughter study. *See* laughter study
  methodology, 79
  modes of appearing, 80
  modifications, 79, 81, 82
  ontological base, original, 6
  relationships, apprehending essential, 80
  relentless drive to be ever thinner study. *See* relentless drive to be ever thinner study.
  specificity enhancement, 77
  structural definition, 82
  suspending belief in existence, 80
  van Kaam's procedural modifications, 81, 82
phenomenology, 17
plagiarism, 20, 22
powering, 99, 105, 199
pragmatism, 35
praxis method, research as. *See* Research as praxis method
protection of participants. *See* specific studies

qualitative descriptive method, 16
  approaches, 58
  assumptions, 57
  case study, 58
  conceptualization of research project, appropriate, 57
  data-gathering techniques, 59
  development, 57
  discipline-specific frame of reference, 6
  epistemology, 58
  interpretation, research, 59
  methodology, 58, 59
  ontological base, original, 6
  participant procedures and selection, 59
  purpose, 57
  recommendations, future research, 59
qualitative descriptive preproject-process-postproject method, 17
  assumptions, 174
  development, 174
  discipline-specific frame of reference, 7
  ontological base, original, 7
  processes, 174, 175
qualitative research method, 15. *See also* grant proposal
appraisal. *See* appraisal, research
quality of life for persons with Alzheimer's disease study, 61
  Bradford Dementia Research Group, 62
  care for oneself, impact of participants' ability to, 62
  communicate with others, impact of participants' ability to, 62
  cotranscendence, 69
  data analysis-synthesis, 65
  data-gathering techniques, 65
  definition, 66–67
  description, importance of participants, 62
  factors impacting quality of life, preliminary findings of, 62
  findings, 65–70, 74
  human becoming theory principles, 63, 64
  influential factors, 62
  location, study, 65
  objectives, research study, 64
  paradoxical rhythm identification, 71
  participants, 64

perspectives, changing, 74
purpose, study, 61
question, research, 64
rhythmicity, 68–69
sentient stages, 62
theme identification, 63, 65–70
questioning, 2, 3, 4

reciprocity, 148
refusal to bear witness, 206
relentless drive to be ever thinner study
    analysis and discussion, 105
    concept emergence, central, 105
    conflictual interrelationship
        embodiment, 105
    discourse, elevation to higher level of,
        102
    discrete passage identification, 101
    focal meaning reformulation, 102, 103
    Giorgi's modification of
        phenomenological inquiry, 100
    Giorgi's phenomenological
        modification analysis, 97
    imaging concept, Parse's, 105
    inquiry implementation, 98
    meaning unit identification, 101
    media impact, print and electronic, 98
    methodology, 100
    nursing knowledge, potential for
        enhancement of, 99
    perspective, researcher's, 99
    phenomenological approach
        application, 98
    powering concept, Parse's, 99, 105
    question, research, 99
    reformulation, subject language, 101
    structural description, 103, 104, 105
    subject selection, 100
    synthesis, presuppositions, 100
    theme development, 101, 102
research as praxis method, 7, 17
    assumptions, 148
    design objectives, 148
    development, 147
    empowerment, 148
    epistemology, 148
    methodology, 148
    negotiation process, 148
    participant information, 148
    person-environment interaction,
        health as manifestation of, 147
    perspective, researchers' specification
        of theoretical, 147

    processes, 148
    reciprocity, 148
    scholarly influence, 147
    tenets, guiding, 148
research question. *See* specific study
restricted entry setting, 129
rhythmicity, 68–69
rich text format, 290
Ricoeur's hermeneutics, 53
Rogerian process of inquiry method, 7,
    17, 239

science of unitary human beings
    development, 237
    energy fields, 237
    epistemology, 238
    methodologies, 239
    nursing as a science and an art,
        designation of, 237
    openness of energy fields, 238
    pandimensionality, 237, 238
    pattern, human field, 238
    principles, 238
    Rogerian process of inquiry method,
        239
    unitary field pattern portrait method,
        240, 241
    unitary pattern appreciation case
        method, 241
sciencing, 1, 2
selective coding, 39
self-transcendence study, 125
    analysis techniques, 114
    assessment, importance of nurse, 124
    Colaizzi's phenomenological research
        method, 113, 114
    descriptions, participant, 114
    design approach, research, 111, 113
    elderly, theoretical application in
        mental health in, 112
    emotional well-being, 112
    findings, study, 122, 123
    Frankl's view of self-transcendence,
        112
    integration, significant statements, 118
    Nazi concentration camp
        demonstration, 112
    non-randomness of selection of
        participants, 124
    nursing implications, 111, 123, 124
    participants, 111
    participant statement formulation,
        116–117, 118

presuppositions, identification of researcher's, 113
purpose of study, 111, 113
question formulation, 113, 114
question, research, 113
structure identification, fundamental, 118
term definition, 111
theme clusters, 118, 119, 120, 121
theme identification, 118
validation, participant, 122
semantic thesaurus searches, 285
sensitivity, theoretical, 38
sentient stages, 62
situatedness, 53
software capabilities, 296, 297
structural transposition, 171, 197, 198, 252, 256, 257
Sunrise Model, 127, 135, 143, 144

taxonomic analysis, application of, 130
theme analysis, application of, 130
theoretical sampling, 38
transcendence. *See* self-transcendence study
transcendental phenomenology. *See* self-transcendence study
truthfulness in reporting, 20

understanding with inspiring envisaging, 172
unitary field pattern portrait method, 17
assumptions, 240
design purposes, 240
discipline-specific frame of reference, 7
ontological base, original, 7
processes, 241
unitary pattern appreciation case method, 7, 241

validation, participant, 122
validity of researcher's interpretation, 124
valuing, integration with human becoming concept of, 261
van Kaam's procedural modification, 81, 82, 89
van Kaam's procedural modification of the phenomenological method application, 89

XML facilitation, 290

Young's spectrum of consciousness, 156, 157